PORTUGUESE
VOYAGES
1498–1663

Flying Fish Meet in the Torrid Zone, from *Navagatio in Brasilium Americae* by
Theodore de Bry. Service Historique de Marine, Vincennes, France.
[Giraudon/Bridgeman Art Library]

"God gave the Portuguese a small country as
cradle but all the world as their grave."
ANTONIO VIEIRA

PORTUGUESE VOYAGES 1498–1663

Edited by
Charles David Ley

Foreword by
Edgar Prestage
Formerly Emeritus Professor of Portuguese Language,
Literature and History in the University of London

**PHOENIX
PRESS**

5 UPPER SAINT MARTIN'S LANE
LONDON
WC2H 9EA

A PHOENIX PRESS PAPERBACK

First published in Great Britain
by J. M. Dent & Sons Ltd in
Everyman's Library in 1947
This paperback edition published in 2000
by Phoenix Press,
a division of The Orion Publishing Group Ltd,
Orion House, 5 Upper St Martin's Lane,
London WC2H 9EA

A CIP catalogue record for this book
is available from the British Library.

Printed in Great Britain by
Clays Ltd, St Ives plc

ISBN 1 84212 109 X

CONTENTS

v

FOREWORD

PORTUGAL owes her place in history to three achievements: the opening of the ocean routes, the colonization of Brazil (a land larger than the United States), and the spread of Christianity in foreign parts, mainly by members of the Society of Jesus; thus Gonçalo de Silveira became the proto-martyr of South-East Africa, Anselmo de Andrade was the first European to enter Tibet, and Saint Francis Xavier, 'the greatest missionary since St. Paul,' reaped a harvest of souls in India, the Moluccas, and Japan, while the good work of Fathers Anchieta and Nobrega is still remembered in Brazil. These achievements are the more remarkable because the population of Portugal numbered less than two millions when she carried her flag, the cross of Christ, over a large part of the globe. Her hardy fishermen and sailors, accustomed to struggle against the full force of the Atlantic for their livelihood, penetrated, year by year, into the unknown, and after less than a century of effort reached India, Brazil, and Labrador. Their losses by shipwreck, hunger, and disease were very great; in the first voyage of Vasco da Gama more than a third of the crews died, mainly from scurvy, and when rounding the Cape of Good Hope many ships went down or were driven on shore. The survivors had to march, often for months, exposed to the daily attacks of savages and wild beasts, until they reached some Portuguese fort on the east coast. The great missionary and preacher Father Antonio Vieira said truly that God gave his countrymen a small land for their birthplace, but all the world to die in.

After the capture in 1415 of Ceuta, the commercial emporium opposite Gibraltar, Prince Henry, son of King John I of Portugal and Philippa of Lancaster, crusader and scientist, established himself on a wind-swept promontory near Cape St. Vincent and became the father of continuous maritime discovery. During forty years he sent out his little ships of twenty-five to fifty tons down the coast of West Africa, with the object of finding a Christian ruler who would help him to fight the Infidel, and in the hope of reaching India, land of spices, since the shorter route by Suez was in Muslim hands. His first prizes were the islands of Porto Santo and Madeira; the outward voyage was straightforward, but winds and tides obliged the seamen to make a wide circuit to return home, and hence they came upon that group of islands the Azores in 1431. At Henry's death in 1460 the farthest south reached was Sierra Leone, but then the pace quickened; in 1488 Bartholomew Dias passed the Cape of Good Hope, in 1498 Vasco da Gama cast anchor off Calicut, in 1500 Pedro Álvares Cabral found Brazil, and in the following year the brothers Corte Real discovered Newfoundland.

The Portuguese (and Columbus, who had learnt his business with them) had made the principal discoveries by sea; there remained those of Australia and New Zealand; they were very close to the former when trading with Timor, and a claim has more than once been made on their behalf, but not proved. Mr. Ley illustrates some of the activities by sea and land in extracts from the best authorities of the time, and I hope that his book will reach a large public. The efforts he describes were more than a small nation could long sustain; exhaustion followed, and the union with Spain in 1580 drew upon Portugal the hostility of countries possessing greater wealth and larger fleets, with fatal results. The defeat of King Sebastian and his army in Morocco in 1578, followed by the Spanish invasion, were regarded by many Portuguese of the time as divine punishments for misdeeds at home and abroad.

In our day Portugal has built up a new colonial empire in East and West Africa, and after fifty years of warfare and unrest has pacified the natives and made them into loyal subjects. Great public works have been undertaken, and the other needs of modern civilization supplied. The mother country is prosperous and has an ever-increasing population of seven millions; in extent of territory Portugal is the fourth colonial power.

EDGAR PRESTAGE.

INTRODUCTION

No one has yet been able satisfactorily to explain the growth and decline of the Portuguese Age of Discovery. There are material, religious, financial, and physical theories offered at every turn to explain why one small country should suddenly, at the very beginning of the Renaissance, carry exploration and conquest to the furthest shores of the unknown world and of the east, and why, almost as suddenly, this age of energy and enthusiasm should end, the hard-won empire shrink, and the genius of Portugal turn from action and heroic prose to that almost oriental, though quite individualistic, contempt for mere doing and that writing of fine lyric poetry which distinguish it to-day; but no theory as to the cause of this change has been widely accepted.

The leading writers of modern Portugal, Eça de Queiroz, Antero de Quental, Gaspar Simões, and José Régio, for example, seem to waver between despair and a kind of cheerful fatalism vaguely inspired by Christian mysticism. Such writers may seem to us strange descendants for the men who went near to discovering the whole world. Should we, as Southey did, detest Portugal's present and idealize her past? I think not.

The men of old Portugal did not build their world in a spirit of facile optimism and refusal to accept the necessarily tragic nature of human life. They were not all thinkers, naturally; many of them, like Álvaro Velho and Luis Vaz de Caminha amongst our present authors, were simple, not very highly cultivated men, who took their modest part in the voyages of discovery and who, no doubt, knew how to endure hardships with that patience which is a key to the Portuguese character. But fine intelligences like Fernão Mendes Pinto and Manuel Godinho combine a dogged persistence in the life of action with a harsh and realistic vision of men, the world, and Portugal. This view of existence was shared by the great poet Camões and runs in a subtle undertone through the apparent patriotic optimism of the *Lusiads*, where it comes out especially strongly in the short digressions. And Gil Vicente's plays, written at the beginning of the sixteenth century, are so satirical that even to-day some of them are not allowed to be acted in Portugal.

The Portuguese people are capable of great patience and persistence; they reject any flattering illusions about life, but, at the same time, they have a strong religious or lyrical feeling. One can easily understand how the men of such a country could gain a

*A 986

world by continued and sustained effort and yet lose it easily
without greatly troubling about its loss.   The period of Portuguese
expansion overseas dates, roughly, from the beginning of the
fifteenth century, when Prince Henry the Navigator sent out his
first ships from Sagres, to the end of the sixteenth century, when
Portugal was under Spanish domination and England and Holland
were becoming great at sea.   The present book does not, however,
attempt to give any consecutive account of Portuguese history
during those crowded years.   We could tell how it is that even
to-day Portugal has colonies scattered all over the world; we could
include the story of how Afonso de Albuquerque, with a mere
handful of men, thousands of miles from their own country, took
by storm large and well-defended towns on the Indian coast, like
Goa and Malacca, in the name of the King of Portugal.   But our
aim is rather to give the human record of the Portuguese voyages.
Here we have the contemporary accounts given by the travellers
themselves, some of them simple narratives, others literary works
of great value.   Some accounts describe famous historical voyages,
such as those of Vasco da Gama to India or of Pedro Álvares Cabral
to Brazil; others describe journeys of no historical importance, such
as those of Mendes Pinto or of the *Santiago*, but the reader will not
find these last any less interesting than the others—on the contrary,
they are much more vivid.   But all the extracts are fine human
documents, a literary expression in prose of the Portuguese who
sailed under Portugal's flag to distant lands, during their country's
great days of colonial adventure.

The only writings given here in full are Caminha's letter and
the story of the wreck of the *São João*.   But in choosing the
extracts I have been careful to avoid anything in the nature of
impertinent prunings, which I think one has no right to make.
Whilst the chapters from an author will not necessarily be consecutive, sentences and parts of sentences will not be omitted.   If
a writer is worth reading he is worth leaving to give his own
narrative in his own way.

The extracts certainly do not form any kind of continuous
narrative, but they do form a rough sequence of the story of the
rise and fall of Portuguese imperial expansion.

The Route to India, 1498.   The example of the classical ages (of
the days of Greece and Rome) deeply stirred and inspired European
man until the decline of classical culture in the nineteenth century
and the growth of scientific learning; especially was this true from
the time of the Renaissance onwards.   To minds fired with personal or national ambitions for conquest or expansion, Alexander
the Great was the most magnificent hero of antiquity.   He it was
who had in times past invaded India, and historians like Plutarch
had shown him surrounded with vast oriental spoils and pomps.

The Romans had tried to copy his example and failed. The dream of oriental dominion had doubtless remained in men's minds throughout the Middle Ages, but it was only with the coming of the Renaissance that it began to seem possible to put that dream into action. Columbus sailed over the Atlantic lured by distant memories of Alexander's eastern excursion, and accidentally discovered America. Bartolomeu Dias, a Portuguese captain, also in quest of the east, had rounded the Cape of Good Hope, but had been forced to turn back before he could reach the shores of India. Vasco da Gama did, however, actually reach India by sea, and thus opened out a new world of commerce or conquest for the Portuguese, whose warlike feats on the Indian coast were far to surpass even Alexander's successes.

The account of da Gama's voyage included in this book reads prosaically enough. Yet the journey here described so unenthusiastically and realistically was to become the theme of Camões's epic, which is the national poem of Portugal. Our extract ends with da Gama in Calicut; the original text goes on to describe most of the voyage home, but breaks off abruptly. It is probable that the account was the log-book of the *São Rafael*, and that it was written by a member of the crew called Álvaro Velho. Velho was a military man and seems to have spent eight years of his life in Sierra Leone, so that we can safely take it that he was a typical Portuguese explorer, a rugged man inured to hardships. His record has no literary merit, but is a capable and accurate document. The translation and notes are by the eminent geographer, the late Dr. E. G. Ravenstein, and were originally published by the Hakluyt Society in 1898.

It seems to me, with reference to the notes, that Ravenstein is a trifle too definite in his rejection of all Velho's evidence of Christianity in Africa and the east. His principal authorities, the cynical opinion of Sir Richard Burton and the obliging information given by a missionary called the Rev. J. J. Jaus, do not seem to me sufficient evidence to justify Ravenstein's uncompromising attitude. For instance, João de Barros, the Portuguese Renaissance historian, states—as Ravenstein tells us—that two men Velho calls 'two Christian captives from India' were Abyssinian Christians. Ravenstein comments that 'the Abyssinian Christians, whatever their shortcomings, do not worship images, as is the practice in the Roman Church.' But the following sentence from Álvares (another of our authors in this book) seems to contradict this: 'Each time that they [the priests] pass before the image [of Our Lady] they make a great reverence to it.' Again, in the important matter of India, Ravenstein does not admit the possibility that the 'church' Vasco da Gama visited in Calicut represented a corrupted form of Christianity, but this was surely not impossible since tradition traces the first introduction of Christianity into India right back to the days of the Apostles. Somewhere in the east the line of oriental Christians originally converted by St. Thomas undoubtedly still existed. Part of the Portuguese quest was to discover what evidences there were of Christianity in India. The ideal would have been to find some Christian monarch like the unlocated Prester John and make some lasting treaty of religious and political alliance with him. It seems strange if the Portuguese were really lightly deceived in such an important part of their mission.

The Discovery of Brazil, 1500. After Vasco da Gama had returned to Lisbon, King Manuel collected another fleet to return to India and further Portuguese interests there. The admiral was Pedro Álvares Cabral, and two of the captains of the other ships were Bartolomeu Dias, the explorer, and Nicolau Coelho, who had accompanied da Gama. Cabral, whether designedly or not is not clear, steered very wide of his course on his way down to the south of Africa, and so came to discover Brazil, which he seems to have considered a large and fertile island. The point where he touched land is some way to the south of the modern town of Bahia.

The letter here printed, which describes the discovery, was written by a gentleman of good family called Luis Vaz de Caminha. Caminha had a position as scribe, first on Cabral's ship, and afterwards in the Portuguese factory which was founded in Calicut as a result of this voyage. In December, however, Caminha was killed when the Indians massacred all the Portuguese at the factory. He was not a literary man, but his account shows force, clarity, and observation. Indeed, the letter in its entirety has been found a suitable item for wireless programmes in modern Portugal.

It will be noticed that the letter insists on religious matters. Cabral and his followers, like most other Portuguese discoverers, belonged to the military Order of Christ, being bound by various vows, among others those of celibacy, though permission to marry was not, in Cabral's time, difficult to obtain. The whole of Caminha's letter, in fact, gives us an example of the Portuguese crusading zeal.

The Lands of Prester John, 1520–6. A nation which was so intent on christianizing the world was naturally greatly desirous of allying itself with that great Christian emperor out beyond Europe known as Prester John. Early travellers like Sir John Mandeville and Marco Polo had spoken of this emperor and priest as existing in the east. The Portuguese identified Prester John with the negus of Abyssinia, but this view does not seem to have been generally accepted in other countries, since we find Shakespeare right at the end of the century writing in *Much Ado about Nothing*: 'Will your grace command me any service to the world's end? I will

on the slightest errand now to the Antipodes that you can devise
to send me on; I will fetch a toothpicker now from the furthest
inch of Asia; bring you the length of Prester John's foot; fetch you
a hair off the great Cham's beard; do you any embassage to the
Pygmies, rather than hold three words' conference with this
harpy.'

King John II sent Pero de Covilhã and Afonso de Paiva in 1487
with orders to find the lands of Prester John.   Covilhã reached
Abyssinia in 1493, and was detained there for the rest of his life.
Yet the emperor of Abyssinia seems to have been definitely im-
pressed by Covilhã, who did not scruple to attend the ceremonies
of the Abyssinian Church; he, or rather, the regent, Queen Helena,
therefore came to wish to have the help of the Christian kingdom
of Portugal against the Mohammedans who used to harass them
and sent an Armenian named Matthew as ambassador to the court
of the king of Portugal to ask for such help.   Finally, in 1515,
Rodrigo de Lima went as Portuguese envoy to Abyssinia.   A priest
called Francisco Álvares (1465–1541) was among his retinue, and
later wrote an account of the journey, which was published in
1540 under the title of *True Information about the Lands of Prester
John*.   It was the duty of Álvares, as a priest, to inquire into the
nature of Abyssinian Christianity.   He seems to have viewed it
with sympathy, and the emperor—Lebna Dengal—also showed a
lively and friendly interest in the nature of the Christianity of his
Portuguese guests.   The emperor wished to detain the ambassador
and his suite as he had detained Covilhã, no doubt fearing the
spread of knowledge about his domains in the outside world.
They, however, sailed for Portugal at the beginning of 1526,
having spent six years in Abyssinia.   It is believed that Álvares
later travelled to Rome to give the Pope an account of Abyssinian
religion.

Álvares's book is what one might expect from a rather practically
minded churchman.   It is very clear, capable, and informative,
a good travel book, though not, strictly speaking, a literary work.
Álvares is not a writer in our modern sense of the word, but he is a
thoroughly educated 'clerk,' accustomed to the use of the pen.

His work is the first European book about Abyssinia and in
every way interesting.   I have chosen four extracts.   Some ex-
planation for their selection is necessary.

The first and longest describes the valley in which all possible
claimants to the throne were imprisoned for life by the emperor.
Apart from its interest in that it gives us a savage and horrible
picture of one side of life in the Abyssinia of those days, the passage
is worth reproducing for English readers because it supplied the
theme for Johnson's *Rasselas, Prince of Abyssinia*.   Johnson would
have read Álvares in the translation given of him in Purchas; but

in his story he has changed the princes' mountain prison into a
'Happy Valley.' Johnson mingles something very like the theme,
of the youth of Buddha with the Portuguese account.

'"Sir," said he, "if you had seen the miseries of the world, you
would know how to value your present state." "Now," said the
prince, "you have given me something to desire; I shall long to
see the miseries of the world, since the sight of them is so necessary
to happiness."'—*Rasselas*, Chapter III.

We are a long way from the barbaric customs which Álvares
describes.

The second passage from Álvares tells how he travelled through
the mountain pass known as Aqui Afagi, or Death of the Asses.
This gives, I feel, an idea of the wildness and inaccessibility of
Abyssinia, and why it was so mysterious to the Europeans of those
days. This passage appeared on the whole more fitting for the
present book than those longer ones in which Álvares gives an
account of Abyssinian religious life with its ceremonies, monasteries, and Lenten observances; some of the monks and nuns used
to spend the nights of Lent lying in cold water.

The third passage shows us the Abyssinian royal family's great
interest in the religion of the Portuguese, and also gives an idea of
how the emperor travelled through the Aqui Afagi.

The fourth is the life story of Pero de Covilhã. It is not very
well told by Álvares, but has some historical interest.

The Furthest East, 1537–58. Easily the most excellent of all the
Portuguese travel books is the *Peregrination* of Fernão Mendes
Pinto (1509–83). It is, in fact, one of the greatest travel books in
the world, and its author certainly a man of genius. It is a very
long book, and the extract here chosen, though itself not short, is
only about a third of the whole work. He was long supposed by
his countrymen to have invented very freely, and the popular
English translation (first edition, 1653) seems to have spread the
same notion here. A character in Congreve's *Love for Love*
remarks: 'Ferdinand Mendes Pinto was but a type of thee, thou
liar of the first magnitude.' Dr. Johnson may have been thinking of Mendes Pinto when he writes of Lobo's book: 'The
reader will here find . . . no Chinese perfectly polite, and completely skilled in all sciences.' But the discoveries of later travellers
and scholars have all gone to prove that nearly everything in
Mendes Pinto is correct. This, since he was a great artist, does not
mean that he did not make certain rearrangements and additions
to the raw facts of his own biography. But that was because he
was interested in the best (and therefore most truthful) presenta-
tion of his subject-matter rather than in the egotistical consideration of whether each page relates his own personal doings exactly
as he did them. That he must have seen at least a great part

of what he describes is certain, as no mere hearsay account could be so generally accurate.

Mendes Pinto sailed to the east in 1537. He later joined the crew of a Portuguese privateer, António de Faria, whose activities along the coasts of non-Portuguese Asia were condoned, like Drake's in America, rather than actively encouraged by the authorities of his country. Actually, the existence of this privateer outside the pages of the *Peregrination* has never been satisfactorily proved, and some Portuguese writers have held the opinion that Faria and Mendes Pinto were really the same person. If this is so, it adds another strange trait to the already very complex nature of this author.

He mingles comprehension of the wrongs done to the orientals with the callousness of his description of the violence with which those wrongs were done. António de Faria meets a gaily ornamented ship bearing an eastern bride to her husband; the bride's ship mistakes the Portuguese for that of the bridegroom and we read the bride's beautiful love-letter of greeting, in which the formality of the east is blended with the luxuriant prose of the Renaissance; but, for all that, Faria captures the bride's ship, massacres the crew, and makes the bride herself a slave.

Again, an oriental tells how he was persuaded by the Portuguese to embrace Christianity, but that, finding himself slighted by them, he abandoned their religion.

A third example is that of the boy whose father's ship, containing all his fortune, was stolen by Faria and he himself taken away and enslaved; he denounces the Portuguese pirate with complete justice—at least, for any modern reader—and tells them to cease continually invoking God, since their deeds are evil.

It is hard to believe that these passages are included by chance. But one wonders whether Mendes Pinto could possibly have realized the extent of the problem raised by this kind of criticism of António de Faria and of the Portuguese. It could be urged that this apparent devil's advocacy was merely instinctive in him because he was a great artist. Marlowe, for instance, admires force in the person of Tamburlaine, and approves of Tamburlaine's trampling on mere intelligent and sensitive figures—on Marlowe's own poetic feeling in them, even. Is Mendes Pinto another case of the same spirit, of the Machiavellian and Nietzschean love of ruthlessness? In such short details as those referred to, Mendes Pinto shows us that he achieved the marvel in his age of understanding how the east must have looked on the encroachments of the west; did he, for all that, wish Portugal to seize more of Asia by violence than she had done?

Our extract begins when António de Faria goes to plunder some tombs of the kings of China. Faria's soft words and harsh deeds

whilst doing so are another example of the half critical and half
consenting attitude of the author (for it is the author who remembered and recorded his words) towards Faria's acts of piracy.
It is almost impossible to read the passage and believe that Mendes
Pinto really thought it was right to plunder and desecrate the
tombs, that he did not in fact take the more enlightened view that
the Chinese monks were serving God to the best of their knowledge.
The best Christian teaching in all ages has justified such a view,
though it obviously becomes unpopular in ages of fanaticism.

The same problem arises when Mendes Pinto speaks of some of
the Chinese religious and charitable institutions which he meets
with after he has been wrecked.   That these descriptions occasion-
ally end by declaring that the Chinese are, after all, miserable
barbarians who are deceived by lying tales proves little; such
declarations would, if nothing else, have been required by the
Inquisition, which censored books.   We even know that the Chief
Chronicler, Francisco de Andrade, did make omissions from and
additions to the text before it was published; he may possibly have
interfered with passages that praised the virtues of the religious
Chinese too boldly.   Maldonado, a Spanish translator of Mendes
Pinto a few years later, said that Andrade had only made matters
worse by his interference.   But it is difficult to be quite sure what
Maldonado meant.

But if Mendes Pinto found Christian feeling and behaviour
amongst the pagan Chinese, he certainly did not regard their
temples and ceremonies as anything but grotesque.   Yet, even the
great high priest, the lama of Lanchow, preaches a sermon full of
something very close to Christian charity, and this contrasts very
favourably with the behaviour of the Portuguese captives who,
amidst all their miseries, squabble and fight as to which of their
families is the oldest.   There are, also, times when Mendes Pinto's
description of the perfection of Chinese customs read almost like
Swiftian satire.

Mendes Pinto not only writes of his travels with genius, he also
managed to see everything which the most efficient newspaper
reporter of to-day might wish to see, if magically transported back
to sixteenth-century Asia.   He is present at the beginning of the
decline of the great Chinese Empire; he sees an unsuccessful
attempt at Tartar invasion with his own eyes.   Not only are he
and his companions the first Europeans to visit Japan, but he is
present at the first introduction of the musket into that country;
the rapid spread and popularity of this invention there he ascribes
to the military spirit of the Japanese.   This means that he actually
saw the beginning of the Europeanization and modernization
of Japan; it began immediately on the first meeting of the Japanese
with Europeans.

This brings our extract to a close, but the *Peregrination* continues with a complicated account of some oriental wars, and a second and third journey to Japan, now in company with the first Jesuit missionaries who went there: he became a Jesuit lay brother after Xavier's death.

Here again, Mendes Pinto was present at the historical moment of the first coming of Christianity to Japan, that furthest corner of the civilized world from Christendom. Christianity existed in India before Vasco da Gama, however wrong Velho may have been in thinking his party had encountered it. Mendes Pinto, as the reader will see, discovered occasional signs of Christianity in China. But it was through Mendes Pinto that Francisco Xavier, a Spaniard whom the Portuguese had protected as the first Christian missionary to the east, decided to sail for Japan; Xavier returned in his ship: Mendes Pinto was a very rich man then and lent money for his Japanese mission; and he tells us of the extreme surprise of the aristocratic and military noblemen of Japan and of the elegant Japanese priests on seeing a man in humble attire and covered with lice treated with such veneration.

The meeting with Xavier seems to have had a very great effect on Mendes Pinto, and to have been the reason for his giving up all his money to the Jesuits and joining their order. He describes Xavier's austerity, death, and miracles very finely. But Mendes Pinto afterwards quarrelled with the Jesuits and left them. Xavier seems to have understood the virtue that lay behind much of the eastern civilization, but the men he had had to choose in the east to work with him were not capable of that remarkable sympathy in a fanatical age. To me it appears clear that it was for that reason, or partly for that reason, that Mendes Pinto left them, for he never ceased to revere Xavier.

Mendes Pinto returned to Portugal in 1558, and it was there that he wrote the *Peregrination*. It is believed that he sent the Pope a copy of one of the ancient Chinese books he speaks of in his work, and this copy may still exist somewhere in the Vatican library. The *Peregrination* was not intended for publication; it was intended for his sons (presumably, for his descendants generally), so that they might have a record of his doings. It was, indeed, to be the family reading-book, from which the younger members could learn their A B C, as he says. He was probably not opposed to publication, only indifferent to it, being contented with being read and remembered by the family he left. He died in 1583, and the *Peregrination* was first published in 1614.

Purchas gives a summary of the book in 1625. The English translation of it, by Henry Cogan, appeared in 1653. He almost certainly used, not the original Portuguese, but Maldonado's Spanish translation of 1620. This is proved by his Introduction,

which is merely a summarized version of the Spaniard's.   Cogan
omitted much of the part of the book referring to Francisco Xavier,
which one can understand in Commonwealth times.   Cogan seems
to have been a strong Royalist.   He also translated Diodorus
Siculus, Mademoiselle de Scudéry, and a book called *The Court
of Rome*.

The Tragic History of the Sea, 1552 and 1585.   In the sixteenth
and seventeenth centuries it was the custom in Portugal to print
booklets describing events of some public interest, such as the
history of famous shipwrecks.   In the eighteenth century, Gomes
de Brito collected several of these accounts dealing with disaster
at sea, and published them under the title of *The Tragic History
of the Sea*.   Most of the losses of ships here described took place
either on the voyage to or on the voyage back from India; the
west coast of India was now largely under the rule of Portugal.
The desire to make rapid gains had gone to the heads of those who
commanded these ships and we find them sailing with their ships
laden to excess or steering by dangerous courses, all in pursuit of
easy fortunes; if they escaped drowning, they often had to trust
themselves to the mercy of hostile tribes on land, who, at least in
West Africa (the scene of so many of these shipwrecks), took everything from them, including their clothes.

What is so remarkable about these works is their frankness—the
absence of any pretence that the shipwrecked crews behaved any
more nobly than they did.   The modern reader will also be surprised to find how crudely religious fervour and violence are mixed
in them.   It is interesting that in *The Tragic History of the Sea* a
Portuguese Jesuit remarks on the mildness and courtesy with which
English privateers like Drake and Cumberland treated the people
they captured; what a pity they are heretics, he adds.

The two voyages here chosen describe shipwrecks on or near
the east coast of Africa.   The first, the wreck of the *São João*, is
very famous, the second less so, but it is written with far greater
power and, one must add, horror.

Manuel de Sousa Sepúlveda was a pioneer in misfortune; not
wishing to die on the beach where he had been cast, he was forced,
against his will, to become an African explorer.   His adventures
among the Kaffirs and his tragic end became extremely famous,
and he is referred to in practically all the subsequent Portuguese
accounts of shipwrecks on the African coast, as well as in Camões's
Lusiad.

The story of the wreck of the *Santiago* continues after our
extract ends, and explains how some others of the shipwrecked
men reached the coast on rafts and in a boat.   The survivors
eventually all found their way to Mozambique, which was and still
is a Portuguese colony.

The account of the disaster of the *São João* was written by a man who had not taken part in the voyage, as the preface shows. The wreck of the *Santiago* is described by a survivor, presumably one of those who went in Melo's boat, named Manuel Godinho Cardoso.

The Jesuits in Abyssinia, 1625–34. As the years went by, the relations between Portugal and Abysinnia grew less cordial. Francisco Álvares, in his day, had been unable to come to any very definite conclusion about the orthodoxy of Abyssinian Christianity; the Reformation had scarcely begun; the Society of Jesus had not been founded. But Father Jerónimo Lobo (1596–1678), a Portuguese Jesuit some hundred years later, visited Abyssinia with very different views. The help given by the Portuguese under Cristóvão da Gama had prevented Abyssinia from being finally overrun by their Mohammedan enemies. Lobo and his fellows knew this, and moreover regarded Abyssinian religion as a dangerous error from which the country must be saved and brought in subjection to Rome. On the other hand, the Abyssinians, though they owed the continuance of their existence as a nation to Portugal, viewed the Portuguese Jesuits with suspicion and hostility, and the efforts of some of the emperors to abolish the old religion and submit to Rome were extremely unpopular and failed completely.

Yet another hundred years later the French were planning a possible colonization of Abyssinia. A certain Le Grand, like others before him, came across the manuscript of Lobo's travels in the library of the monastery of São Roque in Lisbon. He translated this unpublished account into French and in 1728 published it at the beginning of an informative work he did on Abyssinia, describing the history of its religious problems from a somewhat exclusively French point of view. Whilst Johnson was at Pembroke College, Oxford (1728–31), he read this book. He spoke of this to Warren, the Birmingham bookseller, in 1733, suggesting that Warren might like him to make an abridged translation of it. This was published in 1735 and was Johnson's first book. Not only Lobo's account, but all the matter in Le Grand's book is to be found in Johnson's in a condensed form.

His preface (published posthumously in 1787) is such a lively example of its author's style that what refers to Lobo in it has been reproduced in this volume. The translation itself does not bear any definite stamp of the translator. As Boswell says of it: 'This being the first prose work of Johnson, it is a curious object of inquiry how much may be traced in it of that style which marks his subsequent writings with such peculiar excellence; with so happy an union of force, vivacity, and perspicuity. I have perused the book with this view, and have found that here, as I believe in every other translation, there is in the work itself no vestige of the

translator's own style; for the language of translation being adapted
to the thoughts of another person, insensibly follows their cast,
and as it were runs into a mould that is ready prepared.'

  Overland Return from India, 1663. Though the Jesuits in
general did not hold back from any kind of danger, Father Manuel
Godinho wins our special admiration for his coolness and re-
sourcefulness in the face of difficulties, and for the humour with
which he tells us about them. He is also remarkable for having
later left the Society to become an ordinary priest.

  Godinho (1630–1712) was a writer of great intelligence and
writes clearly and incisively. The extract in this volume is taken
from the *Relation of the New Route Father Manuel Godinho took
from India to Portugal in the Year* 1663. His other works deal
with subjects from Portuguese religious life and religious life
generally. Unlike the earlier travellers he expresses himself
almost in a modern manner, for, by 1665, when the book was
published, the Renaissance had quite passed and our present age
had, in a sense, begun. If the prose of modern times has not the
richness of that of the Renaissance, it has a clarity and mathe-
matical precision which mark it; Godinho's style only differs from
that of a good present-day Portuguese writer by a certain baroque
floridity, which is perhaps Jesuitical but is admirably suited to his
own particular style of humour. Though clerical, it is a rollick-
ing, man-of-action's humour, too. He makes the kind of jokes
one would suppose the bishops who led armies in the Middle Ages
to have made. And only a great man could so have united in
himself religion, action, and thought.

  The book opens with a brilliant essay on the decline of Portuguese greatness. Empires, says Godinho—with a Byronic resigna-
tion to the process—decline; the Romans had their day and it
passed, now the Portuguese day is passing, and India is falling into
the hand of the Dutch, and, to a lesser extent, of the English. He
goes on to describe his own return from India; the account is
methodically divided into chapters of narrative and detailed
descriptions of the places he went through. For instance, in the
middle of our extract he devotes a chapter to Babylon (Baghdad)
as he knew it; lack of space does not allow that chapter to be
included here.

  He was evidently bearing home some very important secret
documents. He is not able to reveal what they were, but they
must have had some political importance. The information
about places in his book is carefully and succinctly given, evidently
for possible use by the Portuguese State. He left Ceylon for
Basra by ship disguised as an oriental. He then crossed the desert
on horseback, as we shall see. Finally he returned to Lisbon.
Speed was essential to him, and he did not mind what risks he took

to achieve it.   His errand was also of such importance that he
had been supplied with a large sum of money for the journey.

In the original book, our extract follows on an excellent account
of desert life, and the reasons why the dreaded Alarve Arabs were
so particularly dangerous to travellers.   It was not the chance
encounters with single bodies of Arabs that were so perilous, but
the probability that many of the scattered bands would join together in attacking you if you excited either their anger or their
covetousness.   As the Arab says in *Rasselas*: 'The sons of Ishmael
are the natural and hereditary lords of this part of the continent,
which is usurped by late invaders and low-born tyrants, from whom
we are compelled to take by the sword what is denied to justice.'
This large roving population was spread out all over the desert,
but was capable of swiftly assembling in vast numbers at any
given call.

Conclusion. Our book ends at the beginning of the modern age.
The story of the Portuguese colonial empire does not end here,
but the age of Portuguese discovery and exploration is now over.

Those who in the Middle Ages had sailed out into the Atlantic
had seen a great cloud ahead of them, and perhaps remembering
Dante's Ulysses, had fled home.   But, in 1421, João Gonçalves
Zarco pressed on, and sailed into the cloud, and discovered the
island of Madeira behind it.   That was, in a sense, the beginning.

In 1663, a commission of French clerics with high positions in
the Church arrived in Ceylon; they intended to press on into
China and other parts and regularize the establishment of Christianity there ecclesiastically.   Father Manuel Godinho met them and
told them of the difficulties, the impossibility even, of their as much
as entering the countries they were hoping to bring completely
under the Church.   Godinho repeats his arguments to us; it is
one of the finest passages in his book, and he also knew the Asia
of his day well.   It seemed the east had, for the time, at least,
rejected Christianity.   That was, in a sense, the end.

Other countries have built bigger empires than the Portuguese.
But it was the Portuguese who discovered that an empire could be
built wider than Alexander's, based on sea power.   They were the
first nation to attempt to make Christianity the religion of the
world, and if they had viewed the east with the comprehension
shown by their great writer, Mendes Pinto, instead of laughing
at him and calling him a liar, they would probably have done so.
But Mendes Pinto was too great a man of genius to be understood
immediately.

Any one book is too small to deal adequately with so large a
subject.   The reader is referred to the valuable work done by the
Hakluyt Society and by Professor Edgar Prestage and others to
spread knowledge in England of the Portuguese discoveries.   But

much yet remains to be accomplished in order that the great enterprises of Renaissance Portugal may be thoroughly known amongst us.

CHARLES DAVID LEY.

October 1943.

My thanks are due to the Hakluyt Society for their kind permission to reproduce Dr. Ravenstein's translation of Álvaro Velho, with some of his notes, and Lord Stanley's translation of Francisco Álvares; to Professor Entwistle for his invaluable suggestions as to the selection of material; to Professor Prestage for his kind encouragement and assistance, and for graciously consenting to write the Foreword; and to Dr. Armando Cortesão for his kind assistance and for permission to use in my notes on Mendes Pinto some of the material from his volume on Tomé Pires, before its publication.

C. D. L.

THE ROUTE TO INDIA, 1497–8

(Translated and annotated by Dr. E. G. Ravenstein)

Bibliographical

Roteiro da viagem que em descobrimento da India pelo Cabo da Boa Esperança fez Dom Vasco da Gama. Lisbon. 1838.

TRANSLATION: *Vasco da Gama's First Voyage,* by E. G. Ravenstein, F.R.G.S. Hakluyt Society. 1898.

THE ROUTE TO INDIA

A Journal of the First Voyage of Vasco da Gama in 1497–9.

IN the name of God. Amen!

In the year 1497 King Dom Manuel, the first of that name in Portugal, dispatched four vessels to make discoveries and go in search of spices. Vasco da Gama was the captain-major of these vessels; Paulo da Gama, his brother, commanded one of them and Nicolau Coelho another.[1]

We left Restelo [2] on Saturday, 8th July 1497. May God our Lord permit us to accomplish this voyage in his service. Amen!

On the following Saturday we sighted the Canaries, and in the night passed to the lee of Lançarote. During the following night, at break of day we made the Terra Alta, where we fished for a couple of hours, and in the evening, at dusk, we were off the Rio do Ouro.[3]

The fog during the night grew so dense that Paulo da Gama lost sight of the captain-major, and when day broke we saw neither him nor the other vessels. We therefore made sail for the Cape Verde Islands, as we had been instructed to do in case of becoming separated.

On the following Saturday at break of day we sighted the Ilha do Sal, and an hour afterwards discovered three vessels, which turned out to be the store-ship, and the vessels commanded by Nicolau Coelho and Bartholomeu Diz [Dias], the last of whom sailed in our company as far as the Mine.[4] They, too, had lost sight of the captain-major. Having joined company we pursued our route, but the wind fell, and we were becalmed until Wednesday. At ten o'clock of that day we sighted the captain-major,

---

[1] These vessels, as appears in the course of the Journal, were the *S. Gabriel* (flag-ship), the *S. Rafael* (Paulo da Gama), the *Berrio* (Nicolau Coelho), and a store-ship (Gonçalo Nunes). The author served on board the *S. Rafael*.

[2] In the suburb of Restelo, four miles below the arsenal of Lisbon, stood a chapel or *ermida*, which had been built by Henry the Navigator for the use of mariners. In this chapel Vasco da Gama and his companions spent the night previous to their departure in prayer. After his victorious return, D. Manuel founded on its site the magnificent monastery of Our Lady of Bethlehem or Belém.

[3] For thirty-five miles from Leven Head to Elbow Point, in lat. 24° N., was known to the Portuguese of the time as *terra alta*. The Rio do Ouro is a basin, extending about twenty miles inland and four miles wide at its mouth.

[4] S. Jorge da Mina, the famous fort built on the Gold Coast in 1482, by Diogo d'Azambuja, one of whose captains had been the very Bartholomew Dias who five years afterwards doubled the Cape, and who now returned to the Mine, having been made its captain, in recognition of his great services.

3

about five leagues ahead of us, and having got speech with him in the evening we gave expression to our joy by many times firing off our bombards [1] and sounding the trumpets.

The day after this, a Thursday, we arrived at the island of Santiago [2] and joyfully anchored in the bay of Santa Maria, where we took on board meat, water, and wood, and did the much needed repairs to our yards.

On Thursday, 3rd August, we left in an easterly direction. On 18th August, [3] when about 200 leagues from Santiago going south, the captain-major's main yard broke, and we lay to under foresail and lower mainsail for two days and a night. On the 22nd of the same month, when going south by west, we saw many birds resembling herons. On the approach of night they flew vigorously to the south-south-east, as if making for the land.[4] On the same day, being then quite 800 leagues out at sea [i.e. reckoning from Santiago], we saw a whale.

On Friday, 27th October, the eve of St. Simon and St. Jude, we saw many whales, as also quoquas and seals.[5]

On Wednesday, 1st November, the day of All Saints, we perceived many indications of the neighbourhood of land, including gulf-weed, which grows along the coast.

On Saturday, the 4th of the same month, a couple of hours before break of day, we had soundings in 110 fathoms,[6] and at nine o'clock we sighted the land.[7] We then drew near to each other, and having put on our gala clothes, we saluted the captain-major by firing our bombards, and dressed the ships with flags and standards. In the course of the day we tacked so as to come close to the land, but as we failed to identify it, we again stood out to sea.

On Tuesday we returned to the land, which we found to be low, with a broad bay opening into it. The captain-major sent Pero d'Alenquer in a boat to take soundings and to search for good anchoring ground. The bay was found to be very clean, and to

[1] *Bombardas*, originally catapults, subsequently any piece of ordnance from which stone balls were thrown. In the north of Europe the term was restricted to mortars. Gama, however, carried breech-loading guns, with movable *câmeras* or chambers.

[2] Santiago, the largest of the Cape Verde Islands. The Porta da Praia, within which lies the island of Santa Maria (14° 50′ N.), is no doubt the bay referred to in the text.

[3] The date, 18th August, is obviously wrong.

[4] This is, towards Africa, Gama being at that time considerably to the north of Walvis Bay.

[5] *Lobo marinho*, sea-wolf, a term vaguely applied to all species of seals, as also to the sea-elephant, has been translated throughout as seal.

[6] A Portuguese fathom, or *braça*, is equal to 5 feet, 10 inches.

[7] This was considerably to the north of St. Helena Bay, which was only reached three days later.

afford shelter against all winds except those from the north-west. It extended east and west, and we named it Santa Helena.

On Wednesday [8th November] we cast anchor in this bay, and we remained there eight days, cleaning the ships, mending the sails, and taking in wood.

The river Santiago enters the bay four leagues to the south-east of the anchorage. It comes from the interior (sertão), is about a stone's throw across at the mouth, and from two to three fathoms in depth at all states of the tide.[1]

The inhabitants of this country are tawny-coloured.[2] Their food is confined to the flesh of seals, whales, and gazelles, and the roots of herbs. They are dressed in skins, and wear sheaths over their virile members.[3] They are armed with poles of olive wood to which a horn, browned in the fire, is attached.[4] Their numerous dogs resemble those of Portugal, and bark like them. The birds of the country, likewise, are the same as in Portugal, and include cormorants, gulls, turtle doves, crested larks, and many others. The climate is healthy and temperate, and produces good herbage.

On the day after we had cast anchor, that is to say, on Thursday, we landed with the captain-major, and made captive one of the natives, who was small of stature like Sancho Mexia. This man had been gathering honey in the sandy waste, for in this country the bees deposit their honey at the foot of the mounds around the bushes. He was taken on board the captain-major's ship, and being placed at table he ate of all we ate. On the following day the captain-major had him well dressed and sent ashore.

On the following day fourteen or fifteen natives came to where our ships lay. The captain-major landed and showed them a variety of merchandise, with the view of finding out whether such things were to be found in their country. This merchandise included cinnamon, cloves, seed-pearls, gold, and many other things, but it was evident that they had no knowledge whatever of such articles, and they were consequently given round bells and tin rings. This happened on Friday, and the like took place on Saturday.

On Sunday about forty or fifty natives made their appearance,

[1] Now called Berg River.

[2] Baço, a vague term, meaning also brown or blackish.

[3] The use of such a sheath is universal among the Bantu tribes of southern Africa, but seems now to be more honoured in the breach than the observance among the Hottentots, here spoken of. John of Empoli, who went to India with Afonso de Albuquerque (Ramusio, i), observed such a sheath made of leather with the hair on, among the Hottentots of the Bay of S. Blas.

[4] The shafts of their assegais are made of assegai- or lance-wood (Curtisea faginea), and not of olive wood, and even in John of Empoli's time had iron blades. Their spears for spearing fish, on the other hand, are tipped with the straight horn of the gemsbuck.

and having dined, we landed, and in exchange for the *ceitils* [1] with which we came provided, we obtained shells, which they wore as ornaments in their ears, and which looked as if they had been plated, and fox-tails attached to a handle, with which they fanned their faces. I also acquired for one *ceitil* one of the sheaths which they wore over their members, and this seemed to show that they valued copper very highly; indeed, they wore small beads of that metal in their ears.

On that day Fernão Veloso, who was with the captain-major, expressed a great desire to be permitted to accompany the natives to their houses, so that he might find out how they lived and what they ate. The captain-major yielded to his importunities, and allowed him to accompany them, and when we returned to the captain-major's vessel to sup, he went with the negroes. Soon after they had left us they caught a seal, and when they came to the foot of a hill in a barren place they roasted it, and gave some of it to Fernão Veloso, as also some of the roots which they eat. After this meal they expressed a desire that he should not accompany them any further, but return to the vessels. When Fernão Veloso came abreast of the vessels he began to shout, the negroes keeping in the bush.

We were still at supper; but when his shouts were heard the captain-major rose at once, and so did we others, and we entered a sailing boat. The negroes then began running along the beach, and they came as quickly up with Fernão Veloso as we did, and when we endeavoured to get him into the boat they threw their assegais, and wounded the captain-major and three or four others. All this happened because we looked upon these people as men of little spirit, quite incapable of violence, and had therefore landed without first arming ourselves. We then returned to the ships.

At daybreak on Thursday, 16th November, having careened our ships and taken in wood, we set sail. At that time we did not know how far we might be abaft the Cape of Good Hope. Pero d'Alenquer thought the distance about thirty leagues,[2] but he was not certain, for on his return voyage (when with B. Dias) he had left the Cape in the morning and had gone past this bay with the wind astern, whilst on the outward voyage he had kept at sea, and was therefore unable to identify the locality where we now were. We therefore stood out towards the south-south-west, and late on Saturday we beheld the Cape. On that same day we again stood out to sea, returning to the land in the course of the night. On Sunday morning, 19th November, we once more made for the Cape, but were again unable to round it, for the wind blew from

---

[1] *Ceitil*, a copper coin, worth about one-third of a farthing.
[2] The distance is thirty-three leagues.

the south-south-west, whilst the Cape juts out towards the south-west. We then again stood out to sea, returning to the land on Monday night. At last, on Wednesday at noon, having the wind astern, we succeeded in doubling the Cape, and then ran along the coast.

To the south of this Cape of Good Hope, and close to it, a vast bay, six leagues broad at its mouth, enters about six leagues into the land.[1]

Late on Saturday, 25th November, the day of St. Catherine, we entered the bay (*angra*) of São Brás,[2] where we remained for thirteen days, for there we broke up our store-ship and transferred her contents to the other vessels.[3]

On Friday, whilst still in the bay of São Brás, about ninety men resembling those we had met at St. Helena Bay made their appearance. Some of them walked along the beach, whilst others remained upon the hills. All, or most of us, were at the time in the captain-major's vessel. As soon as we saw them we launched and armed the boats, and started for the land. When close to the shore the captain-major threw them little round bells, which they picked up. They even ventured to approach us, and took some of these bells from the captain-major's hand. This surprised us greatly, for when Bartolomeu Dias was here the natives fled without taking any of the objects which he offered them. Nay, on one occasion, when Dias was taking in water, close to the beach, they sought to prevent him, and when they pelted him with stones, from a hill, he killed one of them with the arrow of a cross-bow. It appeared to us that they did not fly on this occasion, because they had heard from the people at the bay of St. Helena (only sixty leagues distant by sea)[4] that there was no harm in us, and that we even gave away things which were ours.

The captain-major did not land at this spot, because there was much bush, but proceeded to an open part of the beach, when he made signs to the negroes to approach. This they did. The captain-major and the other captains then landed, being attended by armed men, some of whom carried cross-bows. He then made the negroes understand, by signs, that they were to disperse, and to approach him only singly or in couples. To those who approached he gave small bells and red caps, in return for which they presented him with ivory bracelets, such as they wore on their arms, for it appears that elephants are plentiful in this country.

[1] The actual dimensions of False Bay are about five by five leagues.
[2] This is without the shadow of a doubt Mossel Bay.
[3] The thirteen days are counted from 25th November to 7th December, both these days being counted.
[4] The distance by sea is over ninety leagues, that by land sixty-four. 'By sea' is probably a slip of the pen.

We actually found some of their droppings near the watering-place where they had gone to drink.

On Saturday about two hundred negroes came, both young and old. They brought with them about a dozen oxen and cows and four or five sheep. As soon as we saw them we went ashore. They forthwith began to play on four or five flutes,[1] some producing high notes and others low ones, thus making a pretty harmony for negroes who are not expected to be musicians; and they danced in the style of negroes. The captain-major then ordered the trumpets to be sounded, and we, in the boats, danced, and the captain-major did so likewise when he rejoined us. This festivity ended, we landed where we had landed before, and bought a black ox for three bracelets. This ox we dined off on Sunday. We found him very fat, and his meat as toothsome as the beef of Portugal.

On Sunday many visitors came, and brought with them their women and little boys, the women remaining on the top of a hill near the sea. They had with them many oxen and cows. Having collected in two spots on the beach, they played and danced as they had done on Saturday. It is the custom of this people for the young men to remain in the bush with their weapons. The [older] men came to converse with us. They carried a short stick in the hand, attached to which was a fox's tail, with which they fan the face. Whilst conversing with them, by signs, we observed the young men crouching in the bush, holding their weapons in their hands. The captain-major then ordered Martin Afonso, who had formerly been in Manicongo [Congo], to advance, and to buy an ox, for which purpose he was supplied with bracelets. The natives, having accepted the bracelets, took him by the hand, and, pointing to the watering place, asked him why we took away their water, and simultaneously drove their cattle into the bush. When the captain-major observed this he ordered us to gather together, and called upon Martin Afonso to retreat, for he suspected some treachery. Having drawn together we proceeded [in our boats] to the place where we had been at first. The negroes followed us. The captain-major then ordered us to land, armed with lances, assegais, and strung crossbows, and wearing our breast-plates, for he wanted to show that we had the means of doing them an injury, although we had no desire to employ them. When they observed this they ran away. The captain-major, anxious that none should be killed by mischance, ordered the boats to draw together; but to prove that we were able, although unwilling to hurt them, he ordered two bombards to be fired from the poop of the longboat. They were by that time all seated close to the bush, not far from the beach, but the first discharge caused them

[1] The *gora* is the great musical instrument of the Hottentots. It is not a flute or reed-pipe.

to retreat so precipitately that in their flight they dropped the skins with which they were covered and their weapons. When they were in the bush two of them turned back to pick up the articles which had been dropped. They then continued their flight to the top of a hill, driving their cattle before them.

The oxen of the country are as large as those of Alentejo, wonderfully fat and very tame. They are geldings, and hornless. Upon the fattest among them the negroes place a pack-saddle made of reeds, as is done in Castile, and upon this saddle they place a kind of litter made of sticks, upon which they ride. If they wish to sell an ox they pass a stick through his nostrils, and thus lead him.

There is an island in this bay, three bowshots from the land, where there are many seals.[1] Some of these are as big as bears, very formidable with large tusks. These attack man, and no spear, whatever the force with which it is thrown, can wound them. There are others much smaller and others quite small. And whilst the big ones roar like lions, the little ones cry like goats. One day, when we approached this island for our amusement, we counted, among large and small ones, 3,000, and we fired among them with our bombards from the sea. On the same island there are birds as big as ducks, but they cannot fly, because they have no feathers on their wings. These birds, of whom we killed as many as we chose, are called *fotilicaios*, and they bray like asses.[2]

Whilst taking in water in this bay of São Brás, on a Wednesday, we erected a cross and a pillar.[3] The cross was made out of a mizzen-mast, and very high. On the following Thursday, when about to sail, we saw about ten or twelve negroes, who demolished both the cross and the pillar before we left.

Having taken on board all we stood in need of we took our departure, but as the wind failed us we anchored the same day, having proceeded only two leagues.

On Friday morning, the day of the Immaculate Conception, we again set sail. On Tuesday, the eve of Santa Lucia, we encountered a great storm, and ran before a stern-wind with the foresail much lowered. On that day we lost sight of Nicolau Coelho, but at sunset we saw him from the top four or five leagues astern, and it seemed as if he saw us too. We exhibited signal lights and lay to. By the end of the first watch he had come up

[1] This island is still known as Seal Island, although its former visitors no longer make their appearance. The islet lies about half a mile from the land, is only 250 feet in length and 15 feet high.

[2] They are clearly Cape penguins.

[3] The word used by the author is *padrão*, that is, a stone pillar bearing the arms of Portugal and an inscription, such as King John first ordered to be set up by his explorers. None of the 'pillars' set up by Vasco da Gama has been recovered, for the 'pillar' near Malindi is clearly of later date.

with us, not because he had seen us during the day, but because, the wind being scant, he could not help coming in our waters.

On the morning of Friday we saw the land near the Ilheus Chãos (Flat Islands). These are five leagues beyond the Ilha da Cruz (Cross Island). From the bay of São Brás to Cross Island is a distance of sixty leagues, and as much from the Cape of Good Hope to the bay of São Brás. From the Flat Islands to the last pillar erected by Bartolomeu Dias is five leagues, and from this pillar to the Rio do Infante is fifteen leagues.[1]

On Saturday we passed the last pillar, and as we ran along the coast we observed two men running along the beach in a direction contrary to that which we followed. The country here is very charming and well wooded; we saw much cattle, and the further we advanced the more did the character of the country improve, and the trees increase in size.

During the following night we lay to. We were then already beyond the last discovery made by Bartolomeu Dias.[2] On the next day till vespers, we sailed along the coast before a stern-wind, when the wind springing round to the east we stood out to sea. And thus we kept making tacks until sunset on Tuesday, when the wind again veered to the west. We then lay to during the night, in order that we might on the following day examine the coast and find out where we were.

In the morning we made straight for the land, and at ten o'clock found ourselves once more at the Ilheu da Cruz (Cross Island), that is sixty leagues abaft our dead reckoning! This was due to the currents, which are very strong here.[3]

That very day we again went forward by the route we had already attempted, and being favoured during three or four days by a strong stern-wind, we were able to overcome the currents which we had feared might frustrate our plans. Henceforth it pleased God in His mercy to allow us to make headway! We were not again driven back. May it please Him that it be thus alway!

By Christmas Day, 25th December, we had discovered seventy leagues of coast [beyond Dias's furthest]. On that day, after dinner, when setting a studding-sail, we discovered that the mast

[1] The distances given by the author are remarkably correct. From the Cape of Good Hope to Mossel Bay (São Brás) is sixty leagues, as stated by him. Thence to Santa Cruz is fifty-six leagues; from Santa Cruz to the Rio do Infante is twenty-one leagues.
Santa Cruz is the largest of a group of islands in the western part of Algoa Bay. It is four cables in length, rises to a height of 195 feet, and is nearly all bare rock. *There are no springs*. The *Ilheus Chãos* are readily identified with a cluster of low rocky islets about seven leagues to the east. The Cape Padrone of the charts marks the site of the last pillar erected by Dias.
[2] That is, the Rio do Infante, now known as the Great Fish River
[3] The Agulhas current hereabouts runs at the rate of one to four knots an hour to the westward.

had sprung a couple of yards below the top, and that the crack opened and shut. We patched it up with backstays, hoping to be able to repair it thoroughly as soon as we should reach a sheltered port.

On Thursday we anchored near the coast, and took much fish. At sunset we again set sail and pursued our route. At that place the mooring-rope snapped and we lost an anchor.

We now went so far out to sea, without touching any port, that drinking-water began to fail us, and our food had to be cooked with salt water. Our daily ration of water was reduced to a *quartilho*.[1] It thus became necessary to seek a port.

On Thursday, 11th January (1498),[2] we discovered a small river and anchored near the coast. On the following day we went close in shore in our boats, and saw a crowd of negroes, both men and women. They were tall people, and a chief (*senhor*) was among them. The captain-major ordered Martin Afonso, who had been a long time in Manicongo, and another man, to land. They were received hospitably. The captain-major, in consequence, sent the chief a jacket, a pair of red pantaloons, a Moorish cap, and a brace-let. The chief said that we were welcome to anything in his country of which we stood in need: at least, this is how Martin Afonso understood him. That night, Martin Afonso and his companion accompanied the chief to his village, whilst we returned to the ships. On the road the chief donned the garments which had been presented to him, and to those who came forth to meet him he said with much apparent satisfaction: 'Look, what has been given to me!' The people upon this clapped hands as a sign of courtesy, and this they did three or four times until he arrived at the village. Having paraded the whole of the place, thus dressed up, the chief retired to his house, and ordered his two guests to be lodged in a compound, where they were given porridge of millet, which abounds in that country, and a fowl, just like those of Portugal. All the night through, numbers of men and women came to have a look at them. In the morning the chief visited them, and asked them to go back to the ships. He ordered two men to accompany them, and gave them fowls as a present for the captain-major, telling them at the same time that he would show the things that had been given him to a great chief, who appears to be the king of that country. When our men reached the landing place where our boats awaited them, they were attended by quite two hundred men, who had come to see them.

This country seemed to us to be densely peopled. There are many chiefs, and the number of women seems to be greater than that of the men, for among those who came to see us there were

---

[1] Equivalent to three-fourths of a pint.
[2] The MS. says 10th January, but Thursday was the 11th.

forty women to every twenty men.   The houses are built of straw.
The arms of the people include long-bows and arrows and spears
with iron blades.   Copper seems to be plentiful, for the people
wore [ornaments] of it on their legs and arms and in their twisted
hair.   Tin, likewise, is found in the country, for it is to be seen on
the hilts of their daggers, the sheaths of which are made of ivory.
Linen cloth is highly prized by the people, who were always willing
to give large quantities of copper in exchange for shirts.   They
have large calabashes in which they carry sea-water inland, where
they pour it into pits to obtain the salt [by evaporation].

We stayed five days at this place, taking in water, which our
visitors conveyed to our boats.   Our stay was not, however, sufficiently prolonged to enable us to take in as much water as we
really needed, for the wind favoured a prosecution of our voyage.

We were at anchor here, near the coast, exposed to the swell of
the sea.   We called the country Terra da Boa Gente (Land of Good
People) and the river Rio de Cobre (Copper River).

On Monday we discovered a low coast thickly wooded with tall
trees.   Continuing our course we perceived the broad mouth of a
river.[1]   As it was necessary to find out where we were, we cast
anchor.   On Thursday, at night, we entered.   The *Berrio* was
already there, having entered the night before—that is, eight days
before the end of January [i.e. 24th January].[2]

The country is low and marshy, and covered with tall trees
yielding an abundance of various fruits, which the inhabitants eat.

These people are black and well made.   They go naked, merely
wearing a piece of cotton stuff around their loins, that worn by
the women being larger than that worn by the men.   The young
women are good-looking.   Their lips are pierced in three places,
and they wear in them bits of twisted tin.   These people took
much delight in us.   They brought us in their *almadias* [3] what
they had, whilst we went into their village to procure water.

When we had been two or three days at this place two gentlemen (*senhores*) of the country came to see us.   They were very
haughty, and valued nothing which we gave them.   One of them
wore a *touca*,[4] with a fringe embroidered in silk, and the other a
cap of green satin.   A young man in their company—so we understood from their signs—had come from a distant country, and had

---

[1] João dos Santos (*Ethiopia oriental*, II. xx) already identified this river with
the Kiliman River.

[2] A very involved sentence!   Gama arrived off the bar of the Kiliman on
24th January, cast anchor, and sent the smallest of his vessels, the *Berrio*,
within, to take soundings.   On the day after the 25th, he crossed the bar with
the two other vessels.

[3] *Almadia*, a 'dug-out,' properly *el maziyah*, ferry-boat.

[3] Burton (*Commentary*, p. 408) points out that the *touca* is not a turban, but
a kind of cap.   Its shape, however, was not that of the toque of our milliners.

already seen big ships like ours.   These tokens (*senhais*) gladdened our hearts, for it appeared as if we were really approaching the bourne of our desires.   These gentlemen had some huts built on the river bank, close to the ships, in which they stayed seven days, sending daily to the ships, offering to barter cloths which bore a mark of red ochre.   And when they were tired of being there they left in their *almadias* for the upper river.

As to ourselves, we spent thirty-two days [1] in the river taking in water, careening the ships, and repairing the mast of the *Rafael*. Many of our men fell ill here, their feet and hands swelling, and their gums growing over their teeth, so that they could not eat.[2]

We erected here a pillar which we called the pillar of St. Raphael, because it had been brought in the ship bearing that name.   The river we called Rio dos Bons Senhais (River of Good Signs or Tokens).

On Saturday we left this place and gained the open sea.   During the night we stood north-east, so as to keep away from the land, which was very pleasing to look upon.   On Sunday we still stood north-east, and at vesper time discovered three small islands, out in the open, of which two were covered with tall trees, while the third and smallest was barren.   The distance from one island to the other was four leagues.[3]

On the following day we pursued our route, and did so during six days, lying to at night.[4]

On Thursday, 1st March, we sighted islands and the mainland, but as it was late we again stood out to sea, and lay to till morning. We then approached the land, of which I shall speak in what follows.

On Friday morning Nicolau Coelho, when attempting to enter the bay, mistook the channel and came upon a bank.   When putting about ship, towards the other ships which followed in his wake, Coelho perceived some sailing boats approaching from a village on this island, in order to welcome the captain-major and his brother.   As for ourselves we continued in the direction of our proposed anchorage, these boats following us all the while, and making signs for us to stop.   When we had cast anchor in the roadstead of the island from which these boats had come, there approached seven or eight of them, including *almadias*, the people

[1] From 24th January to 24th February, both days included, is thirty-two days.
[2] This disease was evidently scurvy, so fatal to our early navigators.   Castanheda (i. iv) tells us that in this time of trouble Paulo da Gama visited the sick night and day, condoled with them, and freely distributed the medicines which he had brought for his own use.
[3] They are five in number, and form a chain less than five leagues in length. The three southern islands (Silva, do Fogo, and Crown) form a separate group, and are bare, whilst the two northern islands (Casuarina and Epidendron) have trees.   Gama, apparently, missed the two southernmost islands.
[4] These six days are reckoned from 24th February to 1st March.

in them playing upon *anfils*.[1]   They invited us to proceed further
into the bay, offering to take us into port if we desired it.   Those
among them who boarded our ships ate and drank what we did,
and went their way when they were satisfied.[2]

The captain thought that we should enter this bay in order that
we might find out what sort of people we had to deal with; that
Nicolau Coelho should go first in his vessel, to take soundings at
the entrance, and that, if found practicable, we should follow him.
As Coelho prepared to enter he struck the point of the island
and broke his helm, but he immediately disengaged himself and
regained deep water.   I was with him at the time.   When we were
again in deep water we struck our sails and cast anchor at a distance
of two bowshots from the village.[3]

The people of this country are of ruddy complexion and well
made.   They are Mohammedans, and their language is the same
as that of the Moors.[4]   Their dresses are of fine linen or cotton
stuffs, with variously coloured stripes, and of rich and elaborate
workmanship.   They all wear *toucas* with borders of silk embroidered in gold.   They are merchants, and have transactions
with white Moors, four of whose vessels were at the time in port,
laden with gold, silver, cloves, pepper, ginger, and silver rings,
as also with quantities of pearls, jewels, and rubies, all of which
articles are used by the people of this country.   We understood
them to say that all these things, with the exception of the gold,
were brought thither by these Moors; that further on, where we
were going to, they abounded, and that precious stones, pearls, and
spices were so plentiful that there was no need to purchase them as
they could be collected in baskets.   All this we learned through a
sailor the captain-major had with him, and who, having formerly
been a prisoner among the Moors, understood their language.

These Moors, moreover, told us that along the route which we
were about to follow we should meet with numerous shoals; that
there were many cities along the coast, and also an island, one-
half of the population of which consisted of Moors and the other
half of Christians, who were at war with each other.   The island
was said to be very wealthy.

We were told, moreover, that Prester John [5] resided not far

[1] Arabic, *el nafir*, a sort of straight Moorish trumpet or tuba.
[2] They took their visitors for 'Turks,' or at all events for Mohammedans.
All this changed after their true character had been discovered.
[3] It appears from this that Vasco da Gama entered the port immediately on
his arrival, and took a position close to the town.
[4] That is, Arabic.   The 'Moors' of the author are, in fact, either pure Arabs
(white Moors) or Swahilis speaking Arabic.
[5] Vasco da Gama had no doubt received special instructions to inquire for
that Christian potentate.   At one time he was looked for inland from Benin,
but the information received from Pero de Covilhã, whom King John had
dispatched overland to India, in 1487, no less than that furnished by Lucas

from this place; that he held many cities along the coast, and that the inhabitants of those cities were great merchants and owned big ships. The residence of Prester John was said to be far in the interior, and could be reached only on the back of camels. These Moors had also brought hither two Christian captives from India.[1] This information, and many other things which we heard, rendered us so happy that we cried with joy, and prayed to God to grant us health, so that we might behold what we so much desired.

In this place and island of Moncobiquy (Mozambique) there resided a chief (*senhor*) who had the title of sultan, and was like a viceroy. He often came aboard our ships attended by some of his people. The captain-major gave him many good things to eat, and made him a present of hats, *marlotas*,[2] corals, and many other articles. He was, however, so proud that he treated all we gave him with contempt, and asked for scarlet cloth, of which we had none. We gave him, however, of all the things we had.

One day the captain-major invited him to a repast, when there was an abundance of figs and comfits, and begged him for two pilots to go with us. He at once granted this request, subject to our coming to terms with them. The captain-major gave each of them thirty *mitkals*[3] in gold and two *marlotas*, on condition that from the day on which they received this payment one of them should always remain on board if the other desired to go on land. With these terms they were well satisfied.

On Saturday, 10th March, we set sail and anchored out at sea, close to an island,[4] where mass was said on Sunday, when those who wished to do so confessed and joined in the communion.

One of our pilots lived on the island, and when we had anchored we armed two boats to go in search of him. The captain-major went in one boat and Nicolau Coelho in the other. They were met by five or six boats (*barcas*) coming from the island, and crowded with people armed with bows and long arrows and bucklers, who gave them to understand by signs that they were to return to the town. When the captain saw this he secured the

---

Marcos, an Abyssinian priest, who came to Lisbon soon after Covilhã's departure, confirmed the Portuguese in the belief that the 'Prester John' they were in quest of was the emperor of Ethiopia, whose capital at that time was in Shoa (see Álvares).

[1] Barros calls them Abyssinians from the country of Prester John, and says that when they saw the image of the saint which formed the figure-head of the *S. Gabriel*, they knelt down and worshipped. The Abyssinian Christians, whatever their shortcomings, do not worship images, as is the practice of the Roman Church. These captives, therefore, must have been Indians, as stated by our author.

[2] *Marlota*, a short dress of silk or wool worn in Persia and India.

[3] A Mozambique *matikal* (*miskal*) weighs 4·41346 grammes.

[4] The island of S. Jorge.

pilot whom he had taken with him, and ordered the bombards to
fire upon the boats.   Paulo da Gama, who had remained with the
ships, so as to be prepared to render succour in case of need, no
sooner heard the reports of the bombards than he started in the
Berrio.   The Moors, who were already flying, fled still faster, and
gained the land before the *Berrio* was able to come up with them.
We then returned to our anchorage.

The vessels of this country are of good size and decked.   There
are no nails, and the planks are held together by cords,[1] as are also
those of their boats (*barcos*).   The sails are made of palm-matting.[2]
Their mariners have Genoese needles,[3] by which they steer,
quadrants, and navigating charts.

The palms of this country yield a fruit as large as a melon, of
which the kernel is eaten.[4]   It has a nutty flavour.   There also
grow in abundance melons and cucumbers, which were brought
to us for barter.

On the day in which Nicolau Coelho entered the port, the lord
of the place came on board with a numerous suite.   He was
received well, and Coelho presented him with a red hood, in return
for which the lord handed him a black rosary, which he made use
of when saying his prayers, to be held as a pledge.   He then begged
Nicolau Coelho for the use of his boat, to take him ashore.   This
was granted.   And after he had landed he invited those who had
accompanied him to his house, where he gave them to eat.   He
then dismissed them, giving them a jar of bruised dates made into
a preserve with cloves and cumin, as a present for Nicolau Coelho.
Subsequently he sent many things to the captain-major.   All this
happened at the time when he took us for Turks or for Moors from

[1] *Tamica*, popularly known as coir rope.   These 'sewn boats' were already
in use when the *Periplus of the Erythraean Sea* was written, and the town of
Rhapta (from ῥάπτειν, to sew) derived its name from them.

[2] Mats were the wings wherewith they lightly flew,
From certain palm-fronds wove by cunning hand.
Camões, i. 46.—Burton s translation.

[3] The 'Genoese needle' is, of course, the mariner's compass.   The pilots of
the Indian Ocean determined relative latitudes by observing the altitude of
certain stars.   The result was expressed, not in degrees as was done by the
scientific astronomers, but in *isbas* or 'fingers,' each equivalent to $1° 42' 50''$.
The instrument which they used consisted of three staffs.   Two of these were
movable on a hinge, and were directed respectively upon the horizon, and the
star the altitude of which it was desired to determine.   A third staff (or an
octant) was fixed at the end of the horizon staff, and upon it the angle observed
could be read off.   Vasco da Gama brought one of these instruments with him
to Portugal, but the astronomer of Cabral's expedition, who had been instructed
to test its qualities, reported unfavourably.   Yet the results obtained by means
of this instrument by the pilots of the Indian Ocean were very satisfactory, and
the charts prepared by these very practical men were far more correct than the
abortions produced by 'scientific' Arab geographers.

[4] The fruit is the coco-nut.

some foreign land, for in case we came from Turkey he begged to be shown the bows of our country and our books of the law. But when they learnt that we were Christians they arranged to seize and kill us by treachery. The pilot, whom we took with us, subsequently revealed to us all they intended to do, if they were able.

On Sunday we celebrated mass beneath a tall tree on the island [of S. Jorge]. We returned on board and at once set sail, taking with us many fowls, goats, and pigeons, which had been given us in exchange for small glass beads.

On Tuesday we saw high mountains rising on the other side of a cape. The coast near the cape was sparsely covered with trees, resembling elms. We were at that time over twenty leagues from our starting-place, and there we remained becalmed during Tuesday and Wednesday. During the following night we stood off shore with a light easterly wind, and in the morning found ourselves four leagues abaft Mozambique, but we went again forward on that day until the evening, when we anchored once more close to the island [of S. Jorge] on which mass had been celebrated the preceding Sunday, and there we remained eight days waiting for a favourable wind.

During our stay here the king of Mozambique sent word that he wanted to make peace with us and to be our friend. His ambassador was a white Moor and *sharif*,[1] that is, priest, and at the same time a great drunkard.

Whilst at this place a Moor with his little son came on board one of our ships, and asked to be allowed to accompany us, as he was from near Mecca, and had come to Mozambique as pilot of a vessel from that country.

As the weather did not favour us it became necessary once more to enter the port of Mozambique, in order to procure the water of which we stood in need, for the watering-place is on the mainland. This water is drunk by the inhabitants of the island, for all the water they have there is brackish.

On Thursday we entered the port, and when it grew dark we lowered our boats. At midnight the captain-major and Nicolau Coelho, accompanied by some of us, started in search of water. We took with us the Moorish pilot, whose object appeared to be to make his escape, rather than to guide us to a watering-place. As a matter of fact, he either would not or could not find a watering-place, although we continued our search until morning. We then withdrew to our ships.

---

[1] The *sharifs* ('nobles') are the descendants of the Prophet, and although not 'priests,' they enjoy a certain religious rank. Strictly speaking, this title can be claimed only by the head of the family which descends from the Prophet in a direct line. All others can only claim the title of *saiyid*, lord. The 'white' Moors are, of course, true Arabs.

In the evening we returned to the mainland, attended by the same pilot. On approaching the watering-place, we saw about twenty men on the beach. They were armed with assegais, and forbade our approach. The captain-major upon this ordered three bombards to be fired upon them, so that we might land. Having effected our landing, these men fled into the bush, and we took as much water as we wanted. When the sun was about to set we discovered that a negro belonging to João de Coimbra had effected his escape.

On Sunday morning, 24th March, being the eve of Lady Day, a Moor came abreast our ships, and [sneeringly] told us that if we wanted water we might go in search of it, giving us to understand that we should meet with something which would make us turn back. The captain-major no sooner heard this [threat] than he resolved to go, in order to show that we were able to do them harm if we desired it. We forthwith armed our boats, placing bombards in their poops, and started for the village [town]. The Moors had constructed palisades by lashing plants together, so that those behind them could not be seen. They were at the time walking along the beach, armed with assegais, swords,[1] bows, and slings, with which they hurled stones at us. But our bombards soon made it so hot for them that they fled behind their palisades; but this turned out to their injury rather than their profit. During the three hours that we were occupied in this manner [bombarding the town] we saw two men killed, one on the beach and the other behind the palisades. When we were weary of this work we retired to our ships to dine. They at once began to fly, carrying their chattels in *almadias* to a village on the mainland.

After dinner we started in our boats, in the hope of being able to make a few prisoners, whom we might exchange for the two Indian Christians whom they held captive, and the negro who had deserted. With this object in view we chased an *almadia*, which belonged to the *sharif* and was laden with his chattels, and another in which were four negroes.[2] The latter was captured by Paulo da Gama, whilst the one laden with chattels was abandoned by the crew as soon as they reached the land. We took still another *almadia* which had likewise been abandoned. The negroes we took on board our ships. In the *almadias* we found fine cotton stuffs, baskets made of palm fronds, a glazed jar containing butter, glass phials with scented water, books of the Law, a box containing skeins of cotton, a cotton net, and many small baskets filled with millet. All these things, with the exception of the books, which were kept back to be shown to the king, were given by the

[1] *Agonia*, Arabic *el jumbiyah*, a crooked poniard, worn in the waist-belt.
[2] Barros calls these captives 'Moors,' and the author himself does the same at a later stage of his journal.

captain-major to the sailors who were with him and with the other captains.

On Sunday we took in water, and on Monday we proceeded in our armed boats to the village, when the inhabitants spoke to us from their houses, they daring no longer to venture on the beach. Having discharged a few bombards at them we rejoined our ships.

On Tuesday we left the town and anchored close to the islets of São Jorge,[1] where we remained for three days, in the hope that God would grant us a favourable wind.

On Thursday, 29th March, we left these islets of São Jorge, and as the wind was light, we only covered twenty-eight leagues up to the morning of Saturday, the 31st of the month.[2]

In the morning of that day we were once more abreast of the land of the Moors, from which powerful currents had previously carried us.[3]

On Sunday, 1st April, we came to some islands close to the mainland. The first of these we called Ilha do Açoutado (Island of the Flogged One), because of the flogging inflicted upon our Moorish pilot, who had lied to the captain on Saturday night, by stating that these islands were the mainland. Native craft take their course between these islands and the mainland, where the water is four fathoms deep, but we kept outside of them. These islands are numerous, and we were unable to distinguish one from the other; they are inhabited.

On Monday we sighted other islands five leagues off the shore.[4]

On Wednesday, 4th April, we made sail to the north-west, and before noon we sighted an extensive country, and two islands close to it, surrounded with shoals. And when we were near enough for the pilots to recognize these islands, they told us that we had left three leagues behind us an island,[5] inhabited by Christians. We manœuvred all day in the hope of fetching this island, but in vain, for the wind was too strong for us. After this we thought it best to bear away for a city called Mombasa, reported to be four days ahead of us.

The above island was one of those which we had come to discover, for our pilots said that it was inhabited by Christians.

[1] That is São Jorge, and the small islet of Santiago, 1¾ miles to the south.

[2] The text has 30th, but Saturday was the 31st.

[3] These were the Kerimba islands, the southernmost of which is Kizwa, 12° 35′ S. The mainland, being generally low, will rarely be seen when coasting outside the reefs.

[4] These were the islands of Cabo Delgado. None of these, however, is more than nine miles from the mainland.

[5] This island was Quiloa (Kilwa), whose king, at that time, was the most powerful along the coast, Sofala, the Zambesi, Angoshe, and Mozambique being subject to him (*Duarte Barbosa*, p. 10).

When Vasco da Gama attempted to put back he had probably reached Ras Tikwiri, 8° 50′ S.

When we bore away for the north it was already late, and the wind was high. At nightfall we perceived a large island, which remained to the north of us.[1] Our pilot told us that there were two towns on this island, one of Christians and the other of Moors.

That night we stood out to sea, and in the morning we no longer saw the land. We then steered to the north-west, and in the evening we again beheld the land. During the following night we bore away to the north by west, and during the morning watch we changed our course to the north-north-west. Sailing thus before a favourable wind, the *S. Rafael*, two hours before break of day, ran aground on a shoal, about two leagues from the land. Immediately the *Rafael* touched bottom, the vessels following her were warned by shouts, and these were no sooner heard than they cast anchor about the distance of a gunshot from the stranded vessel, and lowered their boats. When the tide fell the *Rafael* lay high and dry. With the help of the boats many anchors were laid out, and when the tide rose again, in the course of the day, the vessel floated and there was much rejoicing.

On the mainland, facing these shoals, there rises a lofty range of mountains, beautiful of aspect. These mountains we called Serras de São Rafael, and we gave the same name to the shoals.[2]

Whilst the vessel was high and dry, two *almadias* approached us. One was laden with fine oranges, better than those of Portugal. Two of the Moors remained on board, and accompanied us next day to Mombasa.

On Saturday morning, the 7th of the month, and eve of Palm Sunday, we ran along the coast and saw some islands at a distance of fifteen leagues from the mainland, and about six leagues in extent. They supply the vessels of the country with masts. All are inhabited by Moors.[3]

On Saturday we cast anchor off Mombasa, but did not enter the

[1] Mafia.

[2] On the homeward voyage, in January 1499, the *S. Rafael* was burnt at these shoals, which are described as lying off the town of Tamugata (Mtangata), and this enables us to fix upon the locality with much certainty. There still is a roadstead or bay called Mtangata, which 'the long roll of the Indian Ocean renders a place of trembling to the coast trader' (Burton, *Journal of the Royal Geographical Society*, 1858, p. 200). A 'town' of this name exists no longer, but Burton describes the ruins of what was once an extensive city near the village of Tongoni.

There are no 'mountains' close to the coast corresponding to the 'Serras de São Rafael,' but the mountains of Usambara, rising twenty to twenty-five miles inland to an altitude of 3,500 feet, are visible in clear weather for a distance of sixty-two miles.

[3] This was Pemba, which, owing to its deep bays, appeared to consist of a number of islands. Its distance from the mainland is only thirty miles (nine leagues), its length, thirty-seven miles. The trees of that island still supply masts for native vessels.

port. No sooner had we been perceived than a *zavra* [1] manned by Moors, came out to us; in front of the city there lay numerous vessels all dressed in flags. And, we, anxious not to be outdone, also dressed our ships, and we actually surpassed their show, for we wanted in nothing but men, even the few whom we had being very ill. We anchored here with much pleasure, for we confidently hoped that on the following day we might go on land and hear mass jointly with the Christians reported to live there under their own *alcaide* [2] in a quarter separate from that of the Moors.

The pilots who had come with us told us there resided both Moors and Christians in this city; that these latter lived apart under their own lords, and that on our arrival they would receive us with much honour and take us to their houses. But they said this for a purpose of their own, for it was not true. At midnight there approached us a *zavra* with about a hundred men, all armed with cutlasses (*tarçados*) and bucklers. When they came to the vessel of the captain-major they attempted to board her, armed as they were, but this was not permitted, only four or five of the most distinguished men among them being allowed on board. They remained about a couple of hours, and it seemed to us that they paid us this visit merely to find out whether they might not capture one or other of our vessels.

On Palm Sunday the king of Mombasa sent the captain-major a sheep and large quantities of oranges, lemons, and sugar-cane, together with a ring, as a pledge of safety, letting him know that in case of his entering the port he would be supplied with all he stood in need of. This present was conveyed to us by two men, almost white, who said they were Christians, which appeared to be the fact. The captain-major sent the king a string of coral beads as a return present, and let him know that he purposed entering the port on the following day. On the same day the captain-major's vessel was visited by four Moors of distinction.

Two men were sent by the captain-major to the king, still further to confirm these peaceful assurances. When these landed they were followed by a crowd as far as the gates of the palace. Before reaching the king they passed through four doors, each guarded by a doorkeeper with a drawn cutlass. The king received them hospitably, and ordered that they should be shown over the city. They stopped on their way at the house of two Christian merchants, who showed them a paper (*carta*), an object of their adoration, on which was a sketch of the Holy Ghost. [3] When they had seen

---

[1] *Zavra* or *zabra*, a dhow, which is a small open vessel, sharp at the stern, with a square sail of matting.

[2] *Alcaide*, from the Arabic *alkadi*, the judge.

[3] Burton (*Camões*, iv. 241) suggests that this picture of the Holy Ghost may have been a figure of Kapot-eshwar, the Hindu pigeon-god and goddess, an incarnation of Shiva and his wife, the third person of the Hindu triad.

all, the king sent them back with samples of cloves, pepper, and corn, with which articles he would allow us to load our ships.

On Tuesday, when weighing anchor to enter the port, the captain-major's vessel would not pay off, and struck the vessel which followed astern. We therefore again cast anchor. When the Moors who were in our ship saw that we did not go on, they scrambled into a *zavra* attached to our stern; whilst the two pilots whom we had brought from Mozambique jumped into the water, and were picked up by the men in the *zavra*. At night the captain-major 'questioned' two Moors[1] whom we had on board, by dropping boiling oil upon their skin, so that they might confess any treachery intended against us. They said that orders had been given to capture us as soon as we entered the port, and thus to avenge what we had done at Mozambique. And when this torture was being applied a second time, one of the Moors, although his hands were tied, threw himself into the sea, whilst the other did so during the morning watch.

About midnight two *almadias*, with many men in them, approached. The *almadias* stood off whilst the men entered the water, some swimming in the direction of the *Berrio*, others in that of the *Rafael*. Those who swam to the *Berrio* began to cut the cable. The men on watch thought at first that they were tunny fish, but when they perceived their mistake they shouted to the other vessels. The other swimmers had already got hold of the rigging of the mizzen-mast. Seeing themselves discovered, they silently slipped down and fled. These and other wicked tricks were practised upon us by these dogs, but our Lord did not allow them to succeed because they were unbelievers.

Mombasa is a large city seated upon an eminence washed by the sea. Its port is entered daily by numerous vessels. At its entrance stands a pillar, and by the sea a low-lying fortress. Those who had gone on shore told us that in the town they had seen many men in irons; and it seemed to us that these must be Christians, as the Christians in that country are at war with the Moors.

The Christian merchants in the town are only temporary residents, and are held in much subjection, they not being allowed to do anything except by the order of the Moorish king.

It pleased God in His mercy that on arriving at this city all our sick recovered their health, for the climate ('air') of this place is very good.

---

[1] These two 'Moors' were undoubtedly two of the four men whom Paulo da Gama had captured at Mozambique, but whom the author previously described as negroes. Of the two pilots who escaped one had been given them by the sultan of Mozambique.

After the malice and treachery planned by these dogs had been discovered, we still remained on Wednesday and Thursday.[1]

We left in the morning, the wind being light, and anchored about eight leagues from Mombasa, close to the shore. At break of day we saw two boats (*barcas*) about three leagues to the leeward, in the open sea, and at once gave chase, with the intention of capturing them, for we wanted to secure a pilot who would guide us to where we wanted to go. At vesper time we came up with one of them and captured it, the other escaping towards the land. In the one we took we found seventeen men, besides gold, silver, and an abundance of maize and other provisions; as also a young woman who was the wife of an old Moor of distinction, who was a passenger. When we came up with the boat they all threw themselves into the water, but we picked them up from our boats.

That same day at sunset, we cast anchor off a place called Malindi, which is thirty leagues from Mombasa. The following places are between Mombasa and Malindi, viz. Benapa, Toca, and Nuguoquioniete.[2]

On Easter Sunday the Moors whom we had taken in the boat told us that there were at this city of Malindi[3] four vessels belonging to Christians from India, and if it pleased us to take them there, they would provide us, instead of them, Christian pilots and all we stood in need of, including water, wood, and other things. The captain-major much desired to have pilots from the country, and having discussed the matter with his Moorish prisoners, he cast anchor off the town, at a distance of about half a league from the mainland. The inhabitants of the town did not venture to come aboard our ships, for they had already learnt that we had captured a vessel and made her occupants prisoners.

On Monday morning the captain-major had the old Moor taken to a sandbank in front of the town, where he was picked up by an *almadia*. The Moor explained to the king the wishes of the captain-major, and how much he desired to make peace with him. After dinner the Moor came back in a *zavra*, accompanied by one of the king's cavaliers and a *sharif*: he also brought three

[1] Castanheda (I. x. 35) says they waited two days in the hope of being able to secure a pilot to take them to Calicut. On crossing the bar they were unable to heave up one of the anchors. The Moors subsequently fished it up and placed it near the royal palace, where D. Francisco de Almeida found it when he took the town in 1505.

[2] Sir J. Kirk suggests to me that these places are Mtwapa, Takaungu, and Kilifi, distorted into Benapa, Toca-nuguo, and Quioniete. Kioni is the native name of the village usually called Kilifi.

[3] The ruins of the ancient town of Malindi lie to the south of the modern village of that name, and are of great extent. They include the remains of a town wall. Persian and Arabic inscriptions have been discovered, but, with the exception of Vasco da Gama's pillar, no traces of occupation by the Portuguese. Malindi Road, or Port Melinda of the Admiralty chart, lies about three miles to the south of the town.

sheep. These messengers told the captain-general that the king would rejoice to make peace with him, and to enter into friendly relations; that he would willingly grant to the captain-major all his country afforded, whether pilots or anything else. The captain-major, upon this, sent word that he proposed to enter the port on the following day, and forwarded by the king's messengers a present consisting of a *balandrau*,[1] two strings of coral, three wash-hand basins, a hat, little bells, and two pieces of *lambel*.[2]

Consequently, on Tuesday we approached nearer to the town. The king sent the captain-major six sheep, besides quantities of cloves, cumin, ginger, nutmeg, and pepper, as also a message, telling him that if he desired to have an interview with him he (the king) would come out in his *zavra*, when the captain-major could meet him in a boat.

On Wednesday, after dinner, when the king came up close to the ships in a *zavra*, the captain-major at once entered one of his boats, which had been well furnished, and many friendly words were exchanged when they lay side by side. The king having invited the captain-major to come to his house to rest, after which he (the king) would visit him on board his ship, the captain-major said that he was not permitted by his master to go on land, and if he were to do so a bad report would be given of him. The king wanted to know what would be said of himself by his people if he were to visit the ships, and what account could he render them? He then asked for the name of our king, which was written down for him, and said that on our return he would send an ambassador with us, or a letter.

When both had said all they desired, the captain-major sent for the Moors whom he had taken prisoner, and surrendered them all. This gave much satisfaction to the king, who said he valued this act more highly than if he had been presented with a town. And the king, much pleased, made the circuit of our ships, the bombards of which fired a salute. About three hours were spent in this way. When the king went away he left in the ship one of his sons and a *sharif*, and took two of us away with him, to whom he desired to show his palace. He, moreover, told the captain that as he would not go ashore he would himself return on the following day to the beach, and would order his horsemen to go through some exercises.

The king wore a robe (royal cloak) of damask trimmed with green satin, and a rich *touca*. He was seated on two cushioned chairs of bronze, beneath a round sunshade of crimson satin attached to a pole. An old man, who attended him as page,

---

[1] *Balandrau*, a surtout worn by the Brothers of Mercy in Portugal.
[2] *Lambel*, a striped cotton stuff which had a large sale at the beginning of the African trade.

carried a short sword in a silver sheath. There were many players on *anafils*, and two trumpets of ivory,[1] richly carved, and the size of a man, which were blown from a hole in the side, and made sweet harmony with the *anafils*.

On Thursday the captain-major and Nicolau Coelho rowed along the front of the town, bombards having been placed in the poops of their longboats. Many people were along the shore, and among them two horsemen, who appeared to take much delight in a sham fight. The king was carried in a palanquin from the stone steps of his palace to the side of the captain-major's boats. He again begged the captain to come ashore, as he had a helpless father who wanted to see him, and that he and his sons would go on board the ships as hostages. The captain, however, excused himself.[2]

We found here four vessels belonging to Indian Christians. When they came for the first time on board Paulo da Gama's ship, the captain-major being there at the time, they were shown an altar-piece representing Our Lady at the foot of the Cross, with Jesus Christ in her arms and the Apostles around her. When the Indians saw this picture they prostrated themselves, and as long as we were there they came to say their prayers in front of it, bringing offerings of cloves, pepper, and other things.[3]

These Indians are tawny men; they wear but little clothing and have long beards and long hair, which they braid. They told us that they ate no beef. Their language differs from that of the Arabs, but some of them know a little of it, as they hold much intercourse with them.

On the day on which the captain-major went up to the town in the boats, these Christian Indians fired off many bombards from their vessels, and when they saw him pass they raised their hands and shouted lustily: 'Christ! Christ!'[4]

[1] The royal trumpet, or *siwa*, was peculiar to the cities ruled by the descendants of the Persians of Shiraz, who settled on this coast in the eleventh and twelfth centuries. They were of ivory, or copper and wood, and consisted of three pieces. The ivory or copper was sometimes most elaborately carved, and bore Arabic texts.

[2] We learn from this passage that the 'king' referred to by the author was in reality the king's son, who acted as regent. He may be supposed to be the sheikh Wagerage (Wajeraj), who in 1515 wrote a letter to King Manuel, in which he begged for permission to send annually *one* vessel to Goa and to Mozambique. He very humbly (or sarcastically?) addresses the king as the 'fountain of the commerce of all cities and kingdoms, the most equitable of sovereigns, and the enricher of all people'; when, indeed, the Portuguese had crippled the trade of Malindi, which had received them with open arms.

[3] Of course they looked upon these Romish images and pictures as outlandish representations of their own gods and idols.

[4] Burton (*Camões*, iv. 420) suggests that they cried 'Krishna,' the name of the eighth Incarnation of Vishnu, the second person of the Hindu Trinity, and the most popular of Indian gods. Sir J. Kirk knows of no word resembling 'Krist' likely to have been called out by these Indians.

That same night they asked the king's permission to give us a night fête; and when night came they fired off many bombards, sent up rockets, and raised loud shouts.

These Indians warned the captain-major against going on shore, and told him not to trust to their 'fanfares,' as they neither came from their hearts nor from their good will.

On the following Sunday, 22nd April, the king's *zavra* brought on board one of his confidential servants, and as two days had passed without any visitors, the captain-major had this man seized, and sent word to the king that he required the pilots whom he had promised. The king, when he received this message, sent a Christian pilot,[1] and the captain-major allowed the gentleman, whom he had retained in his vessel, to go away.

We were much pleased with the Christian pilot whom the king had sent us. We learnt from him that the island of which we heard at Mozambique as being inhabited by Christians was in reality an island subject to this same king of Mozambique; that half of it belonged to the Moors and the other half to the Christians; that many pearls were to be found there, and that it was called Quyluee.[2] This is the island the Moorish pilots wanted to take us to, and we also wished to go there, for we believed that what they said was true.

The town of Malindi lies in a bay and extends along the shore. It may be likened to Alcochete.[3] Its houses are lofty and well whitewashed, and have many windows; on the land side are palm groves, and all around it maize and vegetables are being cultivated.

We remained in front of this town during nine days,[4] and all this time we had fêtes, sham fights, and musical performances ('fanfares').

We left Malindi on Tuesday, the 24th of the month, for a city called Qualecut (Calicut), with the pilot whom the king had given us. The coast there runs north and south, and the land encloses a huge bay with a strait. In this bay,[5] we were told, were to be found many large cities of Christians and Moors, including one called Quambay (Cambay), as also six hundred known islands, and within it the Red Sea and the 'house' [Kaabah] of Mecca.

On the following Sunday we once more saw the north star, which we had not seen for a long time.

[1] This pilot was a native of Gujarat.
[2] The island in question is Kilwa. The information furnished by this Malindi pilot is scarcely more correct than that previously obtained from the Moors.
[3] Alcochete, a town on the left bank of the estuary of the Tagus, above Lisbon.
[4] From 15th to 23rd April is nine days.
[5] The 'bay' is the Arabian Sea, which the 'Strait' of Bab el Mandeb joins to the Red Sea. Cambay (Khambhat), in Gujarat, when the Portuguese first came to India, was one of the most flourishing marts of commerce. The silting up of the gulf accounts, in a large measure, for its commercial decline since then.

On Friday, 18th May,[1] after having seen no land for twenty-three days,[2] we sighted lofty mountains, and having all this time sailed before the wind we could not have made less than 600 leagues. The land, when first sighted,[3] was at a distance of eight leagues, and our lead reached bottom at forty-five fathoms. That same night we took a course to the south-south-west, so as to get away from the coast. On the following day we again approached the land, but owing to the heavy rain and a thunderstorm,[4] which prevailed whilst we were sailing along the coast, our pilot was unable to identify the exact locality. On Sunday we found ourselves close to some mountains,[5] and when we were near enough for the pilot to recognize them he told us that they were above Calicut, and that this was the country we desired to go to.

That night we anchored two leagues from the city of Calicut, and we did so because our pilot mistook Capua,[6] a town at that place, for Calicut. Still further, there is another town called Pandarini.[7] We anchored about a league and a half from the shore. After we were at anchor, four boats (*almadias*) approached us from the land, who asked of what nation we were. We told them, and they then pointed out Calicut to us.

On the following day these same boats came again alongside, when the captain-major sent one of the convicts to Calicut, and those with whom he went took him to two Moors from Tunis, who could speak Castilian and Genoese. The first greeting that he received was in these words: 'May the devil take thee! What brought you hither?' They asked what he sought so far away from home, and he told them he came in search of Christians and of spices. They said: 'Why does not the King of Castile, the King of France, or the Signoria of Venice send hither?' He said that the King of Portugal would not consent to their doing so, and they said he did the right thing. After this conversation they took him to their lodgings and gave him wheaten bread and honey. When he had eaten he returned to the ships, accompanied by one

---

[1] The MS. says 17th, but Friday was the 18th.

[2] From 24th April to 18th May, both days inclusive, is twenty-five days; the African coast was within sight for several days.

[3] Mount Eli (Dely) was probably the land first sighted, a conspicuous hill forming a promontory about sixteen miles to the north of Cananor.

[4] The rains in Malabar begin about April or May, and continue until September or October. They are synchronous with the south-west monsoon, and are heaviest in June, July, and August. The annual rainfall exceeds 150 inches.

[5] Cotta Point, or Cape Kadalur, the 'Monte Formosa,' of the Portuguese, fifteen miles N.N.W. of Calicut.

[6] Castanheda and Barros call this place Capocate. It was seven miles N.N.W. of Calicut, at the mouth of the Elatur River.

[7] Pandaramy (Pandarani) is Batuta's Fandarain. It is identical with Pantharini Kollam, the northern Kollam or Quillan, and boasts one of the nine original mosques built on the Malabar coast by Malik Ibn Dinar. It is fourteen miles N.N.W. of Calicut.

of the Moors, who was no sooner on board, than he said these words: 'A lucky venture, a lucky venture! Plenty of rubies, plenty of emeralds! You owe great thanks to God for having brought you to a country holding such riches!' We were greatly astonished to hear his talk, for we never expected to hear our language spoken so far away from Portugal.

The city of Calicut is inhabited by Christians. They are of tawny complexion. Some of them have big beards and long hair, whilst others clip their hair short or shave the head, merely allowing a tuft to remain on the crown as a sign that they are Christians. They also wear moustaches. They pierce the ears and wear much gold in them. They go naked down to the waist, covering their lower extremities with very fine cotton stuffs. But it is only the most respectable who do this, for the others manage as best they are able.[1]

The women of this country, as a rule, are ugly and of small stature. They wear many jewels of gold round the neck, numerous bracelets on their arms, and rings set with precious stones on their toes. All these people are well disposed and apparently of mild temper. At first sight they seem covetous and ignorant.

When we arrived at Calicut the king was fifteen leagues away. The captain-major sent two men to him with a message, informing him that an ambassador had arrived from the King of Portugal with letters, and that if he desired it he would take them to where the king then was.

The king presented the bearers of this message with much fine cloth. He sent word to the captain bidding him welcome, saying that he was about to proceed to Calicut. As a matter of fact, he started at once with a large retinue.

A pilot accompanied our two men, with orders to take us to a place called Pandarani, below the place [Capua] where we anchored at first. At this time we were actually in front of the city of Calicut. We were told that the anchorage at the place to which we were to go was good, whilst at the place we were then it was bad, with a stony bottom, which was quite true;[2] and, moreover, that it was customary for the ships which came to this country to anchor there for the sake of safety. We ourselves did not feel comfortable, and the captain-major had no sooner received this royal message than he ordered the sails to be set, and we departed. We did not, however, anchor as near the shore as the king's pilot desired.

[1] The visitors thus became at once acquainted with the various castes constituting the population of Calicut, including the Nairs, or fighting caste of Malabar, who eat meat (which shows a servile origin), but wear the thread of the Dwija (twice-born), rank next to the Brahmans, and practise polyandry; and the turbulent Moplah, who are descendants of Arab fathers and native women. These latter are the 'native' Moors.
[2] Off Calicut there are banks and reefs which may endanger the safety of a ship, but the anchorage in the roadstead within them is perfectly safe.

When we were at anchor, a message arrived informing the captain-major that the king was already in the city. At the same time the king sent a *bale*,[1] with other men of distinction, to Pandarani, to conduct the captain-major to where the king awaited him. This *bale* is like an *alcaide*, and is always attended by two hundred men armed with swords and bucklers. As it was late when this message arrived, the captain-major deferred going.

On the following morning, which was Monday, 28th May, the captain-major set out to speak to the king, and took with him thirteen men, of whom I was one.[2] We put on our best attire, placed bombards in our boats, and took with us trumpets and many flags. On landing, the captain-major was received by the *alcaide*, with whom were many men, armed and unarmed. The reception was friendly, as if the people were pleased to see us, though at first appearances looked threatening, for they carried naked swords in their hands. A palanquin was provided for the captain-major, such as is used by men of distinction in that country, as also by some of the merchants, who pay something to the king for this privilege. The captain-major entered the palanquin, which was carried by six men by turns. Attended by all these people we took the road of Calicut, and came first to another town, called Capua. The captain-major was there deposited at the house of a man of rank, whilst we others were provided with food, consisting of rice, with much butter, and excellent boiled fish. The captain-major did not wish to eat, and when we had done so, we embarked on a river close by, which flows between the sea and the mainland, close to the coast.[3] The two boats in which we embarked were lashed together,[4] so that we were not separated. There were numerous other boats, all crowded with people. As to those who were on the banks I say nothing; their number was infinite, and they had all come to see us. We went up that river for about a league, and saw many large ships drawn up high and dry on its banks, for there is no port here.

When we disembarked, the captain-major once more entered his palanquin. The road was crowded with a countless multitude anxious to see us. Even the women came out of their houses with children in their arms and followed us.

[1] *Bale*, in Arabic *wali*, governor. *Alcaide*, in Portuguese, has the same meaning.
[2] Among the thirteen men were Diogo Dias, João de Sá, Gonçalo Pires, Álvaro Velho, Álvaro de Braga, João de Setúbal, João de Palha, and six others, whose names are not recorded. Paulo da Gama and Coelho were left in charge of the vessels, with orders to sail at once for Portugal should any disaster happen to their chief.
[3] This river is the Elatur.
[4] Burton (*Goa*, p. 191) says that even now the usual ferry-boat consists of a platform of planks lashed to two canoes and usually railed round.

When we arrived they took us to a large church,[1] and this is
what we saw:

The body of the church is as large as a monastery, all built of
hewn stone and covered with tiles. At the main entrance rises
a pillar of bronze as high as a mast, on the top of which was perched
a bird, apparently a cock.   In addition to this, there was another
pillar as high as a man, and very stout.   In the centre of the body
of the church rose a chapel, all built of hewn stone, with a bronze
door sufficiently wide for a man to pass, and stone steps leading up
to it.   Within this sanctuary stood a small image which they said
represented Our Lady.[2]   Along the walls, by the main entrance,
hung seven small bells.[3]   In this church the captain-major said
his prayers, and we with him.[4]

We did not go within the chapel, for it is the custom that only
certain servants of the church, called *quafees*,[5] should enter.   These
quafees wore some threads passing over the left shoulder and under
the right arm, in the same manner as our deacons wear the stole.
They threw holy water over us, and gave us some white earth,[6]
which the Christians of this country are in the habit of putting on
their foreheads, breasts, around the neck, and on the forearms.
They threw holy water upon the captain-major and gave him some
of the earth, which he gave in charge of someone, giving them to
understand that he would put it on later.

Many other saints were painted on the walls of the church,

---

[1] This 'church' was, of course, a pagoda or temple. The high pillar in
front of it is used for suspending the flag which indicates the commencement of
the temple festival.   It is of wood, but usually covered with copper or silver.
The cock, which surmounts it, is the symbol of the war-god Subraumainar.
The smaller pillar supports the coco-oil lamps during the festival.—Rev.
J. J. Jaus.

[2] Gois (xl) says that the four priests alone entered this sanctuary, and,
pointing to the image, said: 'Maria, Maria,' upon which the natives prostrated
themselves, whilst the Portuguese knelt, in adoration of the Virgin.   Burton
suggests that this was an image of Gauri, the 'White Goddess,' whilst Charton
(iii. 246) suggests Maha Maja and her son Shakya.

The Rev. J. Jacob Jaus, of the Basel Mission at Calicut, informs me that
there is a local deity called Mari, or Mariamma, much dreaded as the goddess
of smallpox, and highly venerated.   Amma, in Malayalam, means mother.

[3] These bells are struck by the Brahmans when they enter the temple, but
must not be touched by people of inferior castes.

[4] It is just possible that some of the Portuguese doubted whether these Hindu
gods and images represented the saints of their own churches.   Castanheda
(i. 57) says that when João de Sá knelt down by the side of Vasco da Gama, he
said: 'If these be devils, I worship the true God'; at which his chief smiled.
But however this may be, it is equally true that the reports furnished by the heads
of the expedition describe the Hindus as Christians, and that the king believed
them to be so.

[5] The *quafees* are, of course, Brahman priests.   The Rev. J. J. Jaus suggests
kaz (Arabic), meaning judge.

[6] The 'white earth' is a mixture of dust, cow-dung, sacrificial ashes, sandal-
wood, etc., cemented in rice water.

wearing crowns. They were painted variously, with teeth protruding an inch from the mouth, and four or five arms.

Below this church there was a large masonry tank, similar to
many others which we had seen along the road.

After we had left that place, and had arrived at the entrance to
the city, we were shown another church, where we saw things like
those described above. Here the crowd grew so dense that progress along the street became next to impossible, and for this
reason they put the captain into a house, and us with him.

The king sent a brother of the *bale*, who was a lord of this
country, to accompany the captain, and he was attended by men
beating drums, blowing *anafils* and bagpipes, and firing off matchlocks. In conducting the captain they showed us much respect,
more than is shown in Spain to a king. The number of people
was countless, for in addition to those who surrounded us, and
among whom there were two thousand men, they crowded the
roofs and houses.

The further we advanced in the direction of the king's palace,
the more did they increase in number; and when we arrived
there, men of much distinction and great lords came out to meet
the captain, and joined those who were already in attendance upon
him. It was then an hour before sunset. When we reached the
palace we passed through a gate into a courtyard of great size,
and before we arrived at where the king was, we passed four doors,
through which we had to force our way, giving many blows to the
people. When, at last, we reached the door where the king was,
there came forth from it a little old man, who holds a position resembling that of a bishop, and whose advice the king acts upon in
all affairs of the church. This man embraced the captain when he
entered the door. Several men were wounded at this door, and
we only got in by the use of much force.

The king was in a small court, reclining upon a couch covered
with a cloth of green velvet, above which was a good mattress, and
upon this again a sheet of cotton stuff, very white and fine, more
so than any linen. The cushions were after the same fashion.
In his left hand the king held a very large golden cup [spittoon],
having a capacity of half an *almude* [8 pints]. At its mouth this
cup was two *palmas* [16 inches] wide, and apparently it was massive. Into this cup the king threw the husks of a certain herb
which is chewed by the people of this country because of its soothing effects, and which they call *atambor*.[1] On the right side of the
king stood a basin of gold, so large that a man might just encircle

---

[1] *Atambor*, a corruption of the Arabic *al tambur*, the betel-nut. It is the fruit
of *Areca Catechu*, and is universally chewed throughout India, the Indian
archipelago, and southern China. Its juice discolours the teeth, but is said to
make the breath sweet, and to be conducive to health.

it with his arms; this contained the herbs.   There were likewise
many silver jugs.   The canopy above the couch was all gilt.

The captain, on entering, saluted in the manner of the country:
by putting the hands together, then raising them towards Heaven,
as is done by Christians when addressing God, and immediately
afterwards opening them and shutting the fists quickly.   The king
beckoned to the captain with his right hand to come nearer, but
the captain did not approach him, for it is the custom of the country for no man to approach the king except only the servant who
hands him the herbs, and when any one addresses the king he
holds his hand before the mouth, and remains at a distance.   When
the king beckoned to the captain he looked at us others, and
ordered us to be seated on a stone bench near him, where he could
see us.   He ordered that water for our hands should be given us,
as also some fruit, one kind of which resembled a melon, except
that its outside was rough and the inside sweet, whilst another kind
of fruit resembled a fig, and tasted very nice.[1]   There were men
who prepared these fruits for us; and the king looked at us eating,
and smiled; and talked to the servant who stood near him supplying
him with the herbs referred to.

Then, throwing his eyes on the captain, who sat facing him,
he invited him to address himself to the courtiers present, saying
they were men of much distinction, that he could tell them whatever he desired to say, and they would repeat it to him (the king).
The captain-major replied that he was the ambassador of the
King of Portugal, and the bearer of a message which he could only
deliver to him personally.   The king said this was good, and
immediately asked him to be conducted to a chamber.   When
the captain-major had entered, the king, too, rose and joined him,
whilst we remained where we were.   All this happened about sunset.   An old man who was in the court took away the couch as
soon as the king rose, but allowed the plate to remain.   The king,
when he joined the captain, threw himself upon another couch,
covered with various stuffs embroidered in gold, and asked the
captain what he wanted.

And the captain told him he was the ambassador of a king of
Portugal, who was lord of many countries and the possessor of
great wealth of every description, exceeding that of any king of
these parts; that for a period of sixty years his ancestors had annually sent out vessels to make discoveries in the direction of India,
as they knew that they were Christian kings there like themselves.
This, he said, was the reason which induced them to order this
country to be discovered, not because they sought for gold or
silver, for of this they had such abundance that they needed not
what was to be found in this country.   He further stated that the

[1] These fruits were the jack (*Artocarpus integrifolia*) and the banana.

captains sent out travelled for a year or two, until their provisions were exhausted, and then returned to Portugal, without having succeeded in making the desired discovery. There reigned a king now whose name was Dom Manuel, who had ordered him to build three vessels, of which he had been appointed captain-major, and who had ordered him not to return to Portugal until he should have discovered the king of the Christians, on pain of having his head cut off. That two letters had been entrusted to him to be presented in case he succeeded in discovering him, and that he would do so on the ensuing day; and, finally, he had been instructed to say by word of mouth that he [the king of Portugal] desired to be his friend and brother.

In reply to this the king said that he was welcome; that, on his part, he held him as a friend and brother, and would send ambassadors with him to Portugal. This latter had been asked as a favour, the captain pretending that he would not dare to present himself before his king and master unless he was able to present, at the same time, some men of this country.

These and many other things passed between the two in the chamber, and as it was already late in the night, the king asked the captain with whom he desired to lodge, with Christians or with Moors. And the captain replied, neither with Christians nor with Moors, and begged, as a favour that he be given a lodging by himself. The king said he would order it thus, upon which the captain took leave of the king and came to where we were, that is, to a veranda lit up by a huge candlestick. By that time four hours of the night had already gone.[1]

We then all went forth with the captain in search of our lodgings, and a countless crowd with us. And the rain poured down so heavily that the streets ran with water. The captain went on the back of six men [in a palanquin], and the time occupied in passing through the city was so long that the captain at last grew tired, and complained to the king's factor, a Moor of distinction, who attended him to the lodgings. The Moor then took him to his own house, and we were admitted to a court within it, where there was a veranda roofed in with tiles. Many carpets had been spread, and there were two large candlesticks like those at the royal palace. At the top of each of these were great iron lamps, fed with oil or butter, and each lamp had four wicks, which gave much light. These lamps they use instead of torches.

The same Moor then had a horse brought for the captain to take him to his lodgings, but it was without a saddle, and the captain refused to mount it.[2] We then started for our lodgings, and when

---

[1] That is, it was about 10 p.m.
[2] It is still the practice in Calicut to ride horses without a saddle, and no slight seems therefore to have been intended.

we arrived we found there some of our men [who had come from
the ships] with the captain's bed, and with numerous other things
which the captain had brought as presents for the king.

On Tuesday the captain got ready the following things to be sent
to the king, viz. twelve pieces of *lambel*, four scarlet hoods, six
hats, four strings of coral, a case containing six wash-hand basins,
a case of sugar, two casks of oil, and two of honey.   And as it is
the custom not to send anything to the king without the knowledge
of the Moor, his factor, and of the *bale*, the captain informed them
of his intention.   They came, and when they saw the present they
laughed at it, saying that it was not a thing to offer to a king,
that the poorest merchant from Mecca, or any other part of India,
gave more, and that if he wanted to make a present it should be
in gold, as the king would not accept such things.   When the
captain heard this he grew sad, and said he had brought no gold,
that, moreover, he was no merchant, but an ambassador; that he
gave of that which he had, which was his own [private gift] and
not the king's; [1] that if the King of Portugal ordered him to return
he would entrust him with far richer presents; and that if King
Samolin would not accept these things he would send them back
to the ships.   Upon this they declared that they would not forward
his presents, nor consent to his forwarding them himself.   When
they had gone there came certain Moorish merchants, and they
all depreciated the present which the captain desired to be sent
to the king.

When the captain saw that they were determined not to forward
his present, he said, that as they would not allow him to send his
present to the palace he would go to speak to the king, and would
then return to the ships.   They approved of this, and told him
that if he would wait a short time they would return and accompany
him to the palace.   And the captain waited all day, but they never
came back.   The captain was very wroth at being among so
phlegmatic and unreliable a people, and intended, at first, to go
to the palace without them.   On further consideration, however,
he thought it best to wait until the following day.   As to us others,
we diverted ourselves, singing and dancing to the sound of trumpets,
and enjoyed ourselves much.

On Wednesday morning the Moors returned, and took the captain to the palace, and us others with him.   The palace was crowded
with armed men.   Our captain was kept waiting with his conduc-
tors for fully four long hours, outside a door, which was only
opened when the king sent word to admit him, attended by two
men only, whom he might select.   The captain said that he desired
to have Fernão Martins with him, who could interpret, and his

[1] As a matter of fact, Vasco da Gama was very poorly provided with suitable
merchandise.

secretary. It seemed to him, as it did to us, that this separation portended no good.

When he had entered, the king said that he had expected him on Tuesday. The captain said that the long road had tired him, and that for this reason he had not come to see him. The king then said that he had told him that he came from a very rich kingdom, and yet had brought him nothing; that he had also told him that he was the bearer of a letter, which had not yet been delivered. To this the captain rejoined that he had brought nothing, because the object of his voyage was merely to make discoveries, but that when other ships came he would then see what they brought him; as to the letter, it was true that he had brought one, and would deliver it immediately.

The king then asked him what it was he had come to discover: stones or men? If he came to discover men, as he said, why had he brought nothing? Moreover, he had been told that he carried with him the golden image of a Santa Maria. The captain said that the Santa Maria was not of gold, and that even if she were he would not part with her, as she had guided him across the ocean, and would guide him back to his own country. The king then asked for the letter. The captain said that he begged as a favour, that as the Moors wished him ill and might misinterpret him, a Christian able to speak Arabic should be sent for. The king said this was well, and at once sent for a young man, of small stature, whose name was Quaram. The captain then said that he had two letters, one written in his own language and the other in that of the Moors; that he was able to read the former, and knew that it contained nothing but what would prove acceptable, but as to the other he was unable to read it, and it might be good, or contain something that was erroneous. As the Christian was unable to *read* Moorish, four Moors took the letter and read it between them, after which they translated it to the king, who was well satisfied with its contents.

The king then asked what kind of merchandise was to be found in his country. The captain said there was much corn, cloth, iron, bronze, and many other things. The king asked whether he had any merchandise with him. The captain replied that he had a little of each sort, as samples, and that if permitted to return to the ships he would order it to be landed, and that meantime four or five men would remain at the lodgings assigned them. The king said no. He might take all his people with him, securely moor his ships, land his merchandise, and sell it to the best advantage. Having taken leave of the king the captain returned to his lodgings, and we with him. As it was already late no attempt was made to depart that night.

On Thursday morning, a horse without a saddle was brought to the captain, who declined to mount it, asking that a horse of the country, that is a palanquin, might be provided, as he could not ride a horse without a saddle.   He was then taken to the house of a wealthy merchant of the name of Guzerate,[1] who ordered a palanquin to be got ready.   On its arrival the captain started at once for Pandarani, where our ships were, many people following him.   We others, not being able to keep up with him, were left behind.   Trudging thus along we were overtaken by the *bale*, who passed on to join the captain.   We lost our way, and wandered far inland, but the *bale* sent a man after us, who put us on the right road.   When we reached Pandarani we found the captain inside a rest-house, of which there were many along the road, so that travellers and wayfarers might find protection against the rain.

The *bale* and many others were with the captain.   On our arrival the captain asked the *bale* for an *almadia*, so that we might go to our ships; but the *bale* and the others said that it was already late—in fact, the sun had set—and that he should go next day.   The captain said that unless he provided an *almadia* he would return to the king, who had given orders to take him back to the ships, whilst they tried to detain him—a very bad thing, as he was a Christian like themselves.   When they saw the dark looks of the captain they said he was at liberty to depart at once, and that they would give him thirty *almadias* if he needed them.   They then took us along the beach, and as it seemed to the captain that they harboured some evil design, he sent three men in advance, with orders that in case they found the ship's boats and his brother, to tell him to conceal himself.   They went, and finding nothing, turned back; but as we had been taken in another direction we did not meet.

They then took us to the house of a Moor—for it was already far in the night—and when we got there they told us that they would go in search of the three men who had not yet returned. When they were gone, the captain ordered fowls and rice to be purchased, and we ate, notwithstanding our fatigue, having been all day on our legs.

Those who had gone [in search of the three men] only returned in the morning, and the captain said that after all they seemed well disposed towards us, and had acted with the best intentions when they objected to our departure the day before.   On the other hand, we suspected them on account of what had happened at Calicut, and looked upon them as ill-disposed.

When they returned the captain again asked for boats to take him to his ships.   They then began to whisper among themselves, and said that we should have them if we would order our vessels to come nearer the shore.   The captain said that if he ordered his

[1] That is, a man of Gujarat.

vessels to approach his brother would think that he was being held a prisoner, and that he gave this order on compulsion, and would hoist the sails and return to Portugal.   They said that if we refused to order the ships to come nearer we should not be permitted to embark.   The captain said that King Samolin had sent him back to his ships, and that as they would not let him go, as ordered by the king, he should return to the king, who was a Christian like himself.   If the king would not let him go, and wanted him to remain in his country, he would do so with much pleasure.   They agreed that he should be permitted to go, but afforded him no opportunity for doing so, for they immediately closed all the doors, and many armed men entered to guard us, none of us being allowed to go outside without being accompanied by several of these guards.

They then asked us to give up our sails and rudders.   The captain declared that he would give up none of these things: King Samolin having unconditionally ordered him to return to his ships, they might do with him whatever they liked, but he would give up nothing.

The captain and we others felt down-hearted, though outwardly we pretended not to notice what they did.   The captain said that as they refused him permission to go back, they would at least allow his men to do so, as at the place they were in they would die of hunger.   But they said that we must remain where we were, and that if we died of hunger we must bear it, as they cared nothing for that.   While thus detained, one of the men whom we had missed the night before turned up.   He told the captain that Nicolau Coelho had been awaiting him with the boats since last night.   When the captain heard this he sent a man away secretly to Nicolau Coelho, because of the guards by whom we were surrounded, with orders to go back to the ships and place them in a secure place.   Nicolau Coelho, on receipt of this message, departed forthwith.   But our guards, having information of what was going on, at once launched a large number of *almadias* and pursued him for a short distance.   When they found that they could not overtake him they returned to the captain, whom they asked to write a letter to his brother, requesting him to bring the ships nearer to the land and further within the port (roadstead).   The captain said that he was quite willing, but that his brother would not do this; and that even if he consented those who were with him, not being willing to die, would not do so.   But they asked how this could be, as they knew well any order he gave would be obeyed.

The captain did not wish the ships to come within the port, for it seemed to him—as it did to us—that once inside they could easily be captured, after which they would first kill him, and then us others, as we were already in their power.

We passed all that day most anxiously.   At night more people surrounded us than ever before, and we were no longer allowed to walk in the compound, within which we were, but confined within a small tiled court, with a multitude of people around us. We quite expected that on the following day we should be separated, or that some harm would befall us, for we noticed that our gaolers were much annoyed with us. This, however, did not prevent our making a good supper off the things found in the village. Throughout the night we were guarded by over a hundred men, all armed with swords, two-edged battle-axes, shields, and bows and arrows. Whilst some of these slept, others kept guard, each taking his turn of duty throughout the night.

On the following day, Saturday, 2nd June, in the morning, these gentlemen [i.e. the *bale* and others] came back, and this time they 'wore better faces.' They told the captain that as he had informed the king that he intended to land his merchandise, he should now give orders to have this done, as it was the custom of the country that every ship on its arrival should at once land the merchandise it brought, as also the crews, and that the vendors should not return on board until the whole of it had been sold. The captain consented, and said that he would write to his brother to see to it being done. They said this was well, and that immediately after the arrival of the merchandise he would be permitted to return to his ship. The captain at once wrote to his brother to send certain things, and he did so at once. On their receipt the captain was allowed to go on board, two men remaining behind with the things that had been landed.[1]

At this we rejoiced greatly, and rendered thanks to God for having extricated us from the hands of people who had no more sense than beasts, for we knew well that once the captain was on board those who had been landed would have nothing to fear. When the captain reached his ship he ordered that no more merchandise should be sent.

---

[1] These men were Diogo Dias, as factor, and Álvaro de Braga as his assistant.

II. THE DISCOVERY OF BRAZIL. 1500

(Translated by Charles David Ley)

Bibliographical

In *Corografia Brasileira*. By Padre Manuel Aires do Casal. Rio de Janeiro. 1817.

In *Historia da Colonisação Portuguesa do Brasil*. By Carolina Michaëlis de Vasconcelos. Lisbon. 1922.

Carta de Pero Vaz de Caminha. (Reprodução fac-simile, leitura paleográfica, versão em linguagem atual, notas e estudo literário, histórico e topográfico.) By Jaime Cortesão. Rio de Janeiro. 1942.

In *O Descobrimento da América e a suposta Prioridade dos Portuguêses*. By Thomaz Oscar Marcondes de Souza. São Paulo. 1944.

TRANSLATION: In *Cabral's Voyage to Brazil and India*. By William Brooks Greenlee. Hakluyt Society. 1938.

THE DISCOVERY OF BRAZIL

Letter of Pedro Vaz de Caminha, written in Pôrto-Seguro of Vera Cruz on the First Day of May in the Year 1500.

SIRE,

The admiral of this fleet, besides the other captains, will write to Your Majesty telling you the news of the finding of this new territory of Your Majesty's which has just been discovered on this voyage. But I, too, cannot but give my account of this matter to Your Majesty, as well as I can, though I know that my powers of telling and relating it are less than any man's.[1] May it please Your Majesty, however, to let my good faith serve as an excuse for my ignorance, and to rest assured that I shall not set down anything beyond what I have seen and reflected on, either to add beauty or ugliness to the narrative. I shall not give any account of the crew or the ship's course, since that is the pilot's concern, and I should not know how to do so. Therefore, Sire, I begin what I have to tell thus:

And I say that our departure from Belém was, as Your Majesty knows, on Monday, 9th March. On Saturday, the 14th of the same month, between eight and nine o'clock we sailed between the Canary Islands,[2] going in nearest to the Grand Canary. We were becalmed in sight of them the whole day, for some three or four leagues. On Sunday the 22nd of the same month, at about ten o'clock, we came in sight of the Cape Verde Islands,[3] or, to be precise, St. Nicholas's Island, as the pilot, Pero Escobar,[4] declared.

On the following night, the Monday, we discovered at dawn that Vasca de Ataíde and his ship had been lost, though there was no strong or contrary wind to account for this.[5] The admiral sought him diligently in all directions, but he did not appear again. So we continued on our way across the ocean until on the Tuesday of Easter week, which was 21st April, we came across some signs of being near land, at some 660 or 670 leagues from the aforesaid

[1] One should not forget that this is modesty and that Caminha was a highly trained professional scribe.
[2] Recently colonized by the Spanish.
[3] Recently colonized by the Portuguese.
[4] Pilot of the *Berrio* on da Gama's expedition.
[5] He later rejoined them.

island, by the pilot's computation. These signs were a great
quantity of those long seaweeds sailors call *botelho*, as well as
others to which they give the name of 'asses' tails.' On the
following morning, Wednesday, we came across the birds they
call 'belly-rippers.'

This same day, at the hour of vespers we sighted land, that is to
say, first a very high rounded mountain, then other lower ranges of
hills to the south of it, and a plain covered with large trees. The
admiral named the mountain Easter Mount [1] and the country the
Land of the True Cross.

He ordered them to drop the plumb-line, and they measured
twenty-five fathoms. At sunset, about six leagues from the shore,
we dropped anchor in nineteen fathoms, and it was a good clean
anchorage. There we lay all that night. On Thursday morning
we set sail and made straight for land, with the smaller ships leading,
the water being seventeen, sixteen, fifteen, fourteen, thirteen,
twelve, ten and nine fathoms deep, until we were half a league
from the shore. Here we all cast anchor opposite a river mouth.
It must have been more or less ten o'clock when we reached this
anchorage.

From there we caught sight of men [2] walking on the beaches.
The small ships which arrived first said that they had seen some
seven or eight of them. We let down the longboats and the skiffs.
The captains of the other ships came straight to this flagship,
where they had speech with the admiral. He sent Nicolau Coelho [3]
on shore to examine the river.[4] As soon as the latter began to
approach it, men came out on to the beach in groups of twos and
threes, so that, when the longboat reached the river mouth,
there were eighteen or twenty waiting.

They were dark brown and naked, and had no covering for their
private parts, and they carried bows and arrows in their hands.
They all came determinedly towards the boat. Nicolau Coelho
made a sign to them to put down their bows, and they put them
down. But he could not speak to them or make himself understood in any other way because of the waves which were breaking
on the shore. He merely threw them a red cap, and a linen bonnet [5]
he had on his head, and a black hat. And one of them threw him
a hat of large feathers with a small crown of red and grey feathers,
like a parrot's. Another gave him a large bough covered with
little white beads which looked like seed-pearls. I believe that

[1] It retains this name, and is one of the highest mountains in the province
of Bahia.
[2] Tupi Indians.
[3] See da Gama's voyage.
[4] The Caí.
[5] A kind of stocking-cap, with a peak that hangs down and can be moved
towards the sun. Portuguese peasants still wear similar caps.

the admiral is sending these articles to Your Majesty. After this, as it was late, the expedition returned to the ships, without succeeding in having further communication with them, because of the sea.

That night there was such a strong south-easterly wind and squalls that it dragged the ships out of their position, more especially the flagship.   On Friday morning at about eight o'clock, by the pilot's advice, the captain ordered the anchors to be weighed and the sails hoisted.   We went up the coast to the northwards with the longboats and skiffs tied to our sterns, to see if we could find a sheltered spot to anchor in where we could stay to take in water and wood.   Not that these were lacking to us, but so as to be provided with everything now, in good time.   At the hour when we set sail about sixty or seventy men had gradually come up and were seated near the river.   We sailed on, and the admiral told the small ships to run under the shore and to slacken sails if they found a sufficiently protected spot for the ships.

Thus we sailed along the coast, and, ten leagues from the spot where we had weighed anchor, the aforesaid small ships found a ridge of rock which contained a very good, safe port with a very large entrance.   So they went in and struck sails.   The bigger ships came up behind them, and, a little while after sundown, they struck sails also, perhaps at a league from the rocks, and anchored in eleven fathoms.

Our pilot,[1] Afonso Lopes, was in one of the small ships, and he received orders from the admiral to go in the skiff to take the soundings inside the port, for he was a lively and capable man for the work.   He took up two of the men of the country from a canoe.[2]   They were young and well formed and one of them had a bow and six or seven arrows.   There were many others on the shore with bows and arrows, but they did not use them.   Later, in the evening, he took the two men to the flagship where they were received with great rejoicings and festivities.

They are of a dark brown, rather reddish colour.   They have good well-made faces and noses.   They go naked, with no sort of covering.   They attach no more importance to covering up their private parts or leaving them uncovered than they do to showing their faces.   They are very ingenuous in that matter.   They both had holes in their lower lips and a bone in them as broad as the knuckles of a hand and as thick as a cotton spindle and sharp at one end like a bodkin.[3]   They put these bones in from inside the

[1] That is, of the flagship.
[2] *Almadia*. Álvaro Velho also uses the word, which Ravenstein does not translate.
[3] See Álvaro Velho on p. 12 for a similar custom amongst the Africans.

C 986

lip [1] and the part which is placed between the lip and the teeth is made like a rook in chess.   They fit them in in such a way that they do not hurt them nor hinder them talking or eating or drinking.

Their hair is straight.   They shear their hair,[2] but leave it a certain length, not cutting it to the roots, though they shave it above the ears.   One of them had on a kind of wig covered with yellow feathers which ran round from behind the cavity of the skull, from temple to temple, and so to the back of the head; it must have been about a hand's breadth wide, was very close-set and thick, and covered his occiput and his ears.   It was fastened, feather by feather, to his hair with a white paste like wax (but it was not wax), so that the wig was very round and full and regular, and did not need to be specially cleaned when the head was washed, only lifted up.

When they came, the admiral was seated on a chair, with a carpet at his feet instead of a dais.   He was finely dressed, with a very big golden collar round his neck.   Sancho de Toar,[3] Simão de Miranda,[4] Nicolau Coelho, Aires Correia,[5] and the rest of us who were in the ship with him were seated on this carpet.   Torches were lit.   They entered.   However, they made no gesture of courtesy or sign of a wish to speak to the admiral or any one else.

For all that, one of them gazed at the admiral's collar and began to point towards the land and then at the collar as if he wished to tell us that there was gold in the country.[6]   And he also looked at a silver candlestick and pointed at the land in the same way, and at the candlestick, as if there was silver there, too.   We showed them a grey parrot the admiral had brought with him. They took it in their hands at once and pointed to the land, as if there were others there.   We showed them a ram,[7] but they took no notice of it.   We showed them a hen,[8] and they were almost afraid of it and did not want to take it in their hands; finally they did, but as if alarmed by it.   We gave them things to

[1] Their lips were pierced in childhood.
[2] They did this with sharp stones.   Two stones would be used for cutting
[3] A Spaniard.   Many accounts say he was the first European to visit Sofala, and that he discovered Delagoa Bay on the home voyage.   He was captain of a ship.
[4] Another captain.   He accompanied Cabral throughout the voyage.   He was afterwards appointed captain of Sofala, where he died in 1512.
[5] A former shipowner who sold the *Berrio* for da Gama's expedition.   He was going to Calicut to take charge of the ill-fated factory there.
[6] Sugar, coffee, copper, and diamonds are among the chief exports of this part of Brazil to-day.   The Tupi Indians knew gold and silver because native traders brought them from the Andes and the south.
[7] The only sheep native to America were the American big-horns of the Rocky Mountains.
[8] The various species of 'fowls' are, of course, of oriental origin.

eat: bread, boiled fish, comfits, sweetmeats, cakes, honey, dried figs. They would hardly eat anything of all this, and, if they tasted it, they spat it out at once.[1] We brought them wine [2] in a cup; they merely sipped it, did not like it at all, and did not want any more of it. We brought them water in a pitcher, and they each took a mouthful, but did not drink it; they just put it in their mouths and spat it out.

One of them saw the white beads of a rosary. He made a sign to be given them and was very pleased with them, and put them round his neck. Then he took them off and put them round his arm, pointing to the land, and again at the beads and at the captain's collar, as if he meant they would give gold for them.

We took it in this sense, because we preferred to. If, however, he was trying to tell us that he would take the beads and the collar as well, we did not choose to understand him, because we were not going to give it to him. Then he returned the beads to the man who had given them to him. Finally they lay on their backs on the carpet to sleep. They did not try to cover up their private parts in any way; these were uncircumcised and had their hairs well shaved and arranged.

The admiral ordered one of his cushions to be put under either of their heads, and the one in the wig took care that this should not be spoiled. They had a cloak spread over them. They consented to this, pulled it over themselves, and slept.

On the Saturday morning the admiral ordered the sails to be hoisted. We approached the entrance, which was very broad, and some six or seven fathoms in depth. All the ships entered it and anchored in five or six fathoms. The anchorage was so good and fine and safe inside that more than two hundred ships and vessels could lie in it. As soon as the ships had taken up their positions and anchored, all the captains came to this flagship. Now the admiral ordered Nicolau Coelho and Bartolomeu Dias to go on shore and take the two men and let them go with their bows and arrows. He also ordered each of them to be given a new shirt, a red bonnet, a rosary of white beads of bone, which they put on their arms, a varvel, and a bell. And he sent with them, to remain there, a banished youth [3] of the household of Dom João Telo, named Afonso Ribeiro, who was to stay with them there and learn about their lives and their customs. I, also, was told to accompany Nicolau Coelho.

So we went towards the shore, as straight as an arrow. Nearly

[1] All these foods were strange to them. Probably, also, they suspected poison.
[2] The local intoxicant was made from the mandioca root.
[3] A term of banishment to live a while amongst, and learn about, newly discovered tribes was a well-known form of punishment in Portugal in the days of the discoveries. Some English translators prefer the term 'convict' to 'exile.'

two hundred men came up at once there, all naked, with bows and arrows in their hands. The men we had brought with us made signs to them to retire and to put down their bows. They put them down, but they did not retire very far off. Still, they did put them down, and then those we had brought with us went out to them, and the banished youth as well. Once they had left us, they did not stop. They did not wait one for the other, but rather raced each other. They crossed a very full freshwater river there, wading in up to their thighs. And many others went with them, so that they all ran to some groups of palm-trees on the other side of the river, where more again were waiting. There they stopped. The banished man took part in all this, accompanied by a man who had taken him into his care on the exile's leaving the boat and who went with him to the other side. However, they brought him back to us at once; the two we had brought with us came back with him; they were again naked and were not wearing their bonnets.

After this, many more began to arrive. They walked out into the sea towards the boats till they could go no farther. They brought gourds of water to us, and they took some barrels we had with us, filled them with water, and came back with them to the boats. Not that they got so far as absolutely to board the boats, but they came up near to them, and threw these things in, and we caught them. Then they asked us to give them something.

Nicolau Coelho had brought them varvels and bracelets. To some he gave a varvel and to others a bracelet, so that with that fleshing we nearly won them to our service.[1] They gave us some of their bows and arrows in exchange for hats and linen bonnets and for anything we were willing to give them.

The two youths went away and we did not see them again.

Many of the men who were there—practically the greater part of them—had those sticks of bone in their lips. Some of them had their lips pierced and wore wooden pegs in the rifts which looked like the stoppers of wineskins.[2] Others, again, wore three sticks, one in the middle and one at each side. Others were covered with a motley paint, that is to say, half of them was their own colour and half was covered with a black, slightly bluish paint.[3] Others were painted in quarters.

There were three or four girls among them. These were very young and pretty, and had abundant long black hair down their

[1] A metaphor from falconry. Most of the objects given to the Tupis seem to have been originally intended for falconry.
[2] Little wooden stoppers which screw on, about as long as an ordinary nail, but thicker. Wineskins are still used in country districts in Portugal and—very extensively—in Spain.
[3] These 'paints' were the stains from berries and nuts.

backs. Their private parts were tightly knit, well raised, and half free from hairs; thus we were not at all ashamed to look at them.

It was not possible to speak to these people or understand them. There was such a chattering in uncouth speech that no one could be heard or understood. We made signs to them to go away. They did so, and went across the river. Then three or four of our men left the boats and filled I do not know how many water barrels we had brought with us, and so we returned. When they saw us going they made signs to us to come back. We went back, and they sent us the exile, for they did not wish him to remain there with them. He had had a small basin with him and two or three red bonnets, which were to be given to their lord, if they had one. They did not attempt to take anything from him, but sent him back with it all. However, Bartolomeu Dias told him to return and give them, in our sight, to the man who had first taken him into his care. After which he joined us again and we took him back with us.

The man who had taken him into his care was elderly, and he had feathers stuck all over his body as finery, so that he seemed covered with arrows like Saint Sebastian. Others had head-dresses of yellow feathers, or of red, or of green. One of the girls was all dyed from top to toe with that paint of theirs, and she certainly was so well made and so rounded, and her private parts (of which she made no privacy) so comely that many women in our country would be ashamed, if they saw such perfection, that theirs were not equally perfect. None of the men was circumcised, but all just as we are.

After these events we returned and they went away. In the afternoon the admiral went in his longboat and the other captains in theirs, to take their ease round the bay near the beach. Nobody went on shore, because the admiral did not wish to go, in spite of there being nobody there. He only left the boat, as we all did, on a big island there is in the bay, which runs a long way out at low tide. But the island is surrounded by water on every side, so that none can go there except by boat or swimming. There he and all of us took our ease for a good hour and a half. And some sailors had brought a net, and fished; they killed some small fish, but not many. At last we returned to the ships well after nightfall.

On the morning of Low Sunday the admiral decided to go to hear Mass and a sermon on that island. He commanded all the captains to take their places in the boats and come with him —which they did. He ordered a pavilion to be set up on the island and in it a finely adorned altar. Then he had Mass said in the presence of all of us. It was chanted by Friar Henrique and the responses were chanted by the other fathers and priests, who were

all present.   In my opinion every one heard the Mass with great
joy and devoutness.   The admiral stood on the Gospel side with
the banner of the Order of the Knights of Christ,[1] with which he
had left Belém,[2] uplifted before him.

When the Mass was finished, the priest removed his vestments
and mounted a tall chair and we all cast ourselves down on the
sands.   He preached a solemn and edifying sermon on the Gospel.
Finally he spoke of our coming hither and finding this land, as
befitting to the Cross of the Knights of Christ in the service of
which we were voyaging.   This last observation was very timely,
and increased our devotion.

At the time at which we were hearing the Mass and the sermon,
there were more or less the same number of people on the beach as
the day before.   They had their bows and arrows and they were
taking their ease.   First they sat looking at us; but when the Mass
was over, and while we were seated listening to the sermon, many
of them got up and played on horns or shells and began to leap
and dance, for a short while.   Some of them got into two or three
canoes they had there, which were not like those I had seen;
they were merely three beams tied together.[3]   Four, or five, or as
many as wished got into them, but they hardly moved off any distance from the land, only as far out as they could have waded.

After the sermon the admiral and all of us made our way towards
the boats, with our banner uplifted.   We embarked and all made
towards the shore so as to pass along by where those people were.
By the admiral's orders, Bartolomeu Dias went first in his skiff, to
give them back a board from one of their canoes which the sea
had borne away from them.   We all followed him at a stone's
throw.   When they saw Bartolomeu Dias's skiff they all came
down to the water's brink and walked as far out as they could.
He made a sign to them to put down their bows.   Many of them
went and put them down on the ground immediately, but others
did not put them down.

There was one of them there who was always telling the others to
keep away.   Not that it seemed to me that they had any respect
or fear for him.[4]   This man who was keeping them away had his
bows and arrows with him.   He was dyed with red paint on chest,
back, hips, thighs, and all down his legs, but his hypochondries,

---

[1] An Order like the Templars, founded in 1319.   Nearly all the Portuguese
discoverers belonged to this Order.
[2] They had had a ceremonial departure from Belém, like Vasco da Gama's
fleet.
[3] These were approximately six feet in length and two feet in width, and
bound together by sprigs.   Paddles were used.
[4] He was probably an 'elder of the people,' but, even so, the idea of leadership
was very little known amongst the Tupis, whose communities lived in a rough
kind of equality and co-operation.

belly, and stomach were of his own colour. The paint was so red that the water did not eat into it nor wash it away. Rather was he redder than before when he left the water. One of our men left Bartolomeu Dias's skiff and went in among them, but they did not interfere with him, much less did they think of hurting him. Indeed, they gave him gourds of water, and made signs to those in the skiff to come on shore. So Bartolomeu Dias turned his course back towards the admiral. We went to our ships to eat, playing trumpets and bagpipes, and not troubling them further. They sat down on the beach again, and remained there for the time being.

The sea runs out a very long way at low tide on the island where we went to hear Mass and a sermon, and leaves a large expanse of sand and pebbles uncovered. When we were there some men had gone to look for shell-fish, but had not found any. They had, however, found some short thick prawns, one of which was so large and thick, however, that I can say I never saw such a big one. They had also found some cockle and mussel shells but none in a complete state.

Immediately we had eaten, all the captains came to our flagship by the admiral's orders. He took them aside, and I went with them. He asked us all if it seemed advisable to us to send the supply ship to Your Majesty, with the news of the discovery, so that this place might be better explored and known than we could know it, for we should have to continue our journey. Many opinions were given on the matter, but every one, or the majority, agreed in saying that the plan was excellent. On this resolution being taken, the admiral asked if it would then be advisable to take a pair of those men by force so as to send them to Your Majesty, and leave two of the exiles in their places. But they agreed that it was not necessary to take men by force, since those taken anywhere by force usually say of everything that they are asked about that they have it in their country. If we left two of the exiles there, they would give better, very much better information than those men would if we took them; for nobody can understand them, nor would it be a speedy matter for them to learn to speak well enough to be able to tell us nearly so much about that country as the exiles will when Your Majesty sends to them here. Therefore let us not think of taking any one away from here by force, nor of causing scandal. Rather let us conciliate and pacify them and merely leave the two exiles here when we go. All agreed to this, as it seemed the best course.

When we had finished, the admiral said we would go on shore from the boats. Then we could see what the river was like, and also we could take our ease. We all went armed on shore from the boats, taking the banner with us. They were there on the beach at the river mouth, towards which we were going; and before

we arrived they had put down all their bows, as we had taught them
to do, and signed to us to land.   But, as soon as our prows ran
aground, they immediately fled on to the other side of the river,
which is no broader than a skittle alley.   Immediately we had
disembarked some of our men crossed the river [1] and went in
amongst them.   Some of them waited there, others moved away.
In any case, the fact of the matter was that both our people and
theirs moved about in a single group.   They gave away their bows
and arrows for hats and linen caps and whatever else we could
give them.   So many of our men crossed the river and went in
amongst them that they sheered off and moved away.   Some
went inland to where there were others.   The admiral made two
men carry him on their shoulders across the river and called every
one back.   There were not more people than usual on the other
side.   But when they saw the admiral calling up every one around
him, those who were there came up with our people.   It was not
because they recognized him as the Master (indeed, it would seem
that they neither understand nor conceive what this means), but
because many of our people, had by then crossed over on to that
side of the river.   They spoke to us there and brought us several
bows, and beads like the ones I have spoken of.   These they
exchanged for anything, so that our men took many bows, arrows,
and beads back to the ship.

Then the admiral returned to the original bank of the river.
Many at once flocked up to him.   There you could see gallants
painted red, or black, or in quarters, both on body and legs; they
really looked well so.   There were five or six women, too, among
them.   They were young, and their appearance was not bad,
naked like that.   One of them had a thigh painted with that black
paint, from her knee to her hip and her buttocks, and otherwise
she was of her natural colour.   Another was painted round the
backs of her knees and on the palms of her feet; her private parts
were all naked and ingenuously uncovered, and there was no
immodesty at all in this.   There was also a young woman there
carrying a child at her breast tied up in a cloth (of what material,
I do not know) so that nothing could be seen of it but its little legs.
But there was no cloth over the legs and the rest of its mother.

Next the admiral went along up the river which ran beside the
shore.   He waited there for an old man who came up carrying a
canoe paddle.   He went on speaking to us as long as the admiral
was there.   However, nobody ever understood him, nor did he us,
in spite of all we asked him about gold; for we wished to know
if there was any in that land.   The old man's lip was so deeply
pierced that a thick thumb could have been put into the hole.
He wore a valueless green stone in the cleft, which closed it on

[1] The Mutari.

the outside. The admiral ordered it to be taken out. The man said the devil knows what, and tried to put it in the admiral's mouth. We laughed a little and jested about that, but the admiral was displeased and left him. One of our men gave him an old hat for the stone; not that it was worth anything, but just as something to show. Afterwards the admiral had it, I believe, to send to Your Majesty with the other things.

We went along to see the river, the water of which was good and plentiful. There are a few not very high palms along it with very good dates in them. We gathered and ate many. Then the admiral turned back to the river mouth where we had disembarked.

On the other bank of the river a number of them were dancing [1] and making merry, opposite each other, but without touching hands—which they did very well. Diogo Dias,[2] who was an exciseman in Sacavém before, an amusing pleasure-loving fellow, went over on to the other bank of the river, taking with him one of our bagpipe [3] players with his bagpipe. He began dancing with them, taking them by the hand. They laughed and were pleased and danced very well with him to the sound of the bagpipe. After dancing he showed them many kinds of light turns on the ground, and a somersault; they laughed, it surprised them and pleased them. Yet, though he held their attention and diverted them in that way, they soon took fright as wild things from the hills do, and went away inland.

So the admiral and all of us crossed the river and went along the beach whilst the boats went along in near the land. We reached a big freshwater lake which is near the beach. All that coast is marshy inland and there is water in many places there. After we had crossed the river, seven or eight of them went in among the sailors returning to the boats. They took a shark Bartolomeu Dias had killed off with them — took it up, and threw it down on the beach.[4]

As may be seen, whenever up to now they seemed partly tamed, in the passing of them from one hand to the other they fled away like birds from a net. One does not dare raise one's voice to them for fear they may sheer off even more. And yet we do everything that they wish, in order to tame them.

[1] The Tupi dances were usually accompanied by instruments and singing.
[2] Brother of Bartolomeu Dias. Clerk of the *São Gabriel* on da Gama's voyage. He was one of the two left on shore at Pandarini. He was intended as factor at Calicut, but the Indians imprisoned him; though, soon after, they released him and he returned to Portugal.
  On Cabral's voyage he was captain of a caravel. He was driven out of his course whilst returning and accidentally discovered Madagascar. He returned to Lisbon on 27th July 1501.
[3] A form of bagpipe (*gaita*) is found all over northern Portugal and in northern Spain.
[4] They were themselves accustomed to shooting and netting sharks for food.
  * C 986

The admiral gave a red cap to the old man he had spoken to. But he, despite the talk he had had with the admiral and the cap he had been given, made away as soon as the admiral had taken leave and begun to cross the river; he would not come to the other side of the river. The other two whom the admiral had had in the ships and to whom he had given what has already been related never appeared again.[1] I deduce from these facts that they are a savage, ignorant people, and for that very reason they are so timid. For all which, they are healthy and very clean. So that I am even surer that they are like the wild birds or animals whose feathers and hair the air makes finer than when they are domesticated, and whose bodies are as clean, as plump, and as beautiful as they could possibly be. Which all makes me suppose that these people lodge in no houses or dwellings. The air in which they are nurtured makes them what they are. We, at any rate, did not see any houses of theirs nor anything resembling such.[2]

The admiral ordered the exile, Afonso Ribeiro, to go with them again. He went, and was there for some time, but returned in the evening, for they made him come. They would not allow him to stay there, though they gave him bows and arrows, and took nothing that was his. Actually, he said, one of them had taken some yellow beads he was wearing, and run off with them; but he had complained, and the others had pursued the thief, taken them from him, and given them back to the owner again. After which they had told him to go. He said that all he had seen amongst them were some little grottoes of green boughs and large fern leaves like those in the province of Entre Douro e Minho.[3] So, just before nightfall, we returned to our ships to sleep.

On the Monday, after eating, we all went on shore to take in water. Many of them came up, but not so many as the other times. And they brought very few bows with them. They kept at some distance from us at first, but later, and little by little, some intermingled with us, rejoicing to see us and embracing us. They gave us bows for sheets of paper, or for an old cap, or anything else. Though there were others who sheered away at once. Things turned out so well that a good twenty or thirty of our people went with them to a place where there was a large band of them including girls and women. They brought away from there many bows and headpieces of feathers, some green and others yellow, of which I believe the admiral will send you specimens.

Those who went with them say that they were glad to have them

[1] That is, up to the time when Caminha was writing this part of the letter.
[2] But see later references.
[3] The part of Portugal between the river Minho and the river Douro. The Minho divides Spain and Portugal on the north; Oporto is on the Douro. The Minho and Douro provinces are now spoken of separately. It is the most beautiful region of Portugal, and Caminha came from there.

there. We saw them closer to and more at our leisure that day because we had nearly all intermingled. Some were painted in quarters with those paints, others by halves, and others all over, like a tapestry. They all had their lips pierced; some had bones in them, though many had not. Some wore spiky green seed-shells off some tree,[1] which were coloured like chestnut shells, though they were much smaller. These were full of little red berries which, on being squeezed, squirted out a very red juice with which they dyed themselves. The more they wet themselves after being dyed with this red, the redder they become. They were all shaven to above the ears; likewise their eyelids and eye-lashes were shaven. All their foreheads are painted with black paint from temple to temple. This gives the impression of their wearing a ribbon round them two inches wide.

The admiral ordered the exile, Afonso Ribeiro, and the two other exiles to mix in amongst them. And he told Diogo Dias, of Sacavém, to do the same, since he was a merry fellow and knew how to amuse them. He told the exiles to stay there that night. So they all went in amongst those people.

As they afterwards related, they went a good league and a half to a hamlet of nine or ten houses. They said those houses were each as big as this flagship. They were made of wooden planks sideways on, had roofs of straw, and were fairly high. Each enclosed a single space with no partitions, but a number of posts. High up from post to post ran nets,[2] in which they slept. Down below they lit fires [3] to warm themselves.[4] Each house had two little doors, one at one end and one at the other.[5] Our men said that thirty or forty people were lodged in each house, and they saw them there. They gave our men such food as they had, consisting of plenty of *inhame* [6] and other seeds there are in the country which they eat. It was getting late, however, and they soon made all our men turn back, for they would not let any of them stay. They even wanted to come with them, our men said. Our men exchanged some varvels and other small things of little value which they had brought with them for some very large and beautiful red parrots [7] and two small green ones, some caps of green feathers, and a cloth of many colours, also of feathers, a rather beautiful kind

[1] The annatto tree.
[2] Of cotton material.
[3] The spark was obtained from stones or from wood.
[4] They were also a protection against the supernatural.
[5] These huts were lightly built, so that they could be moved from place to place if necessary.
[6] This is the Portuguese for yam. The Brazilian vegetable was, however, different to the African yam to which this name is usually applied; it was, in fact, a species of mandioc.
[7] Macaws.

of material, as Your Majesty will see when you receive all these
things, for the admiral says he is sending them to you.   So our men
came back, and we returned to our ships.

After our meal on the Tuesday we went on shore to fetch water
and wood and to wash our clothes.   There were sixty or seventy
on the beach without bows or anything else when we arrived.
As soon as we landed they came up to us straight away and did not
try to escape.   Also many others came up later, a good two hundred,
and all without bows.   They came in amongst us so readily that
some of them helped us to carry out the wood and put it in the boats.
They vied with our men in doing this, and it gave them great
pleasure.   Whilst we were gathering wood, two carpenters formed
a large cross out of a piece which had been cut for the purpose
the day before.   Many of them came and stood around the carpenters.   I believe they did so more to see the iron tool it was being
made with than to see the cross.   For they have nothing made of
iron and cut their wood and sticks with stones fashioned like wedges
which they fit into a stick between two laths which they tie up
very tightly to make them secure.   (The men who had been to
their houses told us this, because they had seen it there.)   They
were by now so intimate with us that they almost hindered us in
what we had to do.

The admiral sent the two exiles and Diogo Dias back to the
village they had visited (or to others, if they should obtain knowledge of any others), telling them not to come back to the ship to
sleep in any case, even if they were sent away.   So they went off.

Whilst we were cutting timber in the wood, some parrots flew
through the trees.   Some were green, others grey, some big, others
little.   It seems to me, after this, that there must be many of them
in this land, even though there cannot have been more than nine
or ten of those I saw, if so many.   We did not see any other birds
on that occasion, except some rock pigeons which seemed to me
considerably bigger than those in Portugal.   Many say they saw
doves, but I did not see them.   However, as the trees are very tall
and thick and of an infinite variety, I do not doubt but that there
are many birds in this jungle.   Near nightfall we returned to the
ships with our wood.

I believe, Sire, that I have as yet given Your Majesty no account
of how their bows and arrows are made.   The bows are long and
black, and the arrows are long also.   Their heads are of sharpened
cane, as Your Majesty will see from some which I believe the
admiral will send you.

We did not go on land on the Wednesday, because the admiral
spent the whole day in the supply ship having it cleared and as
much as each could take of what was in it carried off to the other
ships.   But they came down on to the beach in great numbers as

we saw from the ships.   There must have been about three hundred of them according to Sancho de Toar, who went there.   Diogo Dias and the exile, Afonso Ribeiro, whom the admiral had ordered the day before to sleep there under any circumstances, had come back after nightfall, because they did not want them to remain there.   They brought green parrots with them and some black birds, almost like magpies, but different in that they had white beaks and short tails.   When Sancho de Toar made for the ship again, some of them wanted to come with him.   But he only allowed two youths to do so who were healthy and vigorous.   He ordered them to be well cleaned and cared for that night.   They ate all the portion they were given [1] and he gave orders, as he said, for them to be provided with a bed with sheets.   They slept and took their ease that night.   Nothing else worth relating happened on that day.

On Thursday, the last day of April, we ate early, almost in the early morning, and then went on shore for more wood and water. Just as the admiral was thinking of leaving this ship, Sancho de Toar came up with his two guests.   As he had not yet eaten, a table-cloth was put down for him and food came for him.   So he ate.   The guests each had a chair to themselves.   They ate very heartily of everything that was given to them, especially cold boiled ham and rice.   They were not given wine, because Sancho de Toar said they did not care for it.

After the meal we all got into the boat, and they did, too.   A cabin boy gave one of them a large, very curly boar's tusk.   He put it into his lip straight away upon taking it, and, since it would not stay fixed there, they gave him a little red wax.   So he arranged the back part to stay firm and put the tusk into his lip so that the curve came out upwards.   He was as pleased with it as if he had been given a wonderful jewel.   As soon as we went on shore, he made off with it at once.   And he did not appear there again.

When we left the boat there must have been eight or ten of them on the beach.   In a little while more began to come.   It seems to me that four hundred or four hundred and fifty must have come on that day.   Some of them brought bows and arrows, but they gave them all away in exchange for caps or anything else they were given.   They ate what we gave them and some of them drank wine, though others would not.   But I should think that if they were made accustomed to it they would drink it very willingly.   They were so healthy and well made and gallant in their paint that it was a pleasure to see them.   They brought us as much wood as they could with the best will in the world and carried it out to the boats.   By now they were tamer and more assured amongst us than we were amongst them.

[1] A sign of greatly increased confidence.

The admiral went with us through the trees a little way till we came to a broad river of abundant waters from which we took in water. This, to our minds, was the same as the one which came down to the beach. We rested a little there and drank and took our ease on its banks amongst the trees. The number, size, and thickness of these trees and the variety of their foliage beggars calculation. There were many palm-trees there from which we gathered several fine dates.

The admiral had said when we had left the boat, that it would be best if we went straight to the cross which was leaning against a tree near the river ready to be set up on the next day, Friday; we ought then all to kneel and kiss it so that they could see the respect we had for it. We did so and signed to the ten or twelve who were there to do the same, and they at once all went and kissed it.

They seem to be such innocent people that, if we could understand their speech and they ours, they would immediately become Christians, seeing that, by all appearances, they do not understand about any faith. Therefore if the exiles who are to remain here learn their speech and understand them, I do not doubt but that they will follow that blessed path Your Majesty is desirous they should and become Christians and believe in our holy religion. May it please God to bring them to a knowledge of it, for truly these people are good and have a fine simplicity. Any stamp we wish may be easily printed on them, for the Lord has given them good bodies and good faces, like good men. I believe it was not without cause that He brought us here. Therefore Your Majesty who so greatly wishes to spread the Holy Catholic faith may look for their salvation. Pray God it may be accomplished with few difficulties.

They do not plough or breed cattle. There are no oxen here, nor goats, sheep, fowls, nor any other animal accustomed to live with man. They only eat this *inhame*, which is very plentiful here, and those seeds and fruits that the earth and the trees give of themselves. Nevertheless, they are of a finer, sturdier, and sleeker condition than we are for all the wheat and vegetables we eat.

While they were there that day they danced and footed it continuously with our people to the sound of one of our tambourines,[1] as if they were more our friends than we theirs. If we signed to them asking them if they wanted to come to our ships they at once came forward ready to come. So that, if we had invited them all, they would all have come. We did not, however, take more than four or five with us that night. The admiral took two, Simão de Miranda one whom he took as a page, and Aires Gomes another, also as a page. One of those whom the admiral took was one of the guests who had been brought him when we

---

[1] Rhythm was the essential basis of their dances.

first arrived here; on this day he came dressed in his shirt [1] and his brother with him.   That night they were very handsomely treated, not only in the way of food, but also to a bed with mattress and sheets, the better to tame them.

To-day, Friday, 1st May,[2] in the morning, we went on shore with our banner.   We made our way up the river and disembarked on the southern bank at a place where it seemed best to us to set up the cross so that it might be seen to the best advantage.   There the admiral marked the place for a pit to be made to plant the cross in.   Whilst they were digging this, he and all of us went for the cross, down the river to where it was.   We brought it from there as in a procession, with the friars and priests singing in front of us.   There were a quantity of people about, some seventy or eighty.   When they saw us coming, some of them went to help us to support the cross.   We passed over the river along by the beach. We then went to set up the cross where it was to be at some two bow-shots from the river.   When we went to do this a good hundred and fifty of those people and more came up.   The cross was then planted, with Your Majesty's arms and motto on it, which had before been fastened to it, and they set up an altar by its side. Friar Henrique said Mass there, and the singing and officiating was done by the others who have been already mentioned.   About fifty or sixty of the people of the place were at the Mass all on their knees as we were.   When the Gospel came and we all stood with uplifted hands, they arose with us, lifted their hands, and stayed like that till it was ended.   After which they again sat, as we did. When God's Body was elevated and we knelt, they all knelt and lifted their hands as we did and were so silent that I assure Your Majesty it much increased our devotion.

They stayed with us thus until the Communion was over.   After the Communion, the friars and priests communicated, as did the admiral and some of us.   Since the sun was very strong some of them arose whilst we were communicating, but others stayed to the end. Amongst those who stayed was a man of fifty or fifty-five years old—or rather he came up amongst those already there and also called others to come.   He went in amongst them and spoke to them pointing to the altar and afterwards at Heaven, as if he were speaking to a good purpose.   We took it so.

When Mass was over, the priest removed his vestments, and mounted on a chair near the altar in his surplice.   He preached to us on the Gospel and about the Apostles whose day it was.   At the end of the sermon he referred to the aim of your most holy and virtuous quest, which caused much devoutness.

[1] Though they had little leadership, their communal life does not seem to have been without notions of property.
[2] St. Philip and St. Jude.

The men who stayed all through the sermon looked at him as we did. The one I have spoken of called others to come. Some came and some went. At the end of the sermon Nicolau Coelho brought a number of tin crucifixes which had remained over from his former journey. It was thought well that those people should each have one hung round their necks. Friar Henrique stood beside the cross for this purpose. There he hung a crucifix round each of their necks, first making him kiss it and raise his hands. Many came for this. All who came, some forty or fifty, had crucifixes hung round their necks.

At last, a good hour after midday, we went to the ships to eat. The admiral took with him the man who had pointed out the altar and Heaven to the others; he also took a brother of his. The admiral did him much honour and gave him a Moorish shirt and his brother a shirt like the others had had.

My opinion and every one's opinion is that these people lack nothing to become completely Christian except understanding us; for they accepted as we do all they saw us do, which makes us consider that they have no idolatry or worship. I believe that if Your Majesty could send someone who could stay awhile here with them, they would all be persuaded and converted as Your Majesty desires. Therefore, if any one is coming out here, let him not omit to bring a clergyman to baptize them. For, by that time, they will have knowledge of our religion through the two exiles who are remaining with them, who also communicated to-day.

Only one woman came with those who were with us to-day. She was young and stayed throughout the Mass. We gave her a cloth to cover herself with and put it around her. But she did not pull it down to cover herself when she sat down. Thus, Sire, the innocence of Adam himself was not greater than these people's, as concerns the shame of the body. Your Majesty will judge if people who live in such innocence could be converted or no if they were taught the things that belong to their salvation.

Our last action was to go and kiss the cross in their presence. We then took our leave and went to eat.

I think, Sire, that two cabin-boys will also stay with the exiles we are leaving here, for they escaped to land in the skiff to-night and have not returned again. We think, I say, that they will stay, because, if God be willing, we are taking our departure from here in the morning.

It appears to me, Sire, that the coast of this country must be a good twenty or twenty-five leagues in length from the most southerly point we saw to the most northerly point we can see from this port. In some parts there are great banks along by the shore, some of which are red and some white; inland it is all flat and very full of large woods. All the coastal country from one point to the other is very flat and very beautiful. As to the jungle, it seemed very large to us seen from the sea; for, look as we would, we could see nothing but land and woods, and the land seemed very extensive. Till now we have been unable to learn if there is gold or silver or any other kind of metal or iron there; we have seen none. However, the air of the country is very healthful, fresh, and as temperate as that of Entre Douro e Minho; we have found the two climates alike at this season. There is a great plenty, an infinitude of waters. The country is so well-favoured that if it were rightly cultivated it would yield everything, because of its waters.

For all that, the best fruit that could be gathered hence would be, it seems to me, the salvation of these people. That should be the chief seed for Your Majesty to scatter here. It would be enough reason, even if this was only a rest-house on the voyage to Calicut. How much more so will it be if there is a will to accomplish and perform in this land what Your Majesty so greatly desires, which is the spreading of our holy religion.

Thus I have given Your Majesty an account of what I have seen in this land. If at some length, Your Majesty will pardon me, since my desire to tell you all made me relate it with such minuteness. And since, Sire, Your Majesty may be sure of my very faithful service in my present duties as in whatever may do you service, I beg of you as a signal favour that you send for Jorge de Ossório, my son-in-law, from the island of São Tomé [1]—I should take this as a great kindness from you.

I kiss Your Majesty's hands.

From this Pôrto-Seguro,[2] in Your Majesty's island of Vera Cruz, to-day, Friday, 1st May 1500.[3]

PERO VAZ DE CAMINHA.

[1] Another exile with a mission; this time to the Cape Verde Islands.
[2] Literally safe port. To-day a town stands there.
[3] The original appears to have been written on successive days. This creates an occasional confusion of tenses which the translator has removed.

III—THE LANDS OF PRESTER JOHN
1520–6

(Translated by Lord Stanley of Alderley)

Bibliographical

Ho Preste Joam das indias.   Verdadera informaçam das terras do Preste Joam.   Lisbon.   1540.

TRANSLATION: *The Voyage of Sir Francis Alvarez . . . made vnto the Court of Prete Iani.*   In *Purchas his Pilgrimes.*   (Anonymous.)   1625.

Narrative of the Portuguese Embassy to Abyssinia.   Translated by Lord Stanley of Alderley.   Hakluyt Society.   1881.

THE LANDS OF PRESTER JOHN

Chapter LVIII. Of the mountain in which they put the sons of the Prester John, and how they stoned us near it

THE above-mentioned valley reaches to the mountain where they put the sons of the Prester John.[1] These are like banished men; as it was revealed to King Abraham, before spoken of, to whom the angels for forty years administered bread and wine for the sacrament, that all his sons should be shut up in a mountain, and that none should remain except the first-born, the heir, and that this should be done for ever to all the sons of the Prester of the country, and his successors:[2] because if this was not so done there would be great difficulty in the country, on account of its greatness, and they would rise up and seize parts of it, and would not obey the heir, and would kill him. He being frightened at such a revelation, and reflecting where such a mountain could be found, it was again told him in revelation to order his country to be searched, and to look at the highest mountains, and that mountain on which they saw wild goats on the rocks, looking as if they were going to fall below, was the mountain on which the princes were to be shut up. He ordered it to be done as it had been revealed to him, and they found this mountain,[3] which stands above this valley, to be the one which the revelation mentioned, round the foot of which a man has to go a journey of two days; and it is of this kind: a rock cut like a wall, straight from the top to the bottom; a man going at the foot of it and looking upwards, it seems that the sky rests upon it. They say that it has three entrances or gates, in three places, and no more; I saw one of these here in this country, and I saw it in this manner:

We were going from the sea to the court,[4] and a young man, a servant of the Prester, whom they call a *calacem*, was guiding us, and he did not know the country well; and we wished to lodge in a town,[5] and they would not receive us; this belonged to a sister

---

[1] The negus's sons. The mountain was called Amba Geshen.
[2] This custom continued for two hundred years; King Naod was the last to be incarcerated. But it was revived in a different locality.
[3] Mount Geshen.
[4] Or, rather, the emperor's camp.
[5] More a collection of huts than a town. According to the Portuguese travellers there were few real houses in Abyssinia, though there were monasteries, and churches marvellously built on the tops of mountains. When Father Pais built the palace at Gondar in 1616 the amazed Abyssinians called it a house upon a house.

of Prester John. The night had not yet advanced much, and he began travelling, telling us to follow him, and that he would get us lodgings. And because he travelled fast on a mule, and on a small path, I told one Lopo da Gama to ride in sight of the *calacem*, and that I would keep him in sight, and the ambassador and the other people would ride in sight of me. And the night closed in when we were quite a league from the road towards the mountain of the princes, and there came forth from all the villages so many people throwing stones at us, that they were near killing us, and they made us disperse in three or four directions. The ambassador had remained in the rear, and he turned back, and others who were about in the middle of the party started off in another direction; and someone there was who dismounted from his mule and fled in panic. Lopo da Gama and I could not turn back, so we went forward and reached another town, which was still better prepared, on account of the noise which they heard behind in the other towns.[1] Here many stones rained upon us, and the darkness was like having no eyes. In order that they might not throw stones at me by hearing the mule's steps, I dismounted and gave the mule to my slave.

God was pleased that an honourable man came up to me, and asked me who I was. I told him that I was a *gaxia neguz*, that is to say, a king's stranger.[2] This man was very tall, and I say honourable, because he treated me well; and he took my head under his arm, for I did not reach any higher, and so he conducted me like the bellows of a bagpipe player,[3] saying, 'Atefra, atefra,' which means 'Do not be afraid, do not be afraid.' He took me with the mule and the slave until he brought me into a vegetable garden which surrounded his house. Inside this garden he had a quantity of poles stuck up one against another, and in the midst of these poles he had a clean resting-place like a hut, into which he put me. As it seemed to me that I was in safety, I ordered a light to be lit; and when they saw the light they rained stones on the hut, and when I put out the light the stone-throwing ceased.[4] The host, as soon as he left me, returned at the noise, and then remained an hour without coming. Whilst he was away, Lopo da Gama heard me, and broke through the bushes, and came to me. On this the host came and said: 'Be quiet, do not be afraid,' and ordered a candle to be lit, and to kill two fowls; and he gave us bread and wine and a hospitable welcome, according to his power.

---

[1] It was even nearer the prison of the princes, and therefore even more diligent in protecting them.
[2] The emperor usually took all foreign visitors into his own protection.
[3] Cf. the reference to bagpipes in Caminha's letter, p. 51.
[4] They were afraid the light was a signal to the princes.

Next day, in the morning, the host took me by the hand and led me to his house, as far as a game of ball,[1] where there were many trees of an inferior kind, and very thick, by which it was concealed as by a wall;[2] and between them was a door, which was locked; and before this door was an ascent to the cliff. This host said to me: 'Look here; if any of you were to pass inside this door, there would be nothing for it but to cut off his feet and his hands, and put out his eyes, and leave him lying there; and you must not put the blame on those who would do this, neither would you be in fault, but those who brought you hither; we, if we did not do this, we should pay with our lives, because we are the guardians of this door.' Lopo da Gama, I, and the *calacem* then at once mounted and rode down to the road, which was below us, a good league off, and we found that none of our party had passed by; and vespers were over, and yet we had not come together.

Chapter LIX. Of the greatness of the mountain in which they put the sons of Prester John, and of its guards, and how the kingdoms are inherited

THE manner they have of shutting up these sons of the kings. Until this King David Prester John, all had five or six wives,[3] and they had sons of them or of most of them. By the death of the Prester, the eldest born inherited; others say that he who appeared to the Prester the most apt, and of most judgment, inherited: others say that he inherited who had the most adherents. Of this matter I will say what I know by hearing it from many.

The King Alexander,[4] the uncle of this David, died without a son, and he had daughters, and they went to the mountain and brought out from it Nahu his brother, who was father of this David. This Nahu brought with him from the mountain a legitimate son, who was, they say, a handsome youth and a good gentleman, but of a strong temper. After that Nahu was in the kingdoms, he had other wives, of whom he had sons and daughters, and at his death they wished to make king that eldest son who had come from the mountain with his father; and some said that he was strong in temper, and would ill-treat the people. Others said that he could not inherit because he had been born as in captivity, and outside

---

[1] A curious manner of measuring distance, common in early Portuguese writers.
[2] He was obviously one of the guards of the prison gates, a post of high responsibility.
[3] The Abyssinian Church frowned on polygamy. But Mohammedan infiltration was responsible for frequent cases of it.
[4] Iskander.

of the inheritance. So they set up as king this David who now reigns, and who at that time was a boy of eleven years of age. The Abima [1] Martos told me that he and the Queen Helena [2] made him king, because they had all the great men in their hands. Thus it appears to me, that beyond primogeniture, adherence enters into the question. Other sons of Nahu, who were infants, remained with the eldest who had come from the mountain with his father, and they took them all back to the said mountain, and so they do with all the sons of the Prester from the time of that King Abraham until now.

They say that this mountain is cold and extensive, and they also say that the top of it is round, and that it takes fifteen days to go round it; [3] and it seems to me that may be so, because on this side, where our road lay, we travelled at the foot of it for two days; and so it reaches to the kingdoms of Ahmara and of Bogrimidi, which is on the Nile, and a long way from here. They say that there are on the top of this mountain yet other mountains which are very high and contain valleys: and they say that there is a valley there between two very steep mountains, and that it is by no means possible to get out of it, because it is closed by two gates, and that in this valley they place those who are nearest to the king, that is to say, those who are still of his own blood, and who have been there a short time, because they keep them with more precaution. Those who are sons of sons, and grandsons, and already almost forgotten are not so much watched over. Withal, this mountain is generally guarded by great guards, and great captains; and a quarter of the people who usually live at the court are of the guards of this mountain and their captains. These captains and guards of the mountain who are at court, lodge apart by themselves and no one approaches them, nor do they go near others, so that no one may have an opportunity of learning the secrets of the mountain. And when they approach the door of the Prester, and he has to receive a message or speak to them, they make all the people go away, and all other affairs cease whilst they are speaking of this.

[1] The patriarch or *abuna* of Abyssinia. He was ordained by the patriarch of Alexandria and sent into the country; he was, moreover, always a foreigner.
[2] See note on p. 70.
[3] In the preceding chapter it was said to be two days' journey in circumference. (Lord Stanley.)

Chapter LXV. How we came to some gates and deep passes difficult to travel, and we went up to the gates, at which the kingdom begins which is named Xoa

ON Monday, 1st October 1520, we travelled on our road through level country of lakes and large pastures for a distance of three or four leagues, all along these dykes,[1] and we went to sleep near them where we had to cross these depths.   Tuesday morning we began to travel for half a league, and we arrived at some gates on a rock which divided two valleys, one to the right, the other to the left hand, and so narrow near the gates that they might hold one cart and no more; with small buttresses, between which the gates shut and close from slope to slope.   Going through this gate one enters at once as into a deep valley, with shale on either side raised more than the height of a lance, as if the edge of the sword had made this, these slopes, and this valley.   The height of these walls has a length of two games of quoits [2] of such narrowness that a man cannot go on horseback, and the mules go scraping the stirrups on both sides, and so steep that a man descends with his hands and feet, and this seems to be made artificially.

Coming out of this narrow pass one travels through a loophole which is about four spans wide, and from one end to the other these clefts are all shale; it is not to be believed, and I would not have believed it, if I had not seen it: and if I had not seen our mules and people pass, I would affirm that goats could not pass there in security.   So we set our mules going there as if one was sending them to destruction, and we after them with hands and feet down the rock, without there being any other road.   This great roughness lasts for a crossbow shot, and they call these here Aqui Afagi, which means death of the asses.   (Here they pay dues.) We passed these gates many times, and we never passed them without finding beasts and oxen dead, which had come from below upwards and had not been able to get up the ascent.   Leaving this pass, there still remains quite two leagues of road sufficiently steep and rocky, and difficult to travel over.   In the middle of this

[1] 'We came to stay Saturday and Sunday, which was the last day of September at a small village of Our Lady, very poor and ill kept, close to which church towards the east commence most wild mountains and deep fosses descending to the greatest abysses men ever saw; nor could their depth be believed, like as the mountains where the Israelites live are scarped from the top, so are these. Below they are of great width, in some places of four leagues, in others five, in others about three. (This is our opinion.)   They say that these dykes run to the Nile, which is very far from here, and higher up we know well that they reach the country of the Moors; they say that in the parts of the Moors they are not so precipitous.   At the bottom of these dykes there are many dwellings and an infinite number of apes, hairy like lions from the breast upwards' (Chapter LXIV).   The 'Moors' are, as elsewhere, the Mohammedans.
[2] *Jôgo da malha.*   Cf. the similar expression in Chapter LVIII.

descent there is a rock hollowed out at the bottom, and water
falls from the top of it (there are always many beggars in this cave).
Thus we descended fully two leagues until reaching a great river
which is named Anecheta, which contains many fish and very
large ones.

From here we travelled, ascending for quite a league, until
reaching a passage which sights another river, at which are other
gates which now are not used; and yet the gates are there still.
Those who pass these dykes and clefts come to sleep here, because
they cannot go in one day from one end to the other. At this
halting-place the friar who conducted us committed a great cruelty,
as though he were not a Christian, or had done it to Moors. Because a *xuum* or captain of some villages which are on a hill above
the place where we were resting did not come up so quickly with the
people who lived there, he sent some men of his, and those who
carried our baggage, to go and destroy for them some great bean
fields which they had by the side of their houses. These men
who went there brought to where we were more than a *moio* [1] of
beans, which were their provisions in this country, because in these
valleys they have nothing except millet and beans. It was a pity
to see such destruction; and because we opposed him, he said
that such was the justice of the country, and also each day he
ordered many of those who carried our baggage to be flogged,
and he took from them mules, cows, and stuffs, saying that so
should be treated whoever served ill.

On Tuesday, 2nd October, we took our road through many
steep rocks (as before) between which we passed very narrow and
bad paths, and dangerous passes; both on one side and on the other
scarped rock, a thing not to be credited. We reached the other
river, a good league from where we slept; this river is great, and
is named Gemaa; it also contains much fish. They say that
both these rivers join together and go to the river Nile. We began
to travel and ascend as great cliffs as we had descended the day
before. In this ascent there will be two leagues; at the end of it
are other gates, and another pass such as from Aqui Afagi. These
gates are always shut, and all who pass through them pay dues.
Neither above nor below is there any other way or passage. Outside of these gates we went to sleep at a plain which is about half a
league from the gates. Already when there, nothing showed of
the dykes, clefts, and cliffs which we had traversed; on the contrary,
all appeared to be a plain on this side and on the further side,
without there being anything in the middle, and there were five
long leagues from one set of gates to the other.

The kingdoms of Amhara and Shoa are divided by these gates
and ravines. These gates are called *Badabaxa*, which means new

[1] *Moyo, modius,* measure of sixty *alqueires,* or bushels. (Lord Stanley.)

land. In these ravines and cliffs there are numerous tribes of
birds, and we could not determine where they breed, nor how they
could bring up their young without their falling down from the
rocks: because whoever saw it would not judge otherwise than
that it was an impossible thing, according to its greatness.

*Chapter XC. How the Prester gave leave to go to the ambassador
and the others, and ordered me to remain alone with the interpreter,
and of the questions about church matters, and how we all sang
compline, and how Prester John departed that night*

WHEN all was concluded, that is to say procession, mass, and communion,[1] the Prester desired the ambassador and all the Franks [2]
to go and dine, and that I should remain alone with one interpreter.
Remaining alone, the old priest came and said that Prester John
said that we observed church matters very well, but what reason
had we for allowing laymen to come into the church the same as
the clergy, and that also he had heard tell that women entered it? [3]
I answered that the church of God was not closed to any Christian,
and that Christ was always with arms open for every Christian
who approached and came to Him, and since He received them in
glory in paradise, how should we not receive them in church, which
is the road to the church of Paradise. With respect to women,
although in former time they did not enter into the sanctuary,[4]
the deserts of Our Lady were and are so great that they had sufficed
to make the feminine gender deserving to enter into the house of
God. And as to ministering at the altar, that men in orders
ministered. They came to say that my reasons seemed good to
him, but he wished to know why, as I was the only priest, and he
who carried the thurible was not a priest, how it was he carried it,
because the incense ought to go in the hand of a priest and of no
other person. I answered that the person who served as a deacon
was a *zagonay*, what they call 'of the gospel,' [5] and that his office
was to carry the thurible.
    There came another message asking if we had that in a book, as
our books were better than theirs, because our books contained
all things.[6] I answered that our books were very perfect, because

    [1] The emperor had requested Álvares to hold a service for him on Christmas
Day.
    [2] Abyssinian or Arabian name for Europeans. See also Godinho, p. 334.
    [3] Only priests entered the Abyssinian churches. The laity communicated
outside.
    [4] Sancta sanctorum. (Lord Stanley.)
    [5] That is, presumably, who recites the Gospel, as deacons do.
    [6] The Abyssinians had very few books. Theologically they followed the
Church of Alexandria, and so would have had little Abyssinian theology.

since the time of the apostles we had always had learned men and
doctors in the holy mother Church, who never did, nor now do,
anything else but compile and bring together those things which
are scattered about in the Holy Scriptures, both by the prophets,
apostles, or evangelists, and by Jesus Christ our Saviour.   They
again told me that they had eighty-one books of the Old and New
Testaments; [1] had we any more?   I told them we had the eighty-
one books, and more than ten times eighty-one drawn from those,
with many declarations and perfections.   They said they well knew
that we had more books than they had: on this account they desired
that I should tell them of books not seen by or known to them.
Thus they kept questioning me, without the two messengers ever
ceasing to go and come, nor I able to sit down, but only to lean upon
a staff until the hour of vespers; and if these questions and answers
had to be written down, two hands of paper would not suffice,
neither could memory retain them for the haste they made.   Some
answers went and other questions came, each in their own fashion,
and in much disorder, because they were not all questions from
Prester John, for some were from his mother, and others from his
wife, and also from Queen Helena. [2]   I answered as God helped me,
I was in such a state of weakness and hunger that I could not
endure it, and instead of an answer, I sent to ask His Highness to
have pity for an old man, [3] who had neither eat nor drunk since
yesterday at midday, nor had slept, and could not stand for weakness.   He sent to say, that since he rejoiced to converse with
me, why did not I rejoice too?   I replied that old age, hunger, and
weakness did not allow of it.   He sent to say that if I wished to
eat he would send it to me, that he had already sent a great deal
to eat to our tent, and if I wished to eat there I might go, or if I
wished to eat here he would order food to be given me.   I told
him I wished to eat at our tent, to rest myself: then they gave me
leave.

While I was on the road, a page reached me half dead with
running; when I heard him come, I thought it was my sins come to
make me turn back.   He told me the Prester sent him to beg me
to send back the hat I had on my head, and to pardon him, and
not be angry at having been so long without eating, and as soon as
I had eaten to come back at once, as he wished to learn more things
from me.   On reaching our tent I was seized with a giddiness,
that the sight left my eyes, and I became quite cold.   An hour and
a half had not passed before he sent to call me, and as it was

[1] This, of course, includes the Apocrypha.
[2] She held sway over the greater part of the kingdom of Gojame, and had been
regent.   It was she who had sent for the Portuguese.   She was the widow of
the Emperor Baeda Maryam.
[3] He was fifty-five years old.

already late, those who knew church matters went with me, and we sung compline, only because there was no place at our tent, and when compline was finished, there came a message to strike our church tent, because Prester John was going away that night, as in effect he did do, in order to pass the bad passages without any one knowing of it.

While we [1] were lying sleeping in our tent, a little more or less than midnight, we heard a great tramping of mules and people passing close to us, and then we heard say that the negus was travelling; and as it seemed to us that we should be left without people, we made ready quickly; and when we arrived at the first pass, there was no remedy for it, and our people made way for us with their lances, and we travelled thus that day with lances in front and lances behind, and we in the middle, not allowing any one to come among us; because otherwise we should never have got together again.   We went and found the king's tent pitched in the middle of the ravines in sight between the meadows, where I before related that the friar ordered the beans to be pulled out, and there slept all the people who were able to pass, and we did not sleep much, for before midnight we heard say that the negus was travelling, and we went after him at once: and we got out of the bad passes before morning.   We heard say that in this night there died in these passes, men, women, and many mules, asses, ponies, and pack oxen; we found many dead.   This is the pass which is named Aqui Afagi, which means death to asses, by which we passed in coming.   It was certain that a great lady died this night, and with her a man who led her mule by the halter, and two who went close to her, and the mule, all of them went over a rock, and were dashed to pieces before they reached the bottom: it could not be otherwise, because the cliffs are, as I before said, something incredible; and whoever sees them, they appear to him more like hell than anything else.   So we made our journey without observing the octaves of Christmas, which they do not observe in this country.   And I before said that the court did not finish moving in four or five days; here they spent more than three weeks in getting through these gates, and the baggage of the Prester was more than a month passing every day.[2]

[1] The Portuguese embassy.
[2] The emperor was constantly moving from place to place in this manner.

Chapter CIII. How Pero de Covilhã,[1] *Portuguese, is in the country of the Prester, and how he came there, and why he was sent*

I HAVE sometimes spoken of Pero de Covilhã, a Portuguese, who is in this country, and have quoted him, and will not desist from quoting him, as he is an honourable person of merit and credit, and it is reasonable that it should be told how he came to this country, and I will relate the cause of it, and what he told me of himself. Firstly, I say that he is my spiritual son, and he told me in confession, and out of it, how thirty-three years had passed that he had not confessed, because he said in this country they do not keep the secret of confession, and he only went to the church and there confessed his sins to God. Besides, he related to me the beginning of his life; first, that he was a native of the town of Colvilhã in the kingdoms of Portugal, and in his youth he had gone to Castile to live with Don Alfonso, Duke of Seville, and at the beginning of the wars between Portugal and Castile he had come with Juan de Guzmán, brother of the said Duke of Seville, to Portugal. This Don Juan had given him to Dom Afonso, king of Portugal, as a groom, and he soon took him as his squire, and he served in that capacity in the said wars, and went with the king to France. When King Dom Afonso died he remained with King Dom João[2] his son, whom he served as squire of the guard until the treasons, when the king sent him to go about Castile, because he could speak Castilian well, in order to learn who were the gentlemen who had gone there. On his return from Castile, the King Dom João sent him to Barbary to buy woollen cloths and to make peace with the king of Tremezen;[3] and returning he was again sent to Barbary, to Muley Belagegi, he who sent the remains of the Infante Dom Fernando.[4] In this journey he carried goods of the King Dom Manuel, who was then duke, to buy horses for him, because the King Dom João intended to give him an establishment, and one Pero Afonso, a veterinary, an inhabitant of Tomar, was going to inspect the horses.

On this arrival coming from Barbary, it was ordained that one Afonso de Paiva, a native of Castelo Branco, should come to these parts, and he waited for Pero de Covilhã to come together. When he came, the king spoke to him in great secrecy, telling him that he expected a great service of him, because he had always found him a good and faithful servant, and fortunate in his acts

[1] 1457–1525.
[2] King Afonso died in 1481.
[3] Or Óran. That is, the Moorish king. Spain was nearly always at war with the Moors of North Africa, and, whenever possible, involved Portugal in the disputes.
[4] The Constant Prince. (Lord Stanley.)

and services; and this service was that he and another companion, who was named Afonso de Paiva, should both go to discover and learn about Prester John, and where cinnamon is to be found, and the other spices which from those parts went to Venice through the countries of the Moors: and that already he had sent on this journey a man of the house of Monteio, and a friar named Frei António, a native of Lisbon, and that they both had arrived at Jerusalem, and that they had returned thence, saying that it was not possible to go to those countries without knowing Arabic, and therefore he requested Pero de Covilhã to accept this journey and to do this service with the said Afonso de Paiva. To which Pero de Covilhã answered, that he regretted that his capacity was not greater, so great was his desire to serve His Highness, and that he accepted the journey with ready willingness. They were dispatched from Santarém on 7th May 1487; King Dom Manuel, who was then duke, was present, and gave them a map for navigating, taken from the map of the world, and it had been made by the licentiate Calçadilha, who is bishop of Viseu, and the doctor Mestre Rodrigo, inhabitant of Pedras Negras, and the doctor Mestre Moyses, at that time a Jew, and this map was made in the house of Pero de Alcaçova; and the king gave four hundred ducats for the expenses of both of them, which he gave out of the chest of the expenses of the garden of Almeirim, the King Dom Manuel, then duke, being present at all this. The King Dom João also gave him a letter of credence for all the countries and provinces in the world, so that in case he saw himself in danger or necessity, this letter of the king's might succour him: [1] and in the presence of the duke he gave them his blessing. Of the said four hundred ducats they took a part for their expenses, and the rest they placed in the hands of Bartolomeo, a Florentine, for it to be given to them in Valencia.

Setting out, they travelled and arrived at Barcelona on the day of Corpus Domini: and they changed their route from Barcelona to Naples, and they arrived at Naples on St. John's Day,[2] and their journey was given them by the sons of Cosmo de' Medici;[3] and from there they passed to Rhodes;[4] and he says that at this time there were not more than two Portuguese in Rhodes, one was named Frei Gonçalo, and the other Frei Fernando, and they lodged with these. From here they passed to Alexandria in a ship of Bartolomé

---

[1] See Gaspar Correia's account of King John's scouts in *Vasco da Gama's Voyages*, pp. 8-11.—Hakluyt Society. (Lord Stanley.)

[2] 24th June.

[3] Lorenzo de' Medici was at the head of the Florentine republic. He was Cosmo's grandson. His brother Giuliano had already died. The passage probably means that the travellers journeyed to Florence from Naples, which city was in Spanish hands.

[4] The seat of the Knights of St. John.

de Paredes: and in order to pass as merchants, they bought much honey, and they arrived at Alexandria. Here both the companions fell ill of fevers; and all their honey was taken by the naib of Alexandria, thinking that they were dying, and God gave them health, and they paid them at their pleasure. Here they bought other merchandise and went to Cairo. Here they remained until they found some Moghreby Moors of Fez and Tremecem, who were going to Aden, and they went with them to Tor, and there they embarked and went to Suaquem,[1] which is on the coast of Abyssinia; and then they went to Aden, and because it was the time of the monsoon, the companions separated, and Afonso de Paiva went to the country of Ethiopia, and Pero de Covilhã to India, agreeing that at a certain time they should both meet in Cairo to come and give an account of what they had found to the king. And Pero de Covilhã departed thence and came to Cananor, and thence to Calicut, and from there he turned back to Goa, and went to Ormuz,[2] and returned to Tor and Cairo in search of his companion, and he found that he was dead.

Whilst he was about to set out on the way to Portugal, he had news that there were there two Portuguese Jews who were going about in search of him; and by great cleverness they heard about each other, and when they had met, they gave him letters from the king of Portugal. These Jews were named, one Rabbi Abraham, a native of Beja, the other Josef, a native of Lamego, and he was a shoemaker. This shoemaker had been in Babylonia, and had heard news or information of the city of Ormuz, and had related it to King Dom João, with which news, he said, the king had been much pleased. And Rabbi Abraham had sworn to the king that he would not return to Portugal without seeing Ormuz with his own eyes. When the letters had been given and read, their contents were, that if all the things for which they had come were seen, discovered, and learned, that they should return and welcome, and they should receive great favours: and if all were not found and discovered, they were to send word of what they had found, and to labour to learn the rest; and chiefly they were to go and see and learn about the great King Prester John, and to show the city of Ormuz to the Rabbi Abraham. Besides the letters, these Jews made requisitions to Pero de Covilhã that he should go and learn about Prester John, and show the city of Ormuz to Rabbi Abraham. Here he at once wrote by the shoemaker of Lamego, how he had discovered cinnamon and pepper in the city of Calicut, and that cloves came from beyond, but that all could be had there; and that he had been in the cities of Cananor, Calicut, and Goa, all on the coast, and to this they could navigate by their coast and the seas

---

[1] Now in the Anglo-Egyptian Sudan.
[2] Portuguese possessions later.

of Guinea, coming to make the coast of Sofala, to which he had also gone, or a great island which the Moors call the island of the moon; [1] they say that it has three hundred leagues of coast, and that from each of these lands one can fetch the coast of Calicut.

Having sent this message to the king by the Jew of Lamego, Pero de Covilhã went with the other Jew of Beja to Aden, and thence to Ormuz, and left him there, and returned thence and came to Jiddah and Meccah and El Medina,[2] where lies buried the Zancarron,[3] and from thence to Mount Sinai. Having seen all well he again embarked at Tor and went as far as outside the strait to the city of Zeila,[4] and thence travelled by land until he reached Prester John, who is very near to Zeila; and he came to the court, and gave his letters to the King Alexander, who then reigned, and he said that he received them with much pleasure and joy, and said that he would send him to his country with much honour. About this time he died, and his brother Nahum reigned, who also received him with much favour, and when he asked leave to go he would not give it. And Nahum died, and his son David reigned, who now reigns; and he says he also asked him for leave and he would not give it, saying that he had not come in his time, and his predecessors had given him lands and lordships to rule and enjoy, and that leave he could not give him, and so the matter remained. This Pero de Covilhã is a man who knows all the languages that can be spoken, both of Christians, Moors, and Gentiles, and who knows all the things for which he was sent; moreover he gives an account of them as if they were present before him.

[1] Madagascar.
[2] He must surely, then, have been disguised as an Arab.
[3] The leg-bone, supposed by popular superstition in Spain to be buried in the great mosque of Cordova. (Lord Stanley.)
[4] Now in British Somaliland.

IV—THE FURTHEST EAST, 1537–58

(Translated by Henry Cogan)

Bibliographical

Peregrinaçam de Fernão Mendes Pinto em que da conta de muytas e muyto estranhas cousas. . . . Lisbon. 1614.

TRANSLATION: *The Voyages and Adventures of Fernand Mendez Pinto* . . . Done into English by H[enry] C[ogan] Gent. Henry Cripps and Lodowick Lloyd. London. 1653.
Reprinted 1663.
Reprinted 1692.
Reprinted (slightly abridged) 1891, by Fisher Unwin, with an Introduction by A. Vambéry.

THE FURTHEST EAST

Chapter XXV. Our arrival at Calempluy,[1] and the description thereof; what happened to António de Faria in one of the hermitages thereof and how we were discovered

HAVING doubled the Cape of Guimai Tarao,[2] two leagues beyond it we discovered a goodly level of ground, situated in the midst of a river, which to our seeming was not above a league in circuit, whereunto António de Faria approached with exceeding great joy, which yet was intermingled with much fear, because he knew not to what danger he and his were exposed. About twelve of the clock at night he anchored within a cannon shot of this island, and the next morning as soon as it was day he sat in council with such of his company as he had called to it; there it was concluded that it was not possible so great and magnificent a thing should be without some kind of guard, and therefore it was resolved that with the greatest silence that might be, it should be rounded all about, for to see what avenues it had, or what obstacles we might meet with when there was question of landing, to the end that accordingly we might deliberate more amply on that we had to do. With this resolution, which was approved by every one, António de Faria weighed anchor, and without any noise got close to the island, and compassing it about exactly observed every particular that presented itself to his sight.

This island was all enclosed with a platform of jasper, six-and-twenty spans high, the stones whereof were so neatly wrought and joined together that the wall seemed to be all of one piece, at which every one greatly marvelled, as having never seen anything till then, either in the Indies or elsewhere, that merited comparison with it. This wall was six-and-twenty spans deep from the bottom of the river to the superficies of the water, so that the full height of it was two-and-fifty spans.[3] Furthermore, the top of the

[1] An island near the Gulf of Nanking. The tombs have never been satisfactorily identified. Possibly Mendes Pinto disguised their whereabouts to prevent further pillaging of them. Father Shurheimer, who is on the whole opposed to Mendes Pinto, makes the following observations: 'Wheeler denkt bei Calemplui mit seinem 17 Königsgräbern an den Wallfahrtsort P'u-to auf den vor Ning-po gelegncn Tschusan-Insel oder an einem Insel im Yang-tse-Kiang . . . Die chinesichen Küstenpiraten, die besonders Japaner anwarben, betrieben auch den Schmuggelhandel mit den Portugiesen'; and Mendes Pinto might, he thinks, have picked up the whole story from them. There seems no need to believe that so vivid an account is secondhand.
[2] In July 1542.
[3] The original compares this wall to a monk's girdle.

platform was bordered with the same stone, cut into great tower-work. Upon this wall, which environed the whole island, was a gallery of balusters of turned copper, that from six to six fathom joined to certain pillars of the same metal, upon each of the which was the figure of a woman holding a bowl in her hand; [1] within this gallery were divers monsters [2] cast in metal, standing all in a row, which holding one another by the hand in manner of a dance encompassed the whole island, being, as I have said, a league about. Amidst these monstrous idols there was likewise another row of very rich arches, made of sundry coloured pieces—a sumptuous work, and wherewith the eye might well be entertained and contented: within was a little wood of orange-trees, without any mixture of other plants, and in the midst a hundred and threescore hermitages dedicated to the gods of the year, of whom these gentiles recount many pleasant fables in their chronicles for the defence of their blindness in their false belief.[3] A quarter of a league beyond these hermitages, towards the east, divers goodly great edifices were seen, separated the one from the other with seven forefronts of houses, built after the manner of our churches; from the top to the bottom as far as could be discerned, these buildings were gilt all over, and annexed to very high towers, which in all likelihood were steeples; their edifices were environed with two great streets arched all along, like unto the frontispieces of the houses; these arches were supported by very huge pillars, on the top whereof, and between every arch, was a dainty prospective.[4] Now in regard these buildings, towers, pillars, and their chapters were so exceedingly gilt all over as one could discern nothing but gold, it persuaded us that this temple must needs be wonderful sumptuous and rich, since such cost had been bestowed on the very walls.

After we had surrounded this whole island, and observed the avenues and entries thereof, notwithstanding it was somewhat late, yet would António de Faria needs go ashore to see if he could get any intelligence in one of those hermitages, to the end he might thereupon resolve either to prosecute his design or return back. So having left a guard sufficient for his two vessels, and Diogo Lobato, his chaplain, captain of them, he landed with forty soldiers and twenty slaves, as well pikes as harquebuses. He also carried with him four of the Chinese, which we took awhile before,

---

[1] Possibly the goddess Amida, with the moon in her hands.
[2] Spirits.
[3] Ancestor worship is the central feature of traditional Chinese religion. The worship of the ancestors of the king (or rather, emperor) was again the centre of ancestor worship in general. The monks approached God through the worship of the dead, and amongst the monks these hermits of the imperial dead must have held a high place. The emperor alone communed directly with God.
[4] A delightful view.

both for that they knew the place well, as having been there at other times, and likewise that they might serve us for truchmen [1] and guides. Being got to the shore unespied of any one, and without noise, we entered the island by one of the eight avenues that it had, and marching through the midst of the little wood of orange-trees we arrived at the gate of the first hermitage, which might be some two musket-shot from the place we disembarked, where that happened unto us which I will deliver hereafter.

António de Faria went directly to the next hermitage he saw before him with the greatest silence that might be, and with no little fear, for that he knew not into what danger he was going to engage himself; which he found shut on the inside. He commanded one of the Chinese to knock at it, as he did two or three times, when at last he heard one speak in this manner: 'Praised be the Creator,[2] who hath enamelled the beauty of the skies; let him that knocks at the gate go about, and he shall find it open on the other side, where let me know what he desires.'

The Chinese [3] went presently [4] about, and entering into the hermitage by a back door, he opened the foregate to António de Faria and let him in with all his followers; there he found an old man that seemed to be a hundred years old; he was apparelled in a long violet-coloured damask gown, and he by his countenance appeared to be a man of quality, as we understood afterwards. Being amazed to see so many men he fell to the ground, where he lay a good while without speaking a word; howbeit at length he began to be better confirmed, and beholding us with a serious look, he gravely demanded of us what we were, and what we would have; whereunto the interpreter answered by the express commandment of António de Faria, that he was a captain stranger, a native of the kingdom of Siam,[5] and that sailing in a junk of his, laden with merchandise, and bound for Liampoo,[6] he had suffered shipwreck, whence he had miraculously escaped with all his company, and for that he had vowed to make a pilgrimage to this holy place, to praise God for preserving him from so great a peril, he was now come to perform his vow; also to crave somewhat of him by way of alms, whereby his poverty might be relieved, protesting within three years to render him twice as much as he should then take from him: whereupon the hermit, named Hiticon, having mused a little on the matter, and fixing his eye on António de Faria, 'Whoever thou art,' said he unto him, 'know that I thoroughly

---

[1] Interpreters.   [2] The Chinese believed in only one God.
[3] An interpreter António de Faria had among his crew.
[4] Immediately.
[5] This may prove that 'António de Faria' and Mendes Pinto were, in fact, the same person. Mendes Pinto frequently found it convenient to say that he came from Siam, as will be seen later in the narrative.
[6] Probably Ning-po.

understand what thou sayest, and that I perceive but too well thy damnable intention, wherewith out of the obscurity of thy blindness, like an infernal pilot, thou carriest both thyself and these others into the profound abysm of the lake of night: for instead of rendering thanks to God for so great a favour as thou confessest He hath showed thee, thou comest hither to rob this holy house. But let me ask thee, if thou executest thy mischievous design, what will the divine justice, thinkest thou, do with thee at the last gasp of thy life? Change then thy perverse inclination, and never suffer the imagination of so great a sin to enter thy thoughts; give credit unto me that tells thee nothing but the very truth, even as I hope to thrive by it all the rest of my life.'

António de Faria, seeming to approve of the counsel which the old hermit gave him, earnestly desired him not to be displeased, assuring him that he had no other means or way left to relieve him and his, but what he could find in that place. To which the hermit, wringing his hands and lifting up his eyes, said weeping: 'Praised be Thou, O Lord, that permittest men to live on the earth, who offend Thee under pretext of seeking means to live, and that vouchsafe not to serve Thee one hour, although they know how assured Thy glory is.' After he had uttered these words, he remained very pensive and much troubled to see the great disorder we used in breaking up the coffins and flinging them out of their places; at length looking upon António de Faria, who stood leaning upon his sword, he entreated him to sit down by him, which he did with a great deal of compliment, not desisting for all that from making signs to his soldiers to persist as they had begun, that was to take the silver which was mingled amongst the bones of the dead in the tombs, that they brake up; whereat the hermit was so grieved as he fell down twice in a swoon from his seat, but being come to himself, he spake thus to António de Faria: 'I will declare unto thee as to a man that seems discreet, the means whereby thou mayst obtain pardon for the sin which thou and thy people now commit, to the end that thy soul may not perish eternally, whenas the last breath of thy mouth shall go out of thy body. Seeing then, as thou sayest, that it is necessity constrains thee to offend in this grievous manner, and that thou hast a purpose to make restitution before thou diest, of that thou takest away from hence; if thou hast time and power, thou mayst do these three things: First, thou must render again what thou now carriest away, that the Sovereign Lord may not turn His mercy from thee. Secondly, thou must with tears ask Him forgiveness for thy fault, which is so odious unto Him, never ceasing to chastise thy flesh both day and night. And thirdly, thou must distribute thy goods to the poor, as liberally as to thyself, giving them alms with prudence and discretion to the end the servant of the night may have nothing to accuse thee of at the last day.[1] Now, for recompense of this counsel, I desire thee to command thy followers to gather together the bones of the saints, that they may not be despised on the earth.'

António de Faria promised him very courteously to perform his request, wherewith the hermit was a little better at quiet than before, but yet not fully satisfied; howbeit he spake him very fair, and assured him that after he had once seen him, he very much repented the undertaking of this enterprise, but his soldiers had threatened to kill him if he returned without executing of it, and this he told him as a very great secret. 'God grant it be so,' replied the hermit, 'for that thou shalt not be so blameworthy as these other monsters of the night,[2] which are so greedy, like to famished dogs, that it seems all the silver in the world is not able to satiate them.'

After we had gathered all the silver together that was in the graves amongst the dead men's bones, and carried it aboard our ships, we were all of opinion not to go any farther to the rest of the hermitages, as well because we knew not the country, as for that it was almost night, upon hope that the next day we might continue our enterprise more at leisure. Now before he re-embarked himself, António de Faria took leave of the hermit, and giving him very good words, he desired him for God's sake not to be offended with that his followers had done, being constrained thereunto by mere necessity: for as for his particular he exceedingly abhorred suchlike actions, adding withal, that at the first sight of him he would have returned back, out of the remorse of conscience, and true repentance; but that his company had hindered him, saying that if he did so, they would surely kill him; so that for to have his life he was compelled to yield and consent thereunto, though he plainly saw that it was a very great sin, in regard whereof he was resolved, as soon as he could rid his hands of them, to go up and down the world to perform such penance as was requisite for the purging of him from so enormous a crime. Hereunto the hermit answered: 'Pleaseth the Lord, who living reigneth above the beauty of the stars, that the knowledge, which by this discourse thou showest to have, be not prejudicial unto thee; for I be assured that he who knows these things, and doth them not, runs a far greater danger than he that sins through ignorance.'[3]

Then one of ours, named Nuno Coelho, who would needs have an oar in our talk, told him that he was not to be angry for a matter of so small importance; whereunto the hermit, beholding him with

---

[1] That Mendes Pinto remembered and recorded these words may show that they were not unconnected, in some obscure way, with his later entering a religious life for a time as a Jesuit lay brother.

[2] Devils.

[3] This is, of course, a Christian doctrine, and one particularly stressed by the Roman Catholics.

so stern a countenance, answered: 'Certainly, the fear which thou
hast of death is yet less, since thou employest thyself in actions as
infamous and black as the soul that is in thy body; and for my part,
I cannot but be persuaded, that all thy ambition is wholly placed
upon money, as but too well appears by the thirst of thy insatiable
avarice, whereby thou wilt make an end of heaping up the measure
of thine infernal appetite.   Continue then thy thieveries, for seeing
then thou must go to hell for that which thou hast already taken
out of this holy house, thou shalt also go thither for those things
which thou shalt steal otherwise, so the heavier the burden shall
be that thou bearest, the sooner shalt thou be precipitated into the
bottom of hell, where already thy wicked works have prepared thee
an everlasting abode.' [1]

Hereupon Nuno de Coelho prayed him to take all things
patiently, affirming that the law of God commanded him so to do.
Then the hermit lift up his hand by way of admiration, and as it
were smiling at what the soldier had said, 'Truly,' answered he,
'I am come to see, that I never thought to see or hear, namely, evil
actions disguised with a specious pretext of virtue, which makes
me believe that thy blindness is exceeding great, since trusting to
good words thou spendest thy life so wickedly, wherefore it is not
possible thou shouldest ever come to heaven, or give any account
to God at the last day, as of necessity thou must do.'   Saying so,
he turned him to António de Faria, without attending further
answer from him, and earnestly desired him not to suffer his company to spit upon and profane the altar, which he vowed was more
grievous to him than the enduring of a thousand deaths; whereupon
to satisfy him, he presently commanded the forbearance of it;
wherewith the hermit was somewhat comforted.

Now because it grew late, António de Faria resolved to leave
the place, but before he departed he held it necessary to inform
himself of certain other particulars, whereof he stood in some doubt,
so that he desired of the hermit how many persons there might be
in all those hermitages; whereunto Hiticon answered,[2] that there
were about three hundred and three score *talagrepos*,[3] besides
forty *menigrepos*,[4] appointed to furnish them with things requisite
for their maintenance, and to attend them when they were sick.
Moreover he asked him whether the King of China came not
sometimes thither; he told him, 'No, for,' said he, 'the king
cannot be condemned by anybody,[5] he is the son of the Sun,' [6]

---

[1] Nuno Coelho was amongst those drowned very shortly afterwards.
[2] It would not have been in keeping with his religious character to conceal
the truth.
[3] Chinese monks.   [4] Chinese friars.
[5] So that he cannot need to do penance by visiting a holy spot.
[6] 'On a throne of new gold the Son of the Sky is sitting among his mandarins.
He shines with jewels and is like a sun surrounded by stars.'   (Tu-fu.)

but contrarily he had power to absolve every one. Then he inquired of him if there were any arms in their hermitages. 'Oh, no,' answered the hermit, 'for all such as pretend to go to heaven have more need of patience to endure injuries, than of arms to revenge themselves.' Being also desirous to know of him the cause why so much silver was mingled with the bones of the dead, 'This silver,' replied the hermit, 'comes of the alms that the deceased carry with them out of this into the other life, for to serve them at their need in the heaven of the moon, where they live eternally.' In conclusion, having demanded of him whether they had any women, he said, that they which would maintain the life of their souls, ought not to taste the pleasures of the flesh, seeing experience made it apparent that the bee which nourisheth herself in a honeycomb doth often sting such as offer to meddle with that sweetness.'[1]

After António de Faria had propounded all these questions, he took his leave of him, and so went directly to his ships, with an intention to return again the next day, for to set upon the other hermitages, where, as he had been told, was great abundance of silver, and certain idols of gold, but our sins would not permit us to see the effect of a business which we had been two months and a half a purchasing with so much labour and danger of our lives,[2] as I will deliver hereafter.

At the clearing up of the day, António de Faria and all of us being embarked, we went and anchored on the other side of the island, about a falcon[3] shot from it, with an intent, as I have before declared, to go ashore again the next morning, and set upon the chapels where the kings of China were interred, that so we might the more commodiously lade our two vessels with such treasures, which peradventure might have succeeded according to our desires, if the business had been well carried, and that António de Faria had followed the counsel was given him, which was, that since we had not been as yet discovered, that he should have carried the hermit away with him to the end he might not acquaint the house of the bonzes[4] with what we had done; howbeit he would never hearken to it, saying that we were to fear nothing that way, by reason the hermit was so old, and his legs so swollen with the gout, as he was not able to stand, much less to go. But it fell out clean contrary to his expectation, for the hermit no sooner saw us embarked, as we understood afterwards, but he

---

[1] He means that marriage (and concubinage) interfere with the mystical life of contemplation of the Deity, to which only those who live a monastic life are fitted.
[2] This refers to the voyage there, previously related in the *Peregrination*.
[3] A kind of light cannon.
[4] Priests.

presently crawled as well as he could to the next hermitage, which was not above a flight [1] shot from his, and giving intelligence of all that had passed, he bad his companion, because himself was not able, to go away with all speed to the bonzes' house to acquaint them with it, which the other instantly performed; so that about midnight we saw a great many of fires lighted on the top of the wall of the temple where the kings were buried, being kindled to serve for a signal to the country about, of some extraordinary danger towards.   This made us ask of our Chinese what they might mean, who answered that assuredly we were discovered, in regard whereof they advised us without any longer stay to set sail immediately.   Herewith they acquainted António de Faria, who was fast asleep, but he straightway arose, and leaving his anchor in the sea, rowed directly, afraid as he was, to the island, for to learn what was done there.

Being arrived near to the quay he heard many bells ringing in each hermitage, together with a noise of men talking, whereupon the Chinese that accompanied him said: 'Sir, never stand to hear or see more, but retire, we beseech you, as fast as you may, and cause us not to be all miserably slain with your further stay.' Howbeit, little regarding or afraid of their words, he went ashore only with six soldiers, having no other arms but swords and targets, and going up the stairs of the quay, whether it were that he was vexed for having lost so fair an occasion, or carried thereunto by his courage, he entered into the gallery that environed the island, and ran up and down in it like a madman, without meeting anybody. That done, and being returned aboard his vessel, much grieved and ashamed, he consulted with his company about what they should do, who were of opinion that the best course we could take was to depart, and therefore they required him to put it accordingly in execution.   Seeing them all so resolved, and fearing some tumults among the soldiers, he was fain to answer that he was also of their mind, but first he thought it fit to know for what cause they should fly away in that manner, and therefore he desired them to stay for him a little in that place, because he would try whether he could learn by some means or other the truth of the matter, whereof they had but a bare suspicion; for which, he told them, he would ask but half an hour at the most, so that there would be time enough to take order for anything before day; some would have alleged reasons against this, but he would not hear them, wherefore having caused them all to take their oaths upon the holy Evangelists, that they would stay for him, he returned to land with the same soldiers that had accompanied him before, and entering into the little wood, he heard the sound of a bell, which addressed him to another hermitage, far richer than that wherein we were the

[1] Arrow.

day before.   There he met with two men, apparelled like monks, with large hoods[1] which made him think they were hermits, of whom he presently laid hold, wherewith one of them was so terrified, as he was not able to speak a good while after.   Hereupon four of the six soldiers passed into the hermitage and took an idol of silver from the altar, having a crown of gold on its head, and a wheel in its hand;[2] they also brought away three candlesticks of silver, with long chains of the same belonging to them.

This performed, António de Faria, carrying the two hermits along with him, went aboard again, and sailing away he propounded divers questions to him of the two that was least afraid, threatening to use him in a strange fashion if he did not tell the truth.   This hermit, seeing himself so menaced, answered that 'A holy man, named Pilau Angiroo, came about midnight to the house of the kings' sepulchres, where knocking in haste at the gate, he cried out, saying: "O miserable men, buried in the drunkenness of carnal sleep, who by a solemn vow have professed yourselves to the honour of the goddess Amida, the rich reward of our labours, hear, hear, hear, O the most wretched men that ever were born; there are strangers come into our island, from the further end of the world,[3] which have long beards, and bodies of iron;[4] these wicked creatures have entered into the holy house of the seven-and-twenty pillars, of whose sacred temple a holy man is keeper, that hath told it me, where after they had ransacked the rich treasures of the saints, they contemptedly threw their bones to the ground, which they profaned with their stinking and infectious spitting, and made a mockery of them like devils, obstinate and hardened in their wretched sins; wherefore I advise you to look well to yourselves, for it is said that they have sworn to kill us all as soon as it is day. Fly away, then, or call some people to your succour, since being religious men you are not permitted to meddle with anything that may shed the blood of man." Herewith they presently arose and ran to the gate, where they found the hermit laid on the ground, and half dead with grief and weariness through the imbecility of his age; whereupon the *grepos* and *menigrepos* made those fires that you saw, and withal sent in all haste to the towns of Corpilem and Fonbana, for to succour them speedily with the forces of the country, so that you may be assured it will not be long before they fall upon this place with all the fury that may be.

[1] Mendes Pinto wrote 'rosaries,' but Cogan translated 'hoods' as being less shocking for his readers.

[2] A figure of one of the kings of China, holding a well-known oriental symbol of life.   'Or ever the silver cord be loosed, or the golden bowl be broken, or the pitcher be broken at the fountain, or the wheel broken at the cistern.' —Eccles. xii. 6.

[3] The Chinese thus expressed their notion of Portugal and Europe.

[4] Armour.

'Now this is all that I am able to say concerning the truth of this affair; wherefore I desire you to return us both into our hermitage with our lives saved, for if you do not so you will commit a greater sin than you did yesterday. Remember also that God, in regard of the continual penance we perform, hath taken us so far into His protection, as He doth visit us almost every hour of the day,[1] wherefore, labour to save yourselves as much as you will, yet shall you hardly do it; for be sure that the earth, the air, the winds, the waters, the beasts, the fishes, the fowls, the trees, the plants, and all things created will pursue and torment you so cruelly, as none but He that lives in Heaven will be able to help you.' [2]

António de Faria, being hereby certainly informed of the truth of the business, sailed instantly away, tearing his hair and beard for very rage to see that through his negligence and indiscretion he had lost the fairest occasion that ever he should be able to meet withal.

Chapter XXVI. Our casting away in the Gulf of Nanquin, with all that befell us after this lamentable shipwreck

WE had already sailed seven days in the Gulf of Nanquin, to the end that the force of the current might carry us the more swiftly away, as men whose safety consisted wholly in flight, for we were so desolate and sad that we scarce spake one to another; in the meantime we arrived at a village called Susequerim, where no news being come either of us or what we had done, we furnished ourselves with some victual, and getting information very covertly of the course we were to hold, we departed within two hours after, and then with the greatest speed we could make we entered into a strait named Xalingau, much less frequented than the gulf that we had passed; here we navigated nine days more, in which time we ran a hundred and forty leagues, then entering again into the said Gulf of Nanquin, which in that place was not above ten or eleven leagues broad, we sailed for the space of thirteen days from one side to another with a westerly wind, exceedingly afflicted, both with the great labour we were fain to endure, and the cruel fear we were in, besides the want we began to feel of victuals.

In this case being come within sight of the mountains of Conxinacau,[3] which are in the height of forty and one degrees, there arose so terrible a south wind, called by the Chinese *tufaon*,[4] as it could not possibly be thought a natural thing, so that our vessels

---

[1] A state of mystical contemplation.   [2] This curse was shortly to be fulfilled.
[3] The Yellow Mountains.   [4] Typhoon.

being low-built, weak, and without mariners, we were reduced to such extremity, that out of all hope to escape we suffered ourselves to be driven along the coast, as the current of the water would carry us, for we held it more safe to venture ourselves amongst the rocks, than to let us be swallowed up in the midst of the sea, and though we had chosen this design as the better and less painful, yet did it not succeed, for after dinner the wind turned to the north-west, whereby the waves became so high, that it was most dreadful to behold; our fear then was so extreme, as we began to cast all that we had into the sea, even to the chests full of silver. That done, we cut down our two masts, and so without masts and sails we floated along all the rest of the day; at length about midnight we heard them in António de Faria's vessel cry: 'Lord, have mercy upon us,' which persuaded us that they were cast away,[1] the apprehension whereof put us in such a fright, as for an hour together no man spake a word.

Having passed all this sad night in so miserable a plight, about an hour before day our vessel opened about the keel, so that it was instantly full of water eight spans high, whereupon perceiving ourselves to sink, we verily believed it was the good pleasure of God that in this place we should finish both our lives and labours. As soon then as it was day we looked out to sea, as far as possibly we could discern, but could no way discover António de Faria, which put us quite out of heart, and so continuing in this great affliction till about ten of the clock, with so much terror and amazement as words are not able to express, at last we ran against the coast, and even drowned as we were, the waves rolled us towards a point of rocks that stood out into the sea, where we were no sooner arrived but that all went to pieces, insomuch that of five-and-twenty Portugals, which we were, there were but fourteen saved, the other eleven being drowned together with eighteen Christian servants and seven Chinese mariners. This miserable disaster happened on a Monday, the 5th of August, in the year one thousand five hundred forty and two, for which the Lord be praised everlastingly.[2]

We fourteen Portugals, having escaped out of this shipwreck by the mere mercy of God, spent all that day and the night following, in bewailing our misfortune and the wretched estate whereunto we were reduced, but in the end consulting together, what course to take for to give some remedy thereunto, we concluded to enter into the country, hoping that far or near we should not fail to meet with somebody, that taking us for slaves, would relieve us

---

[1] In this way Mendes Pinto gives us to understand that he was sailing in another ship, not the flagship.
[2] It was customary for the Portuguese at that time to praise God in this way, both in fortune and misfortune.

with meat, till such time as it should please heaven to terminate
our travels with the end of our lives.   With this resolution we went
some six or seven leagues over rocks and hills, and on the other
side discovered a great marsh, so large and void, as it passed the
reach of our sight, there being no appearance of any land beyond
it, which made us turn back again towards the same place where
we were cast away.   Being arrived there the day after about sunset,
we found upon the shore the bodies of our men which the sea had
cast up, over whom we recommenced our sorrow and lamentations,
and the next day we buried them in the sand to keep them from
being devoured by the tigers, whereof that country is full, which
we performed with much labour and pain, in regard we had no
other tools for that purpose but our hands and nails.   After these
poor bodies were interred we got us into a marsh, where we spent
all the night as the safest place we could choose to preserve us
from the tigers.   From thence we continued our journey towards
the north, and that by such precipices and thick woods, as we had
much ado to pass through them.

Having travelled in this manner three days, at length we arrived
at a little strait without meeting anybody, over the which resolving
to swim, by ill fortune the four first that entered into it, being three
Portugals[1] and a young youth,[2] were miserably drowned, for being
very feeble, and the strait somewhat broad, and the current of the
water very strong, they were not able to hold out any longer when
they came to the midst; so we eleven with three servants that remained, seeing the unfortunate success of our companions, could
do nothing but weep and lament, as men that hourly expected such
or a worse end.   Having spent all that dark night exposed to the
wind, cold, and rain, it pleased our Lord that the next morning
before day we discovered a great fire towards the east, whereupon
as soon as the day broke, we marched fair and softly that way,
recommending ourselves to that Almighty God from whom alone
we could hope for a remedy to our miseries, and so continuing
our journey all along the river the most part of that day, at last
we came to a little wood, where we found five men making a fire
of coals, whom on our knees we besought for God's sake to direct
us to some place where we might get some relief.   'I would,' said
one of them, beholding us with an eye of pity, 'it lay in our power
to help you, but alas! all the comfort we can give you is to bestow
some part of our supper on you, which is a little rice,[3] wherewith
you may pass this night here with us if you will, though I hold

[1] The original adds that the three Portuguese were called Belchior Barbosa
Gaspar Barbosa, and Francisco Borges Caeiro, and that they were all from
Ponte de Lima in the north of Portugal.

[2] Presumably a Chinese, perhaps the one who had been captured and had complained of the hypocrisy of the Portuguese.   See Introduction, p. xv.

[3] This was a rice-growing district, notable for its vast and frequent floods.

it better for you to proceed on your way, and recover the place you see a little below, where you shall find a hospital that serves to lodge such pilgrims as chance to come into these quarters.' Having thanked him for his good address we fell to the rice they gave us, which came but to two mouthfuls apiece, and so took our leaves of them, going directly to the place they had showed us, as well as our weakness would permit.

About an hour within night, we arrived at the hospital, where we met with four men, that had the charge of it, who received us very charitably.   The next morning as soon as it was day they demanded of us what we were, and from whence we came.   Thereunto we answered, that we were strangers, natives of the kingdom of Siam, and that coming from the port of Liampoo to go to the fishing of Nanquin,[1] we were cast away at sea by the violence of a storm, having saved nothing out of this shipwreck but those our miserable and naked bodies.   Whereupon demanding of us again, what we intended to do, and whither we would go, we replied that we purposed to go to the city of Nanquin, there to embark ourselves as rowers in the first *lanteaa* that should put to sea, for to pass unto Canton,[2] where our countrymen, by the permission of the *aytao* of Pequin, exercised their traffic under the protection of the son of the Sun, and Lion crowned in the Throne of the World,[3] wherefore we desired them for God's cause to let us stay in that hospital, until we had recovered our healths, and to bestow any poor clothes on us to cover our nakedness.   After they had given good ear unto us, 'It was reason,' answered they, 'to grant you that which you require with so much earnestness and tears; but in regard the house is now very poor we cannot so easily discharge our duties unto you as we should; howbeit, we will do what we may with a very good will.'   Then, quite naked as we were, they led us all about the village, containing some forty or fifty fires,[4] more or less; the inhabitants whereof were exceeding poor, having no other living but what they got by the labour of their hands, from whom they drew by way of alms some two taels [5] in money, half a sack of rice, a little meal, haricot beans, onions, and a few old rags, wherewith we made the best shift we could; over and above this they bestowed two taels more on us out of the stock of the

[1] Presumably an abbreviated way of saying they were going first to Nanking, and then to the pearl fisheries of Canton.
[2] To the Pearl or West River.
[3] The emperor of China.
[4] Houses.
[5] Crawford . . . thinks that this name comes from the Indian *tola*, a weight chiefly for gold and silver.   It is the trade name for the Chinese ounce and also of the Chinese money of account, often called 'the ounce of silver,' but in Chinese, *liang*.   (I am indebted to the kindness of Dr. A. Cortesão for this note.) The *Oxford English Dictionary* derives it from the Malay *tahil*, a weight, as does also Wyld's *Universal English Dictionary*.

hospital.   But whereas we desired that we might be permitted to
stay there, they excused themselves, saying that no poor might
remain there above three days, or five at the most, unless it were
sick people, or women with child, of whom special care was to be
had, because in their extremities they could not travel without
endangering their lives, wherefore they could for no other persons
whatsoever transgress that ordinance, which had of ancient time
been instituted by the advice of very learned and religious men;
nevertheless, that three leagues from thence, we should in a great
town, called Sileyiacau, find a very rich hospital, where all sorts
of poor people were entertained, and that there we should be far
better looked unto than in their house, which was poor, and
agreeable to the place of its situation, to which end they would
give us a letter of recommendation, by means whereof we should
incontinently be received.

For these good offices we rendered them infinite thanks, and told
them that God would reward them for it since they did it for His
sake, whereupon an old man, one of those four, taking the speech
upon him, 'It is for that consideration alone we do it,' answered
he, 'and not in regard of the world; for God and the world are
greatly different in matters of works, and of the intention which
one may have in the doing of them; for the world, being poor and
miserable as it is, can give nothing that is good, whereas God is
infinitely rich, and a friend to the poor, that in the height of their
afflictions praise Him with patience and humility.   The world is
revengeful, but God is suffering; the world is wicked, God is all
goodness; the world is gluttonous, God is a lover of abstinence;
the world is mutinous and turbulent, God is quiet and peaceable;
the world is a liar and full of dissimulation to them that belong to it,
God is always true, free, and merciful to them that invoke Him
by prayer; the world is sensual and covetous, God is liberal, and
purer than the light of the sun or stars, or than those other lamps
which are far more excellent than they that appear to our eyes,
and are always present before His most resplendent face; the world
is full of irresolution and falsehood, wherewith it entertains itself
in the smoke of its vainglory, whereas God is constant in His
truth, to the end that thereby the humble may possess glory in all
sincerity of heart.[1]   In a word, the world is full of folly and ignorance, contrarily God is the fountain of wisdom; wherefore my
friends, although you be reduced to so pitiful an estate, do you not
for all that distrust His promises; for be assured He will not fail
you, if you do not render yourselves unworthy of His favours,
in regard it was never found that He was at any time wanting to
His; albeit they that are blinded by the world are of another

---

[1] A Chinese version of the seven deadly sins and seven principal virtues.
Mendes Pinto certainly must have seen the analogy.

opinion, whenas they see themselves oppressed with poverty and despised of everybody.'

Having used this speech to us, he gave us a letter of recommendation to the brotherhood of the other hospital, whither we were to go, and so we departed about noon, and arrived at the town an hour or two before sunset. The first thing we did was to go to the house of the repose of the poor, for so the Chinese call the hospitals; there we delivered our letters to the masters of that society, which they term *tanigores*, whom we found all together in a chamber, where they were assembled about the affairs of the poor. After they had received the letter with a kind of compliment that seemed very strange to us, they commanded the register to read it; whereupon he stood up and read thus to them that were sitting at the table: 'We the poorest of the poor, unworthy to serve that sovereign Lord, whose works are so admirable, as the sun, and the stars that twinkle in the sky during the darkness of the night, do testify: having been elected to the succession of this His house of Buatendoo, situated in this village of Catihorao, with all manner of respect and honour, do beseech your humble persons, admitted to the service of the Lord, that out of a zeal of charity you will lodge and favour these fourteen strangers, whereof three are tawny, the other eleven somewhat whiter, whose poverty will manifestly appear to your eyes, whereby you may judge how much reason we have to present this request unto you, for that they have been cast away with all their merchandise in the impetuous waters of the sea, that with their accustomed fury have laid the execution of the Almighty hand upon them, which for a just punishment doth often permit suchlike things to happen; for to show us how dreadful His judgments are, from which may it please Him to deliver us all at the day of death, to the end we may not see the indignation of His face.'

This letter being read, they caused us presently to be lodged in a very neat chamber, accommodated with a table and divers chairs, where after we had been served with good meat, we rested ourselves that night. The next morning the register came along with the rest of the officers, and demanded of us who we were, of what nation, and whereabout we had suffered shipwreck; whereunto we answered as we had done before to those of the village from whence we came, that we might not be found in two tales, and convinced of lying; whereupon having further inquired of us what we meant to do, we told them that our intention was to get ourselves cured in that house, if it pleased them to permit us, in regard we were so weak and sickly as we could scarce stand upon our legs. To which they replied, that they would very willingly see that performed for us, as a thing that was ordinarily done there for the service of God; for the which we thanked them weeping, with so much acknowledgment of their goodness and charity, as the tears stood in their eyes, so that presently sending for a physician, they bid him look carefully to us, for that we were poor folks, and had no other means but what we had from the house. That done, he took our names in writing, and set them down in a great book, whereunto we all of us set our hands, saying, it was necessary it should be so, that an account of the expense was to be made for us.

Having spent eighteen days in this hospital, where we were sufficiently provided for with all things necessary, it pleased God that we thoroughly recovered our healths, so that feeling ourselves strong enough to travel, we departed from thence for to go to a place called Suzoanganee, some five leagues from that hospital, where we arrived about sunset. Now in regard we were very weary, we sat us down upon the side of a fountain that stood at the entrance of that village, being much perplexed and unresolved what way to take. In the meantime, they which came to fetch water, seeing us set there in so sad an equipage, returned with their pitchers empty, and advertising the inhabitants of it, the most of them came presently forth to us; then wondering much, because they had never seen men like unto us, they gathered altogether, as if they would consult thereupon, and after they had a good while debated one with another, they sent an old woman to demand of us what people we were, and why we sat so about that fountain from whence they drew all the water they used. Hereunto we answered that we were poor strangers, natives of the kingdom of Siam, who by a storm at sea were cast upon their country, in that miserable plight wherein they beheld us. 'Tell me,' replied she, 'what course would you have us to take for you, and what resolve you to do, for here is no house for the repose of the poor whereinto you may be received?' To these words one of our company answered, with tears in his eyes, and a gesture conformable to our design,[1] that God, being that which He was, would never abandon us with His almighty hand, but would touch their hearts to take compassion of us and our poverty; and further, that we were resolved to travel in that miserable case we were in till we had the good fortune to arrive at the city of Nanquin, where we desired to put ourselves into the *lanteaas*, there to serve for rowers to the merchants that ordinarily went from thence to Canton and so to get to Cambay,[2] where great store of our country junks usually lay, in which we would embark ourselves. Thereupon having somewhat a better opinion of us than before, 'Seeing you are,' said she, 'such as you deliver, have a little patience till I come again and tell you what these folks resolve to do with you'; wherewith she returned to those country people, which were about some

[1] Copied from what they had observed of Chinese forms of compliment.
[2] On the western coast of Portuguese India.

hundred persons, with whom she entered into a great contestation, but at length she came back with one of their priests, attired in a long gown of red damask, which is an ornament of chiefest dignity among them; in this equipage he came to us with a handful of ears of corn in his hand; then having commanded us to approach unto him, we presently obeyed him with all kind of respect, but he little regarded it, seeing us so poor; whereupon after he had thrown the ears of corn into the fountain, he willed us to put our hands upon them, which we accordingly having done, 'You are to confess,' said he unto us, 'by this holy and solemn oath, that now you take in my presence upon these two substances of bread and water,[1] which the high Creator of all things hath made by His holy will to sustain and nourish all that is born into the world, during the pilgrimage of this life, whether that which you told this woman but now be true, for upon that condition we will give you lodging in this village conformably to the charities we are bound to exercise towards God's poor people; whereas contrarily, if it be not so, I command you in His name that you presently get you gone, upon pain of being bitten and destroyed by the teeth of the gluttonous serpent,[2] that makes his abode in the bottom of the house of smoke.'[3] Hereunto we answered, that we had said nothing but what was most true, wherewith the priest remaining satisfied, 'Since you are,' said he, 'such as you say, come you along boldly with me, and rely on my words.' Then returning with us to the inhabitants of the place, he told them that they might bestow their alms upon us without offence, and that he gave them permission so to do, whereupon we were presently conducted into the village, and lodged in the porch of their pagoda or temple, where we were furnished with all that was needful for us, and had two mats given us to lie upon. The next morning as soon as it was day, we went up and down the street, begging from door to door, and got four taels in silver, wherewith we supplied our most pressing necessities.

After this we went away to another place called Xianguulea, that was not above two leagues from that, with a resolution to travel in that sort, as it were in pilgrimage,[4] to the city of Nanquin, to which it was then some hundred and forty leagues; for we thought that from thence we might go to Canton, where our ships traded at that time, and it may be our design had succeeded, had it not been for ill fortune. About evensong we arrived at that village, where we sat us down under the shadow of a great tree that stood by itself, but it was our ill hap to meet with three boys that kept certain cattle there, who no sooner perceived us, but betaking them to their

[1] This shows us the basis of natural simplicity in Chinese religion as described by Mendes Pinto.
[2] The devil.   [3] Hell.   [4] That is, begging alms like pilgrims.

heels, they cried out: 'Thieves, thieves,' whereat the inhabitants came instantly running out, armed with lances and crossbows, crying out, 'Stop the thieves'; and so perceiving us that fled from them, they mauled us cruelly with stones and staves, in such manner as we were all of us grievously hurt, especially one of our boys that died upon it.   Then seizing on us, they tied our arms behind us, and leading us like prisoners into the village, they so beat and buffeted us with their fists, as they had almost killed us; then they plunged us into a cistern of standing water, that reached up to our waists, wherein were a great number of horse-leeches.

In this miserable place we remained two days, which seemed two hundred years to us, having neither rest nor anything to eat all that time.   At last it was our good fortune that a man of Suzoan-ganee, from whence we came, passing by, chanced to understand how we had been used by those of the village, and thereupon went and told them that they did us great wrong to take us for thieves, for that we were poor strangers, which had been cast away by a storm at sea, wherefore they had committed a great sin to imprison and handle us in that sort.   The report of this man wrought so effectually with them, that we were presently taken out of the cistern, being all gore blood with the sucking of the horse-leeches, and I verily believe that if we had stayed there but one day longer, we had all of us been dead.   So we departed from this place about evening, and bewailing our bad fortune, continued on our voyage.

After our departure from Xianguulea we arrived at a village, inhabited by very poor people, where we met with three men that were pilling [1] flax, who as soon as they saw us forsook their work, and fled hastily away into a wood of fir-trees; there they cried out to those that passed by to take heed of us for that we were thieves; whereupon fearing to incur the same danger whence we so lately escaped, we got us away presently from that place, although it was almost night, and continued our journey, in the rain and the dark, without knowing whither we went, till we came to a gate where cattle were kept, and there we lay the rest of the night upon a little heap of dung.

The next morning as soon as it was day we got again into the way which we had left, and not long after we discovered from the top of a little hill a great plain full of trees, and in the midst thereof a very fair house hard by a river, whither forthwith we went, and sat us down by a fountain that was before the outer gate, where we remained two or three hours without seeing anybody.   At length a young gentleman about sixteen or seventeen years of age came riding upon a very good horse, accompanied with four men on foot, whereof one carried two hares, and another five *nivatores*, which are

[1] Peeling, i.e. 'scutching,' separating the fibres from the woody part of the stalk.

fowls resembling our pheasants, with a goshawk on his fist, and three or four couple of spaniels at their heels; when this gentleman came at us he stayed his horse, to ask us who we were, and whether we would have anything with him.   Hereunto we answered as well as we could, and made him an ample relation of the whole event of our shipwreck, whereat he seemed to be very sorry, as we could gather by his countenance, so that ere he went, 'Stay there,' said he unto us, 'for by and by I will send you what you have need of, and that for His sake that with a glory of great riches lives reigning in the highest of all the heavens.'

A little after he sent an old woman for us, which was apparelled in a long garment, with a chaplet hanging down on her neck; the good dame coming to us, 'The son of him,' said she, 'whom we hold for master in this house, and whose rice we eat, hath sent for you; follow me then with all humility, to the end you may not seem idle fellows to those that shall see you, and such as beg only to be exempted from getting your living by the labour of your hands.' This said, we entered with her into an outward court, all about environed with galleries as if it had been some cloister of religious persons, on the walls whereof were painted divers women on horseback going on hunting with hawks on their fists; over the gate of this court was a great arch very richly engraven; in the midst whereof hung a scutcheon of arms, in the fashion of a shield, fastened to a silver chain; within it was a man painted almost in the form of a tortoise, with the feet up, and the head downwards, and round about it these words were read for a device: 'Ingualec finguau, potim aquarau,' that is to say, 'So is it with all that appertains to me.'   We learnt afterwards that by this monster the figure of the world was represented, which the Chinese depaint in this manner to demonstrate that there is nothing in it but falsehood, and so to disabuse all them that make such account of it by making them to see how all things in it are turned upside down.

Out of this court we went up a broad pair of stairs, made of fair hewed stone, and entered into a great hall, where a woman of about fifty years of age was set upon a tapestry carpet, having two young gentlewomen by her side, that were exceeding fair and richly apparelled, with chains of pearl about their necks, and hard by them was a reverend old man laid upon a little bed, whom one of the two gentlewomen fanned with a ventiloe;[1] at his bed's head stood the young gentleman that had sent for us, and a little further off upon another carpet nine young maids, clothed in crimson and white damask, sat sewing.   As soon as we came before the old man we fell on our knees, and asked an alms of him, beginning our speech with tears, and in the best terms that the time and our necessities could inspire us with; whereupon the old lady, beckoning

[1]Fan.

to us with her hand, 'Come, weep no more,' said she, 'for it
grieves me much to see you shed so many tears; it is sufficient
that I know you desire an alms of us.'   Then the old man that lay in
the bed spake unto us, and demanded whether any of us knew
what was good for a fever.[1]   Whereat the young gentlewoman that
fanned him, not able to forbear smiling, 'Sir,' said she, 'they have
more need that you would be pleased to give order for the satisfying
of their hunger, than to be questioned about a matter which it is
likely they are ignorant of; wherefore methinks it were better first
to give them what they want, and afterwards to talk with them about
that which concerns them less.'   For these words the mother
reprehending her, 'Go to,' said she, 'you will ever be prating
when you should not, but surely I shall make you leave this custom';
whereunto the daughter smiling, replied: 'That you shall when you
please, but in the meantime I beseech you, let these poor strangers
have something to eat.'[2]

For all this the old man would not give over questioning us, for he
demanded of us who we were, of what country, and whither we
were going, besides many other suchlike things.   To which we
answered as occasion required, and recounted unto him how,
when, and in what place we had suffered shipwreck, as also how
many of our company were drowned, and that thus wandering we
travelled up and down not knowing whither to address ourselves.
This answer rendered the old man pensive for awhile, until at
length turning him to his son, 'Well, now,' said he unto him,
'what thinkest thou of that which thou hast heard these strangers
deliver?   It were good for thee to imprint it well in thy memory,
to the end it may teach thee to know God better, and give Him
thanks for that He hath given thee a father, who to exempt thee
from the labours and necessities of this life hath parted with three
of the goodliest things in this country, whereof the least is worth
above a hundred thousand taels, and bestowed them on thee, but
thou art of a humour more inclined to hunt a hare, than to retain
this which I now tell thee.'   The young gentleman made no reply,
but smiling looked upon his sisters.

Then the old man caused meat to be brought unto us before him,
and commanded us to fall to it, as we most willingly did, whereat
he took great pleasure in regard his stomach was quite gone with his
sickness, but his young daughters much more, who with their
brother did nothing but laugh to see us feed ourselves with our
hands, for that is contrary to the custom which is observed through-

---

[1] The Portuguese, as strangers, were often supposed to have magic powers of
healing.   See, later, Mendes Pinto's adventures in Japan and the story of
Pantaleão de Sá, after the wreck of the *S. João*.
[2] We see from this how proficient Mendes Pinto had become in Chinese, or
he would never so have understood familiar conversation.

out the whole empire of China, where the inhabitants at their meat carry it to their mouths with two little sticks made like a pair of scissors.   After we had given God thanks, the old man, that had well observed us, lifting up his hands to heaven, with tears in his eyes, 'Lord,' said he, 'that livest reigning in the tranquillity of Thy high wisdom, I laud Thee in all humility for that Thou permittest men that are strangers, come from the farthest end of the world, and without the knowledge of Thy doctrine, to render Thee thanks and give Thee praise according to their weak capacity, which makes me believe that Thou wilt accept of them with as good a will, as if it were some great offering of melodious music agreeable to Thine ears.' [1]   Then he caused three pieces of linen cloth, and four taels of silver to be given us, willing us withal to pass that night in his house, because it was somewhat too late for us to proceed on our journey; this offer we most gladly accepted, and with compliments after the manner of the country [2] we testified our thankfulness to him, wherewith himself, his wife, and his son rested very well satisfied.

Chapter XXVII. Our arrival at the town of Taypor, where we were made prisoners, and so sent to the city of Nanquin

THE next morning by break of day parting from that place, we went to a village called Finginilau, which was some four leagues from the old gentleman's house, where we remained three days, and then continuing travelling from one place to another, and from village to village, ever declining the great towns, for fear lest the justice of the country should call us in question in regard we were strangers; in this manner we spent almost two months without receiving the least damage from anybody.   Now there is no doubt but we might easily have got to the city of Nanquin in that time if we had had a guide, but for want of knowing the way we wandered we knew not whither, suffering much, and running many hazards. At length we arrived at a village named Chautir, at such a time as they were a solemnizing a sumptuous funeral of a very rich woman, that had disinherited her kindred, and left her estate to the pagod of this village, where she was buried, as we understood by the inhabitants; we were invited then to this funeral, as other poor people were, and according to the custom of the country we did eat on the grave of the deceased.   At the end of three days that we stayed there, which was the time the funeral lasted, we had six

[1] This is immediately after the reference to the Portuguese eating with their hands, and seems to have an almost satirical intention behind it.
[2] The Chinese bow with folded hands.

taels given us for an alms, conditionally that in all our orisons we
should pray unto God for the soul of the departed.

Being gone from this place we continued on our journey to another village, called Guinapalir, from whence we were almost two
months travelling from country to country, until at last our ill
fortune brought us to a town named Taypor,[1] where by chance
there was at that time a *chumbim*, that is to say, one of those super-
intendents of justice that every three years are sent throughout
the provinces for to make report unto the king of all that passeth
there. This naughty man, seeing us go begging from door to
door, called to us from a window where he was, and would know
of us who we were and of what nation, as also what obliged us to
run up and down the world in that manner. Having asked us
these questions in the presence of three registers, and of many other
persons that were gathered together to behold us, we answered
him that we were strangers, natives of the kingdom of Siam, who
being cast away by a storm at sea went thus travelling and begging
our living, to the end we might sustain ourselves with the charity
of good people until such time as we could arrive at Nanquin,
whither we were going with an intent to embark ourselves there in
some of the merchants' *lanteaas* for Canton, where the shipping of
our nation lay. This answer we made unto the *chumbim*, who
questionless had been well enough contented with it, and would
have let us go, had it not been for one of his clerks, for he told them
that we were idle vagabonds, that spent our time in begging from
door to door, and abusing the alms that were given us, and therefore
he was at no hand [2] to let us go free, for fear of incurring the punishment ordained for such as offend in that sort, as is set forth in the
seventh of the twelve books of the statutes of the realm; wherefore
as his faithful servant he counselled him to lay us in good and sure
hold, that we might be forthcoming to answer the law. The
chumbim presently followed his clerk's advice, and carried himself
toward us with as much barbarous cruelty as could be expected
from a pagan such as he was, that lived without God or religion; [3]
to which effect after he had heard a number of false witnesses, who
charged us with many foul crimes, whereof we never so much as
dreamt, he caused us to be put into a deep dungeon, with irons on
our hands and feet, and great iron collars about our necks. In
this miserable place we endured such hunger and were so fearfully
whipped that we were in perpetual pain for six-and-twenty days
together, at the end whereof we were by the sentence of the same
chumbim sent to the parliament of the *chaem* of Nanquin, because

[1] Tai-ping.
[2] On no account.
[3] It is interesting to note that this phrase is applied to the unjust judge, and
not to the charitable *tanigores*.

the jurisdiction of this extended not to the condemnation of any prisoner to death.

We remained six-and-twenty days in that cruel prison, whereof I spake before, and I vow we thought we had been six-and-twenty thousand years there, in regard of the great misery we suffered in it, which was such, as one of our companions called João Rodrigues Bravo died in our arms, being eaten up with lice,[1] we being no way able to help him, and it was almost a miracle that the rest of us escaped alive from that filthy vermin. At length, one morning, when we thought of nothing less, laden with irons as we were, and so weak that we could hardly speak, we were drawn out of that prison, and then being chained one to another, we were embarked with many others, to the number of thirty or forty, that having been convicted for sundry heinous crimes, were also sent to the parliament of Nanquin, where, as I have already declared, is alway residing a *chaem* of justice, which is like to the sovereign title of the viceroy of China.[2] There is likewise a parliament of some five-and-twenty *gerozemos* and *ferucuas*, which are as those we call judges with us, and that determine all causes, as well civil as criminal: so as there is no appeal from their sentence, unless it be unto another court, which hath power even over the king himself, whereunto if one appeals, it is as if he appealed to Heaven. To understand this the better, you must know that although this parliament, and others suchlike, which are in the principal cities of the realm, have an absolute power from the king, both over all criminal and civil causes, without any opposition or appeal whatsoever, yet there is another court of justice which is called the Court[3] of the Creator of All Things, whereunto it is permitted to appeal in weighty and important matters. In this court are ordinarily assisting four-and-twenty *menigrepos*, which are certain religious men, very austere in their manner of living, such as the Capuchins are,[4] and verily if they were Christians, one might hope for great matters from them in regard of their marvellous abstinence and sincerity.[5] There are none admitted into this rank of judges under seventy years of age, and are elected thereunto by the suffrages of their chiefest prelates, most incorruptible men, and so just in all the causes, whereof there are appeals before them, as

---

[1] Many of those imprisoned with Tomé Pires had had the same fate. See Chapter XXIX.

[2] Nanking was a far more important town in those days than it is now. The population, for one thing, was some ten times larger. All the commerce and administration of that part of China was centred in Nanking, since Shanghai was then a place of no importance.

[3] See page 105, 'Breath of the Creator of all Things.' The Portuguese has 'mesa' (table) here, and 'bafo' (breath) later.

[4] Cogan adds 'amongst the papists,' which words do not occur in the original.

[5] It is quite clear that Mendes Pinto is praising their abstinence and sincerity, even though they were not Christians.

it is not possible to meet with more upright, for were it against the
king himself, and against all the powers that may be imagined
in the world, no consideration, how great soever, is able to make
them swerve never so little from that they think to be justice.

Having been embarked in the manner I spake of, the same day
at night we went and lay at a great tower called Potinleu, in one of
the prisons whereof we remained nine days, by reason of the much
rain that fell then upon the conjunction of the new moon.   There
we happened to meet with a Russian prisoner,[1] that received us
very charitably, of whom demanding in the Chinese tongue, which
he understood as well as we,[2] what countryman he was, and what
fortune had brought him thither, he told us that he was of Moscovy,
born in a town named Hiquegens, and that some five years past,
being accused for the death of a man, he had been condemned to
a perpetual prison, but as a stranger he appealed from that sentence to the tribunal of the *aytau* of Batampina,[3] in the city of
Pequin, who was the highest of the two-and-thirty admirals established in this empire, that is, for every kingdom one.   He added
further, that this admiral, by a particular jurisdiction, had absolute
power over all strangers, whereupon he hoped to find some relief
from him, intending to go and die a Christian among the Christians,
if he might have the good hap to be set at liberty.

After we had passed those nine days in this prison, being re-
embarked, we sailed up a great river seven days together, at the
end whereof we arrived at Nanquin.   As this city is the second of
all the empire, so is it also the capital of the three kingdoms of
Liampoo, Faniau, and Sambor.[4]   Here we lay six weeks in prison,
and suffered so much pain and misery as, reduced to the last
extremities, we died insensibly for want of succour, not able to do
anything but look up to heaven with a pitiful eye; for it was our ill
fortune to have all that we had stolen from us the first night we
came thither.   This prison was so great, that there were four thousand prisoners in it at that time, as we were credibly informed, so
that one should hardly sit down in any place without being robbed
and filled full of lice.   Having lain there a month and a half, as I
said, the *anchacy*, who was one of the judges before whom our
cause was to be pleaded, pronounced our sentence at the suit of
the Attorney-General, the tenor whereof was, that having seen
and considered our process, which the *chumbim* of Taypor had

[1] The Russians seem to have been allied to the Tartars.   See a later part of
this account.   Mendes Pinto, however, calls this prisoner an 'alemão' (German),
presumably taking it that this term covered any one from north-eastern Europe.
[2] They had now, apparently, no need of interpreters, as in the days when
they pillaged the hermits.
[3] The chief magistrate of the Yangtse district.
[4] Presumably Ning-po (Liampo), Hangchow (Sambor), and the province in
which Nanking itself stood (Faniau).

sent him, it appeared by the accusations laid to our charge that we were very heinous malefactors, and though we denied many things, yet in justice no credit was to be given unto us, and therefore that we were to be publicly whipped for to teach us to live better in time to come, and that withal our two thumbs should be cut off, wherewith it was evident by manifest suspicions that we used to commit robberies and other vile crimes; and furthermore, that for the remainder of the punishment we deserved, he referred us to the *aytau* of Batampina,[1] unto whom it appertained to take cognizance of such causes, in regard of the jurisdiction that he had of life and death.   This sentence was pronounced in the prison, where it had been better for us to have suffered death than the stripes that we received, for all the ground round about us ran with blood upon our whipping, so that it was almost a miracle that of the eleven which we were, nine escaped alive, for two of our company died three days after, besides one of our servants.

After we had been whipped in that manner I have declared, we were carried into a great chamber that was in the prison, where were a number of sick and diseased persons, lying upon beds, and other ways; there we had presently our stripes washed, and things applied unto them, whereby we were somewhat eased of our pain, and that by men, much like unto the Fraternity of Mercy among us,[2] which only out of charity, and for the honour of God, do tend those that are sick, and liberally furnish them with all things necessary.

Hereafter some eleven or twelve days, we began to be prettily recovered and as we were lamenting our ill fortune, for being so rigorously condemned to lose our thumbs, it pleased God one morning, whenas we little dreamt of it, that we espied two men come into the chamber, of a good aspect, clothed in long gowns of violet-coloured satin, and carrying white rods [3] in their hands; as soon as they arrived, all the sick persons in the chamber cried out: 'Blessed be the ministers of the works of God'; whereunto they answered, holding up their rods: 'May it please God to give you patience in your adversity'; whereupon having distributed clothes and money to those that were next to them, they came unto us, and after they had saluted us very courteously, with demonstration of being moved at our tears, they asked us who we were, and of what country, as also why we were imprisoned there; whereunto we answered weeping, that we were strangers, natives of the kingdom

[1] Whose decision would be sent from Peking.
[2] Cogan has 'among the papists.'   I have substituted 'us' as more suitable, since the modern reader feels quite clearly that Mendes Pinto, a Portuguese and a papist, is speaking—whereas earlier readers regarded the translator as somehow in part the author.
[3] Symbols of peace and purity.   Violet was probably symbolic of the merciful and charitable nature of their ministration.

of Siam, and of a country called Malaca,[1] that being merchants
and well to live, we had embarked ourselves with our goods, and
being bound for Liampoo, we had been cast away just against the
Isles of Lamau,[2] having lost all that we had and nothing left us
but our miserable bodies in the case they now saw us; moreover
we added, that being thus evil entreated by fortune, arriving at the
city of Taypor, the *chumbim* of justice had caused us to be apprehended without any cause, laying to our charge that we were thieves
and vagabonds, who to avoid painstaking went begging from door
to door, entertaining our idle laziness with the alms that were given
us unjustly, whereof the *chumbim* having made informations at his
pleasure, as being both judge and party, he had laid us in irons in
the prison, where for two-and-forty days' space we had endured
incredible pain and hunger, and no man would hear us in our
justifications, as well because we had not wherewithal to give
presents for to maintain our right, as for that we wanted the
language of the country.[3]   In conclusion, we told them how in the
meantime, without any cognizance of the cause, we had been condemned to be whipped, as also to have our thumbs cut off, like
thieves,[4] so that we had already suffered the first punishment,
with so much rigour and cruelty that the marks thereof remained
but too visibly upon our wretched bodies, and therefore we con-
jured them by the charge they had to serve God in assisting the
afflicted that they would not abandon us in this need, the rather
for that our extreme poverty rendered us odious to all the world,
and exposed us to the enduring of all affronts.

These two men, having heard us attentively, remained very
pensive and amazed at our speech; at length lifting up their eyes,
all bathed with tears, to heaven, and kneeling down on the ground,
'O Almighty Lord,' said they, 'that governest in the highest places,
and whose patience is incomprehensible, be Thou evermore
blessed, for that Thou art pleased to hearken unto the complaints
of necessitous and miserable men, to the end that the great offences
committed against Thy divine goodness by the ministers of justice
may not rest unpunished, as we hope that by Thy holy law they
will be chastised at one time or other.'   Whereupon they informed
themselves more amply by those who were about us, of what we
had told them, and presently sending for the register, in whose
hands our sentence was, they straitly commanded him, that

[1] Since the Chinese had called some white and some tawny, they evidently
thought it best to explain this by two different origins.
[2] Probably the islands off Hangchow Bay.   They were trying to conceal the
real place of their shipwreck, lest these Chinese monks should have heard of
their pillaging the tombs.
[3] This may mean that Chinese was too complicated a language for them to be
capable of public pleading in it.
[4] Not only a punishment, but a mode of preventing further thieving.

upon pain of grievous punishment he should forthwith bring them all the proceedings which had been used against us, as instantly he did; now the two officers, seeing there was no remedy for the whipping that we had suffered, presented a petition in our behalf unto the *chaem*, whereunto this answer was returned by the court: 'Mercy hath no place where justice loseth her name, in regard whereof your request cannot be granted.' This answer was subscribed by the *chaem*, and eight *conchalis*, that are like criminal judges.

This hard proceeding much astonished these two proctors for the poor, so named from their office, wherefore, carried with an extreme desire to draw us out of this misery, they presently preferred another petition to the sovereign court of justice, of which I spake in the precedent chapter,[1] where the *menigrepos* and *talagrepos* were judges,[2] an assembly which in their language is called 'The Breath of the Creator of All Things.' In this petition, as sinners, confessing all that we were accused of, we had recourse to mercy, which sorted well for us; for as soon as the petition was presented unto them, they read the process quite through, and finding that our right was overborne, for want of succour, they instantly dispatched away two of their court, who with an express mandate under their hands and seals, went and prohibited the *chaem's* court from intermeddling with this cause, which they commanded away before them. In obedience to this prohibition the *chaem's* court made this decree: 'We, that are assembled in this court of justice of the Lion crowned in the Throne of the World,[3] having perused the petition presented to the four-and-twenty judges of the austere life, do consent that those nine strangers be sent by way of appeal to the court of the *aytau* of *aytaus* in the city of Pequin, to the end that in mercy the sentence pronounced against them may be favourably moderated. Given the seventh day of the fourth moon, in the three-and-twentieth year of the reign of the Son of the Sun.' This decree, being signed by the *chaem* and the eight *conchalis*, was presently brought us by the two proctors for the poor, upon the receipt whereof we told them that we could but pray unto God to reward them for the good they had done us for His sake; whereunto beholding us with an eye of pity, they answered: 'May His celestial goodness direct you in the knowledge of His works, that thereby you may with patience gather the fruit of your labours, as they which fear to offend His holy name.'

After we had passed all the adversities and miseries whereof I have spoken before, we were embarked in the company of some other

---

[1] Cogan forgets that he has made his chapters longer than in the original.
[2] A court of a religious nature. They would thus represent a divine power higher than human justice.
[3] The emperor.

thirty or forty prisoners, that were sent as we were, from this court
of justice to that other sovereign one by way of appeal, there to
be either acquitted or condemned, according to the crimes they
had committed and the punishment they had deserved.   Now a
day before our departure, being embarked in a *lanteaa* and chained
three and three together, the two proctors for the poor came to us,
and first of all furnishing us with all things needful, as clothes and
victuals, they asked us whether we wanted anything else for our
voyage.   Whereunto we answered, that all we could desire of
them was, that they would be pleased to convert that further good
they intended to us into a letter of recommendation unto the
officers of that holy fraternity of the city of Pequin, thereby to
oblige them to maintain the right of our cause in regard (as they
very well knew) we should otherwise be sure to be utterly
abandoned of every one, by reason we were strangers and altogether unknown.   The proctors hearing us speak in this manner,
'Say not so,' replied they, 'for though your ignorance discharges
you before God, yet have you committed a great sin, because the
more you are abased in the world through poverty, the more shall
you be exalted before the eyes of His divine Majesty, if you patiently
bear your trials,[1] whereunto the flesh indeed doth always oppose
itself, being evermore rebellious against the spirit, but as a bird
cannot fly without her wings, no more can the soul meditate without
works.[2]   As for the letter you require of us, we will give it you
most willingly, knowing it will be very necessary for you, to the
end that the favour of good people be not wanting to you in your
need.'   This said, they gave us a sackful of rice, together with four
taels in silver, and a coverlet to lay upon us; then having very
much recommended us unto the *chifuu*, who was the officer of
justice that conducted us, they took their leaves of us in most
courteous manner.   The next morning as soon as it was day they
sent us the letter, sealed with three seals in green wax,[3] the contents
whereof were these:
  'Ye servants of that high lord, the resplendent mirror of an un-
created light,[4] before whom our merits are nothing in comparison
of his, we the least servants of that holy house of Tauhinarel, that
was founded in favour of the fifth prison of Nanquin,[5] with true
words of respect, which we owe unto you, we give your most
humble persons to understand, that these nine strangers, the
bearers of this letter, are men of a far country, whose bodies and

[1] Cogan has 'crosses,' which is obviously incongruous.
[2] The patient endurance of suffering is regarded as an actively virtuous state.
[3] Symbolic of hope or expectation, and therefore suitable to a petition.
[4] The sun was the mirror of God's majesty and the emperor mystically
descended from the sun.
[5] That is, the prison hospital before mentioned.

goods have been so cruelly entreated by the fury of the sea, that according to their report, of ninety and five that they were, they only have escaped shipwreck, being cast by the tempest on the shore of the Isles of Tautaa,[1] upon the coast of the Bay of Sumbor. In which piteous and lamentable case, as we have seen them with our own eyes begging their living from place to place of such as charity obliged to give them something after the manner of good folks, it was their ill fortune without all reason or justice to be apprehended by the *chumbim* of Taypor, and sent to this fifth prison of Faniau,[2] where they were condemned to be whipped, which was immediately executed upon them by the ministers of the displeased arm,[3] as by their process better appeareth. But afterwards, whenas through too much cruelty their thumbs were to be cut off, they with tears besought us, for that sovereign lord's sake, in whose service we are employed, to be assisting unto them, which presently undertaken by us we preferred a petition in their behalf, whereunto this answer was made by the court of the Crowned Lion, that mercy had no place where justice lost her name; whereupon provoked by a true zeal to God's honour, we addressed ourselves to the court of those four-and-twenty of the austere life, who, carried by a blessed devotion, instantly assembled in the holy house of the remedy for the poor, and of an extreme desire they had to succour these miserable creatures, they interdicted that great court from proceeding any further against them, and accordingly the success[4] was agreeable to the mercy of so great a God, for these last judges, revoking the others' first sentence, sent the cause by way of appeal to your city of Pequin with amendment of the second punishment, as you may see more at large by the proceedings; in regard whereof, most reverend and humble brethren, we beseech you all in the name of God to be favourable unto them, and to assist them with whatsoever you shall think necessary for them, that they may not be oppressed in their right, which is a very great sin, and an eternal infamy to us, who again entreat you to supply them with your alms, and bestow on them means to cover their nakedness, to the end they may not perish for want of help, which if you do there is no doubt but that so pious a work will be most acceptable to that Lord above, to whom the poor of the earth do continually pray,[5] and are heard in the highest of heavens, as we hold for an article of faith; on which earth may it please that divine Majesty, for whose sake we do this, to preserve us till death, and to render us worthy of His presence

---

[1] Another name for the islands off the Bay of Hangchow, it seems.
[2] Nanking.
[3] Every officer was considered a member of the great imperial scheme of life.
[4] Event.
[5] By patient and religious endurance of suffering. See above. There seems to have been no particular inquiry into the prisoners' religious beliefs.

in the house of the sun, where He is seated with all His.   Written
in the chamber of the zeal of God's honour, the ninth day of the
seventh moon, and the three-and-twentieth year of the reign of
the Lion crowned in the Throne of the World.'

*Chapter XXVIII.   The marvels of the city of Nanquin, our departure
from thence towards Pequin, and that which happened unto us,
till we arrived at the town of Sempitay*

THIS letter being brought to us very early the next morning, we
departed in the manner before declared, and continued our voyage
till sunset, whenas we anchored at a little village named Minha-
cutem, where the *chifuu* that conducted us was born, and where his
wife and children were at that time, which was the occasion that
he remained there three days,[1] at the end whereof he embarked
himself with his family, and so we passed on in the company of
divers other vessels, that went upon this river unto divers parts
of this empire.   Now though we were all tied together to the bank [2]
of the *lanteaa* where we rowed, yet did we not for all that lose the
view of many towns and villages that were situated along this river,
whereof I hold it not amiss to make some descriptions; to which
effect, I will begin with the city of Nanquin from whence we
last parted.
    This city is under the north in nine-and-thirty degrees and three-
quarters, situated upon the river of Batampina,[3] which signifies
the flower of fish.   This river, as we were told then, and as I
have seen since, comes from Tartaria, out of a lake called Fanistor,[4]
nine leagues from the city of Lansame,[5] where Taborlan, King
of the Tartarians, usually kept his court.   Out of the same lake,
which is eight-and-twenty leagues long, twelve broad, and of a
mighty depth, the greatest rivers that ever I saw take their source.
The first is the same Batampina, that passing through the midst of
this empire of China three hundred and threescore leagues in
length, disembogues into the sea at the Bay of Nanquin in thirty-
six degrees.   The second, named Lechuna,[6] runs with great swiftness all along by the mountains of Pancruum,[7] which separate the
country of Cauchin [8] and the state of Catebenau,[9] in the height of
sixteen degrees.   The third is called Tanquida,[10] signifying, 'the
mother of waters,' that going north-west, traverseth the kingdom

---

[1] Performing pious ceremonies at the tombs of his ancestors.
[2] *Banco* (bench).   [3] Yang-tse-kiang.
[4] Really it rises in the Kuen Lun Mountains in Tibet.
[5] This might be Dolon-Nor in Mongolia, though, on p. 198, Khara-morito
would be a possibility.
[6] Mekong.   [7] Mountains of Annam.
[8] Cochin China.   [9] Tonking.   [10] Salwin.

of Nacataas, a country where China was anciently seated, as I will declare hereafter, and enters into the sea in the empire of Sornau, vulgarly styled Siam, by the mouth of Cuy,[1] one hundred and thirty leagues below Patana. The fourth, named Batobasoy,[2] descends out of the province of Sansim, which is the very same that was quite overwhelmed by the sea in the year 1556, as I purpose to show elsewhere, and renders itself into the sea at the mouth of Cosmim, in the kingdom of Pegu. The fifth and last, called Leysacotay,[3] crosseth the country by east as far as to the archipelago of Xinxipou, that borders upon Moscovy, and falls, as is thought, into a sea that is not navigable, by reason the climate there is in the height of seventy degrees.[4]

Now to return to my discourse: the city of Nanquin, as I said before, is seated by this river of Batampina, upon a reasonable high hill, so as it commands all the plains about it; the climate thereof is somewhat cold, but very healthy, and it is eight leagues about, which way soever it is considered, three leagues broad, and one long; the houses in it are not above two storeys high, and all built of wood; only those of the mandarins are made of hewed stone, and also environed with walls and ditches, over which are stone bridges, whereon they pass to the gates, that have rich and costly arches, with divers sorts of inventions upon the towers, all which, put together, make a pleasing object to the eye, and represent a certain kind of I know not what majesty. The houses of the *chaems, anchacys, aytaus, tutons,* and *chumbims,* which are all governors of provinces or kingdoms, have stately towers, six or seven storeys high, and gilt all over, wherein they have their magazines for arms, their wardrobes, their treasuries, and a world of rich household stuff, as also many other things of great value, together with an infinite of delicate and most fine porcelain, which amongst them is prized and esteemed as much as precious stone, for this sort of porcelain never goes out of the kingdom, it being expressly forbidden by the laws of the country to be sold, upon pain of death, to any stranger, unless to the *xatamaas,* that is, the sophies [5] of the Persians, who by a particular permission buy of it at a very dear rate.

The Chinese assured us that in this city there are eight hundred thousand fires, fourscore thousand mandarins' houses, threescore and two great market-places, a hundred and thirty butchers' shambles, each of them containing fourscore shops, and eight thousand streets, whereof six hundred that are fairer and larger

[1] Bangkok.   [2] Irrawaddy.
[3] This should be the Hwang-ho, but the information about this river is mere fantasy.
[4] The Arctic.   Mendes Pinto's geography is therefore partly correct.
[5] Shahs.

than the rest are compassed about with balusters of copper; we were further assured that there are likewise two thousand and three hundred pagodas, a thousand of which were monasteries of religious persons, professed in their accursed sect, whose buildings were exceeding rich and sumptuous, with very high steeples, wherein there were between sixty and seventy such mighty huge bells, that it was a dreadful thing to hear them rung. There are moreover in the city thirty great strong prisons, each whereof hath three or four thousand prisoners; and a charitable hospital, expressly established to supply the necessities of the poor, with proctors ordained for their defence, both in civil and criminal causes, as is before related. At the entrance into every principal street, there are arches and great gates, which for each man's security are shut every night, and in most of the streets are goodly fountains whose water is excellent to drink. Besides, at every full and new moon, open fairs are kept in several places, whither merchants resort from all parts, and where there is such abundance of all kind of victuals as cannot well be expressed, especially of flesh and fruit. It is not possible to deliver the great store of fish that is taken in this river, chiefly soles and mullets, which are all sold alive,[1] besides a world of sea-fish, both fresh, salted, and dried; we were told by certain Chinese that in this city there are ten thousand trades for the working of silks, which from thence are sent all over the kingdom.[2]

The city itself is environed with a very strong wall, made of fair hewed stone. The gates of it are a hundred and thirty, at each of which there is a porter and two halberdiers, who are bound to give an account every day of all that passes in and out; there are also twelve forts or citadels, like unto ours, with bulwarks and very high towers, but without any ordnance at all. The same Chinese also affirmed unto us that the city yielded the king daily two thousand taels of silver, which amount to three thousand ducats,[3] as I have delivered heretofore. I will not speak of the palace royal, because I saw it but on the outside; howbeit the Chinese tell such wonders of it as would amaze a man, for it is my intent to relate nothing save what we beheld here with our own eyes, and that was so much as I am afraid to write it, not that it would seem strange to those that have seen and read the marvels of the kingdom of China, but because I doubt that they which would compare those wondrous things that are in the countries they have not seen with that little they have seen in their own, will make some question of it, or, it may be, give no credit at all to these

---

[1] 'Hung by a thread through their nose.' Cogan evidently thought this too incredible to translate.
[2] The silk manufacture of Nanking later declined.
[3] *Crusados.* They were worth between half a crown and three shillings.

truths, because they are not conformable to their understanding and small experience.[1]

Continuing our course up this river, the first two days we saw not any remarkable town or place, but only a great number of villages, and little hamlets of two or three hundred fires apiece, which by their buildings seemed to be houses of fishermen and poor people that live by the labour of their hands. For the rest, all that was within view in the country was great woods of fir, groves, forests, and orange-trees, as also plains full of wheat, rice, beans, pease, millet, panic, barley, rye, flax, cotton wool, with great enclosures of gardens, and goodly houses of pleasure belonging to the mandarins and lords of the kingdom. There was likewise all along the river such an infinite number of cattle of all sorts, as I can assure you there is not more in Ethiopia, nor in all the dominions of Prester John; upon the top of the mountains many houses of their sects of gentiles were to be seen adorned with high steeples gilt all over, the glistening whereof was such, and so great, that to behold them afar off was an admirable sight.

The fourth day of our voyage we arrived at a town called Pocasser,[2] twice as big as Canton, compassed about with strong walls of hewed stone, and towers and bulwarks almost like ours, together with a quay on the riverside, twice as long as the shot of a falconet, and enclosed with two rows of iron gates, with very strong gates, where the junks [3] and vessels that arrived there were unladen. This place abounds with all kinds of merchandise, which from thence is transported over all the kingdom, especially with copper, sugar, and alum, whereof there is very great store. Here also, in the midst of a *carrefour* [4] that is almost at the end of the town, stands a mighty strong castle, having three bulwarks and five towers, in the highest of which the present king's father, as the Chinese told us, kept a king of Tartaria nine years prisoner, at the end whereof he killed himself with poison that his subjects sent him, because they would not be constrained to pay that ransom which the king of China demanded for his deliverance. In this town the *chifuu* gave three of us leave to go up and down for to crave the alms of good people, accompanied with four *huppes*, that are as sergeants or bailiffs amongst us, who led us, chained together as we were, through six or seven streets, where we got in alms to the value of about twenty ducats,[5] as well in clothes as money, besides flesh, rice, meal, fruit, and other victuals

---

[1] That is to say, that Chinese civilization was in advance of European at that time. Quite true, but a most daring thing for Mendes Pinto to say.
[2] Probably Chinkiang.
[3] A flat-bottomed ship, often of large dimensions, with a four-cornered sail.
[4] Cross-roads, but the original Portuguese word, *terreiro*, means rather a large square.
[5] As above, *crusados*.

which was bestowed on us, whereof we gave the one half to the *huppes* that conducted us, it being the custom so to do.

Afterwards we were brought to a pagoda, whither the people flocked from all parts that day, in regard of a very solemn feast that was then celebrated there.   This temple or pagoda [1] as we were told, had sometime been a palace royal, where the king [2] then reigning was born; now because the queen his mother died there in childbirth, she commanded herself to be buried in the very same chamber where she was brought to bed, wherefore to honour her death the better, this temple was dedicated to the invocation of Tauhinarel, which is one of the principal sects of the pagans in the kingdom of China, as I will more amply declare whenas I shall [3] speak of the labyrinth of the two-and-thirty laws that are in it. All the buildings of this temple, together with all the gardens and walks that belong to it, are suspended in the air upon three hundred and threescore pillars, every one of the which is of one entire stone of a very great bigness.   These three hundred and threescore pillars are called by the names of three hundred and threescore days of the year, and in each of them is a particular feast kept there with many alms, gifts, and bloody sacrifices, accompanied with music, dancing, and other sports.   Under this pagoda, namely between those pillars, are eight very fair streets, enclosed on every side with grates of copper, and gates for the passage of pilgrims and others that run continually to this feast, as it were to a jubilee.

The chamber above, where the queen lay, was made in the form of a chapel, but round, and from the top to the bottom all garnished with silver, the workmanship whereof was of greater cost than the matter itself.   In the midst of it stood a kind of tribunal, framed round like the chamber, some fifteen steps high, compassed about with six grates of silver, on the top whereof was a great bowl, and upon that a lion of silver, that with his head supported a shrine of gold, three handbreadths square, wherein they said the bones of the queen were, which these blinded ignorants reverenced as a great relic.   Below this tribunal in equal proportion were four bars of silver, that traversed the chamber, whereon hung three-and-forty lamps of the same metal, in memory of the three-and-forty years that this queen lived, and seven lamps of gold in commemoration of seven sons that she had; moreover at the entry into the chapel, just against the door, were eight other bars of iron, whereon also hung a very great number of silver lamps, which the Chinese told us were offered by some of the wives of the *chaems*, *aytaus*, *tutons*, and *anchacys*, who were assistant at the death of the queen, so that in acknowledgment of that honour they sent those lamps thither afterwards.

[1] Mendes Pinto's memory had failed him.   This tower was really in Nanking.
[2] The emperor Yung-lo.   In the original it says, 'grandfather of the king.'
[3] See p. 152.

Without the gates of the temple, and round about six balusters of copper that environed it, were a great many statues of giants, fifteen foot high, cast in brass, all well proportioned with halberds or clubs in their hands, and some of them with battleaxes on their shoulders, which made so brave and majestical a show, as one could never be satisfied enough with looking on them. Amongst these statues, which were in number twelve hundred, as the Chinese affirmed, there were four-and-twenty very great serpents also of brass, and under every one of them a woman seated, with a sword in her hand and a silver crown on her head. It was said that those four-and-twenty women carried the titles of queens, because they sacrificed themselves to the death of this queen, to the end their souls might serve hers in the other life, as in this their bodies had served her body, a matter which the Chinese that draw their extraction from these women hold for a very great honour, insomuch as they enrich the crests of their coats-of-arms with it.   Round about this row of giants was another of triumphant arches, gilt all over, whereon a number of silver bells hung by chains of the same metal, which moved with the air kept such a continual ringing, as one could hardly hear one another for the noise they made.   Without these arches there were likewise at the same distance two rows of copper grates, that enclosed all this huge work, and among them certain pillars of the same metal, which supported lions rampant, mounted upon bowls,[1] being the arms of the kings of China, as I have related elsewhere.   At each corner of the *carrefour* was a monster of brass, of so strange and unmeasurable an height, and so deformed to behold, as it is not possible almost for a man to imagine, so that I think it best not to speak of them, the rather for that I confess I am not able in words to express the form wherein I saw their prodigies; howbeit, as it is not reasonable to conceal these things without giving some knowledge of them, I will say as much as my weak understanding is able to deliver.

One of these monsters, which is on the right hand as one comes into the *carrefour*, whom the Chinese call the serpent glutton of the hollow or profound house of smoke, and that by their histories is held to be Lucifer, is represented under the figure of a serpent of an excessive height, with most hideous and deformed adders coming out of his stomach, covered all over with green and black scars, and a number of prickles on their backs above a span long, like unto porcupines' quills; each of these adders had a woman between his jaws, with her hair all dishevelled and standing on end, as one affrighted.   The monster carried also in his mouth, which was unmeasurable great, a lizard that was above thirty foot long, and as big as a tun, with his nostrils and chaps so full of

[1] The Lion Crowned on the Throne of the World.

blood that all the rest of his body was besmeared with it; this
lizard held a great elephant between his paws, and seemed to gripe
him so hard as his very guts came out of his throat, and all this was
done so proportionably, and to the life, that it made a man tremble
to behold such a deformed figure, and which was scarce possible
for one to imagine. His tail might be some twenty fathom long,
was entortilled about such another monster that was the second
of the four whereof I spake, in the figure of a man, being a hundred
foot high, and by the Chinese called Turcamparoo, who they say
was the son of that serpent; besides that he was very ugly, he stood
with both his hands in his mouth, that was as big as a great gate,
with a row of horrible teeth, and a foul black tongue, hanging out
two fathom long, most dreadful to behold.

As for the other two monsters, one was in the form of a woman,
named by the Chinese Nadelgau, seventeen fathom high and six
thick; this same about the girdlestead before had a face made proportionable to her body, above two fathom broad, and she breathed
out of her mouth and nostrils great flakes, not of artificial, but true
fire, which proceeded, as they told us, from her head, where fire
was continually kept, that in like manner came out of the said face
below. By this figure these idolaters would demonstrate that she
was the queen of the fiery sphere, which according to their belief
is to burn the earth at the end of the world. The fourth monster
was a man, set stooping, which with great swollen cheeks, as big
as the mainsail of a ship, seemed to blow extremely; this monster
was also of an unmeasurable height, and of such a hideous and
ghastly aspect that a man could hardly endure the sight of it; the
Chinese called it Uzanguenaboo, and said that it was he which raised
tempests upon the sea, and demolished buildings, in regard whereof
the people offered many things unto him, to the end he should do
them no harm, and many presented him with a piece of money
yearly, that he might not drown their junks, nor do any of theirs
hurt that went by sea. I will omit many other abuses which their
blindness makes them believe, and which they hold to be so true,
as there is not one of them but would endure a thousand deaths
for the maintenance thereof.

The next day, being gone from the town of Pocasser, we arrived
at another fair and great town, called Xinligau; [1] there we saw many
buildings enclosed with walls of brick, and deep ditches about them,
and at one end of the town two castles, very well fortified with
towers and bulwarks after our fashion; at the gates were drawbridges, suspended in the air with great iron chains, and in the midst

[1] Possibly Yangchow. '. . . la ville de Yang tcheou, l'un des plus célèbres
ports de l'Empire. Peu après il (the canal) entre dans le grand fleuve Yang tse
Kiang à une journée de Nanking.' (*Description de l'Empire de Chine.* Du
Halde. 1735.) They were now, therefore, in the Imperial Canal. (I am,
again, indebted to Dr. Cortesão's kindness for this note and a number following.)

of them a tower five storeys high, very curiously painted with several pictures. The Chinese assured us that in those two castles there was as much treasure as amounted to fifteen thousand pieces of silver, which was the revenue of all this archipelago,[1] and laid up in this place by the king's grandfather now reigning, in memorial of a son of his that was born here, and named Leuquinau, that is to say, 'the joy of all:' those of the country repute him for a saint, because he ended his days in religion, where also he was buried in a temple, dedicated to Quiay Varatel, the god of all the fishes of the sea, of whom these miserable ignorants recount a world of fooleries, as also the laws he invented, and the precepts which he left them, being able to astonish a man, as I will more amply declare when time shall serve. In this town and in another five leagues higher [2] the most part of the silks of this kingdom are dyed, because they hold that the waters of these places make the colours far more lively than those of any other part, and these dyers, which are said to be thirteen thousand, pay unto the king yearly three hundred thousand taels.

Continuing our course up the river, the day after about evening we arrived at certain great plains, where were great store of cattle, as horses, mares, colts, and cows, guarded by men on horseback, that make sale of them to butchers, who afterwards retail them indifferently as any other flesh. Having passed these plains containing some ten or eleven leagues, we came to a town called Junquileu,[3] walled with brick, but without battlements, bulwarks, or towers, as others had, whereof I have spoken before; at the end of the suburbs of this town we saw divers houses built in the water upon great piles, in the form of magazines. Before the gate of a little street stood a tomb made of stone, environed with an iron grate, painted red and green, and over it a steeple framed of pieces of very fine porcelain, sustained by four pillars of curious stone; upon the top of the tomb were five globes, and two others that seemed to be of cast iron, and on the one side thereof were graven in letters of gold, and in the Chinese language, words of this substance: 'Here lies Trannocem Mudeliar, uncle [4] to the king of Malaca, whom death took out of the world before he could be revenged of Captain Afonso Albuquerque,[5] the lion of the robberies of the sea.'

We were much amazed to behold this inscription there; where-

[1] *Anchacilado*, presumably the region governed by an *anchacy*.
[2] This should be Shaopo.
[3] Perhaps Wei-kiué-leoa. The *Comentários* of Afonso de Albuquerque refer to this town as Janquileu and the Malay ambassador is called Tuão Nacem Mudaliar.
[4] More probably first cousin.
[5] 1453-1515. The famous Portuguese admiral who took most of the west coast of India by storm and was later viceroy. He died and was buried at Goa.

fore inquiring what it might mean, a Chinese that seemed more honourable than the rest told us that about some forty years before, this man which lay buried there came thither as ambassador from a prince that styled himself king of Malaca, to demand succour from the son of the Sun against men of a country that hath no name, which came by sea from the end of the world,[1] and had taken Malaca from him; this man recounted many other incredible things concerning this matter, whereof mention is made in a printed book thereof, as also that this ambassador having continued three years at the king's court suing for this succour, just as it was granted him, and that preparations for it were a-making, it was his ill fortune to be surprised one night at supper with an apoplexy, whereof he died at the end of nine days, so that extremely afflicted to see himself carried away by a sudden death before he had accomplished his business, he expressed his earnest desire of revenge by the inscription which he caused to be graven on his tomb, that posterity might know wherefore he was come thither.

Afterwards we departed from this place, and continued our voyage up the river, which thereabouts is not so large as towards the city of Nanquin, but the country is here better peopled with villages, boroughs, and gardens,[2] than any other place, for every stone's-cast we met still with some pagoda, mansion of pleasure, or country house. Passing on about some two leagues further, we arrived at a place encompassed with great iron grates, in the midst whereof stood two mighty statues of brass upright, sustained by pillars of cast metal of the bigness of a bushel, and seven fathom high, the one of a man and the other of a woman, both of them seventy-four spans in height, having their hands in their mouths, their cheeks horribly blown out, and their eyes so staring, as they affrighted all that looked on them. That which represented a man was called Quiay Xingatalor, and the other in the form of a woman was named Apancapatur. Having demanded of the Chinese the explication of these figures, they told us that the male was he, which with those mighty swollen cheeks blew the fire of hell for to torment all those miserable wretches that would not liberally bestow alms in this life; and for the other monster, that she was porter of hell gate, where she would take notice of those that did her good in this world, and letting them fly away into a river of very cold water, called Ochileuday, would keep them hid there from being tormented by the devils, as other damned were. Upon this speech one of our company could not forbear laughing at such a ridiculous and diabolical foolery, which three of their priests or bonzes then present observing, they were so exceedingly offended therewith, as they persuaded the *chifuu* which conducted us that

---

[1] The Portuguese, of course.   [2] Or farms (*quintas*).

if he did not chastise us in such manner as those gods might be
well contented with the punishment inflicted on us for our mockery
of them, both the one and the other would assuredly torment his
soul, and never suffer it to go out of hell; which threatening so
mightily terrified this dog, the *chifuu*, that without further delay
or hearing us speak, he caused us all to be bound hand and foot,
and commanded each of us to have a hundred lashes given him
with a double cord, which was immediately executed with so much
rigour as we were all in a gore blood, whereby we were taught not
to jeer afterwards at anything we saw or heard.

At such time as we arrived here we found twelve bonzes upon
the place, who with silver censers full of perfumes of aloes and
ceniamin [1] censed these two devilish monsters, and chanted out
aloud: 'Help us, even as we serve thee'; whereunto divers other
priests answered in the name of the idol with a great noise: 'So I
promise to do like a good lord.'   In this sort they went as it were
in procession round about the place, singing with an ill-tuned
voice to the sound of a great many bells that were in steeples
thereabouts.   In the meantime there were others, that with drums
and basins made such a din, as I may truly say, put them all
together, was most horrible to hear.

*Chapter XXIX. Our arrival at Sempitay, and our encounter there
with a Christian woman*

FROM this place we continued our voyage eleven days more up the
river, which in those parts is so peopled with cities, towns, villages,
boroughs, forts, and castles, that commonly they are not a flight-
shot distant one from another, besides a world of houses of pleasure,
and temples, where steeples were all gilt, which made such a
glorious show, as we were much amazed at it.   In this manner we
arrived at a town named Sempitay,[2] where we abode five days,
by reason the *chifuu's* wife, that conducted us, was not well.
Here, by his permission, we landed, and chained together as we
were, we went up and down the streets craving of alms, which was
very liberally given us by the inhabitants, who wondering to see
such men as we, demanded of us what kind of people we were, of
what kingdom, and how our country was called.   Hereunto we
answered conformably to that we had often said before, namely
that we were natives of the kingdom of Siam, that going from
Liampoo to Nanquin, we had lost all our goods by shipwreck, and

---

[1] Cinnamon, but the original has *beijoim* (benzoin).
[2] Sumpeichow.

that although they beheld us then in so poor a case, yet we had
been formerly very rich; whereupon a woman who was come
thither amongst the rest to see us, 'It is very likely,' said she,
speaking to them about her, 'that what these poor strangers have
related is most true, for daily experience doth show how those that
trade by sea do oftentimes make it their grave, wherefore it is
best and surest to travel upon the earth and to esteem of it as of that
whereof it hath pleased God to frame us.'   Saying so, she gave
us two *mazes*, which amounts to about sixteen pence of our money,
advising us to make no more such long voyages, since our lives
were so short.

Hereupon she unbuttoned one of the sleeves of a red satin gown
she had on, and baring her left arm, she showed us a cross im-
printed on it, like to the mark of a slave, saying: 'Do any of you
know this sign, which amongst those that follow the way of truth
is called a cross? or have any of you ever heard it named?'   To
this, falling down on our knees, we answered, with tears in our
eyes, that we knew exceeding well.   Then lifting up her hands, she
cried out: 'Our Father, which art in heaven, hallowed be Thy name,'
speaking these words in the Portugal tongue, and because she
could speak no more of our language, she very earnestly desired
us in Chinese to tell her whether we were Christians; we replied
that we were, and for proof thereof, after we had kissed that arm
whereon the cross was, we repeated all the rest of the Lord's prayer,
which she had left unsaid, wherewith being assured that we were
Christians indeed, she drew aside from the rest there present, and
weeping said to us: 'Come along, Christians of the other end of the
world, with her that is your true sister in the faith of Jesus Christ,
or peradventure a kinswoman to one of you, by his side that begot
me in this miserable exile,' and so going to carry us to her house,
the *huppes* which guarded us would not suffer her, saying that if
we would not continue our cravings of alms, as the *chifuu* had permitted us, they would return us back to the ship; but this they spake
in regard of their own interest, for that they were to have the
moiety of what was given us, as I have before declared, and
accordingly they made as though they would have led us thither
again, which the woman perceiving, 'I understand your meaning,'
said she, 'and indeed it is but reason you make the best of your
places, for thereby you live'; so opening her purse, she gave them
two taels in silver, wherewith they were very well satisfied; whereupon, with the leave of the *chifuu*, she carried us home to her house,
and there kept us all the while we remained in that place, making
exceeding much of us, and using us very charitably.

Here she showed us an oratory, wherein she had a cross of wood
gilt, as also candlesticks and a lamp of silver.   Furthermore, she
told us, that she was named Inês de Leiria, and her father Tomé

Pires,[1] who had been great ambassador from Portugal to the king of China,[2] and that in regard of an insurrection with a Portugal captain, made at Canton, the Chinese taking him for a spy and not for an ambassador, as he termed himself, clapped him and all his followers up in prison, where by order of justice five of them were put to torture, receiving so many and such cruel stripes on their bodies, as they died instantly, and that the rest were all banished into several parts,[3] together with her father into this place, where he married with her mother, that had some means; and how he made her a Christian, living so seven-and-twenty years together, and converting many gentiles to the faith of Christ, whereof there were above three hundred then abiding in that town; which every Sunday assembled in her house to say the catechism; whereupon demanding of her what were their accustomed prayers, she answered that she used no other but these, which on their knees,[4] with their eyes and hands lift up to heaven, they pronounced in this manner: 'O Lord Jesus Christ, as it is most true that Thou art the very Son of God, conceived by the Holy Ghost in the womb of the Virgin Mary for the salvation of sinners, so Thou wilt be pleased to forgive us our offences, that thereby we may become worthy to behold Thy face in the glory of Thy kingdom, where Thou art sitting at the right hand of the Almighty. Our Father which art in heaven, hallowed be Thy Name. In the name of the Father, the Son, and the Holy Ghost, Amen.' And so all of them kissing the cross embraced one another, and thereupon returned every one to his own home.[5]

Moreover, she told us that her father had left her many other prayers, which the Chinese had stolen from her, so that she had none left but those before recited; whereunto we replied, that those we had heard from her were very good, but before we went away we would leave her divers other good and wholesome prayers. 'Do so then,' answered she, 'for the respect you owe to so good a God as yours is, and that hath done such things for you, for me, and for all in general.' Then causing the cloth to be laid she gave us a very good and plentiful dinner, and treated us in like sort every meal, during the five days we continued in her house, which, as I said before,[6] was permitted by the *chifuu* in regard of a present

[1] Tomé Pires was born about 1468. In 1511 he sailed for the East where he wrote *Suma Oriental*.
[2] In 1517.
[3] This was in 1523. The original continues: '. . . where they died eaten of lice, of whom only one was left alive, called Vasco Calvo, from a place in our country by name Alcouchete—so she had heard her father say many times, with the tears in his eyes in speaking of him.' (For Vasco Calvo, see Chapter XXXVII.)
[4] The original adds, 'before that cross.'
[5] 'And they lived so together in great conformity and friendship without any sort of hatreds or rivalries between them.'
[6] This phrase is not in the original, and is incorrect.

that this good woman sent his wife, whom she earnestly entreated so to deal with her husband, as we might be well entreated, for that we were men of whom God had a particular care, as the *chifuu's* wife promised her to do with many thanks to her for the present she had received.

In the mean space, during the five days we remained in her house, we read the catechism seven times to the Christians, wherewithal they were very much edified; beside, Christóvão Borralho made them a little book in the Chinese tongue, containing the paternoster, the creed, the ten commandments,[1] and many other good prayers. After these things we took our leaves of Inês de Leiria and the Christians, who gave us fifty taels in silver, which stood us since in good stead, as I shall declare hereafter, and withal Inês de Leiria gave us secretly fifty taels more, humbly desiring us to remember her in our prayers to God.

After our departure from the town of Sempitay we continued our course upon the river of Batampina, unto a place, named Lequimpau, containing about eleven or twelve thousand fires and very well built, at least we judged so by that we could discern, as also enclosed with good walls, and curtains [2] round about it. Not far from it was an exceeding long house, having within it thirty furnaces on each side, where a great quantity of silver was melted, which was brought in carts from a mountain, some five leagues off, called Tuxenguim. The Chinese assured us, that above a thousand men wrought continually in that mine to draw out the silver, and that the king of China had in yearly revenue out of it about five thousand *picos*. This place we left about sunset, and the next day in the evening we arrived just between two little towns, that stood opposite one to another, the river only between, the one named Pacau, and the other Nacau, which although they were little, yet were they fairly built, and well walled with great hewed stone, having a number of temples, which they call pagodas, all gilt over, and enriched with steeples and vanes [3] of great price, very pleasing and agreeable to the eye.

[The end of Chapter XXIX and beginning of Chapter XXX relate the legendary story of the founding of the Chinese Empire, which Mendes Pinto had often heard read from a Chinese book.]

[1] Also the Ave Maria and the Salve Regina which Cogan omits.
[2] Fortifications.
[3] Cogan has 'fanes.'

CHAPTER XXX. *Many things that we saw as we passed along*

BEING departed from those two towns Pacau and Nacau we continued our course up the river, and arrived at another town, called Mindoo, somewhat bigger than those from whence we parted, where about half a mile off was a great lake of salt water, and a number of salt-houses round about it. The Chinese assured us that this lake did ebb and flow like the sea, and that it extended above two hundred leagues into the country,[1] rendering the king of China in yearly revenue one hundred thousand taels, only for the third of the salt was drawn of it; as also that the town yielded him another one hundred thousand taels for the silk alone that was made there, not speaking at all of the camphor, sugar, porcelain, vermilion, and quicksilver, whereof there was very great plenty; moreover, that some two leagues from this town were twelve exceeding long houses, like unto magazines, where a world of people laboured in casting and purifying of copper, and the horrible din which the hammers made there was such, and so strange, as if there were anything on earth that could represent hell this was it; wherefore being desirous to understand the cause of this extraordinary noise, we would needs go to see from whence it proceeded, and we found that there were in each of these houses forty furnaces, that is twenty of either side, with forty huge anvils, upon every of which eight men beat in order, and so swiftly as a man's eye could hardly discern the blows, so as three hundred and twenty men wrought in each of these twelve houses, which in all the twelve houses made up three thousand eight hundred and forty workmen, beside a great number of other persons that laboured in other particular things; whereupon we demanded how much copper might be wrought every year in each of these houses, and they told us, one hundred and ten, or six-score thousand *picos* whereof the king had two-thirds, because the mines were his, and that the mountain from whence it was drawn was called Coretum Baga, which signifies a river of copper, for that from the time since it was discovered, being above two hundred years, it never failed, but rather more and more was found.

Having passed about a league beyond those twelve houses up the river, we came to a place enclosed with three ranks of iron grates, where we beheld thirty houses, divined into five rows, six in each row, which were very long and complete, with great towers

---

[1] The original has, 'being some two hundred leagues inland.' Cogan altered this, perhaps because he had learned that the lakes are, in fact, much nearer the coast than that.

full of bells of cast metal, and much carved work, as also gilt
pillars, and the frontispieces of fair hewed stone, whereupon many
inventions were engraved.   At this place we went ashore by the
chifuu's permission that carried us, for that he had made a vow to
this pagod, which was called *Bigay potim*, that is to say, god of a
hundred and ten thousand gods, *Corchoo fungane, ginaco ginaca*,
which according to their report signifies strong and great above
all others, for one of the errors wherewith these wretched people
are blinded is, that they believe every particular thing hath its
god, who hath created it,[1] and preserves its natural being, but that
this *Bigay potim* brought them all forth from under his armpits,
and that from him as a father they derive their being, by a filial
union, which they term *bija porentesay*; and in the kingdom of
Pegu, where I have often been, I have seen one like unto this,
named by those of the country Ginocoginana, the god of all greatness, which temple was in times past built by the Chinese, whenas
they commanded in the Indias, being according to their sup-
putation from the year of our Lord Jesus Christ 1013 to the year
1072, which by account it appears that the Indias were under the
empire of China but only fifty and nine years, for the successor of
him that conquered it, called Oxivagan, voluntarily abandoned it
in regard of the great expense of money and blood that the unprofitable keeping of it cost him.   In those thirty houses, whereof
I formerly spake, were a great number of idols of gilt wood; and
a like number of tin, latten, and porcelain, being indeed so many,
as I should hardly be believed to declare them.

Now we had not passed above five or six leagues from this place
but we came to a great town, about a league in circuit, quite
destroyed and ruinated, so that asking the Chinese what might be
the cause thereof, they told us that this town was anciently called
Cohilouzaa, that is, the flower of the field, and had in former times
been in very great prosperity, and that about one hundred forty
and two years before, a certain stranger, in the company of some
merchants of the port of Tanaçarim in the kingdom of Siam,
chanced to come thither, being as it seems a holy man, although
the bonzes said he was a sorcerer, by reason of the wonders he
did, having raised up five dead men, and wrought many other
miracles, whereat all men were exceedingly astonished; and that
having divers times disputed with the priests he had so shamed
and confounded them, as fearing to deal any more with him, they
incensed the inhabitants against him, and persuaded them to put
him to death, affirming that otherwise God would consume them
with fire from heaven, whereupon all the townsmen went unto the
house of a poor weaver, where he lodged, and killing the weaver,

[1] Or rather, spirit.   Buddhism and Confucianism had, however, become very
corrupt at this time in China.

with his son and two sons-in-law of his, that would have defended him, the holy man came forth to them, and reprehending them for this uproar, he told them amongst other things, that the God of the law, whereby they were to be saved, was called Jesus Christ, who came down from heaven to the earth for to become a man, and that it was needful He should die for men, and that with the price of His precious blood, which He shed for sinners upon the cross, God was satisfied in His justice, and that giving Him the charge of heaven and earth, He had promised Him, that whosoever professed His law with faith and good works should be saved, and have everlasting life; and withal, that the gods whom the bonzes served and adored with sacrifices of blood, were false, and idols, wherewith the devil deceived them. Hereat the churchmen entered into so great fury that they called unto the people, saying: 'Cursed be he that brings not wood and fire for to burn him,' which was presently put in execution by them, and the fire beginning exceedingly to rage, the holy man said certain prayers,[1] by virtue whereof the fire incontinently went out, wherewith the people being amazed cried out: 'Doubtless the God of this man is most mighty, and worthy to be adored throughout the whole world'; which one of the bonzes hearing, who was ringleader of this mutiny, and seeing the townsmen retire away in consideration of that they had beheld, he threw a stone at the holy man, saying: 'They which do not as I do, may the serpent of the night engulf them into hell fire.' At these words all the other bonzes did the like, so that he was presently knocked down dead with the stones they flung at him, whereupon they cast him into the river, which most prodigiously stayed its course from running down, and so continued for the space of five days together that the body lay in it. By means of this wonder many embraced the law of that holy man, whereof there are a great number yet remaining in that country.

Whilst the Chinese were relating this history unto us, we arrived at a point of land, where going to double cape, we descried a little place environed with trees, in the midst whereof was a great cross of stone very well made, which we no sooner espied, but transported with exceeding joy, we fell on our knees before our conductor, humbly desiring him to give us leave to go on shore, but this heathen dog refused us, saying that they had a great way yet to the place where they were to lodge, whereat we were mightily grieved; howbeit God of His mercy even miraculously [2] so ordered it, that being gone about a league further, his wife fell in labour,

---

[1] In the original, 'made the sign of the cross, and said certain words which they do not now remember.' Cogan has substituted a procedure less displeasing to the puritans of his time.

[2] This is, as I see it, the second intervention of the supernatural in our extract, the first being the shipwreck of António de Faria.

so as he was constrained to return to that place again, it being a
village of thirty or forty houses, hard by where the cross stood.
Here we went on land, and placed his wife in a house where some
nine days after she died in child-bed, during which time we went
to the cross, and prostrating ourselves before it with tears in our
eyes, the people of the village beholding us in this posture, came
to us, and kneeling down also, with their hands lift up to heaven,
they said: 'Christo Jesu, Jesu Christo, Maria micauvidau late
impone moudel,' which, in our tongue, signifies, 'Jesus Christ,
Jesus Christ, Mary always a Virgin conceived him, a Virgin brought
him forth, and a Virgin still remained'; whereunto we weeping
answered, that they spake the very truth; then they asked us if
we were Christians; we told them we were, which as soon as they
understood they carried us home to their houses, where they
entertained us with great affection.

Now all these were Christians and descended of the weaver in
whose house the holy man was lodged, of whom demanding
whether that which the Chinese had told us was true, they showed
us a book that contained the whole history thereof at large, with
many other wonders wrought by that holy man, who they said was
named Matthew Escandel, and that he was a hermit of Mount
Sinai, being a Hungarian by nation, and born in a place called
Buda.   The same book also related that nine days after this saint
was buried, the said town of Cohilouzaa, where he was murdered,
began to tremble in such sort as all the people thereof in a mighty
fright ran out into the fields, and there continued in their tents,
not daring to return unto their houses, for they cried out all with
one common consent: 'The blood of this stranger craves vengeance
for the unjust death the bonzes have given him, because he preached
the truth unto us.'   But the bonzes rebuked and told them that
they committed a great sin in saying so; nevertheless, they willed
them to be of good cheer, for they would go all to Quiay Tiguarem,
god of the night, and request him to command the earth to be
quiet, otherwise we[1] would offer him no more sacrifices.   Immediately whereupon all the bonzes went accordingly in procession to
the said idol, which was the chiefest in the town, but none of the
people durst follow them, for fear of some earthquake, which
the very next night, about eleven of the clock, as those devilish
monsters were making their sacrifices with odoriferous perfumes
and other ceremonies accustomed amongst them, increased so
terribly, that by the Lord's permission, and for a just punishment
of their wickedness, it quite overthrew all the temples, houses,
and other edifices of the town to the ground, wherewith all the
bonzes were killed, not so much as one escaped alive, being in
number above four thousand, as the book delivereth, wherein

[1] That is, the bonzes.

it is further said, that afterwards the earth opening, such abundance of water came forth, as it clean overwhelmed and drowned the whole town, so that it became a great lake, and above a hundred fathom deep; moreover they recounted many other very strange particulars unto us, and also however since that time the place was named Fiunganorsee, that is, the chastisement of heaven, whereas before it was called Cohilouzaa, which signifies the flower of the field, as I have declared heretofore.

After our departure from the ruins of Fiunganorsee, we arrived at a great town, called Junquinilau,[1] which is very rich, abounding with all kind of things, fortified with a strong garrison of horse and foot, and having a number of junks and vessels riding before it. Here we remained five days to celebrate the funeral of our *chifuu's* wife, for whose soul he gave us by way of alms both meat and clothes, and withal freeing us from the oar, permitted us to go ashore without irons, which was a very great ease unto us.

Having left this place we continued our course up the river, beholding still on either side a world of goodly great towns environed with strong walls, as also many fortresses and castles all along the water's side; we saw likewise a great number of temples, whose steeples were all gilt, and in the fields such abundance of cattle that the ground was even covered over with them, so far as we could well discern. Moreover, there were so many vessels upon this river, especially in some parts, where fairs were kept, that at first sight one would have thought them to be populous towns, besides other lesser companies of three hundred, five hundred, six hundred, and a thousand boats, which continually we met withal on both sides of the river, wherein all things that one could imagine were sold. Moreover, the Chinese assured us that in this empire of China, the number of those which lived upon the rivers was not less than those that dwelled in the towns, and that without the good order which is observed to make the common people work [2] and to constrain the meaner sort to supply themselves unto trades for to get their living, they would eat up one another.

Now it is to be noted that every kind of traffic and commerce is divided among them into three or four forms, as followeth: They which trade in ducks, whereof there are great quantities in this country, proceed therein diversely; some cause their eggs to be hatched for to sell the ducklings, others fat them when they are great for to sell them dead after they are salted; these traffic only with the eggs, others with the feathers, and some with the heads, feet, gizzards, and entrails, no man being permitted to trench upon his companion's sale, under the penalty of thirty lashes, which no

[1] Possibly Tientsin.
[2] That is, the almost perfect system of the distribution of work practised in China at that time.

privilege can exempt them from. In the same manner, concerning
hogs, some sell them alive and by wholesale, others dead and by
retail, some make bacon of them, others sell their pigs, and some
again sell nothing but the chitterlings, the sweetbreads, the blood,
and the haslets; which is also observed for fish, for such a one
sells it fresh, that cannot sell it either salted or dried, and so of
other provisions, as flesh, fruit, fowls, venison, pulse, and other
things, wherein such rigour is used, as there are chambers expressly
established, whose officers have commission and power to see
that they which trade in one particular may not do it in another,
if it be not for just and lawful courses, and that on pain of thirty
lashes. There be others likewise that get their living by selling
fish alive, which to that purpose they keep in great well-boats,
and so carry them into divers countries, where they know there is
no other but salt fish. There are likewise all along this river of
Batampina,[1] whereon we went from Nanquin to Pequin, which is
distant one from the other one hundred and fourscore leagues,
such a number of engines for sugar, and presses for wine and oil,
made of divers sorts of pulse and fruit, as one could hardly see any
other thing on either side of the water. In many other places
also there were an infinite company of houses, and magazines full
of all kinds of provision that one could imagine, where all sorts of
flesh are salted, dried, smoked, and piled up in great high heaps,
as gammons of bacon, pork, lard, geese, ducks, cranes, bustards,
ostriches,[2] stags, cows, buffalos, wild goats, rhinoceroses, horses,
tigers, dogs, foxes, and almost all other creatures that one can
name, so that we said many times amongst ourselves, that it was not
possible for all the people of the world to eat up all those provisions.

We saw likewise upon the same river, a number of vessels
which they call *panouras*, covered from the poop to the prow with
nets, in manner of a cage, three inches high, full of ducks and
geese,[3] that were carried from place to place to be sold. When
the owners of those boats would have these fowl to feed, they
approach to the land, and where there are rich meadows or marshes
they set forth planks; opening the doors of those cages, they beat
three or four times upon a drum, which they have expressly for
that purpose, whereupon all these fowl, being six or seven thousand
at the least, go out of the boat with a mighty noise, to fall to feeding
all along the water's side. Now when the owner perceives that
these fowl have fed sufficiently, and that it is time to return them,
he beats the drum the second time, at the sound whereof they gather

[1] Mendes Pinto had not noticed that they had long left the Yangtse for the
Grand Canal.
[2] If these birds were really sold in China they must have been imported from
some distant country, such as Arabia.
[3] From time immemorial the Chinese have excelled all other nations in the
rearing of many and various species of ducks and geese.

all together, and re-enter with the same noise as they went out, wherein it is strange to observe that they return all in again, not so much as one missing. That done, the master of the boat parts from that place, and afterwards, when he thinks it is time for them to lay, he repairs towards land, and where he finds the grounds dry, and good grass, he opens the doors, and beats the drum again, at which all the fowl of the boat come forth to lay, and then at such time as the master judges that these fowl have laid, he beats his drum afresh, and suddenly in haste they all throng into the boat, not so much as one remaining behind. Thereupon two or three men get ashore with baskets in their hands, whereinto they gather up the eggs, till they have gotten eleven or twelve baskets full, and so they proceed on their voyage to make the sale of their ware, which being almost spent, to store themselves anew, they go for to buy more unto them that breed them, whose trade it is to sell them young, for they are not suffered to keep them when they are great, as the others do, by reason, as I have said before, no man may deal in any commodity for which he hath not permission from the governors of the towns. They that get their living by breeding of ducks have near to their houses certain ponds, where many times they keep ten or eleven thousand of these ducklings, some bigger, some lesser.

Now for to hatch the eggs, they have in very long galleries twenty and thirty furnaces full of dung, wherein they bury two hundred, three hundred, and five hundred eggs together, then stopping the mouth of each furnace that the dung may become the hotter, they leave the eggs there till they think the young ones are disclosed, whereupon putting into every several furnace a capon [1] half pulled,[2] and the skin stripped from off his breast, they leave him shut up therein for the space of two days, at the end whereof being all come out of the shell, they carry them into certain places underground made for that purpose, setting them bran soaked in liquor, and so being left there loose some ten or eleven days, they go afterwards of themselves into the ponds, where they feed and bring them up for to sell them unto those former merchants, who trade with them into divers parts, it being unlawful for one to trench upon another's traffic, as I have before related, so that in the markets and public places, where provisions for the month are sold, if any that sell goose eggs do chance to be taken seized with hens' eggs and it is suspected that they sell of them, they are

[1] A method of training capons to bring up young chickens is described by Goldsmith in his *Animated Nature*: '. . . they pluck the feathers off his breast, and rub the bare skin with nettles; they then put the chickens to him, which presently run under his breast and belly, and probably rubbing his bare skin gently with their heads, allay the stinging pain which the nettles had just produced,' etc.

[2] Plucked.

presently punished with thirty lashes on the bare buttocks, without hearing any justification they can make for themselves, being as I have said, found seized of them, so that if they will have hens' eggs for their own use, to avoid incurring the penalty of the law they must be broken at one end, whereby it may appear that they keep them not to sell, but to eat. As for them that sell fish alive, if any of their fish chance to die, they cut them in pieces, and salting them sell them at the price of salt fish, which is less than that of fresh fish, wherein they proceed so exactly, that no man dares pass the limits which are prescribed and ordained by the *conchalis* of the state, upon pain of most severe punishment, for in all this country the king is so much respected, and justice so feared, as no kind of person, how great soever, dares murmur, or look awry at an officer, no, not at the very *huppes* which are as the bailiffs or beadles amongst us.

Chapter XXXI. The order which is observed in the moving towns that are made upon the rivers, and that which further befell us

WE saw likewise all along this great river a number of hogs both wild and domestic that were kept by certain men on horseback, and many herds of tame red deer,[1] which were driven from place to place like sheep, to feed, all lamed of their right legs, to hinder them from running away, and they are lamed so when they are but calves, to avoid the danger that otherwise they might incur of their lives. We saw also divers parks, wherein a world of dogs were kept to be sold to the butchers, for in these countries they eat all manner of flesh, whereof they know the price, and of what creatures they are, by the choppings they make of them. Moreover, we met with many small barques, whereof some were full of pigs, others of tortoises, frogs, otters, adders, eels, snails, and lizards, for as I have said, they buy there of all that is judged good to eat; now to the end that such provisions may pass at an easier rate, all that sell them are permitted to make traffic of them in several fashions; true it is, that in some things they have greater franchises than in others, to the end that by means thereof no merchandise may want sale. And because the subject I now treat of dispenses me to speak of all, I will relate that which we further observed there, and whereat we were much abashed, judging thereby how far men suffer themselves to be carried by their interests and extreme avarice.

[1] A species of reindeer.

You must know then that in this country there are a many of such as make a trade of buying and selling men's excrements, which is not so mean a commerce amongst them, but that there are many of them grow rich by it, and are held in good account; now these excrements serve to manure grounds that are newly grubbed, which is found to be far better for that purpose than the ordinary dung. They which make a trade of buying it go up and down the streets with certain clappers, like our spital men,[1] whereby they give to understand what they desire without publishing of it otherwise to people, in regard the thing is filthy of itself; whereunto I will add thus much, that this commodity is so much esteemed amongst them, and so great a trade driven of it, that into one seaport sometimes there comes in one tide two or three hundred sails laden with it. Oftentimes also there is such striving for it as the governors of the place are fain to interpose their authority for the distribution of this goodly commodity, and all for to manure their grounds, which, soiled with it, bear three crops in one year.

We saw many boats likewise laden with dried orange peels, wherewith in victualling houses they boil dog's flesh, for to take away the rank savour and humidity of it, as also to render it more firm. In brief, we saw so many *vancans*, *lanteaas*, and *barcasses* in this river, laden with all kinds of provision that either the sea or land produces, and that in such abundance, as I must confess I am not able to express it in words; for it is not possible to imagine the infinite store of things that are in this country, of each whereof you shall see two or three hundred vessels together at a time, all full, especially at the fairs and markets that are kept upon the solemn festival days of their pagodas, for then all the fairs are free, and the pagodas for the most part are situated on the banks of rivers, to the end all commodities may the more commodiously be brought thither by water.

Now when all these vessels come to join together, during these fairs, they take such order, as they make as it were a great and fair town of them, so that sometimes you shall have of them a league in length, and three-quarters of a league in breadth, being composed of above twenty thousand vessels, besides *balons*, *guedees*, and *manchuas*, which are small boats, whose number is infinite. For the government hereof there are threescore captains appointed, of which thirty are to see good order kept, and the other thirty are for the guard of the merchants that come thither, to the end they may sail in safety. Moreover, there is above them a *chaem*, who hath absolute power both in civil and criminal causes, without any appeal or opposition whatsoever, during the fifteen

---

[1] These would be the 'lazars,' those who were suspected of having leprosy, and who would be sent out from the hospitals to beg. The original says, 'como quem pede para São Lázaro.'

days that this fair lasts, which is from the new to the full moon. And indeed more come to see the policy, order, and beauty of this kind of town than otherwise, for, to speak the truth, the framing of it in that manner with vessels, makes it more to be admired than [1] all the edifices that can be seen upon the land.

There are in this moving town two thousand streets, exceeding long and very strait, enclosed on either side with ships, most of which are covered with silks, and adorned with a world of banners, flags, and streamers, wherein all kind of commodities that can be desired are to be sold.   In other streets are as many trades to be seen as in any town on the land, amidst the which they that traffic go up and down in little *manchuas*, and that very quietly, and without any disorder.   Now if by chance any one is taken stealing, he is instantly punished according to his offence.   As soon as it is night, all these streets are shut up with cords athwart them, to the end none may pass after the retreat sounded; in each of these streets there are at least a dozen of lanterns, with lights burning, fastened a good height on the masts of the vessels, by means whereof all that go in and out are seen,[2] so that it may be known who they are, from whence they come, and what they would have, to the end the *chaem* may the next morning receive an account thereof.   And truly, to behold all these lights together in the night, is a sight scarce able to be imagined, neither is there a street without a bell and a sentinel, so as when that of the *chaem's* ship is heard to ring, all the other bells answer it, with so great a noise of voices adjoined thereunto, that we were almost beside ourselves at the hearing of a thing which cannot be well conceived, and that was ruled with such good order.   In every of these streets, even in the poorest of them, there is a chapel to pray in, framed upon great *barcasses*, like to galleys, very neat, and so well accommodated, that for the most part they are enriched with silks and cloth of gold.   In these chapels are their idols, and priests which administer their sacrifices and receive the offerings that are made them, wherewith they are abundantly furnished for their living.   Out of each street, one of the most account, or chiefest merchant, is chosen to watch all night in his turn with those of his squadron, besides the captains of the government, who in *balons* walk [3] the round without, to the end no thief may escape by any avenue whatsoever, and for that purpose these guards cry as loud as they can that they may be heard.

Amongst the most remarkable things we saw one street, where

---

[1] Cogan has here mistranslated.   The original runs: 'During the fifteen days that this fair lasts, which is from the new to the full moon, the policy, order, and beauty of this kind of town is more worth seeing . . . than . . .'

[2] There was, of course, very little street lighting in Europe then.

[3] This is a mistranslation.   'Go' would be better.

there were above a hundred vessels laden with idols of gilt wood of divers fashions, which were sold for to be offered to the pagodas, together with a world of feet, thighs, arms, and heads, that sick folks bought to offer in devotion.[1]   There also we beheld other ships, covered with silk hangings, where comedies and other plays were represented to entertain the people withal, which in great numbers flocked thither.   In other places, bills of exchange for heaven were sold, whereby these priests of the devil promised them many merits, with great interest, affirming that without these bills they could not possibly be saved, for that God, say they, is a mortal enemy to all such as do not some good to the pagodas, whereupon they tell them such fables and lies as these unhappy wretches do oftentimes take the very bread from their mouths to give it them.   There were also other vessels all laden with dead men's skulls, which divers men bought for to present as an offering at the tombs of their friends, when they should happen to die; for, say they, as the deceased is laid in the grave in the company of these skulls, so shall his soul enter into heaven, attended by those unto whom those skulls belonged, wherefore when the porter of paradise shall see such a merchant with many followers, he will do him honour, as to a man that in this life hath been a man of quality, for if he be poor, and without a train, the porter will not open to him, whereas contrarily the more dead men's skulls he hath buried with him, the more happy he shall be esteemed. There were many boats likewise, where there were men that had a great many of cages, full of live birds, who playing on divers instruments of music, exhorted the people with a loud voice, to deliver those poor creatures of God that were there in captivity, whereupon many came and gave them money for the redemption of those prisoners, which presently they let out of the cages, and then as they flew away, the redeemers of them cried out to the birds: 'Pichau pitanel catan vacaxi,' that is, 'Go, and tell God[2] how we serve Him here below.'   In imitation of these, there are others also, who in their ships kept a great many of little live fishes in great pots of water, and like the sellers of birds invite the people for God's cause to free those poor innocent fishes, that had never sinned, so that divers bought many of them, and casting them into the river, said: 'Get ye gone, and tell there below[3] the good I have done you for God's sake.'   To conclude all, the vessels where these things are exposed to sale are seldom less in number than two hundred, besides thousands of others, which sell such-like wares in a far greater quantity.

[1] Mendes Pinto must have been quite accustomed to the *ex votos* of his own country.
[2] In the heavens.
[3] In the house of smoke.

We saw likewise many *barcasses* full of men and women that
played upon divers sorts of instruments and for money gave them
music that desired it.   There were other vessels laden with horns,
which the priests sold, therewith to make feasts in heaven, for
they say that those were the horns of several beasts, which were
offered in sacrifice to the idols out of devotion, and for the performance of vows that men had made in divers kind of misfortunes and sicknesses, wherein they had at other times been;
and that as the flesh of those beasts had been given here below
for the honour of God to the poor, so the souls of them for whom
those horns were offered do in the other world eat the souls of those
beasts to whom those horns belonged, and thereunto invite the
souls of their friends, as men use to invite others here on earth.
Other vessels we saw covered with blacks[1] and full of tombs, torches,
and great wax lights, as also women in them, that for money would
be hired to weep and lament for the dead; others there were, called
pitaleus, that in great barques kept divers kinds of wild beasts to
be showed for money, most dreadful to behold, as serpents, huge
adders, monstrous lizards,[2] tigers, and many others suchlike.
We saw in like sort a great number of stationers, which sold all
manner of books that could be desired, as well concerning the
creation of the world, whereof they tell a thousand lies, as touching
the states, kingdoms, islands, and provinces of the world, together
with the laws and customs of nations, but especially of the kings
of China, their number, brave acts, and of all things else that
happened in each of their reigns.   Moreover, we saw a great many
of the light, swift foists,[3] wherein were men very well armed, who
cried out with a loud voice, that if any one had received an affront,
whereof he desired to be avenged, let him come unto them, and
they would cause satisfaction to be made him.   In other vessels
there were old women, that served for midwives, and that would
bring women speedily and easily abed, as also a many of nurses,
ready to be entertained [4] for to give children suck.   There were
barques likewise very well adorned and set forth, that had in them
divers reverend old men and grave matrons, whose profession
was to make marriages, and to comfort widows, or such as had
lost their children, or suffered any other misfortune.   In others
there were a number of young men and maids, that lacked masters
and mistresses, which offered themselves to any that would hire
them.   There were other vessels that had in them such as undertook to tell fortunes,[5] and to help folks to things lost.
In a word, not to dwell any longer upon every particular that
was to be seen in this moving town, for then I should never have

---

[1] In the original *do*, literally 'woe' or 'mourning.'   [2] Crocodiles.
[3] Light galleys propelled by oars and sails.   [4] Employed.
[5] *Cristaleiras*, readers of crystals.

done, it shall suffice me to say, that nothing can be desired on land, which was not to be had in their vessels, and that in greater abundance than I have delivered, wherefore I will pass from it to show you that one of the principal causes why this monarchy of China, that contains two-and-thirty kingdoms, is so mighty, rich, and of so great commerce, is, because it is exceedingly replenished with rivers, and a world of canals that have been anciently made by the kings,[1] great lords, and people thereof, for to render all the country navigable, and so communicate their labours with one another. The narrowest of these canals have bridges of hewed stone over them, that are very high, long, and broad, whereof some are of one stone, eighty, ninety, nay, a hundred spans long, and fifteen or twenty broad, which doubtless is very marvellous, for it is almost impossible to comprehend by what means so huge a mass of stone could be drawn out of the quarry without breaking, and how it should be transported to the place where it was to be set. All the ways and passages, from cities, towns, and villages, have very large causeways made of fair stone, at the ends whereof are costly pillars and arches, upon which are inscriptions with letters of gold, containing the praises of them that erected them; moreover there are handsome seats placed all along for poor passengers to rest themselves on. There are likewise innumerable aqueducts and fountains everywhere, whose water is most wholesome and excellent to drink. And in divers parts there are certain wenches of love that out of charity prostitute themselves to travellers which have no money, and although amongst us this is held for a great abuse and abomination, yet with them it is accounted a work of mercy, so that many on their death-beds do by their testaments bequeath great revenues for the maintenance of this wickedness, as a thing very meritorious for the salvation of their souls; moreover, many others have left lands for the erecting and maintaining of houses in deserts and uninhabited places, where great fires are kept all the night to guide such as have strayed out of their way, as also water for men to drink, and seats to repose them in, and that there may be no default herein, there are divers persons entertained with very good means, to see these things carefully continued, according to the institution of him that founded them for the health of his soul.

By these marvels which are found in the particular towns of this empire, may be concluded what the greatness thereof might be were they joined all together; but for the better satisfaction of the reader, I dare boldly say, if my testimony may be worthy of credit, that in one-and-twenty years' space, during which time, with a world of misfortune, labour, and pain, I traversed the greatest

[1] Kublai Khan is reported to have made the Grand Canal up which Mendes Pinto was travelling.

part of Asia, as may appear by this my discourse, I had seen in some countries a wonderful abundance of several sorts of victuals and provisions which we have not in our Europe, yet without speaking what each of them might have in particular, I do not think there is in all Europe so much as there is in China alone. And the same may be said of all the rest, wherewith heaven hath favoured this climate, as well for the temperature of the air, as for that which concerns the policy and riches, the magnificence and greatness of their estate.[1] Now that which gives the greatest lustre unto it is their exact observation of justice, for there is so well ruled a government in this country, as it may justly be envied of all others in the world. And to speak the truth, such as want this particular have no gloss, be they otherwise never so great and commendable. Verily, so often as I represent unto myself those great things which I have seen in this China, I am on the one side amazed to think how liberally it hath pleased God to heap upon this people the goods of the earth, and on the other side I am exceedingly grieved to consider how ungrateful they are in acknowledging such extraordinary favours; for they commit amongst themselves an infinite of most enormous sins, wherewithal they incessantly offend the divine goodness, as well in their brutish and diabolical idolatries as in the abominable sin of sodomy, which is not only permitted amongst them in public, but is also accounted for a great virtue according to the instructions of their priests.

Chapter XXXII. Our arrival at the city of Pequin, together with our imprisonment, and that which moreover happened unto us there; as also the great majesty of the officers of their court of justice

AFTER we were departed from that rare and marvellous town whereof I have spoken, we continued our course up the river, until at length on Tuesday, the nineteenth of October in the year 1541, we arrived at the great city of Pequin, whither, as I have said before, we had been remitted by appeal. In this manner chained three and three together, we were cast into a prison, called Gofaniauserca, where for our welcome we had at the first dash thirty lashes apiece given us, wherewith some of us became very sick.

Now as soon as the *chifuu* who conducted us thither had presented the process of our sentence, sealed with twelve seals, to

---

[1] We know now that this is true, but even Johnson in the eighteenth century could not credit it. See his Preface to *Lobo*.

the justice of the *aytau*, which is their parliament, the twelve *conchalys* of the criminal chamber, unto whom the cognizance of our cause appertained, commanded us presently away to prison, whereupon one of those twelve, assisted by two registers, and six or seven officers, whom they term *huppes*, and are much like our catchpoles here, terrified us not a little, as he was leading us thither, for giving us very threatening speeches. 'Come,' said he unto us, 'by the power and authority which I have from the *aytau* of Batampina, chief president of the two-and-thirty judges of strangers, within whose breast are the secrets of the Lion crowned on the Throne of the World enclosed, I enjoin and command you to tell me what people you are, as also of what country, and whether you have a king, who for the service of God, and for the discharge of his dignity, is inclined to do good to the poor, and to render them justice,[1] to the end that with tears in their eyes, and hands lifted up, they may not address their complaints to that sovereign Lord, which hath made the bright enamel of the skies, and for whose holy feet all they that reign with Him serve but for sandals.'

To this demand we answered him, that we were poor strangers, natives of the kingdom of Siam, who being embarked with our merchandise for Liampoo, were cast away in a great storm at sea, from whence we escaped naked with the loss of all that we had, and how in that deplorable estate we were fain to get our living by begging from door to door till such time as at our arrival at the town of Taypor, the *chumbim*, then resident there, had arrested us for prisoners without cause, and so sent us to the city of Nanquin, where by his report we had been condemned to the whip, and to have our thumbs cut off, without so much as once deigning to hear us in our justifications, by reason whereof lifting up our eyes to heaven, we had been advised to have recourse with our tears to the four-and-twenty judges of austere life, that through their zeal to God they might take our cause in hand, since by reason of our poverty we were altogether without support, and abandoned of all men; which with a holy zeal they incontinently effected by revoking the cause, and annulling the judgment that had been given against us; and that these things considered we most instantly besought him that for the service of God he would be pleased to have regard to our misery and the great injustice that was done us, for that we had no means in this country, nor person that would speak one word for us.

The judge remained some time in suspense upon that we had said to him; at length he answered that we need say no more to him; 'for it is sufficient that I know you are poor, to the end this affair may go another way than hitherto it hath done, nevertheless

[1] The duties of the emperor of China.

to acquit me of my charge, I give you five days' time, conformably to the law of the third book, that within in the said term you may retain a proctor to undertake your cause, but if you will be advised by me, you shall present your request to the *tanigores* of the sacred office, to the end that, carried by a holy zeal of the honour of God, they may out of compassion of your miseries take upon them to defend your right.'

Having spoken thus, he gave us a tael in way of alms, and said further to us: 'Beware of the prisoners that are here, for I assure you that they make it their trade to steal all that they can from any one'; whereupon entering into another chamber where there were a great number of prisoners, he continued there above three hours in giving them audience, at the end whereof he sent seven-and-twenty men that the day before had received their judgment to execution, which was inflicted upon them by whipping to death, a spectacle so dreadful to us, and that put us in such a fright, as it almost set us besides ourselves.

The next morning, as soon as it was day, the jailors clapped irons on our feet and manacles on our hands, and put us to exceeding great pain, but seven days after we had endured such misery, being laid on the ground one by another and bewailing our disaster, for the extreme fear we were in of suffering a most cruel death, if that which we had done at Calempluy should by any means chance to be discovered, it pleased God that we were visited by the *tanigores* of the house of mercy, which is of the jurisdiction of this prison, who are called in their language *co filem guaxy*. At their arrival all the prisoners bowing themselves, said with a lamentable tone: 'Blessed be the day wherein God doth visit us by the ministry of his servants'; whereunto the *tanigores* made answer with a grave and modest countenance: 'The almighty and divine hand of Him that hath formed the beauty of the stars keep and preserve you.' Then approaching to us, they very courteously demanded of us what people we were, and whence it proceeded that our imprisonment was more sensible [1] to us than to others. To this speech we replied with tears in our eyes, that we were poor strangers, so abandoned of men, as in all that country there was not one that knew our names, and that all we could in our poverty say to entreat them to think of us for God's sake, was contained in a letter that we had brought them from the chamber of the society of the house of Quinay Hinarel, in the city of Nanquin; whereupon Christóvão Borralho presenting them with the letter, they received it with a new ceremony, full of all courtesy, saying: 'Praised be He who hath created all things, for that He is pleased to serve Himself of sinners here below, whereby they may be recompensed at the last day of all days, by satisfying them double their labour with

[1] Obs. for acutely felt, painful.

the riches of His holy treasures, which shall be done, as we believe, in as great abundance as the drops of rain fall from the clouds to the earth.' After this, one of the four, putting up the letter, said unto us, that as soon as the chamber of justice for the poor was open, they would all of them give an answer to our business, and see us furnished with all that we had need of, and so they departed from us.

Three days after they returned to visit us in the prison, and in the next morning coming to us again, they asked us many questions answerable to a memorial which they had thereof, whereunto we replied in every point according as we were questioned by each of them, so as they remained very well satisfied with our answers; then calling the register to them, who had our papers in charge, they inquired very exactly of him, touching many things that concerned us, and withal required his advice about our affair; that done, having digested all that might make for the conversation of our right into certain heads, they took our process from him, saying, they would peruse it all of them together in their chambers of justice with the proctors of the house, and the next day return it him again, that he might carry it to the *chaem*, as he was resolved before to do.

Not to trouble myself with recounting in particular all that occurred in this affair, until such time as it was fully concluded, wherein six months and a half were employed, during the which we continued still prisoners in such misery, I will in few words relate all that befell us unto the end. Whenas our business was come before the twelve *conchalys* of the criminal court, the two proctors of the house of mercy most willingly took upon them to cause the unjust sentence, which had been given against us, to be revoked. Having gotten then all the proceedings to be disannulled, they by petition remonstrated unto the *chaem* who was the president of that court, how we could not for any cause whatsoever be condemned to death, seeing there were no witnesses of any credit that could testify that we had robbed any man, or had ever seen us carry any offensive weapons contrary to the prohibition made against it by the law of the first book,[1] but that we were apprehended quite naked, like wretched men, wandering after a lamentable shipwreck, and that therefore our poverty and misery was worthy rather of a pitiful compassion than of that rigour wherewith the first ministers of the arm of wrath had caused us to be whipped; moreover, that God alone was the judge of our innocency, in Whose name they required him once, twice, nay, many times, to consider that he was mortal, and could not last long, for that God had given him a perishable life, at the end whereof he was to render an account of that which had been required of him, since by a solemn oath

[1] Another proof of the high state of civilization of the Chinese.

he was obliged to do all that should be manifest to his judgment, without any consideration of men of the world, whose custom it was to make the balance sway down, which God would have to be upright, according to the integrity of His divine justice.[1]

To this petition the king's proctor opposed himself, as he that was our adverse party, and that in certain articles, which he framed against us, set forth, how he would prove by ocular witnesses, as well of the country, as strangers, that we were public thieves, making a common practice of robbing, and not merchants, such as we pretended to be; whereunto he added, that if we had come to the coast of China with a good design, and with an intent to pay the king his due in his custom houses, we would have repaired to the ports where they were established by the ordinance of the *aytau* of the government, but for a punishment, because we went from isle to isle, like pirates, Almighty God, that detests sin and robbery, had permitted us to suffer shipwreck, that so falling into the hands of the ministers of His justice, we might receive the guerdon of our wicked works, namely, the pains of death, whereof our crimes rendered us most worthy. In regard of all which, he desired we might be condemned according to the law of the second book, that commanded it in express terms; and that if for other considerations, no way remarkable in us, we could by any law be exempted from death, yet nevertheless, for that we were strangers and vagabonds, without either faith, or knowledge of God, that alone would suffice at leastwise to condemn us to have our hands and noses cut off, and so to be banished for ever into the country of Ponxileytay, whither such people as we were wont to be exiled, as might be verified by divers sentences given and executed in like cases,[2] and to that effect, he desired the admittance of his articles, which he promised to prove within the time that should be prescribed him.

These articles were presently excepted against by the proctor of the court of justice established for the poor, who offered to make the contrary appear within a certain term, which to that end, and for many other reasons alleged by him in our favour, was granted him, wherefore he required that the said articles might not be admitted, especially for that they were infamous, and directly contrary to the ordinances of justice. Whereupon the *chaem* ordered that his articles should not be admitted, unless he did prove them by evident testimonies, and such as were conformable to the divine law, within six days next ensuing, and that upon pain in case of contravention not to be admitted to any demand of a longer

[1] Unbiased judgment of this kind was extremely rare in the Europe of those days.
[2] The Chinese equivalent to our vagrancy laws. It was, however, understood that the vagrant was wandering 'with evil intent.'

delay. The said term of six days being prescribed the king's proctor, he, in the meantime, producing no one proof against us, nor any person that so much as knew us, came and demanded a delay of other six days, which was flatly denied him, in regard it but too well appeared that all he did was only to win time, and therefore he would by no means consent unto it, but contrarily he gave the proctor for the poor five days' respite to allege all that further he could in our defence. In the meantime, the king's proctor declaimed against us in such foul and opprobrious terms, as the *chaem* was much offended thereat, so that he condemned him to pay us twenty taels of silver, both for his want of charity,[1] and for that he could not prove any one of the obligations which he had exhibited against us.

Three days being spent herein, four *tanigores* of the house of the poor, coming very early in the morning to the prison, sent for us into the infirmary, where they told us that our business went very well, and how we might hope that our sentence would have a good issue, whereupon we cast ourselves at their feet, and with abundance of tears desired God to reward them for the pains they had taken in our behalf. Thereunto one of them replied: 'And we also most humbly beseech Him to keep you in the knowledge of His law,[2] wherein all the happiness of good men consists'; and so they caused two coverlets to be given us, for to lay upon our beds in the night, because the weather was cold, and withal bid us that we should not stick to ask anything we wanted, for that God Almighty did not love a sparing hand in the distributing of alms for His sake. A little after their departure came the register, and showing us the *chaem's* order, whereby the king's proctor was condemned to pay us twenty taels, gave us the money, and took an acquittance under our hands for the receipt of it. For which giving him a world of thanks, we entreated him for his pains to take as much thereof as he pleased, but he would not touch a penny, saying: 'I will not for so small a matter lose the recompense which I hope to gain from God,[3] for the consideration of you.'[4]

We passed nine days in great fear, still expecting to have our sentence pronounced, whenas one Saturday morning two *chumbims* of justice came to the prison for us, accompanied with twenty officers, by them called *huppes*, carrying halberds, partisans, and

---

[1] This was one of the most serious sins by the Chinese code of morals.
[2] The knowledge of God and of the moral law is considered as independent of religious belief.
[3] This conception of a claim upon God is quite different from Christian ideas.
[4] Cogan here omits a chapter which tells how the Portuguese prisoners tried on the *tanigores* one of the, to them, recognized forms of bribery, and how the *tanigores* reproved them but excused them, since they were barbarians. This is one of the more critical chapters, and it is interesting to note that Cogan, in Commonwealth times, did not care to include it.

other arms, which made them very dreadful to the beholders. These men, tying us all nine together in a long iron chain, led us to the *caladigan*, which was the place where audience was given, and where execution was done on delinquents.   Now how we got thither, to confess the truth, I am not able to relate, for we were at that instant so far besides ourselves, as we knew not what we did, or which way we went, so as in that extremity all our thought was how to conform ourselves to the will of God, and beg of Him with tears that for the merit of His sacred passion, He would be pleased to receive the punishment that should be inflicted on us for the satisfaction of our sins.

At length, after much pain and many affronts, that were done us by many which followed after us with loud cries, we arrived at the first hall of the *caladigan*, where were four-and-twenty executioners whom they call the ministers of the arm of justice, with a great many of other people, that were there about their affairs.   Here we remained a long time, till at length upon the ringing of a bell, other doors were opened, that stood under a great arch of architecture, very artificially wrought, and whereon were a number of rich figures.   On the top a monstrous lion of silver was seen, with his fore and hind feet upon a mighty great bowl, made of the same metal, whereby the arms of the king of China are represented, which are ordinarily placed on the forefront of all the sovereign courts where the *chaems* preside, who are as viceroys amongst us.   Those doors being opened, as I said before, all that were there present entered into a very great hall, like the body of a church, hung from the top to the bottom with divers pictures, wherein strange kinds of execution done upon persons of all conditions after a most dreadful manner were constrained, and under every picture was this inscription: 'Such a one was executed with this kind of death for committing such a crime'; so that in beholding the diversity of these fearful portraitures one might see in it, as it were, a declaration of the kind of death that was ordained for each crime, as also the extreme rigour which the justice there observed in such executions.

From this hall we went into another room far richer and more costly, for it was gilt all over, so that one could not have a more pleasing object, at leastwise if we could have taken pleasure in anything, considering the misery we were in.   In the midst of this room there was a tribunal, whereunto one ascended by seven steps, environed with three rows of balusters of iron, copper, and ebony; the tops whereof were beautified with mother of pearl. At the upper end of all was a cloth of state of white damask, fringed about with a deep caul[1] fringe of green silk and gold; under this state sat the *chaem* with a world of greatness and majesty;

[1] Net.

he was seated in a very rich chair of silver, having before him a little table, and about him three boys on their knees, sumptuously apparelled, with chains of gold, one of the which (namely, he in the middle) served to give the *chaem* the pen wherewithal he signed; the other two took the petitions that were preferred, and presented them on the table, that they might be signed; on the right hand in another place somewhat higher, and almost equal with the *chaem*, stood a boy, some ten or eleven years old, attired in a rich robe of white satin, embroidered with roses of gold, having a chain of pearl three double about his neck, and hair as long as a woman's, most neatly plaited with a fillet of gold,[1] all enamelled with green,[2] and powdered over with great seed-pearl. In his hand he held, as mark of that which he represented, a little branch of roses, made of silk, gold thread, and rich pearls, very curiously intermixed;[3] and in this manner he appeared so gentle, handsome, and beautiful, as no woman, how fair soever, could overmatch him; this boy leaned on his elbow upon the *chaem's* chair, and figured mercy. In the like manner, on the left hand was another goodly boy, richly apparelled in a coat of carnation satin, all set with roses of gold, having his right arm bared up to the elbow, and dyed with a vermilion as red as blood, and in that hand holding a naked sword, which seemed also to be bloody: moreover, on his head he wore a crown, in fashion like to a mitre, hung all with little razors, like unto lancets, wherewith surgeons let men blood; being thus gallantly set forth, and of most beautiful presence, yet he struck all that beheld him with fear, in regard of that he represented, which was justice. For they say that the judge, which holds the place of the king, who presents God on earth, ought necessarily to have those two qualities, justice and mercy; and that he which doth not use them is a tyrant, acknowledging no law, and usurping the power that he hath.

The *chaem* was apparelled in a long gown of violet satin,[4] fringed with green silk and gold, with a kind of scapular about his neck, in the midst of which was a great plate of gold, wherein a hand holding a very even pair of balance was engraven, and the inscription about it: 'It is the nature of the Lord Almighty to observe in His justice, weight, measure, and true account, therefore take heed to what thou doest, for if thou comest to sin thou shalt suffer for it eternally.' Upon his head he had a kind of round bonnet, bordered about with small sprigs of gold, all enamelled violet and

[1] Cogan omits: 'and crimson, scattered over with pearls of great price, and on his feet sandals.'
[2] Cogan omits: 'and gold.'
[3] Presumably white roses, to signify mercy. Gold means excellence and nobility. The pearl is a symbol of wisdom, for it is taken from under the water at the risk of him who dives for it.
[4] Like the *tanigores* when they visited the hospital. See p. 103.

green, and on the top of it was a little crowned lion of gold, upon
a round bowl of the same metal; by which lion crowned, as I have
delivered heretofore, is the king signified, and by the bowl the
world, as if by these devices they would denote that the king is the
Lion crowned on the Throne of the World.   In his right hand he
held a little rod of ivory, some three spans long, in manner of a
sceptre; upon the top of the three first steps of this tribunal stood
eight ushers with silver maces on their shoulders, and below were
threescore Mogors [1] on their knees, disposed into two [2] ranks, carrying halberds in their hands, that were neatly damasked with gold.
In the vanguard of these same stood, like as if they had been the
commanders or captains of this squadron, the statues of two
giants, of a most gallant aspect, and very richly attired, with their
swords hanging in scarfs, and mighty great halberds in their
hands, and these the Chinese in their language call *gigaos*; on
the two sides of this tribunal below in the room were two very
long tables, at each of which sat twelve men, whereof four were
presidents or judges, two registers, four solicitors, and two *conchalys*, which are, as it were, assistants to the courts: one of these
tables was for criminal, and the other for civil causes, and all
the officers of both these tables were apparelled in gowns of white
satin, that were very long, and had large sleeves, thereby demon-
strating the latitude and purity of justice; the tables were covered
with carpets of violet damask, and richly bordered about with
gold; the *chaem's* table, because it was of silver, had no carpet on
it, nor anything else but a cushion of cloth of gold and a standish.

Now all these things put together, as we saw them, carried a
wonderful show of state and majesty.   But to proceed, upon the
fourth ringing of a bell, one of the *conchalys* stood up, and after a
low obeisance made to the *chaem*, with a very loud voice that he
might be heard of every one, he said: 'Peace there, and with all
submission hearken, on pain of incurring the punishment ordained
by the *chaems* of the Government for those that interrupt the
silence of sacred justice.'   Whereupon this same sitting down
again, another arose, and with the like reverence, mounting up to
the tribunal where the *chaem* sat, he took the sentences from him
that held them in his hand, and published them aloud one after
another, with so many ceremonies and compliments, as he employed above an hour therein.   At length coming to pronounce
our judgment, they caused us to kneel down, with out eyes fixed
on the ground and our hands lifted up, as if we were praying unto
heaven, to the end that in all humility we might hear the publication
thereof, which was thus:

'Bitau Dicalor, the new *chaem* of this sacred court, where
justice is rendered to strangers, and that by the gracious pleasure

---

[1] Mogols.   [2] Cogan has 'three,' which is wrong.

of the son of the Sun, the Lion crowned on the Throne of the World, unto whom are subjected all the sceptres and crowns of the kings that govern the earth, ye are subjected under his feet by the grace and will of the most High in heaven; having viewed and considered the appeal made to me by these nine strangers, whose cause was commanded hither by the city of Nanquin, by the four-and-twenty of austere life, I say, by the oath I have taken upon my entry into the charge, which I exercise for the *aytau* of Batampina, the chief of two-and-thirty that govern all the people of this empire, that the ninth day of the seventh moon, in the fifteenth year of the reign of the son of the Sun, I was presented with the accusations, which the *chumbim* of Taypor sent me against them, whereby he chargeth them to be thieves, and robbers of other men's goods, affirming that they have long practised that trade, to the great offence of the Lord above, who hath created all things; and withal that without any fear of God they used to bathe themselves in the blood of those that with reason resisted them, for which they have already been condemned to be whipped and have their thumbs cut off, whereof the one hath been put in execution; but when they came to have their thumbs cut off, the proctors for the poor, opposing it, alleged in their behalf, that they were wrongfully condemned, because there was no proof of that wherewith they were charged, in regard whereof they required for them, that instead of judging them upon a bare show of uncertain suspicions, valuable testimonies might be produced, and such as were conformable to the divine laws and the justice of heaven; whereunto answer was made by that court, how justice was to give place to mercy, whereupon they that undertook their cause made their complaint to the four-and-twenty of austere life, who both out of very just considerations and the regard they had to the little support they could have, for that they were strangers, and of a nation so far distant from us, as we never heard of the country where they say they were born,[1] mercifully inclining to their lamentable cries, sent them and their cause to be judged by this court, wherefore omitting the prosecution thereof here by the king's proctor, who being able to prove nothing whereof he accused them, affirms only that they are worthy of death for the suspicion and jealousy they have given of themselves, but in regard [2] sacred justice, that stands upon considerations which are pure and agreeable to God, admits of no reasons from an adverse party, if they be not made good by evident proofs, I thought it not fit to allow of the king's proctor's accusations, since he could not prove what he had alleged, whereupon insisting on his demand, without showing either any just

[1] They must therefore have spoken of Portugal. Hitherto they had apparently only claimed to have come from Siam.
[2] Inasmuch as.

causes or sufficient proof concerning that he concluded against those strangers, I condemned him in twenty taels of silver amends to his adverse parties, being altogether according to equity, because the reasons alleged by him were grounded upon a bad zeal, and such as were neither just nor pleasing to God, whose mercy doth always incline to their side that are poor and feeble on the earth, whenas they invoke Him with tears in their eyes, as is daily and clearly manifested by the pitiful effects of His greatness; so that having thereupon expressly commanded the *tanigores* of the house of mercy to allege whatsoever they could say on their behalf, they accordingly did so within the time that was prefixed them for that purpose; and so all proceedings having received their due course the cause is now come to a final judgment.   Wherefore, everything duly viewed and considered, without regard had to any human respect, but only to the merit and equity of their cause, and according to the resolution of the laws, accepted by the twelve *chaems* of the Government in the fifth book of the will and pleasure of the son of the Sun, who in such cases out of his greatness and goodness hath more regard to the complaints of the poor than to the insolent clamours of the proud of the earth; [1] I do ordain and decree that these nine strangers shall be clearly quit and absolved of all that which the king's proctor hath laid to their charge, as also of all the punishment belonging thereunto, condemning them only to a year's exile, during which time they shall work for their living in the reparations of Quansy,[2] and whenas eight months of the said year shall be accomplished, then I expressly enjoin all the *chumbims, conchalys, monteos,* and other ministers of their government, that immediately upon their presenting of this my decree unto them, they give them a passport and safe conduct, to the end they may freely and securely return into their country, or to any other place they shall think fit.'

After this sentence was thus published in our hearing, we all cried out with a loud voice: 'The sentence of thy clear judgment is confirmed in us, even as the purity of thy heart is agreeable to the son of the Sun.'   This said, one of the *conchalys*, that sat at one of the tables, stood up, and having made a very low obeisance to the *chaem*, he said aloud five times one after another, to all that press of people, which were there in great number: 'Is there any one in this court, in this city, or in this kingdom, that will oppose this decree, or the deliverance of these nine prisoners?'   Whereunto no answer being made, the two boys that represented justice and mercy touched the ensigns which they held in their hands to-

---

[1] All this speech from a heathen is very much in agreement with Christian principles, but not at all in accordance with the practice of Christian countries at that time.
[2] Kiang-si.

gether, and said aloud: 'Let them be freed and discharged according to the sentence very justly pronounced for it'; whereupon one of those ministers, whom they call *huppes*, having rung a bell thrice, the two *chumbims* of execution, that had formerly bound us, unloosed us from our chain, and withal took off our manacles, collars, and the other irons from our legs, so that we were quite delivered, for which we gave infinite thanks to our Lord Jesus Christ, because we always thought that for the ill conceit men had of us, we should be condemned to death. From thence so delivered as we were, they led us back to the prison, where the two *chumbims* signed our enlargement in the jailor's book; nevertheless, that we might be altogether discharged, we were to go two months after to serve a year according to our sentence, upon pain of becoming slaves for ever to the king, conformable to his ordinances. Now because we would presently have gone about to demand the alms of good people in the city, the *chifuu*, who was as grand provost of that prison, persuaded us to stay till the next day, that he might first recommend us to the *tanigores* of mercy, that they might do something for us.

Chapter XXXIII. What passed betwixt us and the tanigores of mercy, with the great favours they did us; and a brief relation of the city of Pequin, where the king of China kept his court

THE next morning the four *tanigores* of mercy came to visit the infirmary of this prison, as they used to do; where they rejoiced with us for the good success of our sentence, giving us great testimony how well contented they were with it, for which we returned them many thanks, not without shedding abundance of tears, whereat they seemed to be not a little pleased, and willed us not to be troubled with the term we were condemned to serve in, for they told us that instead of a year we should continue but eight months there, and that the other four months, which made the third part of our punishment, the king remitted it by way of alms for God's sake, in consideration that we were poor, for otherwise if we had been rich, and of ability, we should have had no favour at all,[1] promising to cause this diminution of punishment to be endorsed on our sentence, and besides that they would go and speak to a very honourable man for us, that was appointed to be the chief marshal, or *monteo*, of Quansy, the place where we were to serve, to the end he might show us favour, and cause us to be truly paid for the time we should remain there. Now because this man was naturally a friend to the poor, and inclined to do them

---

[1] This would certainly not have been done in Europe then.

good, they thought it would be fit to carry us along with them to
his house, the rather for that it might be he would take us into his
charge; we gave them all very humble thanks for the good offer of
theirs, and told them that God would reward this charity [1] they
showed us for his sake; whereupon we accompanied them to the
monteo's house, who came forth to receive us in his outward court,
leading his wife by the hand, which he did, either out of a greater
form of compliment, or to do the more honour to the *tanigores*,
and coming near them he prostrated himself at their feet, and said:
'It is now, my lord, and holy brethren, that I have cause to rejoice,
for that it hath pleased God to permit, that you His holy servants
should come unto my house, being that which I could not hope
for, in regard I held myself unworthy of such favour.'

After the *tanigores* had used many compliments and ceremonies
to him, as is usual in that country, they answered him thus: 'May
God, our sovereign Lord, the infinite source of mercy, recompense
the good thou dost for the poor with blessing in this life; for
believe it, dear brother, the strongest staff whereon the soul doth
lean to keep her from falling so often as she happens to stumble,
is the charity which we use towards our neighbour, whenas the
vainglory of this world doth not blind the good zeal whereunto
His holy law doth oblige us, and that thou mayst merit the blessed
felicity of beholding His face, we have brought thee here these
nine Portugals, who are so poor, as none in this kingdom are like
to them; wherefore we pray thee that in the place whither thou art
going now, as *monteo*, thou wilt do for them all that thou thinkest
will be acceptable to the Lord above, in whose behalf we crave
this of thee.'

To this speech the *monteo* and his wife replied in such courteous
and remarkable terms, as we were almost besides ourselves to hear
in what manner they attributed the success of their affairs to the
principal cause of all goodness, even as though they had the light
of faith, or the knowledge of the Christian verity. Hereupon they
withdrew into a chamber, into which we went not, and continued
there about half an hour; then as they were about to take leave
of one another, they commanded us to come in to them, where the
tanigores spake to them again about us, and recommending us unto
them more than before, the *monteo* caused our names to be written
down in a book that lay before him,[2] and said unto us: 'I do this,
because I am not so good a man as to give you something of mine
own, nor so bad as to deprive you of the sweat of your labour,
whereunto the king hath bound you, wherefore even at this instant
you shall begin to get your living, although you do not serve as

---

[1] The Portuguese and Chinese, therefore, felt themselves in agreement as to
the God they worshipped.
[2] As his retainers.

yet, for the desire I have that this may be accounted to me for an
alms, so that now you have nothing to do but to be merry in my
house, where I will give order that you shall be provided of all that
is necessary for you.   Besides this, I will not promise you anything, for the fear I am in of the showing some vanity by my
my promise, and so the devil may make use thereof as of an advantage, to lay hold on me, a matter that often arrives through the
weakness of our nature; [1] wherefore let it suffice you for the present
to know, that I will be mindful of you for the love of these holy
brethren here, who have spoken to me for you.'   The four *tanigores* thereupon taking their leave, gave us four taels, and said
unto us: ' Forget not to render thanks unto God for the good success
you have had in your business, for it would be a grievous sin in
you not to acknowledge so great a grace.'

Thus were we very well entertained in the house of this captain
for the space of two months that we remained there, at the end
whereof we parted from thence, for to go to Quansy, where we
were to make up our time, under the conduct of this captain, who
ever after used us very kindly, and showed us many favours, until
that the Tartars entered into the town, who did a world of mischief
there, as I will more amply declare hereafter.

Before I recount that which happened unto us after we were
embarked with those Chinese that conducted us, and that gave
us great hope of setting us at liberty, I think it not amiss to make a
brief relation here of the city of Pequin, which may truly be
termed the capital of the monarchy of the world, as also of some
particulars I observed there, as well for its arches and policy, as
for that which concerns its extent,[2] its government, the laws of
the country, and the admirable manner of providing for the good
of the whole state, together in what sort they are paid, that serve
in the time of war, according to the ordinances of the kingdom,
and many other things like unto these, though I must needs confess that herein I shall want [3] the best part, namely, wit and capacity
to render a reason in what climate it is situated, and in the height
of how many degrees, which is a matter the learned and curious
most desire to be satisfied in; but my design having never been
other (as I have said heretofore) than to leave this my book unto
my children, that therein they may see [4] the sufferings I have
undergone, it little imports me to write otherwise than I do, that
is, in a gross and rude manner; for I hold it better to treat of these
things in such sort as nature hath taught me, than to use hyperboles,

---

[1] Practically a Christian point of view.
[2] Nearly twenty miles in circumference.
[3] Lack.
[4] In the original, 'therein they may *learn their alphabet* and see . . .'   This
is perhaps Cogan's most serious omission.

and speeches from the purpose, whereby the weakness of my poor
understanding may be made more evident.

Howbeit, since I am obliged to make mention of this matter,
by the promise I have made of it heretofore, I say, that this city,
which we call Paquin and they of the country Pequin, is situated
in the height of forty and one degrees [1] of northerly latitude; the
walls of it are in circuit (by the report of the Chinese themselves,
and as I have read in a little book, treating of the greatness thereof
and entitled *Aquesendoo*, which I brought since along with me into
Portugal [2] thirty large leagues, namely ten long and five broad;
some others hold that it is fifty, namely seventeen in length and
eight in breadth: and forasmuch as they that entreat of it are of
different opinions, in that the one make the extent of it thirty
leagues, as I have said before, and others fifty, I will render a
reason of this doubt, conformable to that which I have seen myself.
It is true, that in the manner it is now built, it is thirty leagues in
circuit, as they say, for it is environed with two rows of strong walls,
where there are a number of towers and bulwarks after our fashion;
but without this circuit, which is of the city itself, there is another
far greater, both in length and breadth, that the Chinese affirm
was anciently all inhabited, but at this present there are only some
boroughs and villages, as also a many of fair houses or castles
about it, amongst the which there are sixteen hundred that have
great advantages over the rest, and are the houses of the proctors
of the sixteen hundred cities and most remarkable towns of the
two-and-thirty kingdoms of this monarchy, who repair unto this
city at the general assembly of the estates, which is held every three
years for the public good.

Without this great enclosure, which (as I have said) is not com-
prehended in the city, there is, in a distance of three leagues broad
and seven long, fourscore thousand tombs of the mandarins,
which are little chapels all gilded within, and compassed about with
balusters of iron and latten, the entries whereinto are through very
rich and sumptuous arches: near to these chapels there are also
very great houses, with gardens and tufted woods of high trees,
as also many inventions of ponds, fountains, and aqueducts;
whereunto may be added, that the walls of the enclosure are on
the inside covered with fine porcelain, and on the vanes are many
lions portrayed in gold, as also in the squares of the steeples,
which are likewise very high, and embellished with pictures. It
hath also five hundred very great palaces, which are called the
houses of the son of the Sun, whither all those retire that have
been hurt in the wars for the service of the king, as also many other

---

[1] More properly forty degrees. But the accuracy is surprising, especially
coming after his sarcasm.
[2] Supposed to be now in the Vatican library

soldiers, who in regard of age or sickness are no longer able to bear arms, and to the end that during the rest of their days they may be exempted from incommodity, each of them receives monthly a certain pay to find himself withal, and to live upon. Now all these men of war, as we learned of the Chinese, are ordinarily a hundred thousand, there being in each of those houses two hundred men according to their report.

We saw also another long street of low houses, where there were four-and-twenty thousand oar-men, belonging to the king's *panoures*; and another of the same structure a good league in length, where fourteen thousand taverners that followed the court dwelt; as also a third street like unto the other two, where live a great number of light women, exempted from the tribute which they of the city pay, for that they are courtesans, whereof the most part had quitted their husbands for to follow the wretched trade; and if for that cause they come to receive any hurt,[1] their husbands are grievously punished for it, because they are there as in a place of freedom, and under the protection of the *tuton* of the court, lord steward of the king's house. In this enclosure do likewise remain all the laundresses, by them called *mainatos*, which wash the linen of the city, who as we were told are above a hundred thousand, and live in this quarter, for that there are divers rivers there, together with a number of wells, and deep pools of water, compassed about with good walls. Within this same enclosure, as the said *Aquesendoo* relates, there are thirteen hundred gallant and very sumptuous houses of religious men and women, who make profession of the four principal laws[2] of those two-and-thirty which are in the empire of China, and it is thought that in some of these houses there are above a thousand persons, besides the servants, that from abroad do furnish them with victuals and other necessary provisions.

We saw also a great many houses, which have fair buildings of a large extent, with spacious enclosures, wherein there are gardens, and very thick woods, full of any kind of game, either for hawking or hunting, that may be desired; and these houses are as it were inns, whither come continually in great number people of all ages and sexes, as to see comedies, plays, combats, bull-baitings, wrestlings, and magnificent feasts, which the *tutons*, *chaems*, *conchalys*, *aytaus*, *bracalons*, *chumbims*, *monteos*, *lanteas*, lords, gentlemen, captains, merchants, and other rich men, do make for to give content to their kindred and friends. These houses are bravely furnished with rich hangings, beds, chairs, and stools, as likewise with huge cupboards of plate, not only of silver, but of

---

[1] That is, by the husbands' revenging themselves on them. 'Se êles por isto lhe fizerem algum mal.'
[2] Piety, austerity, humility, and duty.

gold also; and the attendants that wait at the table are maids ready to be married, very beautiful, and gallantly attired; howbeit, all this is nothing in comparison of the sumptuousness and other magnificences that we saw there. Now the Chinese assured us there were some feasts that lasted ten days after the *carachina*, or Chinese manner, which in regard of the state, pomp, and charge thereof, as well in the attendance of servants and waiters, as in the costly fare of all kind of flesh, fowl, fish, and all delicacies, in music, in sports of hunting and hawking, in plays, comedies, tilts, tourneys, and in shows both of horse and foot, fighting and skirmishing together, do cost above twenty thousand taels. These inns do stand in at least a million of gold, and are maintained by certain companies of very rich merchants who in way of commerce and traffic employ their money therein, whereby it is thought they gain far more than if they should venture it to sea.[1]

It is said also that there is so good and exact an order observed there, that whensoever any one will be at a charge that way, he goes to the *sipatom* of the house, who is the superintendent thereof, and declares unto him what his design is, whereupon he shows him a book, all divided into chapters, which treats of the ordering and sumptuousness of feasts, as also the rates of them, and how they shall be served in, to the end, that he who will be at the charge, may choose which he pleases. This book, called *Pinetoreu*, I have seen, and heard it read, so that I remember how, in the three first chapters thereof, it speaks of the feasts whereunto God is to be invited, and of what price they are; and then it descends to the king of China, of whom it says, that by a special grace of heaven, and right of sovereignty, he hath the government of the whole earth, and of all the kings that inhabit it. After it hath done with the king of China, it speaks of the feasts of the *tutons*, which are the ten sovereign dignities that command over the forty *chaems*, who are as the viceroys of the state. These *tutons* also are termed the beams of the Sun, for, say they, as the king of China is the son of the Sun, so the *tutons*, who represent him, may rightly be termed his beams, for that they proceed from him, even as the rays do from the sun; but setting aside the brutishness of these gentiles, I will only speak of the feast whereunto God is to be invited, which I have seen some to make with much devotion, though for want of faith, their works can do them little good.

[1] The venturing of money only in sea traffic was, of course, one of the principal causes of the Portuguese decline.

Chapter XXXIV. The order which is observed in the feasts that are made in certain inns; and the state which the chaem of the two-and-thirty universities keeps; with certain remarkable things in the city of Pequin

THE first thing whereof mention is made in the preface of that book, which treats of feasts, as I have said before, is the feast that is to be made unto God here upon earth, of which it is spoken in this manner: 'Every feast, how sumptuous soever it be, may be paid for with a price more or less conformable to the bounty of him that makes it, who for all his charge bestowed on it reaps no other recompense than the praise of flatterers and idle persons; wherefore, O my brother,' saith the preface of the said book, 'I counsel thee to employ thy goods in feasting of God in His poor, that is to say, secretly to supply the necessities of good folks, so that they may not perish for want of that which thou hast more than thou needest. Call to mind also the vile matter wherewith thy father engendered thee, and that too, which is far more abject, wherewith thy mother conceived thee, and so thou wilt see how much inferior thou art even to the brute beasts, which without distinction of reason apply themselves to that whereunto they are carried by the flesh; and seeing that in the quality of a man thou wilt invite thy friends, who possibly by to-morrow may not be, to show that thou art good and faithful, invite the poor creatures of God, of whose groans and necessities He like a pitiful father taketh compassion, and promiseth to him that doth them good infinite satisfaction in the house of the Sun, where as an article of faith we hold that His servants shall abide for evermore in eternal happiness.' [1]

After these words and other suchlike, worthy to be observed, the *sipatom*, who, as I told you, is the chief of them that govern this great labyrinth, shows him all the chapters of the book, from one end to the other, and bids him look what manner of men or lords he will invite, what number of guests, and how many days he will have the feast to last; for, addeth he, the kings and *tutons*, at the feasts that are made for them, have so many messes of meat, so many attendants, such furniture, such chambers, such vessels, such plate, such sports, and so many days of hawking and hunting, all which amounts to such a sum of money. Then if he will not bestow so much the *sipatom* shows him in another chapter the feasts which are ordinarily made for the *chaems, aytaus, ponchalys, bracalons, anchacys, conchalys, lanteas,* or for captains and rich

---

[1] This is very similar to Christian precepts. 'The poor creatures of God' is the equivalent of the Russian 'God's poor.'

men, whereas other kind of persons of meaner condition have
nothing else to do but to sit down and fall to on free cost, so that
there are usually fifty or threescore rooms full of men and women
of all sorts.[1]   There are also in other rooms most excellent and
melodious consorts[2] of music, namely of harps, viols, lutes, ban-
dores, cornets, sackbuts, and other instruments which are not in
use amongst us.   If it be a feast of women, as it often falls out to
be, then are the waiters on the table likewise women, or young
damsels, richly attired, who for that they are maids, and endued
with singular beauty, it happens many times that men of extraordinary quality fall in love with them, and do marry them.

Now for a conclusion of that which I have to say of these inns,
of all the money, which is spent upon such feasts, four in the
hundred, whereof the *sipatom* pays the one half and they that make
the feasts the other, is set apart for the entertainment of the table
of the poor, whereunto for God's sake all manner of people are
admitted that will come to it.   Moreover, they are allowed a
chamber and a good bed, but that only for the space of three days,
unless they be women with child, or sick persons, which are not
able to travel; for in that case they are entertained a longer time,
because regard is had unto the people according to the need they
are in.

We saw also in this outward enclosure, which, as I have delivered,
environs all the other city, two-and-thirty great edifices or colleges,
distant about a flight-shot the one from the other, where such as
apply themselves to the study of the two-and-thirty laws, which are
professed in the two-and-thirty kingdoms of this empire, do reside.
Now in each of these colleges, according as we could guess by the
great number of persons that we saw there, there should be above
ten thousand scholars; and indeed the *Aquesendoo*, which is the
book that treats of these things, makes them amount in the whole
to four hundred thousand.   There is likewise, somewhat apart
from the rest, another far greater and fairer edifice, of almost a
league in circuit, where all those that have taken degrees, as well
in their theology as in the laws of the government of this monarchy,
do live.

In this university there is a *chaem*, who commands over all the
heads of the colleges, and is called by a title of eminent dignity,
xileyxitapou, that is to say, lord of all the nobles.   This *chaem*,
for that he is more honourable and of an higher quality than all
the rest, keeps as great a court as any *tuton*; for he hath ordinarily
a guard of three hundred Mogors, four-and-twenty ushers that go

[1] Cogan here omits a sentence detailing the different rooms in the house.
[2] This old word for concert has two senses, that of a body of performers in
ensemble, and the modern one of a performance by a number of players or
singers simultaneously.

with silver maces before him, and six-and-thirty women, which mounted on white ambling nags, trapped with silk and silver, ride playing on certain very harmonious instruments of music, and singing to the tune thereof, make a pleasing consort after their manner. There are also led before him twenty very handsome spare horses, without any other furniture than their cloths of silver tinsel, and with headstalls full of little silver bells, every horse being waited on by six halberdiers and four footmen very well apparelled. Before all this train goes four hundred *huppes*, with a number of great long chains, which, trailing on the ground, make such a dreadful rattling and noise as does not a little terrify all that are within hearing. Then next to them marches twelve men on horseback called *peretandas*, each of them carrying an umbrella of carnation satin, and other twelve that follow them with banners of white damask, deeply indented, and edged about with golden fringe. Now after all this pomp comes the *chaem* sitting in a triumphant chariot, attended by threescore *conchalys*, *chumbims*, and *monteos*, such as amongst us are the chancellors, judges, and counsellors of the courts of justice, and these go all on foot, carrying upon their shoulders scimitars rightly garnished with gold. Last of all follow lesser officers, that are like unto our registers, examiners, auditors, clerks, attorneys, and solicitors, all likewise on foot, and crying out unto the people with a loud voice for to retire themselves into their houses, and clear the streets, so as there may be nothing to hinder or trouble the passage of this magnificence.

But the most observable thing herein is, that close to the person of the *chaem*, march two little boys on horseback, one on the right hand, the other on the left, richly attired, with their ensigns in their hands, signifying justice and mercy, whereof I have spoken heretofore. That on the right side, representing mercy, is clothed in white, and that on the left, representing justice, is apparelled in red; the horses whereon these little boys are mounted have on them foot-cloths of the same colour their garments are, and all their furniture and trappings are of gold, with a kind of net-work over them, made of silver thread. After each of these children march six young youths, about fifteen years of age, with silver maces in their hands, so that all these things together are so remarkable, as there is no man that beholds them, but on the one side trembles for fear, and on the other side remains astonished at the sight of so much greatness and majesty.

Now that I may not longer dwell on that which concerns this great enclosure, I will pass over in silence many other marvels that we saw there, consisting in rich and fair buildings, in magnificent pagodas, in bridges placed upon great pillars of stone on either side whereof are rails or grates of iron, finely wrought, and in highways

that are straight, broad, and all very well paved, whereof I think
fit not to speak, for by that which I have already said, one may
easily judge of what I have omitted, in regard of the resemblance
and conformity that is between them; wherefore I will only entreat,
and that as succinctly as I can, of certain buildings which I saw in
this city, chiefly of four that I observed more curiously than the
rest, as also of some other particularities that well deserve to be
insisted upon.

This city of Pequin, whereof I have promised to speak more
amply than yet I have done, is so prodigious, and the things therein
remarkable, as I do almost repent me for undertaking to discourse
of it, because, to speak the truth, I know not where to begin, that
I may be as good as my word; for one must not imagine it to be
either as the city of Rome, or Constantinople, or Venice, or Paris,
or London, or Seville, or Lisbon, or that any of the cities of Europe
are comparable unto it, how famous or populous soever they be:
nay, I will say further, that one must not think it to be like to
Grand Cairo in Egypt, Tauris in Persia, Amadabad in Cambaya,
Bisnagar in Narsingua, Goura in Bengala, Ava in Chaleu, Tim-
plan in Calaminhan, Martaban and Bagou in Pegu, Guimpel and
Tinlau in Siammon, Odia in the kingdom of Sornau, Passarvan
and Dema in the island of Jaoa, Pangor in the country of the
Lequiens, Usingea in the Grand Cauchin, Lansame in Tartaria,
and Meaco in Japan, all which cities are the capitals of many great
kingdoms; for I dare well affirm, that all those same are not to be
compared to the least part of the wonderful city of Pequin, much
less to the greatness and magnificence of that which is most excellent in it, whereby I understand her stately buildings, her inward
riches, her excessive abundance of all that is necessary for the
entertaining of life, also the world of people, the infinite number of
barques and vessels that are there—the commerce, the courts of
justice, the government and the state of the *tutons, chaems, anchacys, aytaos, ponchalys,* and *bracalons,* who rule whole kingdoms and very spacious provinces, with great pensions, and are
ordinarily resident in this city, or others for them, whenas by the
king's command they are sent about affairs of consequence.

But setting these things aside, whereof yet I intend to speak more
amply when time shall serve, I say that this city (according to
that which is written of it, both in the *Aquesendoo* before mentioned,
and all the chronicles of the kingdom of China) is thirty leagues in
circuit, not comprehending therein the buildings of the other
enclosure that is without it, and is environed with a double wall,
made of good strong freestone, having three hundred and threescore gates, each of which hath a small fort, composed of two high
towers, with its ditches and drawbridges; and at every gate is a
register and four porters with halberds in their hands, who are

bound to give account of all that goes in and out. These gates, by the ordinance of the *tuton*, are divided according to the three hundred and threescore days of the year, so that every day in his turn hath the feast of the invocation of the idol, whereof each gate bears the name, celebrated with much solemnity.

This great city hath also within that large enclosure of her walls, as the Chinese assured us, three thousand and three hundred pagodas or temples, wherein are continually sacrificed a great number of birds and wild beasts, which they hold to be more agreeable unto God than such as are kept tame in houses, whereof their priests render reasons to the people, therewith persuading them to believe so great an abuse for an article of faith. The structures of these pagodas whereof I speak are very sumptuous, especially those of the orders of the *menigrepos, conquiays,* and *talagrepos,* who are the priests of the four sects of Xaca, Amida, Gizom, and Canom, which surpass in antiquity the other two-and-thirty of that labyrinth of the devil, who appears to them many times in divers forms, for to make them give more credit to his impostures and lies.[1] The principal streets of this city are all very long and broad, with fair houses of two or three storeys high, and enclosed at both ends with balusters of iron and latten; the entrance into them is through lanes, that cross these great streets, at the ends whereof are great arches, with strong gates, which are shut in the night, and on the top of the arches there are watch-bells. Each of these streets hath its captain and officers, who walk the round in their turns, and are bound every ten days to make report into the town house of all that passeth in their quarters, to the end that the *ponchalys* or *chaems* of the Government may take such order therein as reason requires.

Moreover this great city (if credit may be given to that which the said book, so often before mentioned by me, records) hath a hundred and twenty canals, made by the kings and people in former times, which are three fathom deep, and twelve broad, crossing through the whole length and breadth of the city, by the means of a great number of bridges, built upon arches of strong freestone, at the end whereof there are pillars, with chains that reach from the one to the other, and resting-places for passengers to repose themselves in: it is said that the bridges of these hundred and twenty canals or aqueducts are in number eighteen hundred and that if one of them is fair and rich, the other is yet more, as well for the fashion as for the rest of the workmanship thereof.

The said book affirms, that in this city there are sixscore piazzas

[1] 'How abundantly do spiritual beings display their powers! They cause all men under heaven to fast and purify themselves, and put on their richest dresses to engage in their sacrifices. Then, like overflowing water, they seem to be over the heads and on the right and left of their worshippers.' (Confucius.)

or public places, in each of the which is a fair kept every month. Now during the two months' time that we were at liberty in this city, we saw eleven or twelve of these fairs, where were an infinite company of people, both on horseback and on foot, that out of boxes hanging about their necks sold all things that well-near can be made, as the haberdashers of small wares do amongst us, besides the ordinary shops of rich merchants, which were ranged very orderly in the particular streets, where was to be seen a world of silk stuffs, tinsels, cloth of gold, linen and cotton cloth, sables, ermines, musk, aloes, fine porcelain, gold and silver plate, pearl, seed pearl, gold in powder, and ingots and such other things of value, whereat we nine Portugals were exceedingly astonished. But if I should speak in particular of all the other commodities that were to be sold there, as of iron, steel, lead, copper, tin, latten, coral, cornelian, crystal, quicksilver, vermilion, ivory, cloves, nutmegs, mace, ginger, tamarinds, cinnamon, pepper, cardamom, borax, honey, wax, sanders, sugar, conserves, acates,[1] fruit, meal, rice, flesh, venison, fish, pulse, and herbs; there was such abundance of them, as it is scarce possible to express it in words.

The Chinese also assured us that this city hath a hundred and threescore butchers' shambles, and in each of them a hundred stalls, full of all kinds of flesh that the earth produceth for that these people feed on all, as veal, mutton, pork, goat, the flesh of horses, buffaloes, rhinoceroses, tigers, lions, dogs, mules, asses,[2] otters, chamois,[3] badgers, and finally of all other beasts whatsoever. Furthermore, besides the weights which are particularly in every shambles, there is not a gate in the city that hath not its scales, wherein the meat is weighed again, for to see if they have their due weight that have bought it, to the end that by this means the people may not be deceived. Besides those ordinary shambles there is not scarce a street but hath five or six butchers' shops in it, where the choicest meat is sold; there are withal many taverns, where excellent fare is always to be had, and cellars full of gammons of bacon, dried tongues, powdered geese, and other savoury viands, for to relish one's drink, all in so great abundance, that it would be very superfluous to say more of it; but what I speak is to show how liberally God hath imparted to these miserable blinded wretches the good things which He hath created on the earth, to the end that His holy name may therefore be blessed for evermore.

[1] Cates, choice dainties.
[2] The wild ass, or onager, whose flesh is held in high esteem by orientals.
[3] More probably, a species of reindeer.

Chapter XXXV. The prison of Xinanguibaleu, wherein those are kept which have been condemned to serve at the reparations of the wall of Tartaria; and another enclosure called the Treasure of the Dead, with the revenues whereof this prison is maintained

DESISTING now from speaking in particular of the great number of the rich and magnificent buildings which we saw in this city of Pequin, I will only insist on some of the edifices thereof, that seemed more remarkable to me than the rest, whence it may be easy to infer what all those might be, whereof I will not make any mention here to avoid prolixity; and of these neither would I speak, were it not that our Lord may one day permit that the Portugal nation, full of valour and of lofty courage, may make use of this relation for the glory of our great God, to the end that by these human means and the assistance of His divine favour, it may make those barbarous people understand the verity of our holy Catholic faith, from which their sins have so far eloigned them, as they mock at all that we say to them thereof. Hereunto I will add that they are extravagant and senseless, as they dare boldly affirm that only with beholding the face of the son of the Sun, which is their king, a soul would be more happy than with all other things of the world besides, which persuades me that if God of His infinite mercy and goodness would grant that the king of the people might become a Christian, it would be an easy matter to convert all his subjects, whereas otherwise I hold it difficult for so much as one to change his belief, and all by reason of the great awe they are in of the law, which they fear and reverence alike, and whereof it is not to be believed how much they cherish the ministers.

But to return to my discourse: the first building which I saw of those that were most remarkable, was a prison, which they call Xinanguibaleu, that is to say, the enclosure of the exiles; the circuit of this prison is two leagues square, or little less, both in length and breadth: it is enclosed with a very high wall without any battlements; the wall on the outside is environed with a great deep ditch full of water, over the which are a many of drawbridges, that are drawn up in the night with certain iron chains, and so hang suspended on huge cast pillars; in this prison is an arch of strong hewed stone abutting in two towers, in the tops whereof are six great sentinel bells, which are never rung but all the rest within the said enclosure do answer them, which the Chinese affirm to be above a hundred, and indeed they make a most horrible din. In this place there are ordinarily three hundred thousand prisoners, between seventeen and fifty, whereat we were much amazed, and indeed we had good cause, in regard it is a thing so unusual and extraordinary.

Now desiring to know of the Chinese the occasion of so marvellous a building, and of the great number of prisoners that were
in it; they answered us that after the king of China, named
Crisnagol Docotay,[1] had finished a wall of three hundred leagues'
space betwixt this kingdom of China and that of Tartaria,[2] as I
have declared otherwhere, he ordained by the advice of his people
(for to that effect he caused an assembly of his estates to be held)
that all those which should be condemned to banishment should
be sent to work in the repairing of this wall, and that after they
had served six years together therein, they might freely depart,
though they were sentenced to serve for a longer time, because the
king pardoned them the remainder of the term by way of charity
and alms; but if during those years they should happen to perform any remarkable act or other thing, wherein it appeared they
had advantage over others, or if they were three times wounded in
the sallies they should make, or if they killed some of their enemies,
they were then to be dispensed with for all the rest of their time,
and that the *chaem* should grant them a certificate thereof, where it
should be declared why he had delivered them, and how he had
thereby satisfied the ordinances of war.   Two hundred and ten
thousand men are to be continually entertained in the work of
the wall, by the first institution, whereof defalcation is made of a
third part, for such are dead, maimed, and delivered, either for
their notable actions, or for that they had accomplished their time:
and likewise whenas the *chaem*, who is as the chief of all those,
sent to the *pitaucamay*, which is the highest court of justice, to
furnish him with that number of men, they could not assemble
them together as soon as was necessary, for that they were divided
in so many several places of that empire, which is prodigiously
great, as I have delivered before, and that withal a long time was
required for the assembling them together, another king, named
Goxiley Aparau, who succeeded to that Crisnagol Docotay, ordained
that the great enclosure should be made in the city of Pequin, to
the end that as soon as any were condemned to the work of this
wall they should be carried to Xinanguibaleu for to be there altogether, by which means they might be sent away without any delay,
as now is done.   So soon as the court of justice hath committed
the prisoners to this prison, whereof he that brings them hath a
certificate, they are immediately left at liberty, so that they may
walk at their pleasure within this great enclosure, having nothing
but a little plate of a span long and four fingers broad, wherein
these words are engraven: 'Such a one of such a place hath been
condemned to the general exile for such a cause; he entered such
a day, such a month, such a year.'   Now the reason why they make
every prisoner to carry this plate for a testimony of their evil

[1] Che-Hwang-te.   [2] Now Mongolia.

actions, is, to manifest for what crime he was condemned, and at what time he entered, because every one goes forth conformably to the length of time that shall be since he entered in. These prisoners are held for duly delivered when they are drawn out of captivity for to go and work at the wall, for they cannot upon any cause whatsoever be exempted from the prison of Xinanguibaleu, and the time they are there is counted to them for nothing, in regard they have no hope of liberty but at that instant when their turn permits them to work in the reparations, for then they may be sure to be delivered, according to the ordinance whereof I have made mention before.

Having now delivered the occasion whereof so great a prison was made, before I leave it I hold it not amiss to speak of a fair which we saw there, of two that are usually kept every year, which those of the country call Gunxineu Apparau Xinanguibaleu, that is to say, the rich fair of the prison of the condemned; These fairs are kept in the months of July and January, with very magnificent feasts, solemnized for the invocation of their idols; and even there they have their plenary indulgences, by means whereof great riches of gold and silver are promised them in the other world. They are both of them frank and free, so as the merchants pay no duties, which is the cause that they flock thither in such great number, as they assured us that there were three millions of persons there; and forasmuch as I said before, that the three hundred thousand that are imprisoned there are at liberty, as well as those that go in and out, you shall see what course they hold to keep the prisoners from getting forth amongst others. Every one that is free and comes in hath a mark set on the wrist of his right arm with a certain confection made of oil, bitumen, lacquer, rhubarb,[1] and alum, which being once dry cannot be any ways defaced, but by the means of vinegar and salt mingled together very hot; and to the end that so great a number of people may be marked, on both sides of the gates stand a many of *chanipatoens*, who with stamps of lead, dipped in this bitumen, imprints a mark on every one that presents himself unto them, and so they let him enter; which is only practised on men, not upon women, because none of that sex are ever condemned to the labour of the wall. When therefore they come to go out of the gates, they must all have their arms bared where this mark is, that the said *chanipatoens*, who are the porters and ministers of this affair, may know them, and let them pass; and if by chance any one be so unhappy as to have that mark defaced by any accident, he must even have patience, and remain with the other prisoners, in regard there is no way to get him out of this place if he be found without that mark. Now those *chanipatoens* are so dextrous and well versed in it, that a

[1] China cultivates the best medicinal rhubarb in the world.

hundred thousand men may in an hour go in and out without
trouble, so that by this means the three hundred thousand prisoners
continue in their captivity, and none of them can slip away amongst
others to get out.

There are in this prison three great enclosures like great towns,
where there are a number of houses, and very long streets, without
any lanes; and at the entrance into each street there are good gates,
with their sentinel bells aloft, together with a *chumbim* and twenty
men for a guard; within a flight-shot of those enclosures are the
lodgings of the *chaem* who commands all this prison, and those
lodgings are composed of a number of fair houses, wherein are
many out-courts, gardens, ponds, halls, and chambers, enriched
with excellent inventions, able to lodge a king at his ease, how great
a court soever he have.   In the two principal of these towns there
are two streets, each of them about a flight-shot long, which
abut upon the *chaem's* lodgings, arched all along with stone, and
covered overhead like the hospital at Lisbon, but that they far
surpass it.   Here are all things to be sold that one can desire, as
well for victual and other kind of provisions, as for all sorts of
merchandise and rich wares.[1]   In those arched streets, which are
very spacious and long, are these two fairs kept every year, whither
such an infinite multitude of people resort, as I have declared
before.   Moreover, within the enclosure of this prison are divers
woods of tall and high trees, with many small streams and ponds
of clear sweet water for the use of the prisoners, and to wash their
linen, as also sundry hermitages and hospitals, together with twelve
very sumptuous and rich monasteries, so that whatsoever is to be
had in a great town may in great abundance be found within the
enclosure, and with advantage in many things, because the most
part of these prisoners have their wives and children there, to whom
the king gives a lodging answerable to the household or family
which each one hath.

The second of those things which I have undertaken to relate
is another enclosure we saw, almost as big as the former, compassed
about with strong walls and great ditches.   This place is called
Muxiparan, which signifies the treasure of the dead, where are
many towers of hewed carved stone, and steeples diversely painted.
The walls on the top are instead of battlements environed with
iron grates, where there are a number of idols of different figures,
as of men, serpents, horses, oxen, elephants, fishes, adders, and
many other monstrous forms of creatures which were never seen,
some of brass, and iron, and others of tin and copper; so that this

---

[1] Cogan omits: 'as goldsmiths or silversmiths and other most rich merchants
who there have their shops, and yet who may not avail themselves of their
riches to leave going to fulfil their sentences when their appointed time shall
arrive.'

infinite company of several figures joined together is one of the most remarkable and pleasantest things that can be imagined.

Having passed over the bridge of the ditch we arrived at a great court that was at the first entrance, enclosed round about with huge gates, and paved all over with white and black stones in chequer work, so polished and bright, as one might see himself in them as in a looking-glass. In the midst of this court was a pillar of jasper six-and-thirty spans high, and as it seemed all of one piece, on the top whereof was an idol of silver in the figure of a woman, which with her hands strangled a serpent that was excellently enamelled with black and green. A little further at the entrance of another gate, which stood between two very high towers, and accompanied with four-and-twenty pillars of huge great stone, there were two figures of men, each of them with an iron club in his hand, as if they had served to guard that passage, being a hundred and forty spans high, with such hideous and ugly visages, as makes them even to tremble that behold them: the Chinese called them *Xixipatou Xalican*, that is to say, the blowers of the house of smoke. At the entering into this gate there were twelve men with halberds and two registers, set at a table, who enrolled all that entered there, unto whom every one paid a matter of a groat: when we were entered within this gate, we met with a very large street, closed on both sides with goodly arches, as well in regard of the workmanship as the rest, round about the which hung an infinite company of little bells of latten, by chains of the same metal, that moved by the air, made such a noise as one could with much ado hear one another. This street might be about half a league long, and within these arches, on both sides of the way, were two rows of low houses, like unto great churches, with steeples all gilt, and divers inventions of painting. Of these houses the Chinese assured us there was in that place three thousand, all which from the very top to the bottom were full of dead men's skulls, a thing so strange, that in every man's judgment a thousand great shops could hardly contain them. Behind these houses, both on the one side and the other, were two great mounts [1] of dead men's bones, reaching far above the ridges of the houses, full as long as the street, and of a mighty breadth. These bones were ordered and disposed one upon another so curiously and aptly, that they seemed to grow there. Having demanded of the Chinese whether any register was kept of these bones, they answered there was, for the *talagrepos*, unto whose charge the administration of these three thousand houses was committed, enrolled them all; and that none of these houses yielded less than two thousand taels revenue out of such lands, as the owners of these bones had bequeathed to them for their souls' health; and that the rent of all

[1] Mounds.

these three thousand houses together amounted unto five millions of gold yearly, whereof the king had four, and the *talagrepos* the other for to defray the expenses of this fabric; and that the four appertained to the king, as their support, who dispensed them in the maintenance of the three hundred thousand prisoners of Xinanguibaleu.

Being amazed at this marvel, we began to go along this street, in the midst whereof we found a great piazza, compassed about with two huge grates of latten, and within it was an adder of brass enfolded into I know not how many boughts,[1] and so big that it contained thirty fathom in circuit, being withal so ugly and dreadful as no words are able to describe it. Some of us would estimate the weight of it, and the least opinions reached to a thousand quintals,[2] were it hollow within, as I believe it was. Now although it was of an unmeasurable greatness, yet was it in every part so well proportioned, as nothing can be amended, whereunto also the workmanship thereof is so correspondent, that all the perfection which can be desired from a good workman is observed in it. This monstrous serpent, which the Chinese call the gluttonous serpent of the house of smoke, had on the top of his head a bowl of iron, two-and-fifty foot in circumference, as if it had been thrown at him from some other place. Twenty paces further was the figure of a man of the same brass in the form of a giant, in like manner very strange and extraordinary, as well for the greatness of the body as the hugeness of the limbs. This monster held an iron bowl just as big as the other aloft in both his hands, and beholding the serpent with a frowning and angry countenance, he seemed as though he would throw this bowl at him. Round about this figure was a number of little idols all gilt on their knees, with their hands lifted up to him, as if they would adore him.

All this great edifice was consecrated to the honour of this idol, called Muchiparon, whom the Chinese affirmed to be the treasurer of all the dead men's bones, and that when the gluttonous serpent before mentioned came to steal them away, he made at him with that bowl which he held in his hands, whereupon the serpent in great fear fled immediately away to the bottom of the profound house of smoke, whither God had precipitated him for his great wickedness; and further that he had maintained a combat with him three thousand years already, and was to continue the same three thousand years more, so that from three thousand to three thousand years he was to employ five bowls wherewith he was to make an end of killing him. Hereunto they added, that as soon as this serpent should be dead, the bones that were there assembled would

[1] Bights, loops.
[2] According to Woodhouse's *Measures, Weights & Moneys* (1881), the Portuguese quintal was equal to 129·516 pounds avoirdupois.

return into the bodies to which they appertained formerly, and so should go and remain for ever in the House of the Moon.   To these brutish opinions they join many others suchlike, unto which they give so much faith, that nothing can be able to remove them from it, for it is the doctrine that is preached unto them by their bonzes, who also tell them that the true way to make a soul happy, is to gather these bones together into this place, by means whereof there is not a day passes but that a thousand or two of these wretches' bones are brought thither.   Now if some for their far distance cannot bring all the bones whole thither, they will at leastwise bring a tooth or two, and so they say that by way of an alms they make as good satisfaction as if they brought all the rest, which is the reason that in all these charnel-houses there is such an infinite multitude of these teeth, that one might lade many ships with them.

We saw in a great plain without the walls of this city another building, very sumptuous and rich, which they call Nacapirau, that is to say, the Queen of Heaven, for it is the opinion of these blinded wretches that our Lord above is married like the kings here below, and that the children which He hath had by the Nacapirau, are the stars we see twinkling in the firmament by night, and that when any exhalation comes to dissolve in the air, they say that it is one of his children that is dead, whereof his other brothers are so grieved, that they shed such abundance of tears as the earth is watered therewith, by which means God provides us of our living, as it were in manner of alms bestowed for the souls of the deceased.   But letting pass these and other such-like fooleries, I will only entreat of such particulars as we observed in this great edifice, whereof the first was one hundred and forty convents of this accursed religion, both of men and women, in each of which there are four hundred persons, amounting in all to six-and-fifty thousand, besides an infinite number of religious servants, that are not obliged to their vow of profession, that are within, who for a mark of their priestly dignity are clothed in violet, with green stoles [1] on them, having their head, beard, and eyebrows shaven, and wearing beads about their necks to pray with, but for all that they crave no alms, by reason they have revenue enough to live on.[2]   The next was an enclosure within this huge building, a league in circuit, the walls whereof were built upon arches, vaults, of strong hewed stone, and underneath them were galleries, environed all about with balusters of latten; within this enclosure at a gate, through which we passed, we saw under most deformed

[1] Portuguese, 'altirnas verdes sobracadas, que são como entre nós as estolas.' Cogan (according to the text of the first edition) has translated 'stars,' but this must surely be a printer's error.

[2] Cogan has omitted a short passage here.   Mendes Pinto tells us that the Tartar king afterwards took possession of the Nacapirau building and had thirty thousand Chinese killed.

figures the two porters of hell, at least they believe so, calling the
one Bacharon, and the other Quagifau, both of them with iron
clubs in their hands, and so hideous and horrible to see to that it
is impossible to behold them without fear.

Having passed this gate under a chain that went across from
the breast of one of these devils to the other, we entered into a very
fair street, both for breadth and length, enclosed at either end
with many arches, diversely painted, on the top whereof were all
along two rows of idols to the number of five thousand. Now
we could not well judge of what matter these idols were made;
howsoever, they were gilt all over, and upon their heads they wore
mitres of sundry inventions. At the end of this street was a great
square place, paved with black and white stone, and compassed
about with four rows of giants in brass, each of them fifteen foot
high, with halberds in their hands, and their hair and beards all
gilt, which was not only a very pleasing object to the eye, but also
represented a kind of majestical greatness. At the end of this
place was Quiay Huyan, the god of rain,[1] which idol was so huge,
that with his head he touched the battlements of the tower, being
above twelve fathom high; he was likewise of brass, and both from
his mouth, head, and breast, at six-and-twenty several places
came out streams of water. Having passed between his legs,
which stood straddling at a great distance one from another, we
entered into a large room, as long as a church, where there were
three aisles set with [2] very big and high pillars of jasper; all along
the walls thereof on both sides were a many of idols, great and
little in divers forms all gilt, sited and disposed in such order as
they took up all the breadth and length of the walls, and seemed at
first sight to be all gold. At the end of this room or temple upon
a round tribunal, whereunto one ascended by fifteen winding stairs,
was an altar, proportionable to the same tribunal, whereon stood the
image of Nacapirau, in the likeness of a very fair woman, with her
hair hanging upon her shoulders, and her hands lifted up to
heaven. Now for that she was gilt all over with fine gold, and
that with a great deal of art and care, she glistened in that manner
as it was impossible to continue looking on her, so dazzled were a
man's eyes with the rays that darted from her. Round about this
tribunal on the first four stairs were the statues of twelve kings of
China in silver, with crowns on their heads and maces on their
shoulders; a little lower were three rows of idols gilt, kneeling on
their knees, and holding up their hands and all about hung a number
of silver candlesticks with seven branches apiece.

[1] Cogan omits the words 'leaning on a staff.'
[2] Cogan has '*ships* set *upon*.' The Portuguese word *nave* certainly means
a ship, but when applied to church architecture, its meaning is 'nave' as
in English.

When we were out of this we went through another street all arched like that by which we entered in, and from this we passed through two other streets full of very stately buildings, and so came to a gate that stood between four high towers, where there was a *chifuu*, with thirty halberdiers, and two registers, which wrote down the names of all that went in and out, as they did ours, and so we gave them about a groat for our passage out.

Chapter XXXVI. Of an edifice, situated in the midst of the river, wherein were the hundred and thirteen chapels of the kings of China,[1] with the public granaries established for the relief of the poor

To give an end to the matter whereof I entreat, which would be infinite if I should recount everything in particular, amongst the great number of marvellous buildings which we saw, the most remarkable to my seeming was an enclosure, seated in the midst of the river of Batampina, containing some league in circuit in an island, and environed with fair hewed stone, which on the outside was about eight-and-thirty foot high above the water, and on the inside even with the ground, being encompassed with two rows of balusters of latten, whereof the outermost were but six foot high, for the commodity of such as would rest themselves there, and the innermost were nine foot high, having six lions of silver standing upon huge bowls, which are the arms of the king of China, as I have said elsewhere. Within the enclosure of these balusters stood in very goodly order a hundred and thirteen chapels after the fashion of bulwarks all round, in each of which was a rich tomb of alabaster, placed with much art upon the heads of two silver serpents, which in regard of the many boughts wherein they were entertained seemed to be snakes, though they had the visages of women, and three horns on their heads, the explication whereof we could not possibly learn. In each of these chapels were thirteen branched candlesticks with seven great lights apiece in them, so that, to compute the whole, the candlesticks of these hundred and thirteen chapels amount to a thousand four hundred thirty and nine.

In the midst of a great place, environed round about with three rows of winding stairs and two ranks of idols, was a very high tower, with five steeples diversely painted, and silver lions on the top of all. Here the Chinese told us were the bones of those hundred and thirteen kings that had been transported thither from these chapels below; and it is the opinion of these brutish people that

[1] The Ming temple was visited twice a year by the emperor ;who there worshipped the spirits of his ancestors.

these bones, which they hold for great relics, do feast one another at every new moon; in regard whereof these barbarians use on that day to offer unto them a great charger full of all kind of fowl, as also rice, beef, pork, sugar, honey, and all other sorts of victual that one can name; wherein their blindness is such, as in recompense of these meats, which the priests take unto themselves, they imagine that all their sins are forgiven them, by way as it were of a plenary indulgence. In this tower likewise we saw an exceeding rich chamber, covered on the inside all over from the top to the bottom with plates of silver. In this chamber were the statues of those hundred and thirteen kings of China all of silver, where in each of them were the bones of each several king enclosed. Now they hold, according as they are made to believe by their priests, that these kings thus assembled together converse every night one with another, and pass away the time in sundry sports, which none is worthy to see but certain bonzes, whom they term *cabizundes*, a title amongst them of the most eminent dignity, such it may be as the cardinals of Rome. To this beastly ignorance the wretches add many other blind tales, which they are assuredly persuaded are very clear and manifest truths. Within this great enclosure we counted in seventeen places three hundred and forty bells of cast metal, namely twenty in each place, which are all rung together on those days of the moon wherein they say these kings do visit and feast one another.

Near to this tower in a very rich chapel, built upon seven-and-thirty pillars of fair hewed stone, was the image of the goddess Amida, made of silver, having her hair of gold, and seated upon a tribunal fourteen steps high, that was all overlaid with fine gold. Her face was very beautiful, and her hands were heaved up towards heaven; at her armpits hung a many of little idols not above half a finger long filed [1] together, whereupon demanding of the Chinese what those meant, they answered us, that after the waters of heaven had overstrode the earth, so that all mankind was drowned by a universal deluge, God seeing that the world would be desolate, and nobody to inhabit it, he sent the goddess Amida, the chief lady of honour to his wife Nacapirau, from the heaven of the moon, that she might repair the loss of drowned mankind, and that then the goddess having set her feet on a land from which the waters were withdrawn, called Calempluy (which was the same island, whereof I have spoken heretofore, in the Strait of Nanquin, where António de Faria went on land, she was changed all into gold, and in that manner standing upright with her face looking up unto heaven, she sweat out at her armpits a great number of children, namely males out of the right, and females out of the left, having no other place about her body whence she might

[1] Threaded.

bring them forth, as other women of the world have, who have sinned, and that for a chastisement of their sin, God by the order of nature hath subjected them to a misery full of corruption and filthiness, for to show how odious unto Him the sin was that had been committed against Him. The goddess Amida having thus brought forth these creatures, which they affirm were thirty-three thousand three hundred thirty and three, two parts of them females, and the other males, for so say they the world was to be repaired, she remained so feeble and faint with this delivery, having nobody to assist her at her need, that she fell down dead in the place, for which cause the moon at that time in memory of this death of hers, whereat she was infinitely grieved, put herself into mourning, which mourning they affirm to be those black spots we ordinarily behold in her face, occasioned indeed by the shadow of the earth, and that when there shall be so many years run out as the goddess Amida brought forth children, which were, as I have delivered, thirty-three thousand three hundred thirty and three, then the moon will put off her mourning, and afterwards be as clear as the day. With these and suchlike fopperies did the Chinese so turmoil us as we could not choose but grieve to consider how much those people, which otherwise are quick of apprehension, and of good understanding, are abused in matter of religion with such evident and manifest untruths.

After we were come out of this great place where we saw all these things, we went unto another temple of religious votaries, very sumptuous and rich, where they told us the mother of the then reigning king, named Nhay Camisama, did abide, but thereunto we were not permitted to enter, because we were strangers. From this place through a street arched all along, we arrived at a quay called Hichario Topileu, where lay a great number of vessels, full of pilgrims from divers kingdoms, which came incessantly on pilgrimage to this temple, for to gain, as they believe, plenary indulgences, which the king of China and the *chaems* of the government do grant unto them, besides many privileges and franchises throughout the whole country, where victuals are given them abundantly and for nothing.

I will not speak of many other temples or pagodas which we saw in this city whilst we were at liberty, for I should never have done to make report of them all; howbeit I may not omit some other particulars, that I hold very fit to be related before I break off this discourse; whereof the first were certain houses, in several parts of this city, called *laginampurs*, that is to say, the school of the poor, wherein fatherless and motherless children that are found in the streets are taught to write and read, as also some trade, whereby they may get their living;[1] and of these houses or schools there are

[1] Cogan has considerably abbreviated the following account.

about some five hundred in this city.   Now if it happen that any
of them through some defect of nature cannot learn a trade, then
have they recourse to some means for to make them get their living
according to each one's incommodity; as for example, if they be
blind they make them labour in turning of handmills; if they be
lame of their feet they cause them to make laces, ribbon, and suchlike manufactures; if they be lame of their hands, then they make
them earn their living by carrying of burdens; but if they be lame
both of feet and hands, so that nature hath wholly deprived them
of means to get their living, then they shut them up in great
convents, where there are a number of persons that pray for the
dead, amongst whom they place them, and so they have their
share of half the offerings that are made there, the priests having
the other half; if they be dumb, then they are shut up in a great
house, where they are maintained with the amerciaments that the
common sort of women, as oyster-wives and suchlike, are condemned in for their scolding and fighting one with another.   As
for old queans [1] that are past the trade, and such of the younger
sort as by the lewd exercise thereof are become diseased with the
pox or other filthy sickness, they are put into other houses where
they are very well looked unto, and furnished abundantly with all
things necessary, at the charge of the other women that are of the
same trade, who thereunto pay a certain sum monthly, and that
not unwillingly, because they know that they shall come to be so
provided for themselves by others, and for the collecting of this
money there are commissioners expressly deputed in several parts
of the city.

There are also other houses much like unto monasteries, where
a great many of young maids, that are orphans, are bred up, and
these houses are maintained at the charge of such women as are
convicted of adultery; for, say they, it is most just, that if there be
one which hath lost herself by her dishonesty, there should be
another that should be maintained by her virtue.   Other places
there are also, where decayed old people are kept at the charge of
lawyers that plead unjust causes, where the parties have no right;
and of judges, that for favouring one more than another, and corrupted with bribes, do not execute justice as they ought to do;
whereby one may see with how much order and policy these
people govern all things.

In the prosecution of my discourse it will not be amiss here to
deliver the marvellous order and policy which the kings of China
observe in furnishing their states abundantly with provisions and
victuals for the relief of the poor people, which may very well
serve for an example of charity and good government to Christian
kingdoms and commonwealths.   Their chronicles report, that a

[1] Prostitutes.

certain king, great-grandfather to him that then reigned in China, named Chausiran-Panagor, very much beloved of his people for his good disposition and virtues, having lost his sight by an accident of sickness, resolved to do some pious work that might be acceptable to God, to which effect he assembled his estates, where he ordained that for the relief of the poor there should be granaries established in all the towns of his kingdom for wheat and rice, that in the time of dearth (which many times happened) the people might have wherewithal to nourish themselves that year, and to that purpose he gave the tenth part of the duties of his kingdom by a grant under his hand, which when he came to sign accordingly with a golden stamp, that he ordinarily used because he was blind, it pleased God to restore him perfectly to his sight again, which he enjoyed still as long as he lived.   By this example, if it were true, it seemed that our Lord Jesus Christ would demonstrate, how acceptable the charity that good men exercise towards the poor is to Him, even though they be gentiles, and without the knowledge of the true religion.   Ever since there have been always a great many of granaries in this monarchy, and that to the number of an hundred and fourteen thousand.   As for the order which the magistrates observe in furnishing them continually with corn, it is such as followeth: A little before reaping-time all the old corn is distributed forth to the inhabitants, as it were by way of love, and that for the term of two months; after this time is expired, they unto whom the old corn was lent return in as much new, and withal six in the hundred over and above for waste, to the end that this store may never fail: but when it falls out to be a dear year, in that case the corn is distributed to the people without taking any gain or interest for it, and that which is given to the poorer sort, who are not able to repay what hath been lent to them, is made good out of the rents which the countries pay to the king as an alms bestowed on them by his special grace.

Touching the king's revenues, which are paid in silver *picos*, they are divided into three parts, whereof the first is for the maintenance of the king and his state, the second for the defence of the provinces, as also for the provisions of magazines and armies, and the third to be laid up and reserved in a treasury that is in this city of Pequin, which the king himself may not touch, unless it be upon occasion for defence of the kingdom, and to oppose the Tartars, Cauchins,[1] and other neighbouring princes, who many times make grievous war upon him.   This treasure is by them called *chidampur*, that is to say, 'the wall of the kingdom,' for they say that by means of this treasure being well employed and carefully managed, the king need lay no impositions upon the people,

---

[1] From Cochin China.

so that they shall not be any ways vexed and oppressed, as it happens in other kingdoms for want of this providence.

Now by this that I have related one may see, how in all the great monarchy the government is so excellent, the laws so exactly observed and every one so ready and careful to put the prince's ordinances in execution, that Father Xavier,[1] having well noted it, was wont to say, that if ever God would grant him the grace to return unto Portugal, he would become a suitor to the king for to peruse over the rules and ordinances of those people, and the manner how they govern both in time of war and peace; adding withal that he did not think the Romans ever ruled so wisely in all the time of their greatest prosperity, and that in matter of policy the Chinese surpassed all other nations of whom the ancients have written.[2]

Chapter XXXVII. The great number of officers and other people which are in the king of China's palace; with our going to Quansy to accomplish the time of our exile and what befell us there

OUT of the fear I am in lest coming to relate in particular all those things which we saw within the large enclosure of this city of Pequin, they that shall chance to read them may call them in question, and not to give occasion also unto detractors, who judging of things according to the little world they have seen, may hold those truths for fables, which mine own eyes have beheld, I will forbear the delivery of many matters that possibly might bring much contentment to more worthy spirits who, not judging of the riches and prosperity of other countries by the poverty and misery of their own, would be well pleased with the relation thereof.   Howbeit, on the other side I have no great cause to blame those who shall not give credit to that which I say, or make any doubt of it, because I must acknowledge that many times when I call to mind the things that mine eyes have seen, I remain confounded therewith, whether it be the grandeurs of this city of Pequin, or the magnificence wherewith this gentile king is served, or the pomp of the *chaems* and *anchacys* of the government or the dread and awe wherein

---

[1] The following passage has been omitted by Cogan for religious reasons: 'The holy Father Xavier, light of his age in all the orient, whose virtues and saintly reputation have made him to be so well known throughout the world that it becomes me not here to speak of him.'
[2] This shows that Xavier agreed with Mendes Pinto in admiring some part of Chinese civilization.   It was Xavier's successors who quarrelled with Mendes Pinto.

all men are of these ministers, or the sumptuousness of their temples and pagodas, together with all the rest that may be there, for within the only enclosure of the king's palace there are above a thousand eunuchs, three thousand women, and twelve thousand men of his guard, unto whom the king gives great entertainment and pensions: also twelve *tutons*, dignities that are sovereign above all others, whom, as I have already declared, the vulgar call 'the beams of the sun.' Under these twelve *tutons*, there are forty *chaems* or viceroys, besides many other inferior dignities, as judges majors, governors, treasurers, admirals, and generals, which they term *anchacys*, *aytaus*, *ponchalys*, *lanteas*, and *chumbims*, whereof there are above five hundred always residing at the court, each of them having at the least two hundred men in his train, which for the most part to strike the greater terror are of divers nations, namely, Mogors, Persians, Corazones,[1] Moems,[2] Calaminhams,[3] Tartars, Cauchins, and some Braamas[4] of Chaleu[5] and Tangou;[6] for in regard of valour, they make no account of the natives, who are of a weak and effeminate complexion, though otherwise I must confess they are exceeding able and ingenious in whatsoever concerneth mechanic trades, tillage, and husbandry; they have withal a great vivacity of spirit, and are exceeding proper and apt for the inventing of very subtle and industrious things. The women are fair and chaste, and more inclined to labour than the men; the country is fertile in victual, and so rich and abounding in all kind of good things, as I cannot sufficiently express it, and such is their blindness as they attribute all those blessings to the only merit of their king and not to the divine Providence, and to the goodness of that sovereign Lord who hath created all things.

From this blindness and incredulity of these people are these great abuses and confused superstitions derived, which are ordinary amongst them, and wherein they observe a world of diabolical ceremonies; for they are so brutish and wicked as to sacrifice human blood, offering it up with divers sorts of perfumes and sweet savours. Moreover, they present their priests with many gifts, upon assurance from these wretches of great blessings in this life, and infinite riches and treasure in the other; to which effects the same priests grant them I know not what certificates, as it were bills of exchange, which the common people call *cuchimiocos*, that after their death they may serve above in heaven to procure for them a recompense of a hundred for one; wherein these miserable creatures are so blinded, that they save the very meat and drink from their own mouths to furnish those accursed priests of Satan with all things necessary, believing that these goodly bills they have from them will assuredly return them that benefit.

[1] Khorassanians.   [2] Perhaps from southern Manchuria or from India.
[3] Arakanese.   [4] Burmese.   [5] Shan.   [6] Perhaps Tongking.

G 586

There are also priests of another sect, called Naustolins, who, contrary to those others, preach and affirm with great oaths, that reasonable creatures live and die like beasts and therefore that they are to make merry and spend their goods jovially whiles life shall last, there being no other after this, as all but fools and ignorants are to believe.

There is another sect, named Trimechau, who are of opinion that so long time as a man shall live in this world, so long shall he remain underground, until at length by the prayers of their priests his soul shall reassume the body of a child of seven days old, wherein he shall live again till he shall grow so strong as to re-enter into the old body, which he had left in the grave, and so be transported into the heaven of the moon, where they say he shall live many years, and in the end be converted into a star, which shall remain fixed above in the firmament for ever.

Another sect there is called Gizom, who believe that only the beasts, in regard of their sufferings and the labour which they endure in this life, shall possess heaven after their death, and not man, that leadeth his life according to the lusts of the flesh, robbing, killing, and committing a world of other offences, by reason whereof, say they, it is not possible for him to be saved, unless at the hour of death he leave all his estate to the pagodas, and to the priests that they may pray for him; whereby one may see that all the intentions of their diabolical sects is not founded but upon a very tyranny, and upon the interests of the bonzes, who are they that preach this pernicious doctrine to the people, and persuaded them with many fables to believe it; in the meantime these things seem so true to these wretches that hear them, as they very willingly give them all their goods, imagining that thereby only they can be saved, and freed from those punishments and fears, wherewithal they threaten them if they do otherwise.

I have spoken here of no more than these three sects, omitting the rest of the two-and-thirty which are followed in this great empire of China, as well because I should never have done (as I have said heretofore) if I would relate them all at large, as for that by these it may be known what the others are, which are nothing better, but in a manner even the very same; wherefore leaving the remedy of such evils and great blindness to the mercy and providence of God unto whom only it appertains, I will pass on to the declarations of the miseries we endured during our exile in the town of Quansy, until such time as we were made slaves by the Tartars, which happened in the year 1544.

We had been now two months and a half in this city of Pequin, whenas on Saturday, the thirteenth of July [1] 1554, we were carried away to the town of Quansy, there to serve all the time that we were

[1] Cogan has 'July,' but it was January, according to Mendes Pinto.

condemned unto. Now as soon as we arrived there, the *chaem* caused us to be brought before him, and after he had asked us some questions, he appointed us to be of the number of fourscore halberdiers, which the king assigned him for his guard; this we took as a special favour from God, both in regard this employment was not very painful, as also because the entertainment was good, and the pay of it better, being assured besides that at the same time we should recover our liberty.[1]

Thus lived we about a month very peaceably, and well contented for that we met with a better fortune than we expected, whenas the devil, seeing how well all we nine agreed together (for all that we had was in common amongst us, and whatsoever misery any one had we shared it with him like true brothers), he so wrought that two of our company fell into a quarrel, which proved very prejudicial to us all. This division sprung from a certain vanity too familiar with the Portugal nation, whereof I can render no other reason, but that they are naturally sensible of anything that touches upon honour. Now see what the difference was: Two of us nine falling by chance in contest about the extraction of the Madureiras and the Fonsecas,[2] for to know which of these two houses was in most esteem at the king of Portugal's court, the matter went so far, that from one word to another they came at length to terms of oyster-wives, saying one to the other, 'Who are you?' and again, 'Who are you?' So that thereupon they suffered themselves to be so transported with choler, that one of them gave the other a great box on the ear, who instantly returned him a blow with his sword, which cut away almost half his cheek; this same feeling himself hurt caught up a halberd, and therewith ran the other through the arm; this disaster begot such part-taking amongst us, as of nine that we were seven of us found ourselves grievously wounded. In the meantime the *chaem* came running in person to this tumult with all the *anchacys* of justice, who laying hold of us gave us presently thirty lashes apiece, which drew more blood from us than our hurts. This done, they shut us up in a dungeon underground, where they kept us six-and-forty days with heavy iron collars about our necks, manacles on our hands, and irons on our legs, so that we suffered exceedingly in this deplorable estate.

This while our business was brought before the king's attorney, who having seen our accusations, and that one of the articles made faith[3] that there were sixteen witnesses against us, he stuck not to say that we were people without the fear or knowledge of God,

---

[1] More correctly, 'gain a further liberty.'
[2] Evidently the surnames of two of the disputants. They are two old Portuguese family names.
[3] Attested.

who did not confess him otherwise with our mouths than as any
wild beast might do if he could speak; [1] that these things pre-
supposed it was to be believed that we were men of blood, of a
language, of a law, of a nation, of a country, and of a kingdom, the
inhabitants whereof wounded and killed one another most cruelly
without any reason or cause, and therefore no other judgment
could be made of us, but that we were the servants of the most
gluttonous serpent of the profound pit of smoke, as appeared by
our works, since they were no better than such as that accursed
serpent had accustomed to do, so that according to the law of
the third book of the will of the son of the Sun, called Nileterau,
we were to be condemned to a banishment from all commerce of
people as a venomous and contagious plague; so that we deserved
to be confined to the mountains of Chabaguay, Sumbor, or Lamau,
whither such as we were used to be exiled, to the end they might
in that place hear the wild beasts howl in the night, which were of
as vile a breed and nature as we.

From this prison we were one morning led to a place, called
by them Pitau Calidan, where the *anchacy* sat in judgment with a
majestical and dreadful greatness. He was accompanied by divers
chumbims, *huppes*, *lanteas*, and *sipatons*, besides a number of other
persons; there each of us had thirty lashes apiece more given us,
and then by public sentence we were removed to another prison,
where we were in better case yet than in that out of which we came,
howbeit for all that we did not a little detest amongst ourselves both
the Fonsecas and the Madureiras, but much more the devil,
that wrought us this mischief. In this prison we continued almost
two months, during which time our stripes were thoroughly
healed, howbeit we were exceedingly afflicted with hunger and
thirst.

At length it pleased God that the *chaem* took compassion of us,
for on a certain day, wherein they use to do works of charity
for the dead, coming to review our sentence he ordained, that in
regard we were strangers, and of a country so far distant from
theirs, as no man had any knowledge of us, nor that there was any
book or writing which made mention of our name, and that none
understood our language; [2] as also that we were accustomed and
even hardened to misery and poverty, which many times puts the
best and most peaceable persons into disorder, and therefore might
well trouble such as made no profession of patience in their
adversities,[3] whence it followed that our discord proceeded rather
from the effects of our misery than from any inclination unto
mutiny and tumult, wherewith the king's attorney charged us;

[1] A terrible condemnation.
[2] They cannot therefore have thought the prisoners came from Siam.
[3] That is, not practising Taoism.

and furthermore representing unto himself what great need there was of men for the ordinary service of the state, and of the officers of justice, for which provision necessarily was to be made, he thought fit that the punishment for the crimes we had committed should in the way of an alms bestowed in the king's name be moderated, and reduced to the whipping which we had twice already had, upon condition nevertheless that we should be detained there as slaves for ever, unless it should please the *tuton* otherwise to ordain of us. This sentence was pronounced against us, and though we shed a many of tears to see ourselves reduced unto this miserable condition wherein we were, yet this seemed not so bad unto us as the former.

After the publication of this decree we were presently drawn out of prison, and tied three and three together, then led to certain iron forges, where we passed six whole months in strange labours and great necessities, being in a manner quite naked, without any bed to lie on, and almost famished. At last after the enduring of so many evils, we fell sick of a lethargy,[1] which was the cause, in regard it was a contagious disease, that they turned us out of doors for to go and seek our living until we became well again. Being thus set at liberty we continued four months sick, and begging the alms of good people from door to door, which was given us but sparingly by reason of the great dearth that then reigned over all the country, so as we were constrained to agree better together, and to promise one another by a solemn oath that we took, to live lovingly for the future as good Christians should do, and that every month one should be chosen from amongst us to be as it were a kind of chief, whom, by the oath we had taken, all the rest of us were to obey as their superior, so that none of us was to dispose of himself, nor do anything without his command or appointment; and those rules were put into writing by us, that they might be the better observed; as indeed God gave us the grace to live ever afterward in good peace and concord, though it were in great pain, and extreme necessity of all things.

We had continued a good while living in peace and tranquillity, according to our forementioned agreement, whenas he, whose lot it was to be our chief that month, named Cristóvão Borralho, considering how necessary it was to seek out some relief for our miseries by all the ways that possibly we could, appointed us to serve weekly two and two together, some in begging up and down the town, some in getting water and dressing our meat, and others in fetching wood from the forest, both for our own use and to sell. Now one day myself and one Gaspar de Meireles being enjoined to go to the forest, we rose betimes in the morning and went forth

---

[1] A form of sleeping sickness, not, however, nearly so fatal as the West African variety.

to perform our charge; and because this Gaspar de Meireles was a pretty musician, playing well on a cittern,[1] whereunto he accorded his voice, which was not bad, being parts that are very agreeable to those people,[2] in regard they employ the most part of their times in [3] the delights of the flesh, they took great pleasure in hearing of him, so as for that purpose they invited him very often to their sports, from whence he never returned without some reward, wherewith we were not a little assisted.

As he and I then were going to the wood, and before we were out of the town, we met by fortune in one of the streets with a great many of people, who full of jollity were carrying a dead corpse to the grave with divers banners and other funeral pomp, in the midst whereof was a consort of music and voices. Now he that had the chief ordering of the funeral, knowing Gaspar de Meireles, made him stay, and putting a cittern into his hands, he said unto him: 'Oblige me, I pray thee, by singing as loud as thou canst, so as thou mayst be heard by this dead man whom we are carrying to burial, for I swear unto thee that he went away very sad for that he was separated from his wife and children, whom he dearly loved all his lifetime.'

Gaspar de Meireles would fain have excused himself, alleging many reasons thereupon to that end, but so far was the governor of the funeral from accepting them, that contrarily he answered him very angrily: 'Truly, if thou wilt not deign to benefit this defunct with the gift that God hath given thee, of singing and playing on this instrument, I will no longer say that thou art a holy man,[4] as we all believed hitherto, but that the excellency of that voice which thou hast comes from the inhabitants of the house of smoke, whose nature it was at first to sing very harmoniously, though now they weep and wail in the profound lake of the night, like hunger-starved dogs that gnashing their teeth and foaming with rage against men, discharge the froth of their malice by the offences which they commit against Him that lives in the highest of the heavens.' After this ten or eleven of them were so earnest with Gaspar de Meireles, as they made him play almost by force, and led him to the place where the deceased was to be burnt, according to the custom of those gentiles.

In the meantime, seeing myself left alone without my comrade, I went along to the forest for to get some wood according to my commission, and about evening returning back with my load on my back I met with an old man in a black damask gown furred

[1] Portuguese, *viola* (viol).
[2] Popular Portuguese music in those days (like popular southern Spanish music to-day) was Moorish in origin, and therefore in the oriental tradition.
[3] Cogan omits 'banquets.'
[4] That is, that his gift was of God.

clean through with white lamb, who being all alone, as soon as he espied me, he turned a little out of the way, but perceiving me to pass on without regarding him, he cried [1] so loud to me that I might hear him, which I no sooner did, but casting my eye that way, I observed that he beckoned to me with his hand, as if he called me, whereupon imagining there was something more than ordinary herein, I said unto him in the Chinese language: 'Potau-quinay?' which is, 'Dost thou call me?' whereunto returning no answer, he gave me to understand by signs that in effect he called me; conjecturing then that there might be some thieves thereabouts, which would bereave me of my load of wood, I threw it on the ground to be the better able to defend myself, and with my staff in my hand, I went fair and softly after him, who seeing me follow him began to double his pace athwart a little path, which confirmed me in the belief I had before that he was some thief, so that turning back to the place where I left my load, I got it up again on my back as speedily as I could, with a purpose to get into the great highway that led unto the city.   But the man, guessing at my intention, began to cry out [2] louder to me than before, which making me turn my look towards him, I presently perceived him on his knees, and showing me afar off a silver cross about a span long, or thereabout, lifting up withal both his hands unto heaven; whereat being much amazed, I could not imagine what this man should be.   In the meantime he with a very pitiful gesture ceased not to make signs unto me to come to him; whereupon somewhat recollecting myself, I resolved to go and see who he was, and what he would have, to which end with my staff in my hand I walked towards him, where he stayed for me.   Whenas then I came near him, having always thought him before to be a Chinese, I wondered to see him cast himself at my feet, and with tears and sighs to say thus unto me: 'Blessed and praised be the sweet name of our Lord Jesus Christ, who after so long an exile hath showed me so much grace, as to let me see a Christian man, that professeth the law of my God fixed on the cross.'

I must confess that when I heard so extraordinary a matter, and so far beyond my expectation, I was therewith so surprised that scarcely knowing what I said, 'I conjure thee,' answered I unto him, 'in the name of our Lord Jesus to tell me who thou art.' At these words this unknown man, redoubling his tears, 'Dear brother,' replied he, 'I am a poor Christian, by nation a Portugal, and named Vasco Calvo, brother to Diogo Calvo, who was some-time captain of Dom Nuno Manoel his ship, and made a slave here in this country about seven-and-twenty years since, together with one Tomé Pires, whom Lopo Soares sent as ambassador into

---

[1] In the original, 'he spat.'   A Portuguese spit is very noisy.
[2] Again, 'spit.'

this kingdom of China, and that since died miserably by the occasion of a Portugal captain.' Whereupon coming thoroughly to myself again, I lifted him up from the ground where he lay weeping like a child; and shedding no fewer tears than he, I entreated him that we might sit down together, which he would hardly grant, so desirous he was to have me go presently with him to his house, but sitting down by me he began to discourse the whole success [1] of his travels, and all that had befallen him since his departure from Portugal, till that very time, as also the death of the ambassador Tomé Pires, and of all the rest, whom Fernão Peres de Andrada had left at Canton to go to the king of China, which he recounted in another manner than our historians have delivered it.

After we had spent the remainder of the day in entertaining one another with our past adventures, we went to the city, where having showed me his house, he desired me that I would instantly go and fetch the rest of my fellows, which accordingly I did, and found them all together in the poor lodging where we lay, and having declared unto them what had befallen me, they were much abashed at it, as indeed they had cause, considering the stratagems of the accident, so they went presently along with me to Vasco Calvo's house, who waiting for us, gave us such hearty welcome, as we could not choose but weep for joy. Then he carried us into a chamber where was his wife,[2] with two little boys and two girls of his; she entertained us very kindly, and with as much demonstration of love as if she had been the mother or daughter to either of us. After this we sat down at the table, which he had caused to be covered, and made a very good meal of many several dishes provided for us.[3]

Supper done, his wife arose very courteously from the table, and taking a key which hung at her girdle, she opened the door of an oratory, where there was an altar, with a silver cross, as also two candlesticks, and a lamp of the same, and then she and her four children falling down on their knees, with their hands lift up to heaven, began to pronounce these words very distinctly in the Portugal tongue: 'O thou true God, we wretched sinners do confess before thy Cross, like good Christians, as we are, the most sacred Trinity, Father, Son, and Holy Ghost, three Persons and one God; and also we promise to live and die in Thy most holy Catholic faith, like good and true Christians, confessing and believing so much of Thy holy truth as is held and believed by thy Church. In like manner we offer up unto Thee our souls, which Thou hast redeemed with Thy most precious blood, for

---

[1] Succession.
[2] She must certainly have been Chinese, like Inês de Leiria's mother.
[3] Cogan omits the words, 'at which we had much ado to keep from weeping.'

to be wholly employed in Thy service all the time of our lives, and then to be yielded unto Thee at the hour of our death, as to our Lord and God, unto whom we acknowledge they appertain both by creation and redemption.' After this confession they said the Lord's Prayer and the Creed,[1] which they pronounced very distinctly, whereat we could not choose but shed a world of tears to see these innocents, born in a country so far remote from ours, and where there was no knowledge of the true God, thus to confess his law in such religious terms. This being done, we returned, because it was three of the clock in the morning, to our lodging, exceedingly astonished at that we had seen, as at a thing which we had great reason to admire.

Chapter XXXVIII. A Tartar commander enters with his army into the town of Quansay, and that which followed thereupon; with the nauticor's besieging the castle of Nixiamcoo, and the taking of it by the means of some of us Portugals

We had been now eight months and a half in this captivity, wherein we endured much misery and many incommodities, for that we had nothing to live upon but what we got by begging up and down the town, whenas one Wednesday, the third of July in the year 1544, a little after midnight there was such a hurly-burly amongst the people, that to hear the noise [2] and cries which were made in every part, one would have thought the earth would have come over and over, which caused us to go in haste to Vasco Calvo his house, of whom we demanded the occasion of so great a tumult, whereunto with tears in his eyes he answered us, that certain news were come how the king of Tartary was fallen upon the city of Pequin with so great an army, as the like had never been seen since Adam's time. In this army, according to report, were seven-and-twenty kings, under whom marched eighteen hundred thousand men, whereof six hundred thousand were horse, which were come by land from the cities of Lansame, Fanistor, and Mecuy, with fourscore thousand rhinoceroses [3] that draw the waggons, wherein

---

[1] Cogan again omits the Ave Maria and Salve Regina.
[2] Cogan omits 'ringing of bells.'
[3] ' In some parts of the continent of Asia, where the natives are more desirous of appearing warlike than showing themselves brave, these animals are tamed, and led into the field to strike terror into the enemy; but they are always unmanageable and restive animals, and probably more dangerous to the employers, than those whom they are brought to oppose.'—Goldsmith's *Animated Nature*, III. xi.

was all the baggage of the army; as for the other twelve hundred
thousand, which were foot, it was said that they arrived by sea
in seventeen thousand vessels, down through the river of Batampina; by reason whereof the king of China, finding himself too
weak for the resisting of such great forces, had with a few retired
himself to the city of Nanquin.   And that also it was reported
for a certain, that a *nauticor*, one of the chiefest Tartar commanders,
was come to the forest of Manicataran,[1] not above a league and
a half from Quinsay, with an army of threescore and two thousand
horse, wherewith he marched against the town, that in all likelihood he would be there within two hours at the furthest.

These news so troubled us that we did nothing but look one
upon another, without being able to speak a word to any purpose;
howbeit, desiring to save ourselves, we prayed Vasco Calvo to
show us what means he thought we might use to effect it, who sad
and full of grief thus answered us: 'O that we were in our country
between Laura and Carucha,[2] where I have often been, and should
be there now in safety, but since it cannot be so, all that we can do
for the present is to recommend ourselves to God, and to pray
unto Him to assist us; for I assure you that an hour ago I would
have given a thousand taels in silver to any one that could have got
me from hence, and saved me with my wife and children, but there
was no possibility for it, because the gates were then all shut up,
and the walls round about environed with armed men, which the
chaem hath placed there to withstand the enemy.'   So my fellows
and I, that were nine in number, passed the rest of the night there
in much affliction and unquietness, without any means of counsel-
ling one another, or resolving on what we were to do, continually
weeping for the extreme fear we were in of what should become
of us.

The next morning a little before sunrising the enemy appeared
in a most dreadful manner; they were divided into seven very
great battalions, having their ensigns quartered with green and
white, which are the colours of the king of Tartaria; marching in
this order to the sound of their trumpets, they arrived at a pagoda
called Petilau Namejoo, a place of good receipt,[3] in regard of the
many lodgings it had, which was not much distant from the walls.
In their vanguard they had a number of light horse, who ran con-
fusedly up and down with their lances in their rests.   Being in
this sort come to see the pagoda, they stayed there about half an
hour, and then marching on till they were within a harquebus-
shot of the walls, they suddenly ran to them with such hideous

[1] Near the Maling mountains.
[2] Vasco Calvo was referring to places in the woods near Quansy and not to
towns in Portugal, as Cogan seems to imagine.
[3] Providing good accommodation.

cries, as one would have thought that heaven and earth would have
come together, and rearing up above two thousand ladders, which
for that purpose they had brought along with them, they assaulted
the town on every side with a most invincible courage.   Now
though the besieged at the beginning made some resistance, yet
was it not able to hinder the enemy from effecting his design, for
by the means of certain iron rams breaking up the four principal
gates, they rendered themselves masters of the town after they had
slain the *chaem*, together with a great number of mandarins and
gentlemen that were run thither to keep them from entering.
Thus did these barbarians possess themselves of this miserable
town, whereof they put all the inhabitants they could meet withal
to the sword, without sparing any; and it was said that the number
of the slain amounted to threescore thousand persons, amongst
whom were many women and maids of very great beauty, which
appertained to the chiefest lords of the place.

After the bloody massacre of so much people, and that the town
was fired, the principal houses overthrown, and the most sumptuous
temples laid level with the ground, nothing remaining on foot
during[1] the disorder, the Tartars continued there seven days, at
the end whereof they returned towards Pequin, where their king
was, and from whence he had sent them to this execution, carrying
with them a world of gold and silver only, having burnt all the
merchandise they found there, as well because they knew not how
to transport it away, as for that the Chinese should not make any
benefit of it.   Two days after their departure they arrived at a
castle, named Nixiamcoo, where the *nauticor* of Lansame, their
general, pitched his camp and entrenched himself on all sides with
an intention to take it by assault the next day to be revenged on the
Chinese there, for that upon his passing by there towards Quansay,
they had cut off a hundred of his men by an ambuscade.

After the army was encamped and entrenched, and that the
general had placed sure guards and sentinels in all places, he retired
to his tent, whither he sent for the seventy captains that commanded his army, unto whom upon their arrival he discovered his
resolution, which being well approved of they fell into deliberation
in what manner the castle should be assaulted the day following,
which concluded on, the next morning as soon as it was light the
soldiers began to march towards the castle, divided into fourteen
battalions.   Being come within a flight-shot of it, with the sound
of trumpets and most hideous cries, they reared up their ladders
against the walls, and courageously mounted up; but in the heat
of this assault, where every one showed his valour, the one in
bravely attempting, and the other in well defending, the Tartar
in less than two hours lost above three thousand of his men, which

[1] This is a mistranslation for 'nothing being left standing after.'

made him sound a retreat in great disorder, and he passed the rest
of that day in burying the dead and curing of the wounded,
whereof, there being a great number, the most part died not long
after, for that the arrows wherewith they were hurt had been
smeared by the Chinese with so strange and deadly poison, as
there was no remedy to be found for it.   In the meantime the
Tartar commanders seeing the ill success of this assault, and fearing
the king would be offended at so great a loss for so small an occasion, persuaded the general to call another council, wherein it
might be considered, whether it would be most expedient for the
king's honour to persist in the siege of that place, or to give it over,
whereupon this affair coming accordingly into deliberation it was
a long time debated with such diversity of opinions, as they were
not able to conclude upon anything, so that it was thought fit,
in regard it was then late, to put off the assembly till the next day.
This resolution taken, every man retired to his quarter.

   Now we being led away amidst a great many of other slaves,
with whom we had escaped out of the fire of the town, it fell out,
whether for our good or for our greater misfortune, we could not
then tell, that we were under the guard, as prisoners of war, of
one of that assembly, a rich and honourable man, who returning
to his tent with three other persons of like quality to himself,
whom he had invited to supper, it chanced after they were risen
from table that one of them espied us, where we stood chained in
a corner of the tent, and perceiving us to weep [1] was so moved that
he demanded of us what people we were, what the name of our
country was, and how we came to be slaves to the Chinese; whereunto we gave such an answer, as the Tartar, engaging himself
further in this discourse, inquired of us whether our king was
inclined to the wars, and whether we did use to fight in our country;
to whom one of our companions, named Jorge Mendes, replied
that we did, and that we had been trained up from our infancy in
a military course of life; which so pleased the Tartar, that calling
his two friends unto him, ' Come hither,' said he, ' and have the
patience to hear what these prisoners can say; for believe me, they
seem to be men of understanding'; whereupon the other two came
near, and hearing us relate some part of our misfortunes, it begat
a desire in them to ask us other questions, wherein having satisfied
them the best that we could, one of them that seemed more curious
than the rest, addressing himself to Jorge Mendes spake thus:
' Since you have seen so much of the world as you say, if there were
a one amongst you that could find out any device or stratagem of
war, whereby the *mitaquer* (for so was the *nauticor* called) might
take this castle, I vow to you that he would become your prisoner,
whereas you are his.'   Then Jorge Mendes, never considering

   [1] Mistranslation.   'Perceiving us to understand him.'

with what imprudence he spoke, nor understanding what he said, nor into what danger he was putting himself, boldly answered him: 'If my lord *mitaquer* will in the name of the king give it us under his hand that we shall have a safe conduct to convey us by sea to the isle of Ainan,[1] from whence we may freely return into our country, possibly I may be the man that will show him how he shall take the castle with little ado.' This speech being heard and maturely considered by one of the three, a man in years and of great authority, as having the honour to be much esteemed and beloved of the *mitaquer*, 'Think well of what thou sayest,' replied he to Jorge Mendes, 'for I assure thee if thou doest it, that whatsoever thou demandest shall be granted thee, aye, and more too.'

Hereupon the rest of us seeing what Jorge Mendes was going to undertake, as also how far he engaged himself in his promise, and that the Tartars began already to ground some hope thereupon, we thought fit to reprehend him for it, and to tell him that he was not to hazard himself so at random by promising a thing that might bring us into the danger of our lives. 'I fear nothing less,' said he unto us, 'for as for my life, in the estate where now I am, I make so little account of it, that if any of these barbarians would play for it at primero,[2] I would with three of the worst cards in the pack venture it upon the first encounter; for I am confident that all the benefit they can expect from us will never oblige them to grant us either life or liberty,[3] so that for my particular I had as lief die to-day as to-morrow; judge you only by that which you saw them do at Quansay, whether you are likely to be better dealt withal now.'

The Tartars were much abashed to see us thus in contestation one with another, and to hear us talk so loud, which is not usual amongst them, wherefore they reprehended us very seriously, saying, that it was for women to speak aloud, who could not put a bridle to their tongue, nor a key to their mouths, and not for men, that carry a sword and are made for the wars.[4] Howbeit, if it were so that Jorge Mendes could execute what he had propounded, the *mitaquer* could not refuse him anything he could demand. This said, the Tartars retired every one to his lodging, for that it was eleven of the clock at night, the first watch being newly past, and the captains of the guard beginning then to walk the round about the camp at the sound of divers instruments, as is the custom in semblable occasions.

[1] Hai-nan.

[2] A gambling card game, popular in the sixteenth and seventeenth centuries.

[3] Unwarrantably free. 'For it is clearly to be perceived that these are not people to give us our lives against the ransom they hope for for us like the Moors in Africa.'

[4] Even the Tartars have something for which to reprove their European prisoners.

The same of the three Tartar commanders which I said before was so esteemed of by the *mitaquer*, had no sooner learnt of Jorge Mendes that he could tell how to take the castle of Nixiamcoo, but that he went presently to acquaint the general with it, and making the matter greater than it was, he told him that he could do no less than send for him to hear his reasons, which peradventure would persuade him to give credit unto him, and in case it proved not so, yet was there nothing lost thereby. The *mitaquer* being well pleased with this advice, sent incontinently a command to the *tileymay*, which was the captain under whose guard we were, for to bring us unto him, as presently he did.

Being then arrived, chained as we were, at the *mitaquer's* tent, we found him set in council with the seventy commanders of the army about two hours after midnight. At our coming he received us with an affable countenance, yet grave and severe, and causing us to approach nearer unto him, he commanded part of our chains to be undone, then asked us if we would eat, whereunto we answered most willingly, for that in three days together we had not so much as tasted a bit of anything, whereat the *mitaquer* was very much offended, and sharply reproving the *tileymay* for it, willed two great platters of sodden rice and ducks cut in small pieces to be set before us, whereto we fell with such an appetite, like men that were almost famished, as those of the company, who took great pleasure to see us feed so, said to the *mitaquer*: 'Whenas you had nothing else, my lord, but to cause these to come before you for to slack their hunger, verily you had done very much for them, by saving them from a languishing death, which otherwise they could not have avoided, and so you might have lost these slaves, of whom the service or sale might have been some way profitable unto you, for if you will not make use of them at Lansame, you may sell them for a thousand taels at least.'

Hereat some began to laugh, but the *mitaquer* commanded more rice to be given us, together with some apples and other things, conjuring us again to eat, as a thing which he took pleasure to see us do, wherein we most willingly gave him satisfaction. After we had fed well, he began to talk with Jorge Mendes about that which had been told him of him, and of the means that were to be used for taking the castle, making him many great promises of honours, pensions, favour with the king, and liberty for all the rest of his fellows, with other such offers, as passed all measure; for he swore unto him that if by his means God should give him the victory, whereby he sought nothing but to be revenged on his enemies for the blood which they had shed of his men, he should every way be like unto himself, or at least to any of his children whichsoever. Herewith Jorge Mendes found himself somewhat perplexed, because he held it almost impossible for him to bring it to effect;

howsoever he told him, that not to hold him longer in hand,[1] he did not think but if he might view the castle with his own eyes, he might then peradventure let him know how it might be taken, wherefore if his lordship pleased, he would the next morning consider it all about, and thereupon render him an account what course was to be taken therein. The *mitaquer*, and all the rest, allowed very well of his answer, and greatly commending him for it, sent us to be lodged in a tent not far from his, where we spent the rest of the night under a sure guard. You may judge now in what fear we were, knowing that if the business did not succeed according to the desire of these barbarians, they would cut us all in pieces, for that they were a people which for never so small a matter would not stick to kill twenty or thirty men, without any regard either of God or anything else.

The next morning about eight of the clock, Jorge Mendes and two of us that were appointed to accompany him went to survey the place with thirty horse for our safeguard. Whenas Jorge Mendes had well observed the situation thereof, as also that part whereby it might most commodiously be assaulted, he returned to the *mitaquer*, that expected him with impatience, to whom he gave an account of what he had seen, and facilitated the taking of the castle with little hazard, whereat the *mitaquer* was so over-joyed that he presently caused the rest of our irons, and the chains wherewith we were fastened by the neck and feet, to be taken off, swearing to us by the rice he did eat, that as soon as he came to Pequin, he would present us to the king and infallibly accomplish all that he had promised us, for the more assurance whereof he confirmed it by a deed under his hand, that was written in letters of gold, to make it more authentical. That done, he sent for us to dinner, and would needs have us to sit with him at table, doing us many other honours according to their manner, which greatly contented us, but on the other side we were in no little fear, lest this affair should not for our sins have a success answerable to that hope the *mitaquer* had already conceived of it. The rest of this day the commanders spent in resolving upon the order that was to be observed for assaulting the castle, wherein Jorge Mendes was the sole director.

First of all, then, an infinite company of bavins [2] and faggots was gotten together for to fill up the ditches; there were also three hundred ladders made, very strong, and so large, that three men might easily mount up on them afront without encumbering one another; likewise there was a world of panniers, dossers,[3] and baskets provided, together with a great multitude of mattocks and

[1] Keep him longer in suspense.
[2] Fascines, long cylindrical faggots used for filling up ditches, etc.
[3] A dosser or dorser is a kind of pannier.

spades, that were found in the villages and boroughs thereabout, which the inhabitants had deserted upon the bruit of this war, and all the soldiers of the army made preparation of such things as they should need the next day when the assault was to be given. In the meantime Jorge Mendes rode always by the *mitaquer's* side, who showed him many great favours, which we perceived had begotten in him a stately carriage, far different from that he was wont to have, whereat we wondering some of us (who envious of another's good fortune, and out of an ill nature [1]), could not choose but murmur, saying one to another, as it were in disdain, and in a kind of jeering: 'What think you of this dog? Verily, he will be the cause that either to-morrow morning we shall be all cut in pieces, or if the business he hath undertaken succeed as we desire, it is probable that he will be in such credit with these barbarians, that we shall account it for a happiness to be his servants'; [2] and this was the talk which we had amongst us.

The next day all the army was put into order, and divided into twelve battalions, whereof they made twelve files, and one counter-file in the vanguard that encompassed the whole camp in manner of a half moon: upon the wings were the foremost with all that mass of bavins, ladders, baskets, mattocks, spades, and other materials to fill up the ditch and make it equal with the rest of the ground. Marching in this manner they arrived at the castle, which they found strongly manned, and with a number of flags and streamers waving upon the battlements.

The first salutation between the besiegers and the besieged was with arrows, darts, stones, and pots of wild-fire,[3] which continued about half an hour, then the Tartars presently filled the ditch with bavins and earth and so reared up their ladders against the wall, that now, by reason of the filling up of the ditch, was not very high. The first that mounted up was Jorge Mendes, accompanied with two of ours, who as men resolved had set up their rest,[4] either to die there, or to render their valour remarkable by some memorable act, as in effect it pleased our Lord that their resolution had a good success, for they not only entered first, but also planted the first colours upon the wall, whereat the *mitaquer*, and all that were with him, were so amazed, as they said one to another: 'Doubtless if these people did besiege Pequin as we do, the Chinese which defend that city would sooner lose their honour than we shall make them to do it with all the forces we have.' In the meantime all the

[1] A more correct translation of this parenthesis would be: 'for our ill nature is ever envious of another's good fortune.'

[2] The words 'all our lives' have been omitted.

[3] First used by the Greeks of the Byzantine Empire. Probably its ingredients were nitre, sulphur, and naphtha.

[4] To set up one's rest was a term used in the game of primero, meaning to venture one's final stake.

Tartars that were at the foot of the ladders followed the three Portugals, and carried themselves so valiantly, what with the example of a captain that had showed them the way, as out of their own natural disposition, almost as resolute as those of Japan, that in a very short space above five thousand of them were got upon the walls, from whence with great violence they made the Chinese to retire; whereupon so furious and bloody a fight ensued between either party, that in less than half an hour the business was fully decided, and the castle taken, with the death of two thousand Chinese and Mogors that were in it, there being not above sixscore of the Tartars slain.   That done, the gates being opened, the *mitaquer*, with great acclamations of joy, entered, and causing the Chinese colours to be taken down, and his own to be advanced in their places, he with a new ceremony of rejoicing at the sound of many instruments of war, after the manner of the Tartars, gave rewards to the wounded, and made divers of the most valiant of his followers knights, by putting bracelets of gold about their right arms; and then about noon he with the chief commanders of his army, for the greater triumph, dined in the castle, where he also bestowed bracelets of gold upon Jorge Mendes and the other Portugals, whom he made to sit down at table with him.

After the cloth was taken away, he went out of the castle with all his company, and then causing all the walls of it to be dismantled, he razed the place quite to the ground, setting on fire all that remained with a number of ceremonies which was performed with great cries and acclamations to the sound of divers instruments of war.   Moreover, he commanded the ruins of this castle to be sprinkled with the blood of his enemies, and the heads of all of them that lay dead there to be cut off; [1] as for his own soldiers that were slain, he caused them to be triumphantly buried, and such as were hurt to be carefully looked unto; this done, he retired, with a huge train and in great pomp, to his tent, having Jorge Mendes close by him on horseback.   As for the other eight of us, together with many brave noblemen and captains, we followed him on foot. Being at his tent, which was richly hung, he sent Jorge Mendes a thousand taels for a reward, and to us but a hundred apiece, whereat some of us, that thought themselves to be better qualified, were very much discontented, for that he was more respected than they by whose means, as well as his, the enterprise had been so happily achieved, [2] though by the good success thereof we had all obtained honour and liberty.

[1] Thus destruction was sown in the ruins and the bodies rendered useless as habitations for spirits.
[2] A mistranslation.   The passage should run, 'for that he, by whose means the enterprise had been so happily achieved, was more respected than they.'

*Chapter XXXIX. The mitaquer departs from the castle of Nixi-
amcoo, and goes to the king of Tartary's camp before Pequin;
with that which we saw till we arrived there; and the mitaquer's
presenting us unto the king*

THE next day the *mitaquer*, having nothing more to do where he
was, resolved to take his way towards the city of Pequin, before
which the king lay, as I have delivered before; to this effect, having
put his army into battle array, he departed from thence at eight of
the clock in the morning, and marching leisurely to the sound
of his warlike instruments, he made his first station about noon
upon the bank of a river, whose situation was very pleasant, being
all about environed with a world of fruit trees, and a many goodly
houses, but wholly deserted, and bereaved of all things which
the barbarians might anyway have made booty of. Having
passed the greatest heat of the day there, he arose and marched
on until about an hour in the night [1] that he took up his lodging
at a pretty good town, called Lautimey, which likewise we found
deserted, for all this whole country was quite dispeopled for fear
of the barbarians, who spared no kind of person, but wheresoever
they came put all to fire and sword, as the next day they did by
this place, and many other along this river, which they burnt down
to the ground; and that which yet was more lamentable, they set
on fire and clean consumed to ashes a great large plain, being
above six leagues about, and full of corn ready to be reaped.
This cruelty executed, the army began again to move, composed
as it was of some threescore and five thousand horse (for as touching
the rest they were all slain, as well at the taking of Quansay, as in
that of the castle of Nixiamcoo), and went on to a mountain, named
Pommitay, where they remained that night; the next morning
dislodging from thence, they marched on somewhat faster than
before, that they might arrive by day at the city of Pequin, which
was distant about seven leagues from that mountain.

At three of the clock in the afternoon we came to the river of
Palamxitau, where a Tartar captain, accompanied with a hundred
horse, came to receive us, having waited there two days for that
purpose. The first thing that he did was the delivering of a letter
from the king to our general, who received it with a great deal of
ceremony. From this river to the king's quarter, which might be
some two leagues, the army marched without order as being unable
to do otherwise, partly as well in regard of the great concourse of
people, wherewith the ways were full in coming to see the general's
arrival, as for the great train which the lords brought along with
them, that overspread all the fields.

[1] An hour after nightfall. The original Portuguese says 'half an hour.'

In this order, or rather disorder, we arrived at the castle of
Lautir, which was the first fort of nine that the camp had for the
retreat of the spies:[1] there we found a young prince, whom the
Tartar had sent thither to accompany the general, who alighting
from his horse, took his scimitar from his side and on his knees
offered it unto him, after he had kissed the ground five times,
being the ceremony or compliment ordinarily used amongst them;
the prince was exceedingly pleased with this honour done unto
him, which with a smiling countenance, and much acknowledgment of words, he testified unto him.   This past, the prince with a
new ceremony stepped two or three paces back, and lifting up his
voice with more gravity than before, as he that represented the
person of the king, in whose name he came, said unto him: 'He,
the border of whose rich vesture my mouth kisseth, and that out
of an incredible greatness mastereth the sceptres of the earth, and
of the isles of the sea, sends thee word by me, who am his slave,
that thy honourable arrival is no less agreeable unto him than the
summer's sweet morning is to the ground, whenas the dew doth
comfort and refresh our bodies, and therefore would have thee
without further delay to come and hear his voice mounted on his
horse, whose trappings are garnished with jewels taken out of his
treasury, to the end that riding by my side, thou mayest be made
equal in honour to the greatest of his court, and that they which
behold thee marching in this sort, may acknowledge that the right
hand of him is mighty and valiant unto whom the labours of
war giveth this recompense.' Hereupon the *mitaquer*, prostrating
himself on the earth, with his hands lifted up, answered him thus:
'Let my head be a hundred times trampled on by the sole of his
feet, that all those of my race may be sensible of so great a favour,
and that my eldest son may ever carry it for a mark of honour.'
Then mounting on the horse which the prince had given him,
trapped with gold and precious stones, being one of those that the
king used to ride on himself, they marched on with a great deal of
state and majesty.   In this pomp were many spare horses led,
richly harnessed; there were also a number of ushers, carrying
silver maces on their shoulders, and six hundred halberdiers on
horseback, together with fifteen chariots, full of silver cymbals
and many other ill-tuned barbarous instruments, that made so
great a din, as it was not possible to hear one another.   Moreover,
in all this distance of way, which was a league and a half, there were
so many men on horseback, as one could hardly pass through the
crowd in any part thereof.   The *mitaquer* being thus in triumph
arrived at the first trenches of the camp, he sent us by one of his

---

[1] A mistranslation. *Espia* here is a watch-tower and not a spy.   'Which was
the first fortress of some nine watch-towers which the countryside had and which
had in it a great force of soldiers.'

servants to his quarter, where we were very well received, and
abundantly furnished with all things necessary for us.

Fourteen days after we arrived at this camp, the *mitaquer*, our
general, sent for us to his tent, where in the presence of some of his
gentlemen he said unto us: 'To-morrow morning about this time
be you ready, that I may make good my word unto you, which is
to let you see the face of him whom we hold for our sovereign
lord, a grace that is done you out of a particular respect to me; and
this His Majesty doth not only grant unto you, but your liberty
also, which I have obtained of him for you and which in truth I
am no less glad of, than of the taking of Nixiamcoo, the particulars
whereof you may relate unto him, if you come to be so happy as
to be questioned by him about it. Withal I assure you that I shall
take it for a great satisfaction, if when you shall return into your
country, you will remember that I have kept my word with you,
and that therein I have showed myself so punctual, as it may be
I would not for that consideration demand of the king some other
thing more profitable for me, that you may know this was that
which I only desired. Also the king hath done me the honour to
grant me presently, and that with such exceeding demonstration
of favour, as I must confess I am thereby more obliged unto you
than you are to me.'

Having spoken thus unto us, we prostrated ourselves upon the
ground, and in this sort answered him: 'My lord, the good which
you have pleased to do us is so great, that to go about to thank you
with words (as the world useth to do) in the state we now are in,
would rather be an ingratitude than a true and due acknowledgment; so that we think it better to pass it by in silence within the
secret of that soul which God hath put into us. And therefore,
since our tongues are of no use to us herein, and that they cannot
frame words capable to satisfy so great an obligation as this is,
wherein all of us stand for ever so infinitely engaged unto you, we
must with continual tears and sighs beg of the Lord which made
heaven and earth, that He will reward you for it; for it is He that
out of His infinite mercy and goodness hath taken upon Him to
pay that for the poor, which they of themselves are not able to
discharge; it is He, then, that will thoroughly recompense you and
your children for this good office you have done us, and whereby
you merit to have a share in His promises, and to live long and
happily in this world.'

Amongst those which accompanied the *mitaquer* at that time,
there was one named Bonquinadau, a man in years, and of the
principallest lords of the kingdom, who in this army commanded
over the strangers and rhinoceroses that served for the guard of
the camp. This same, unto whom more respect was borne than
to all the rest that were present, had no sooner heard our answer

but lifting up his eyes to heaven he said: 'Oh, who could be so happy as to be able to ask of God the explication of so high a secret, whereunto the weakness of our poor understanding cannot arrive; for I would fain know from whence it comes, that He permits people so far eloigned from the knowledge of our truth, to answer on the sudden in terms so agreeable to our ears, that I dare well say, nay, I will venture my head on it, that concerning things of God and heaven they know more sleeping than we do broad awake, whence it may be inferred that there are priests amongst them that understand the course of the stars, and the motions of the heavens, far better than our bonzes of the house of Lechuna.[1] Whereupon all that were about him answered: 'Your greatness hath so much reason for it, that we were obliged to behold it as an article of our faith, wherefore we think it were fit that these strangers should not be suffered to go out of our country, where, as our masters and doctors, they might teach us such things they know of the world.' 'That which you advise,' replied the *mitaquer*, 'is not much amiss, and yet the king would never permit it for all the treasures of China, because if he should, he would then violate the truth of his word, and so lose all the reputation of his greatness, wherefore you must excuse me if I do not propound things unto him that cannot be'; whereupon turning himself towards us, 'Go, get you gone,' said he unto us, 'and to-morrow morning fail not to be ready for to come again when I shall send for you.'

These words exceedingly contented us as there was great cause they should; and accordingly the next day he sent us nine horses very well furnished, upon which we mounted and so went to his tent. He in the meantime had put himself into a *piambre* (that is somewhat like to a litter) drawn with two horses richly harnessed; round about him for his guard marched threescore halberdiers, six pages apparelled in his livery mounted on white curtals,[2] and we nine on horseback a little more behind. In this manner he went on towards the place where the king was, whom he found lodged in the great and sumptuous edifice of the goddess Nacapirau, by the Chinese called the queen of heaven, whereof I have spoken at large in the thirty-fifth chapter. Being arrived at the first trenches of the king's tent, he alighted out of his litter, and all the rest likewise off from their horses, for to speak to the *nautaran*, of whom with a kind of ceremony, after the fashion of the gentiles, he craved leave to enter, which was presently granted him. Thereupon the *mitaquer*, being returned into his litter, passed through the gates in the same manner as before, only we and the rest of his followers waited upon him on foot. When he came to

---

[1] Lanchow, the residence of a Buddhist lama.
[2] Horses with docked tails.

a low and very long gallery, where there was a great number of gentlemen, he alighted again out of his litter, and told us that we were to attend him there, for that he would go and know whether it were a fit time to speak with the king or no.

We stayed there then about an hour, during the which some of the gentlemen that were in the gallery observing us to be strangers, and such kind of people as they had never seen the like, they called us, and very courteously bid us to sit down by them, when having spent some time in beholding certain tumblers showing feats of activity we perceived the *mitaquer* coming forth with four very beautiful boys, attired in long coats after the Turkish fashion, guarded [1] all over with green and white, and wearing about the small of their legs little hoops of gold in the form of irons and shackles. [2] The gentlemen that were present, as soon as they saw them, rose up on their feet, and drawing out their cutlasses, which they wore by their sides, they laid them on the ground with a new kind of ceremony, saying three times: 'Let the Lord of our heads live a hundred thousand years.'

In the meanwhile, as we lay with our heads bending to the ground, one of those boys said aloud unto us: 'You men of the other end of the world, rejoice now for that the hour is come wherein your desire is to be accomplished, and that you are to have the liberty which the *mitaquer* promised you at the castle of Nixiamcoo; wherefore arise from off the earth, and lift up your hands to heaven, rendering thanks unto the Lord, who during the night of our peaceable rest enamels the firmament with stars, seeing that of Himself alone, without the merit of any flesh, He hath made you to encounter in your exile with a man that delivers your persons.'

To this speech, prostrated as we were on the ground, we returned him this answer by our truchman: 'May Heaven grant us so much happiness, as that His foot may trample on our heads'; whereunto he replied: 'Your wish is not small, and may it please God to accord you this gift of riches.'

These four boys, and the *mitaquer*, whom we followed, passed through a gallery, erected upon five-and-twenty pillars of brass, and entered into a great room, where there were a number of gentlemen, and amongst them many strangers, Mogors, Persians, Berdios, Calaminhams, and Bramaas. After we were out of this room, we came to another, [3] where there were many armed men, ranged into five files all along the room with cutlasses on their shoulders that were garnished with gold. These stayed the *mitaquer* a little, and with great compliments asked him some

---

[1] Trimmed, ornamented.
[2] This is a most romantic liberty with the text. The original says, 'wearing slippers of gold on their feet.'
[3] Called Tigihipan.

questions, and took his oath upon the maces the boys carried, which he performed on his knees, kissing the ground three several times, whereupon he was admitted to pass on into a great place like a quadrangle;[1] there we saw four ranks of statues of brass, in the form of wild men, with clubs and crowns of the same metal gilt. These idols or giants were each of them six-and-twenty spans high, and six broad, as well on the breast as on the shoulders; their countenances were hideous and deformed, and their hair curled like to negroes.

The desire we had to know what these figures signified made us to demand it of the Tartars, who answered us, that they were the three hundred and threescore gods which framed the days of the year, being placed there expressly to the end that in their effigies they might be continually adored, for having created the fruits which the earth produceth; and withal that the king of Tartary had caused them to be transported thither from a great temple called Angicamoy which he had taken in the city of Xipatom, out of the chapel of the tombs of the kings of China,[2] for to triumph over them, whenas he should happily return into his country, that the whole world might know how in despite of the king of China he had captivated his gods.

Within this place whereof I speak, and amidst a plantation of orange-trees that was environed within a fence of ivy,[3] roses, rosemary, and many other sort of flowers, which we have not in Europe, was a tent pitched upon twelve balusters of the wood of camphor, each of them wreathed about with silver in the fashion of knotted card-work, bigger than one's arm. In this tent was a low throne in the form of an altar, garnished with branched work of fine gold, and over it was a cloth of state, set thick with silver stars; where also the sun and moon were to be seen, as also certain clouds, some of them white, and others of the colour of those which appear in the time of rain, all enamelled so to the life, and with such art, that they beguiled all those that beheld them, for they seemed to rain indeed, so as it was impossible to see a thing more complete, either for the proportions or colours. In the midst of this throne upon a bed lay a great statue of silver called Abicau Nilancor, which signifies the god of the health of kings, that had been also taken in the temple of Angicamoy. Now round about the same statue were four-and-thirty idols of the height of a child of five or six years old, ranged in two files, and set on their knees, with their hands lifted up towards this idol, as if they would adore him.

At the entry into this tent there were four young gentlemen

[1] Or cloister.
[2] The tombs of the Ming dynasty, some miles to the north of Peking.
[3] This would not be, strictly speaking, ivy, but a species of pelargonium.

richly clad, who, with each of them a censer in his hand, went
two and two about, then at the sound of a bell prostrated themselves
on the ground, and censed one another, saying with a loud voice:
'Let our cry come unto thee as a sweet perfume, to the end thou
mayest hear us.' For the guard of this tent, there were threescore halberdiers, who at a little distance environed it all about.
They were clothed with gilt leather, and had morions [1] on their
heads curiously engraven; all which were very agreeable and
majestical objects.

Out of this place we entered into another division, where there
were four chambers very rich and well furnished, in the which were
many gentlemen, as well strangers as Tartars. From thence passing on whither the *mitaquer* and the young boys conducted us, we
arrived at the door of a great low room, in form like to a church,
where stood six ushers with their maces, who with a new compliment to the *mitaquer* caused us to enter, but kept out all others.

In this room was the king of Tartaria, accompanied with many
princes, lords, and captains, amongst whom were the kings of
Pafua, Mecuy, Capinper, Raja [2] Benan, Anchesacotay, and others
to the number of fourteen, who in rich attire were all seated some
three or four paces from the foot of the tribunal. A little more
on the one side were two-and-thirty very fair women, who playing
upon divers instruments of music made a wonderful sweet consort. The king was set on his throne under a rich cloth of state,
and had about him twelve young boys kneeling on their knees
with little maces of gold like sceptres, which they carried on their
shoulders; close behind him was a young lady extremely beautiful
and wonderfully richly attired, with a ventiloe in her hand, wherewith she ever and anon fanned him. This same was the sister
of the *mitaquer* our general, and infinitely beloved of the king,
for whose sake therefore it was that he was in such credit and
reputation throughout the whole army. The king was much
about forty years of age, full stature, somewhat lean, and of a good
aspect; his beard was very short, his moustaches after the Turkish
manner, his eyes like to the Chinese, and his countenance severe
and majestical. As for his vesture, it was violet-colour, in fashion
like to a Turkish robe embroidered with pearl; upon his feet he
had green sandals wrought all over with gold purl, [3] and great pearls
among it, and on his head a satin cap of the colour of his habit,
with a rich band of diamonds and rubies intermingled together.

Before we passed any farther, after we had gone ten or eleven
steps in the room, we made our compliment by kissing of the
ground three several times, and performing other ceremonies,
which the truchmen taught us. In the meantime the king commanded the music to cease, and addressing himself to the *mitaquer*,

[1] Hat-shaped helmets without beaver or visor.   [2] Rajah.   [3] Twisted cord.

'Ask these men of the other end of the world,' said he unto him,
'whether they have a king, what is the name of their country, and
how far distant it is from this kingdom of China where now I am.'
Thereupon one of ours, speaking for all the rest, answered that
our country was called Portugal, that the king thereof was exceeding rich and mighty, and that from thence to the city of Pequin
was at the least three years' voyage.[1]

This answer much amazed the king, because he did not think
the world had been so large, so that striking his thigh with a wand
that he had in his hand and lifting up his eyes to heaven, as though
he would render thanks unto God, he said aloud, so as every one
might hear him: 'O Creator of all things; are we able to comprehend the marvels of Thy greatness, we that at the best are but poor
worms of the earth?[2] Fuxiquidane, fuxiquidane, let them approach,
let them approach.' Thereupon beckoning to us with his hand,
he caused us to come even to the first degree[3] of the throne, where
the fourteen kings sat, and demanded of him again, as a man astonished, 'Pucau, pucau?'—that is to say, 'How far, how far?'
whereunto he answered as before, that we should be at least three
years in returning to our country. Then he asked why we came
not rather by land than by sea, where so many labours and dangers
were to be undergone.[4] Thereunto he replied that there was too
great an extent of land, through which we were not assured to
pass, for that it was commanded by kings of several nations.
'What come you to seek for, then,' added the king, 'and wherefore
do you expose yourselves to such dangers?' Then having rendered
him a reason to this last demand with all the submission that
might be,[5] he stayed a pretty while without speaking, and then
shaking his head three or four times, he addressed himself to an
old man that was not far from him and said: 'Certainly we must
needs conclude, that there is either much ambition or little justice
in the country of these people, seeing they come so far to conquer
other lands.' To this speech the old man, named Raja Benan,
made no other answer but that it must needs be so, for men, said
he, who have recourse unto their industry and invention to run
over the sea for to get that which God hath not given them, are

---

[1] Their nation could be frankly avowed to the Tartars. Indeed, the Portuguese conquests on the Indian coast were something very small compared to
the Tartars' conquests and the Mogul conquest.

[2] These words in their original tongue were, according to Mendes Pinto, as
follows: 'Julicavão, julicavão minaydotoreu pisinão himacor dauulquitaroo
xinapoco nifando hoperau vuxido vultanitirau companoo foragrem hupuchiday
purpuponi hincau, hincau.'

[3] Step.

[4] Though the Tartar dominions were wide and sometimes stretched right
across Asia, they were never a sea-going people.

[5] He seems to have acknowledged that the Portuguese came to conquer
other lands.

necessarily carried thereunto either by extreme poverty, or by an
excess of blindness and vanity, derived from much covetousness,
which is the cause why they renounce God and those that brought
them into the world.

This reply of the old man was seconded with many jeering words
by the other courtiers, who made great sport upon this occasion,
that very much pleased the king.   In the meantime the women fell
to their music again, and so continued, till the king withdrew into
another chamber in the company of these fair musicians and that
young lady which fanned him, not so much as one of those great
personages daring to enter besides.   Not long after, one of those
twelve boys that carried the sceptres before mentioned, came to
the *mitaquer*, and told him from his sister, that the king commanded him not to depart away, which he held for a singular
favour, by reason this message was delivered to him in the presence
of those kings and lords that were in the room, so that he stirred
not, but sent us word that we should go unto our tent with this
assurance, that he would take care the son of the Sun [1] should be
mindful of us.

*Chapter XL. The King of Tartaria's raising of his siege from before
Pequin, for to return into his country, and that which passed
until his arrival there*

WE had been now full three-and-forty days in this camp, during
which time there passed many fights and skirmishes between the
besiegers and the besieged, as also two assaults in the open day
which were resisted by them within with an invincible courage
like resolute men as they were.   In the meantime the king of
Tartaria, seeing how contrary to his hope so great an enterprise
had been wherein he had consumed so much treasure, called his
council of war to be assembled, in the which were present the seven-
and-twenty kings that accompanied him, and likewise many
princes and lords, and the most part of the chief commanders of
the army.   In this council it was resolved, that in regard winter
was at hand, and that the rivers had already overflowed their banks
with such force and violence, as they had ravaged and carried away
most of the trenches and palisades of the camp, and that moreover
great numbers of the soldiers died daily of sickness, and for want
of victuals, that therefore the king could not do better than to
raise his siege, and be gone before winter came, for fear, lest staying

[1] It seems that the Tartar hierarchy was very similar to the Chinese.   Certainly that of the Japanese was so.

longer, he should run the hazard of losing himself and his army. All these reasons seemed so good to the king, that without further delay he resolved to follow this counsel, and to obey the present necessity, though it were to his great grief. So that incontinently he caused all his infantry and ammunition to be embarked, then having commanded his camp to be set on fire, he himself went away by land with three hundred thousand horse, and twenty thousand rhinoceroses.

Now after they had taken an account of all the dead, they appeared to be four hundred and fifty thousand, the most of whom died of sickness, as also a hundred thousand horses and threescore thousand rhinoceroses, which were eaten in the space of two months and an half wherein they wanted victual; that so of eighteen hundred thousand men wherewith the king of Tartaria came out of his country to besiege the city of Pequin, before the which he lay six months and a half, he carried home some seven hundred and fifty thousand less than he brought forth, whereof four-and-fifty thousand died of sickness, famine, and war, and three hundred thousand went and rendered themselves unto the Chinese, drawn thereunto by the great pay which they gave them, and other advantages of honour and presents which they continually bestowed on them; whereat we are not to marvel, seeing experience doth show how that alone is of far more power to oblige men than all other things in the world.

After the king of Tartaria was gone from this city of Pequin, upon a Monday, the seventeenth of October, with three hundred thousand horse, as I have related before, the same day about evening he went and lodged near to a river, called Quaytragun, and the next morning an hour before day the army began to march at the sound of the drums, fifes, and other instruments of war, according to the order prescribed them. In this manner he arrived a little before night at a town, named Guijampee, which he found altogether depopulated. After his army had reposed there about an hour and a half, he set forth again, and marching somewhat fast he came to lodge at the foot of a great mountain, called Liampeu,[1] from whence he departed towards morning. Thus marched he eight leagues a day for fourteen days together, at the end whereof he arrived at a good town, named Guauxitim,[2] which might contain about eleven or twelve thousand fires. There he was counselled to furnish himself with victuals, whereof he had great need, for which purpose therefore he begirt it round, and scaling it in the open day, he quickly made himself master of it,

[1] Presumably in the Nan-kau range.
[2] Champing. Though one cannot pronounce with certainty in the case of any of these eastern place-names reproduced from memory and in Portuguese spelling.

and put it to the sack with so cruel a massacre of inhabitants, as my fellows and I were ready to swoon for very astonishment.

Now after that the wood and fire had consumed all things, and that the army was abundantly provided of ammunition and victual, he departed at the break of day; and though he passed the next morning in the view of Caixiloo,[1] yet would not he attack it, for that it was a great and strong town, and by situation impregnable, having heard besides that there were fifty thousand men within it, whereof ten thousand were Mogors, Cauchins, and Champaas,[2] resolute soldiers, and much more warlike than the Chinese. From thence passing on he arrived at the walls of Singrachirau,[3] which are the very same that, as I have said heretofore, do divide those two empires of China and Tartaria; there meeting with no resistance he went and lodged on the further side of it at Panquinor,[4] which was the first of his own towns, and seated some three leagues from the said wall, and the next day he marched to Xipator,[5] where he dismissed the most part of his people. In this place he stayed not above seven days, which he spent in providing pay for his soldiers, and in the execution of certain prisoners he had taken in that war and brought along with him. These things thus expedited, he, as a man not very well pleased, embarked himself [6] for Lansame in sixscore *laulees*, with no more than ten or eleven thousand men. So in six days after his embarking, he arrived at Lansame, where not permitting any reception to be made him he landed about two hours within night.

The king abode in this city of Lansame until such time as all his forces, as well horse as foot, were arrived there, which was within six-and-twenty days; then having all his army together, he went on to another city, far greater and fairer, called Tuymican,[7] where he was visited by some princes his neighbours, and by the ambassadors of many other kings and sovereigns of more remoter countries, of which the chiefest were six great and mighty monarchs, namely Xataanas, the sophy of Persia; Siamon, emperor of the Gueos, whose country [8] borders on that of Bramaa and Tanguu; the Calaminham, 'Lord of the indomitable force of the Elephant of the Earth,' as I shall deliver hereafter, when I come to treat of him and his state;[9] the *sournau* of Odiaa, that names himself the king of Siam, whose dominion runs seven hundred leagues along the coast with that of Tanauserin,[10] and on the Champaa side with

---

[1] Mi-yun.   [2] From Sinkiang.
[3] Ku-pei-kow.   [4] Pao-ngan.
[5] This might be Ta-tung. The Tartars' journey here seems a little obscure.
[6] On the river Hwang-ho, presumably.
[7] Töng-ko, or, it might be, Wei-chang.
[8] Perhaps Assam.
[9] Chapters CLXIII–CLXV in the original, not included here.
[10] Tenasserim.

the Malayos, Berdios, and Patanes, and through the heart of the country with Passioloca,[1] Capimper, and Chiammay,[2] as also with the Lauhos[3] and Gueos, so that this prince alone hath seventeen kingdoms within his state, by reason whereof for to make himself the more redoubted amongst the gentiles, he causeth himself to be styled 'The Lord of the White Elephant'; the fifth was the great Mogor,[4] whose state is within the heart of the country, near to the Corazones, a province bordering upon Persia,[5] and the kingdom of Dely[6] and Chitor; and the last an emperor of a country named Caran,[7] as we were informed there, the bounds of whose sovereignty are at the mountains of Goncalidau,[8] sixty degrees further on, where a certain people live, whom they of the country call Moscovites, whereof we have some in this city, which were fair of complexion, well shapen, and apparelled with breeches, cassocks, and hats, like to the Flemings which we see in Europe, the chiefest of them wearing gowns lined with sables, and the rest with ordinary furs.[9]

The ambassador of this emperor of Caran was more remarkable in his entry than all the rest. He had for his guard about six-score men, armed with arrows and partisans damasked with gold and silver, and all attired alike in violet and green. After them marched on horseback twelve ushers, carrying silver maces, before whom twelve horses were led that had carnation clothes on them, bordered about with gold and silver. They were followed by twelve huge tall men, that seemed to be giants, clothed with tigers' skins as wild men are used to be painted, each of them hold-ing in his hand a great greyhound by a silver chain. Then appeared twelve little pages, mounted on white hackneys, having green velvet saddles, trimmed with silver lace and fringe; they were all apparelled alike in crimson satin cassocks, lined with martens, breeches and hats of the same and great chains of gold scarf-wise about them; these twelve boys were all of one equal stature, so fair of face, so well favoured, and of so sweet a proportion of body, as I believe there have been never any seen more accomplished. For himself, he was seated in a chariot with three wheels on each

---

[1] Pitsunalok.   [2] Chiengmai.   [3] Laos.
[4] Great Mogul.   The Tartars had penetrated to India at the beginning of the century.
[5] Peshawar, possibly.   [6] Delhi.
[7] Is this a confusion for Kazan?   The original, in every case, refers to the emperor himself as Caran.   Cf. 'the Calaminhan' (p. 198) and 'the Cauchin' (p. 211).
[8] Ural Mountains.
[9] Cogan omits: 'We noted in them that they have some words of the Latin tongue in their speech, and that if they chance to sneeze they say three times, "Dominus, Dominus, Dominus." But for all else that we could note they were more like to idolaters and gentiles than to those who have a knowledge of true religion, being withal much given to filthy lewdness.'

side, garnished all over with silver. Round about this *pirange* (for so was this chariot called) there were forty footmen in jerkins and breeches of green and red cloth, laced all over with carnation silk lace, having swords by their side above three fingers broad, with the hilts, handles, and chapes [1] of silver, and hunting horns hanging in silver chains, baldric-wise about them; and on their heads they wore caps, with feathers in them full of silver spangles: thus was the equipage of this ambassador so sumptuous and stately, that one might very well conclude he belonged to some very rich and mighty prince.

Now going one day as attendants on the *mitaquer*, who went to visit him from the king, amongst other things that we saw in his lodging, we observed there for one of the greatest rarities in that country, five chambers hung all with very rich arras, such as we have in Christendom, and no question brought from thence. In each of these chambers was a cloth of state of gold or silver tinsel, and under it a table with a basin and ewer of silver of a very costly fashion; also a chair of state of rich violet stuff trimmed with gold fringe, and at the foot of it a cushion of the same, all upon an exceeding large foot-pace [2] of tapestry; there was also a chafing-dish of silver, with a perfuming pot of the same, out of the which proceeded a most delicate odour. At the door of each of those five chambers stood two halberdiers, who permitted persons of quality to enter that came thither to see them. In another very great room in form like to a gallery, there was upon a very high and large foot-pace a little table placed, covered with a damask table-cloth, edged about with gold fringe, and upon a silver plate a napkin with a fork and a spoon of gold, as also two little salt-cellars of the same metal. Now about ten or eleven paces on the one side from this table were two cupboards of plate of all kind of fashions, and other vessels of great value. Moreover at the four corners of this table were four cisterns about the bigness of a bushel, with their kettles fastened to them with chains all of silver, as also two very great candlesticks of the same with white wax candles in them but not lighted. There were also at the door of the room twelve handsome halberdiers, clothed in mantles like to Irish [3] rug, with scimitars by their sides, all covered over with plates of silver, which guard (as ordinarily it is with them) were very haughty and rude in their answers to all that speak to them.

Although this ambassador was come thither in the way of visit as the rest, yet the principal subject of his embassy was to treat of a marriage between the emperor of Caran and a sister of the Tartar, named Meica Vidau, that is to say, a rich sapphire, a lady

[1] Metal plates of scabbards.
[2] Dais.
[3] Cogan's addition. Irish rug was a kind of coarse frieze.

about some thirty years of age, but very handsome, and exceeding charitable to the poor, whom we saw divers times in this city at the chiefest feasts, which these people use to solemnize at certain times of the year, after the manner of the gentiles. Howbeit, setting aside all this, whereof I had not spoken but that it seemed more remarkable unto me than all the rest, I will return to my former discourse, as well concerning our liberty, as the voyage that we made even to the islands of the Sea of China, whither the emperor of Tartaria caused us to be conveyed, to the end that such as shall come after us may attain to the knowledge of a part of those things, whereof it may be they have never heard spoken until this present.

Chapter XLI. In what manner we were brought again before the king of Tartaria; with our departure from that kingdom; and all that we saw and that befell us in our voyage till our arrival at the court of the king of Cauchinchina

AFTER some time had been spent in the celebrations of certain remarkable feasts, that were made for joy of the conclusion of a marriage betwixt the Princess Meica Vidau, the king's sister, and the emperor of Caran, the Tartar by the advice of his captains resolved to return anew to the siege of Pequin, which he had formerly quitted, taking the ill success that he had there as a great affront to his person; to this effect then he caused all the estates of his kingdom to be assembled, and also made a league with all the kings and princes bordering on his dominions. Whereupon considering with ourselves how prejudicial this might prove to the promise had been made us for the setting of us at liberty, we repaired to the *mitaquer*, and represented unto him many things that made for our purpose, and obliged him to keep his word with us; to the which he returned us this answer: 'Certainly you have a great deal of reason for that you say, and I have yet more not to refuse you that which you demand of me with so much justice; wherefore I resolve to put the king in mind of you, that you may enjoy your liberty, and the sooner you shall be gone from hence, the sooner you shall be freed from the labours which the time begins to prepare for us in the enterprise that His Majesty hath newly undertaken by the counsel of some particulars,[1] who for that they know not how to govern themselves have more need to be counselled than the earth hath need of water to produce the fruits that are sowed in her; but to-morrow morning I shall put the king in mind of you and your poverty, and withal I shall present unto

[1] Individuals.

him how you have poor fatherless children, as you have heretofore told me, to the end he may be thereby incited to cast his eyes upon you, as he is accustomed to do in like cases, which is none of the least marks of his greatness.'

Hereupon he dismissed us for that day, and the next morning he went to Pontiveu, which is a place where the king useth to give audience to all such as have any suit to him.   There beseeching His Majesty to think of us, he answered him, that as soon as he dispatched away an ambassador to the king of Cauchinchina, he would send us along with him for so he had resolved to do.   With this answer the *mitaquer* returned to his house, where we were ready attending his coming, and told us what the king had promised him, wherewithal not a little contented we went back to our lodging. There in the expectation of the good success of this promise we continued ten days with some impatience, at the end whereof the *mitaquer* by the king's express command carried us with him to the court, where causing us to approach near to His Majesty, with those ceremonies of greatness which are observed in coming before him, being the same we used at Pequin, after he had beheld us with a gentle eye, he bid the *mitaquer* ask of us whether we would serve him, and in case we would, he should not only be very well pleased with it, but he would also give us better entertainment and more advantageous conditions than all the strangers that should follow him in this war.   To this demand the *mitaquer* answered very favourably for us, how he had often heard us say, that we were married in our country, and had a great charge of children, who had no other means to maintain them, but what we got with our labour, which was poorly enough, God knows.

The king heard this speech with some demonstration of pity, so that looking on the *mitaquer*, 'I am glad,' said he, 'to know that they have such good cause to return home as they speak of, that I may with the more contentment acquit me of that which thou hast promised them in my name.'   At these words the *mitaquer* and all we that were with him lifting up our hands, as to a testimony of our thankfulness unto him, we kissed the ground three times, and said: 'May thy feet rest themselves upon a thousand generations, to the end that thou mayst be lord of the inhabitants of the earth.'[1]   Hereat the king began to smile, and said to a prince that was near him: 'These men speak as if they had been bred amongst us.'   Then casting his eyes on Jorge Mendes, who stood before all us next to the *mitaquer*, 'And thou,' said he unto him, 'in what condition art thou, wilt thou go or stay?' Whereupon Mendes, who had long before premeditated his answer, 'Sir,' replied he, 'for me, that have neither wife nor children to bewail

---

[1] This form of exaggeration here used by the Portuguese is, of course, etiquette in addressing eastern sovereigns.

my absence, the thing I most desire in the world is to serve Your Majesty, since you are pleased therewith, whereunto I have more affection than to be *chaem* of Pequin one thousand years together.'

At this the king smiled again, and then dismissed us, so that we returned very well satisfied to our lodging, where we continued three days in a readiness to depart, at the end of which by the mediation of the *mitaquer*, and means of his sister, who, as I have said before, was wonderfully beloved of the king, His Majesty sent us for the eight that we were two thousand taels, and gave us in charge to his ambassador, whom he sent to the city of Uzamquee[1] in Cauchenchina, in the company of the same king of Cauchenchina's ambassador. With him we departed from thence five days after, being embarked in the vessel wherein he went himself. But before our departure Jorge Mendes gave us a thousand ducats, which was easy for him to do, for that he had already six thousand of yearly rent; withal he kept us company all that day, and at length took his leave of us, not without shedding many a tear for grief that he had so exposed himself to a voluntary exile.

Being departed from this city of Tuymican on the ninth day of May, in the year one thousand five hundred forty and four, we came to lodge that night at a university in a pagoda called Guatipamor,[2] where the two ambassadors were very well entertained by the *tuyxivau* of the house, which is as the rector thereof, and the next morning when it was broad day, both of them continued their course down the river, each one in his own ship, besides other two wherein their stuff was.

About two hours in the night we arrived at a little town named Fuxanguim,[3] well fortified with towers and bulwarks after our manner, as also with very broad ditches, and strong bridges of hewed stone; there was likewise great store of artillery, or cannons of wood, made like unto the pumps of ships, behind the which they put boxes of iron, that held their charge and were fastened unto them with iron bands; as for the bullets which they shot, they were like unto those of falconets, and half black.[4]   Being much amazed to see this, we demanded of the ambassador who it was that had invented those kind of guns,[5] whereunto they answered that it was certain men called Almains, and of a country named Muscovy, who by a very great lake of salt water came down to this town in nine vessels rowed with oars, in the company of a widow woman, lady of a place called Guaytor, who they said was chased out of her country by a king of Denmark, so that flying for refuge with three sons of hers, the great-grandfather of this king

---

[1] Saigon.   [2] Probably Shi-tsui-tze.   [3] Perhaps Ping-lo.
[4] The Portuguese says 'meias esperas' (pieces of artillery).
[5] Gunpowder was, of course, used in China some centuries before it was in Europe.

of Tartaria made them all great lords, and gave them certain
kinswomen of his in marriage, from whom are extracted the
chiefest families of this empire.   The next morning we párted from
this town and that night lay at another more nobler, named Linxau.[1]

Five days [2] we continued our voyage down this river, and then
we arrived at a great temple, called Singuafatur, [3] where we saw
an enclosure of above a league in circuit, in which were builded a
hundred threescore and four houses, very long and broad, after
the fashion of arsenals, all full up to the very tiles of dead men's
heads, whereof there was so great a number, that I am afraid to
speak it, for that it will hardly be credited.   Without each of these
houses were also great piles of the bones of these heads, which were
three fathom higher than the ridges of them, so that the house
seemed to be buried, no other part of them appearing but the
frontispiece where the gate stood; not far from thence upon a
little hill on the south side of them was a kind of a platform,
whereunto one went up by certain winding stairs of iron, and
through four several doors.   Upon this platform was the tallest,
the most deformed and dreadful monster that possibly can be
imagined, standing upon his feet, and leaning against a mighty
tower of hewed stone; he was made of cast iron, and of so great
and prodigious a stature, that by guess he seemed to be above
thirty fathom high, and more than six broad, notwithstanding the
which deformity he was exceedingly well proportioned in all his
limbs, only his head was somewhat too little for so great a body.
This monster held in both his hands a bowl of the same iron,
being six-and-thirty spans about.

Beholding so strange and monstrous a thing, we demanded of the
Tartar ambassador the explication thereof, who willing to satisfy our
curiosity, 'If you knew,' answered he, 'what the power of this god
is, and how needful it is for you to have him to friend, certainly
you would think it well employed if you presented him with all
your means, how great soever they might be, and gave them to
him rather than to your own children; for you must know that this
great saint, which you see there, is the treasurer of the bones of all
those that are born into the world, to the end that at the last day,
when men come to be born again, he may give to every one the
same bones which he had upon earth, for he knows them all, and
can tell in particular to what body each of those bones belong.
Whereupon you are further to understand, that he who in this life
shall be so unadvised as not to honour him, nor present him with
something, will be but in an ill case in the other world, for this saint
will then give him some of the rottenest bones he can meet withal,

[1] Ning-hsia.
[2] Cogan adds 'after,' but this is an obvious mistranslation.
[3] Chung-wei.

and one or two less than he should have, by means whereof he will become deformed, lame, or crooked, and therefore if you will follow my counsel, you shall make yourselves of his fraternity, by offering something unto him, and you will find by experience the good that will redound to you thereof hereafter.'

We desired also to know of him what the bowl which this monster held in his hand signified; whereunto he answered us that he held it to fling it at the head of the gluttonous serpent, that lived in the profound abysm of the house of smoke, when he should come thither to steal away any of those bones.   After this we inquired of him how this monster was called, and he told us that his name was Pachinarau dubeculem Pinanfaque, and that it was threescore and fourteen thousand years since he was begotten on a tortoise, called Miganja, by a sea-horse, that was a hundred and thirty fathom long, named Tybrem Vucam, who had been king of the giants of Fanius.   He told us likewise many other brutish fooleries and absurdities, which those of that country believe as their creed, and wherewith the devil precipitates them all into hell.   Moreover, this ambassador assured us that the gifts which were presented to this idol amounted to above two hundred thousand taels of yearly rent, without comprising therein what came from chapels and other foundations of obits [1] from the principal lords of the country, the revenue whereof was far greater than that of the gifts.   For a conclusion he told us that this same idol had ordinarily twelve thousand priests attending on his service, who were maintained with meat, drink, and clothing, only to pray for the dead, that is to say, for those unto whom these bones appertained.

We were also assured that these priests never went out of this enclosure without the permission of their superiors, but that there was still without six hundred servants, who took care for the providing of all things necessary for them; and further that it was not lawful for these priests, save once a year, to break within this enclosure the vow which they had made of chastity, but without the same they might whore their pleasure with whomsoever they would, without committing any sin.   There was also a seraglio there, wherein many women, appointed for that purpose, were shut up, whom their governesses permitted to have to do with the priests of this beastly and diabolical sect.

Continuing our voyage from this pagoda or monastery of gentiles, whereof we have spoken, the next day we arrived at a very fair town, called Quanginau,[2] which stands on the bank of the river. In this place the ambassadors stayed three whole days for to furnish themselves with certain things they wanted, as also for to see the feastings and joy that was made at that time upon the entry of the

---

[1] Revenues left by the dead for these purposes.   [2] Tsiug-yüen.

talapicor of Lechuna, which is their pope, who was going then
unto the king for to comfort him about the ill success he had in
China. Amongst other graces which this *talapicor* bestowed on
the inhabitants of this town, in recompense of the charge they had
been at for his reception, he granted unto them that they might
be all priests, and administer their sacrifices in what places soever
they were, and likewise that they might therefore receive the same
entertainment and gifts that were accustomed to be given unto
their priests, without any difference between them and those that
upon examination had been promoted to that dignity. Moreover he gave them power to grant bills of exchange for heaven unto
all such as should do them good here below. To the ambassador
of Cauchinchina he granted as a most singular favour, that he might
legitimate any that would pay him for it, and also confer on the
lords of the court titles and marks of honour as far forth as if he
had been king; whereof the foolish ambassador was so proud, as
setting aside covetousness, though it were a vice he was naturally
inclined unto, he employed all that ever he had there in gifts upon
those priests, and besides, not contented therewith, he for that end
borrowed of us the two thousand taels the king had given us, which
afterwards he paid us again with interest after fifteen in the hundred.

After these matters the two ambassadors resolved to continue
their voyage, but before their departure they went to visit the
talapicor in a pagoda where he was lodged, for in regard of his
greatness, and that he was held for a saint, he might not abide
with any man, but with the king only. Now as soon as he understood of the ambassadors coming to him he sent them word not to
go away that day, because he was to preach at the church of certain
religious women of the invocation of Pontimaqueu; this they took
for a great honour, and incontinently went to the pagoda, where
the sermon was to be.

At their arrival they found such a concourse of people, that they
were constrained to remove the pulpit to another very great place,
which in less than an hour was environed with scaffolds, hung
about with silk stuff, whereon the one side were the ladies, richly
apparelled, and on the other the prioress, called Vanguenarau,
with all the *menigrepas*, or religious women of the pagoda, being
in number above three hundred. After the *talapicor* was gone up
into the pulpit, and that he had made an exterior show of much
holiness, ever and anon lifting up his hands and eyes to heaven,
he began his sermon in this manner: [1]

'Like as it is the property of water to cleanse all things, and of

---

[1] As Lanchow is really in China, though apparently then in the Tartar dominions, the lama may be supposed to have spoken Chinese, which would
explain Mendes Pinto's understanding him so well.

the sun to warm all creatures, so it is the property of God through a celestial and divine nature to do good unto all; wherefore we are all bound, as well in general and particular, to imitate this our Lord, who hath created and doth nourish us, by doing that unto those who stand in need of the good of this world, as we would that they should do unto us, for that by this work we are more pleasing unto Him than by any other whatsoever. For as the good father of a family rejoiceth to see his children made much of, and presents given to them, so our heavenly Lord, who is the true father of us all, rejoiceth at such time as with a zeal of charity we communicate one with another; whereby it is evident that the covetous man who shuts his hand, when the poor ask something of him which they want, constrained thereunto by necessity, and that turns him another way without assisting them, shall be treated in the same manner by a just judgment of God, and driven down into the bottom of the sink of the night, where like a frog he shall croak without ceasing, being tormented by the hunger of his covetousness. This being so, I do advise and enjoin you all, since you have ears to hear me, that you do that which the law of the Lord obligeth you to do, which is, that you give of that whereof you have too much to the poor, who have not wherewith to feed themselves, to the end God may not be wanting to you when you shall be at the last gasp of your life. Go to, then, let this charity be so remarkable and universal in you, that the very fowls of the air may taste of your liberality. And this you ought to do to keep the poor, having need of what you possess in excess, from being forced by their necessity to rob other men of their goods, whereof you would be no less blameable than if you killed an infant in the cradle. I commend also unto your remembrance that which is written in the book of our truth, touching the good you are bound to do unto the priests that pray for you, to the end they may not perish for want of the good you ought to do unto them, which would be as great a sin before God, as if you should cut the throat of a little white heifer when she is sucking of her dam, by the death of whom a thousand souls would die, which are buried in her as in a golden tomb, in expectation of the day which is to accomplish the promise that was made unto them, wherein they shall be transformed into white pearls for to dance in heaven, like unto the motes which are in the beams of the sun.'

Having uttered these things, he added many others thereunto, and delivering a world of extravagancies and fooleries, he bestirred himself in such manner as was a wonder to behold, so that we eight Portugals were exceedingly amazed at the extreme devotion of these people, and how that in lifting up their hands to heaven, they ever and anon repeated this word: 'Taiximida,' that is to say, 'So we believe.'

In the meantime one of our fellows, named Vicente Morosa, hearing the auditors so often use that word 'Taiximida,' said in imitation of them, 'Such may thy life be'; and that with such a grace and so settled a countenance, not seeming any way to jeer him, that not one in the assembly could forbear laughing. He in the meanwhile continued still firm, and more and more confirmed, seeming even to weep out of an excess of devotion. Now his eyes being always fixed on the *talapicor*, he whensoever he chanced to look on him could not choose but do as the rest did, so that upon the conclusion of his sermon all that heard him fell to laughing outright. The prioress herself and all the *menigrepas* of her monastery could not contain themselves in their serious humour, imagining that the faces which the Portugal made, and his actions, were so many effects of his devotion and good meaning; for if one had thought it to be otherwise, and that he had done it out of derision, no question but he had been so chastised, as he should never have been able to mock again.

When the sermon was ended the *talapicor* returned to the pagoda where he lodged, being accompanied with the most honourable of all the assembly, together with the ambassadors, unto whom all the way as he went he ceased not to commend the devotion of the Portugals. 'Look,' said he, 'there is not so much as these people, who live like beasts, and without the knowledge of our truth, but see well enough that there is nothing but what is godly in that I have preached'; whereunto all answered that it was as he said.

The day after we parted from the town of Quanginau, and continued our voyage down the river for the space of four[1] days, during the which we saw a number of towns and great boroughs on either side of us, at the end whereof we arrived at a city called Lechuna, the chiefest of the religion of these gentiles, and such it may be as Rome is amongst us.

In this city was a very sumptuous temple, where there were many remarkable edifices, in the which seven-and-twenty kings or emperors of this monarchy of Tartaria have been buried. Their tombs are in chapels, wonderful rich, as well for the excellency of their workmanship, which is of an infinite cost, as for that they are within covered all over with plates of silver, wherein there are divers idols of different forms made also of silver. On the north side a little apart from the temple was an enclosure worthy the observation, both for its extent and the fortification thereof; within it were two hundred and fourscore monasteries, as well of men as of women, dedicated to certain idols, and for the service of all these pagodas or temples there are ordinarily, as we were assured, two-and-forty thousand priests and *menigrepos*, not comprising therein those which were lodged without the enclosure for

---
[1] Cogan has 'fourteen.'

the service of these false priests. We observed that in these two hundred and fourscore houses there was an infinite company of pillars of brass, and upon the top of each pillar are idols of the same metal gilt, besides those which likewise were there all of silver. These idols are the statues of them whom in their false sect they hold for saints, and of whom they recount such fopperies as would make a man wonder to hear them; for they give unto each of them a statue, more or less rich and gilded, according to the degrees of virtue which they have exercised in this life. And this they do expressly, that the living may be incited to imitate them, to the end there may be as much done unto them when they are dead.[1]

In one of these monasteries of the invocation of Quiay Frigau, that is to say, the god of the motes of the sun, was a sister of the king's, the widow of Raja Benan, prince of Pafua, whom the death of her husband had made resolve to shut herself up in this monastery, with six thousand women that had followed her thither, and she had taken upon her, as the most honourable title she could think on, the name of 'The Broom of the House of God.' The ambassadors went to see this lady, and kissed her feet as a saint; she received them very courteously, and demanded many things of them with great discretion, whereunto they rendered such answers as became them; but coming to cast her eyes upon us, who stood somewhat far off, and understanding that never any of our nation was seen in those parts before, she inquired of the ambassadors of what country we were. They answered, that we were come from a place at the other end of the world, whereof no man there knew the name. At those words she stood much amazed, and causing us to come nearer, she questioned us about many things, whereof we gave her such an account as greatly contented her and all that were present. In the meantime the princess wondering at the answers which one of ours made her, 'They speak,' said she, 'like men that have been brought up amongst people who have seen more of the world than we have.' So after she had heard us talk a while of some matters that she had propounded unto us, she dismissed us with very good words, and caused a hundred taels to be given us in way of an alms.

The ambassadors, having taken their leave of her, continued their voyage down along the river, so that at the end of five days we arrived at a great town, called Rendacalem,[2] situated on the uttermost confines of the kingdom of Tartaria. Out of this place we entered upon the state of the Xinaleygrau, and therein we

[1] Ancestor-worship.
[2] Probably Feng-hsiang. They seem to have reached the other Hwang-ho River in the province of Shensi, though how they reached there, by canal, or possibly by road as well, is not quite clear. They were now in China proper.

proceeded on four days together, until such time as we came to a town named Voulem,[1] where the ambassadors were very well entertained by the lord of the country, and abundantly furnished with all things necessary for their voyage, as also with pilots to guide them in those rivers.

From thence we pursued our course for seven days together, during the which we saw not anything worthy of note, and at length came to a strait, called Quatenqur,[2] whereinto the pilots entered, as well to abridge their voyage, as to avoid the encounter of a famous pirate, who had robbed those parts of most of their wealth. Through this strait running east, as also east-north-east, and sometimes east-south-east, according to the windings of the water, we arrived at the lake of Singapamor, called by them of the country Cunebetea,[3] which was, as our pilots affirmed, six-and-thirty leagues in extent, where we saw so many several sorts of birds, that I am not able to recount them. Out of this lake of Singapamor (which as an admirable masterpiece nature hath opened in the heart of this country) do four very large and deep rivers proceed, whereof the first is named Ventrau, that runneth eastward through all the kingdoms of Sornau and Siam, entering into the sea by the bar[4] of Chiamtabuu, in six-and-twenty degrees; the second, Jangumaa, that going south and south-east, traverseth also the greatest part of this country, as likewise the kingdom of Chiammay, the Laos, Gueos, and another part of Dambambuu, disemboguing into the sea by the bar of Martavan, in the kingdom of Pegu, and there is in distance from the one to the other by the degrees of this climate, above seven hundred leagues. The third, called Pumphileu, passeth in the same manner through all the countries of Capimper and Sacotay, and turning above that second river runs quite through the empire of Monginoco, and a part of Meleytay and Sovady, rendering itself into the sea by the bar of Cosmim, near to Arracan. The fourth, which in all likelihood is as great as the rest, is not known by any name, neither could the ambassadors give us any reason for[5] it; but it is probable, according to the opinion of divers, that it is Ganges in the kingdom of Bengala, so that by all the discoveries which have been made in these oriental countries it is conceived that there is not a greater river than it.

---

[1] Hsi-ngan.
[2] This must have been part of either the Han-kiang or the Yang-tse-kiang River. The pirates were river pirates.
[3] Lake Tung-ting-hu, it seems. Mendes Pinto's information about directions and about the rivers running out of this lake are not reliable. The Chinese rivers interlace their courses so frequently that it is possible to reach most points of China by water. Besides, canals supply nature's oversights.
[4] Estuary.
[5] Account of.

Having crossed this lake we continued our course for the space of seven days, till we came to a place named Caleypute,[1] the inhabitants whereof would by no means permit us to land, for the ambassadors endeavouring to do so, they entertained us with such store of darts and stones from the shore, as we thought us not a little happy in that we could save ourselves from danger of it. After we had gotten out of this place, much vexed with the bad entreaty [2] we had received there, that which most afflicted us was to see ourselves unprovided of things we were greatly in need of, but by the counsel of our pilots we sailed by another river far larger than the strait which we had left,[3] and that by the space of nine days, at the end whereof we arrived at a very good town, called Tarem,[4] the lord of which was subject to the Cauchin, who received the ambassadors with great demonstrations of love, and furnished them abundantly with all that they wanted.

The next day we departed from thence about sunset, and continuing our voyage down the river, about seven days after we came to an anchor in the port of Xolor,[5] which is a very fair town, where all the enamelled porcelain which is carried to China is made. There the ambassadors stayed five days, during which time they caused their ships, that were very heavy, to be hauled ashore by the force of boats. That done, and provision made of all things necessary, they went to see certain mines, which the king of Cauchin hath in that place, from whence great store of silver is drawn, and the ambassadors being desirous to know how much silver those mines yielded every year, they were answered that the whole amounted to some six thousand *picos*, which make eight thousand quintals of our weight.

After our departure from the town of Xolor we still continued our course for five days together down that great river, and saw all along that while a many of great boroughs and goodly towns; for in that climate the land is better than otherwhere, very well peopled, and full of riches; withal the rivers are frequented with a world of vessels, and the fields very well tilled and replenished with abundance of wheat, rice, all kind of pulse, and exceeding great sugar-canes, whereof there is marvellous store in all that country.[6] The gentlemen there are ordinarily clothed in silk, and mounted on horses handsomely furnished; as for the women, they are exceeding white and fair. Now it was not without much labour, pain, and danger, that we passed those two channels, as also the river of Ventinau, by reason of the pirates that usually are

[1] This might be Wu-chow.   [2] Treatment.
[3] The Si-kiang.   [4] Possibly Tai-ping.
[5] Hanoi, in the delta of the Song-koi or Red River. It was originally directly on the sea-coast, but some thousand years before Mendes Pinto visited it.
[6] This being a river-delta, the soil is particularly fertile.

* H 986

encountered there; nevertheless we at the length arrived at the town of Manaquileu,[1] which is situated at the foot of the mountains of Chomay upon the frontiers of the two kingdoms of China and Cauchenchina, where the ambassadors were both well received by the governor thereof.

The next morning departing from that place they went and lay in a town, named Tinanquaxi,[2] which appertained to an aunt of the king's, whom they went to visit. She gave them a very kind reception, and withal told them for news that the king her nephew was newly returned from the war of the Tinocouhos,[3] and wonderfully well pleased with his good success therein; whereunto she added many particularities, which they were glad to hear, especially when she assured them that the king, after he had dismissed the forces that he had carried out with him, was gone with a small train to the city of Fanaugrem,[4] where he intended to spend some time in hunting and fishing, and then to go and winter at Usamguee, the capital city of this empire of Cauchin. Whenas they had consulted awhile upon these news, they resolved to send their four vessels away to Usamguee, and themselves to travel by land to Fanaugrem, where they understood the king was. This deliberation taken they put incontinently into execution and that by the advice of this princess, who for that purpose caused them to be furnished with horses for themselves and their people, as also with eight rhinoceroses for the transportation of their baggage.

They began their journey then about three days after, and having travelled fourscore and six leagues in the space of thirteen days, and that with much toil and labour, by reason of certain mountains which they were to pass, that were of a long extent, and very rough and stony, in the end they arrived at a great lodging, called Taraudachit,[5] seated upon the bank of a river. There they passed the night, and the next morning they parted thence for to go to a town named Lindau Panoo,[6] where they were very well received by the captain thereof, a kinsman of the ambassadors of Cauchenchina, who was come not about six days before from Fanaugrem, where the king remained still, being not more than fifteen leagues from that place. After that this captain hath told this ambassador his kinsman some other news of the court, and of the success of the war, he further advertised him that a son-in-law of his was dead, for the love of whom his daughter, the wife of the deceased, had cast herself into a pile of flaming fire, where with her husband's body she was consumed to ashes, at which all her kindred exceedingly rejoiced, for that by so generous an end she had given proof

[1] This might be Nam-dinh.   [2] This might be Ninh-binh.
[3] The people of Tonquin.   [4] Possibly Kenmarat.
[5] Savam-Naklet.   [6] Perhaps Ban-muk-dahan.

of what she had ever been.[1] The ambassador himself, her father, testified also no little content for the same, saying: 'Now it is, O my daughter, that I know assuredly thou art a saint, and that thou servest thy husband in heaven, wherefore I promise and swear to thee, that for so memorable an end, wherein thou hast given an infallible proof of the royal blood whereof thou art descended, I will in memory of thy goodness build thee such a magnificent and honourable house, as shall make thee desire to come from where thou art, for to recreate thyself in it, in imitation of those blessed souls which we hold have heretofore done the like.'

This said, he fell flat down with his face on the ground, and in that posture continued till the day following, whenas he was visited by all the religious men of the place, who comforted him with full assurance that his daughter was a saint, so that all of them granted him permission to erect a statue of silver unto her. These speeches of the priests greatly pleased the ambassador, who very much acknowledged the same unto them, giving money both to them and to all the poor that were thereabout. At this place we spent nine days in celebrating the funerals of the defunct, and then departing we went the next day to a certain monastery called Latiparau, that is to say, the remedy of the poor, where the two ambassadors remained three days in expectation of news from the king, whom they had already advertised of their arrival. Now his answer to them was, that they should go to a town, named Agimpur, three leagues from the place where they were, and but one from Fanaugrem, whither he would send for them when time served.

Chapter XLII. The reception of the Tartarian ambassador by the king of Cauchenchina, with the said king's going from thence to the city of Usamguee, and his triumphal entry thereinto

THE king, being advertised by his ambassador that he brought another along with him from the king of Tartaria, sent for him not long after from Agimpur by the brother of the queen his wife, a very valiant and rich prince.[2] He was mounted on a chariot with three wheels on a side, adorned all within with plates of silver, and drawn by four white horses, whose furniture was all embroidered with gold. This chariot, which they of the country call *fiambra*,

---

[1] Suttee, or the voluntary self-immolation of widows on the funeral piles of their husbands. The practice is usually connected with Hinduism, but this is an instance of it among Buddhists.

[1] Mendes Pinto adds his name, Passilau Vacan.

was waited on by threescore footmen, half on the one side and half
on the other, clothed in green leather, with scimitars by their sides,
whose scabbards were garnished with gold, and before them went
twelve ushers bearing their maces on their shoulders. After the
footmen followed certain others carrying halberds trimmed with
silver, in gowns and breeches of green and white silk, and with
scimitars by their sides; these fellows seemed very haughty and
proud, so that by their outward behaviours, which in all their
actions appeared to be like unto their surly dispositions, they
rendered themselves somewhat terrible to others. Thirty paces
after this guard marched fourscore elephants exceeding well furnished, with chairs and castles adorned with silver which they
carried on their backs, and on their teeth [1] their *panoures*, or warlike
defences, together with many little bells of the same metal hanging
about their necks. Before these elephants which were said to be
the king's guard, rode a number of men-at-arms in very good
equipage, and in the vanguard of all this train went twelve chariots
with cymbals of silver and covered with silk.

When this prince was come in this stately manner to the ambassador of Tartaria, who attended him, and that they had performed
all such compliments one to another as are usual amongst them,
the prince gave the ambassador the chariot wherein he came
thither, and mounting on a gallant courser, he placed himself on
the right hand of him, and the king's ambassador on the left.
In this pomp, and with the same order as before, as also with the
sound of divers instruments of music, they arrived at the first
court of the king's house, where the *broquem*, captain of the guard
of the palace, attended them, being accompanied with many noblemen, besides a number on horseback, which stood ranked in two
files all along the court. After they had with a new ceremony
been complimented withal, they went on foot to the palace gate,
where they encountered with an old man, above fourscore years
of age, who was said to be the king's uncle. This same, being
waited upon by divers great lords, was no sooner perceived by
the ambassadors, but with a new kind of compliment they kissed the
scimitar that hung by his side, whereupon he returned them the
like, together with an honour, which is of no little estimation amongst
them, that was to hold his hand upon their heads, so long as they
were prostrated on the ground before him. Then having caused
the Tartar to rise, and to march even cheek by jowl with him, he
led him through a very long hall to a door which was at the end
thereof, where after he had knocked three times, one demanded
of him who he was, and what he would have; whereunto answering
very soberly, 'Here is come,' said he, 'out of an ancient custom of
true amity, an ambassador from the great Xinarau of Tartaria,

---

[1] Tusks.

to demand audience of Prechau Guimian, whom we all hold for the lord of our heads.' This answer being returned, the door was opened, into which they presently entered; the prince marched foremost with the ambassador of Tartaria, whom he held by the hand, and a little behind them went the other belonging to the king, with the captain of the guard, then followed all the company by three and three.

Having gone through that room, where there was none but certain of the guard on their knees with halberds, we went into another room far more spacious and fair than the former, in the which we saw threescore and four statues of brass, and nineteen of silver, all tied by the neck with iron chairs. At so extraordinary a thing as this being much abashed, we demanded of one of their *grepos*, or priests, the reason of it, who answered us, that the statues which we beheld there were the fourscore and three gods of the Tinocouhos, whom the king in the late war had taken from them out of a temple where they were placed; 'for,' added he, 'there is nothing in the world held in more esteem or for a greater honour by the king, than to triumph over the gods of his enemies, which he hath led away captive in despite of them.' Whereupon inquiring further of him why they were set there, he replied that it was to have them in a readiness against the time that the king should make his entry into Usamguee, whither he purposed shortly to go, for to make a show of them so chained in his triumph as a special mark of the victory he had gained.

After we were at the end of this room where the idols were, we entered into another very great one, where we saw a number of very fair women, who were set all along, some employed in curious needleworks, and others singing and playing upon certain instruments of music, very pleasing to hear. Passing on, we arrived at the door of the king's chamber, where we found six women, which were as it were porters there, and carried silver maces. In this room was the king, in the company of a few ancient men, and a great number of young women, to the tune of whose music certain little girls sung very harmoniously. The king was set on a throne of eight steps high in the manner of an altar, over the which was a cloth of state supported by pillars, all covered over with gold engraven; near to him were six little children upon their knees with sceptres in their hands, and a little further off stood a woman reasonably well in years, which fanned him ever and anon, and had a great garland about her neck. This prince was about some five-and-thirty years of age, and of a goodly presence. He had full eyes, auburn hair and beard, a grave look, and in all points the countenance of a generous king.

As soon as the ambassadors came into the room they prostrated themselves three times on the ground, and at the third time the

king's lay still flat all along, whilst the Tartar passed on; who
being come near to the first step of the throne where the king
sat, he said unto him with so loud a voice as all there present might
hear him: 'O thou the prop of all the forces of the earth, and the
breath of the high God which hath created all things, may the
majestical being of thy greatness prosper for ever and ever, so that
thy sandals may serve for hairs to the heads of kings, making thee
like to the bones and flesh of the great prince of the silver mountains,
by whose commandment I come to visit thee, as thou mayst perceive by this his letter sealed with his royal arms.'

When he had made an end of speaking thus, the Cauchin, beholding him with a smiling countenance, 'May the sun,' answered
he, 'put a conformity between the desires of the king thy master,
and mine, and that by the sweet heat of his amorous rays, to the
end that the great amity, which is betwixt us, may endure and
continue firm till the last noise the sea shall make, that so the Lord
may be eternally praised in His peace.' At these words all the
lords that were in the room answered with one voice: 'So grant it
may be, O Lord Almighty, that givest a being to the night and the
day.' Then the same women, which played before, beginning their
music again, the king used no further speech, but only in kindly
entertaining [1] the ambassador, 'I will,' said he, 'read my brother
Xinarau's letter and return an answer thereunto according to thy
desire, to the end thou mayst go from me contented.' The ambassador made him no reply, but prostrated himself again at the
foot of the royal throne, laying his head three times on the upper-
most step where the king's feet stood. That done, the captain
of the guard took him by the hand, and led him to his house, where
he lodged during the three days that he abode there, at the end
whereof the king departed thence for to go to Usamguee.

In regard of the king's journey to Usamguee, the Tartar ambassador had audience but once by the way, in the which he moved
him about our particular,[2] according to the express commandment
he had received from his master for that purpose, and it was said
that the king heard him very willingly, answering that he would
do what he desired, and therefore willed him to put him in mind
of it, when the time should serve, to the end we might not lose the
opportunity of the season for our voyage. With this good news
the ambassador acquainted us at his return, and demanded of us
for this good office he had done us, that we would write him out
some of those prayers which we made to our God, whose slave, he
said, he infinitely desired to be, in regard of the great excellencies
which he had heard us deliver of Him. This we not only granted
him very readily, but also gave him infinite thanks besides for this

[1] A mistranslation. It should be 'on withdrawing he said to . . .'
[2] Appealed to him about our case.

his great favour showed unto us, which we made more account of than all the benefits that had been propounded unto us by the king of Tartaria if we would have continued in his service.

After the king was departed from the city of Fanaugrem, he proceeded on in his journey, travelling but only six leagues a day, by reason of the great number of persons that he carried along with him.   The first day he dined at a little town called Benau,[1] where he stayed until the evening, and then went to lodge at a monastery named Pomgatur.   The next morning he departed from thence, and so with not above three thousand horse in his train, he prosecuted his journey for nine days together, passing by many goodly towns, at least they seemed to be so, without permitting any reception to be made him by any of them.[2]   In this manner he arrived at the city of Lingator,[3] seated on a river of fresh water, which for the breadth and deepness of it is frequented with much shipping; there he abode five days, for that he found himself somewhat indisposed with the tediousness of the journey.   From this place he departed before day, taking no greater company with him than thirty horse, and so withdrawing himself from the communication of so much people as continually importuned him, he spent most part of the time as he went by the way in hawking and hunting; those of the countries by which he passed providing game always ready for him.   In this sort going on he slept most commonly amidst very thick woods in tents pitched for him to that purpose. Being arrived at the river of Baguetor, he passed down the same in certain vessels, called *laulees* and *jangaas*, which were there ready for him, till he came to a town named Natibasoy, where about evening he landed without any kind of pomp.

The rest of his journey he made by land, so that at the end of thirteen days he arrived at Usamguee, where he had a most magnificent reception.   At his entry thereinto there marched before him, as it were in triumph, all the spoils which he had taken in the wars, whereof the principal, and those which he made most reckoning of, were twelve chariots laden with the idols, of whom I have spoken heretofore, and whereof the forms were different as they use to have them in their pagodas.   Of these idols there were threescore and four of brass, which seemed to be giants, and nineteen of silver of the same stature, for, as I have delivered before, these people glory in nothing so much as to triumph over those idols, that so they may say that in despite of their enemies he had made their gods his slaves.   Round about these twelve chariots went divers priests by three and three, weeping and bound with iron chains.

---

[1] Perhaps Bassak.
[2] Cogan omits 'for he said popular feasts gave occasion for tyrannical officers to rob the people, which did God great disservice.'
[3] Possibly Stung-treng.

After them followed forty other chariots, each of them being drawn
by two rhinoceroses, and full from the bottom to the top of an
infinite company of arms and trailed colours.[1]   In the tail of them
there were twenty more, carrying each of them a very great chest,
barred with iron, and wherein, as we were told, was the treasure
of the Tinocouhos.   In the same order marched all other things
which are used to be most esteemed of in such triumphant entries,
as two hundred elephants armed with castles, and warlike *panoures*,
which are certain swords that are fastened to their teeth when
they fight, and a great number of horses laden with sacks full of
dead men's heads and bones; so that in this entry this king of
Cauchin presented to the view of his people all that he had gained
from his enemies in the battle he had given them.

After we had been a full month in this city, during which time
we had seen a world of stately shows, sports, and several sorts of
rejoicing, accompanied with most costly feasts and banquets, set
forth and made not only by the greater persons, but by the common
people also, the Tartar ambassador, that had brought us thither,
moved the king again about our voyage, whereunto he gave us so
gracious an ear that he presently commanded we should be furnished with a vessel for to carry us to the coast of China, where we
hoped to meet with some Portugal ship, that might transport
us to Malaca, and from thence to the Indias, which accordingly
was done, whereupon without further delay we prepared all things
necessary for our departure.

*Chapter XLIII. Our departure from the city of Usamguee, and our
adventures till our arrival at the isle of Tanixumaa, which is
the first land of Japan; with our going ashore there*

UPON the 12th of January we departed from the city of Uzamguee,
exceedingly rejoicing at our escape from so many labours and
crosses, which we before had sustained, and embarked ourselves
upon a river [2] that was above a league broad, down the which we
went seven days together, beholding in the meantime on either side
thereof many fair towns and goodly boroughs, which by the outward appearance we believed were inhabited by very rich people,
in regard of the sumptuousness of the buildings, not only of particular houses, but much more of the temples, whose steeples were
all covered over with gold, as likewise in regard of the great number
of barques and vessels, that were on this river, abundantly fraught
with all sorts of provisions and merchandise.

[1] The colours of the defeated were carried towards the ground.
[2] This must have been the Me-kong.   They were travelling inland again.

Now when we were come to a very fair town, called Quange-paruu,[1] containing some eighteen or twenty thousand fires, the *naudelum*, who was he that conducted us by the express commandment from the king, stayed there twelve days to trade in exchange of silver and pearl; whereby he confessed to us that he had gained fourteen for one, and that if he had been so advised as to have brought salt thither, he had doubled his money above thirty times: we were assured that in this town the king had yearly out of the silver mines above two thousand five hundred *picos*,[2] which are forty thousand quintals of our weight, besides the huge revenue that he drew out of many other different things. This town hath no other fortification than a weak brick wall, eight foot high, and a shallow ditch some thirty foot broad. The inhabitants are weak and unarmed, having neither artillery nor anything for their defence, so that five hundred resolute soldiers might easily take it.[3]

We parted from this place on Tuesday morning and continued our course thirteen days, at the end whereof we got to the port of Sanchau,[4] in the kingdom of China.[5] Now because there was no shipping of Malaca there, for they were gone from thence nine days before, we went seven leagues further to another port named Lampacau,[6] where we found two junks of Malaya, one of Patana, and another of Lugor. And whereas it is the quality of us Portugals to abound in our own sense, and to be obstinate in our opinions, there arose amongst us eight so great a contrariety of judgment about a thing, wherein nothing was so necessary for us as to maintain ourselves in peace and unity, that we were even upon the point of killing one another. But because the matter would be too shameful to recount in the manner as it passed, I will say no more but that the *necoda* of the lorcha which had brought us thither from Usamguee, amazed at this so great barbarousness of ours, separated himself from us in such displeasure, that he would not charge himself either with our messages or letters, saying that he had rather the king should command his head to be

[1] I am inclined to think this was Luang-Brabang. River transport was rapid and we are not told how long they had been travelling. The aim was eventually to reach the Chinese coast by the complicated system of interlaced rivers and canals.

[2] Cogan has 'fifteen hundred.' This is too much of a discrepancy with the information on page 211 that six thousand *picos* were equal to eight thousand quintals. In any case, however, these can be only approximate equivalents.

[3] The town was far from the capital and near silver mines. Mendes Pinto offers it to his countrymen.

[4] An island near Macau. They must, by then, have travelled several hundreds of miles. On the rivers, a constant and steady progress could be kept up day and night.

[5] Cogan omits the words, 'which is the island where the holy Father Francisco [Xavier] later came to die.'

[6] Macau.

cut off, than to offend God in carrying with him anything whatsoever that belonged to us.

Thus different as we were in opinions, and in very bad terms
amongst ourselves, we lingered above nine days in this little island,[1]
during which time the three junks departed without vouchsafing
to take us in, so that we were constrained to remain in these soli-
tudes, exposed to many great dangers, out of which I did not think
that ever we could have escaped, if God had not been extraordinarily merciful unto us; for having been there seventeen days
in great misery and want, it happened that a pirate named Sami-
pocheca arrived in this place, who having been defeated went
flying from the fleet of the *aytau* of Chincheo,[2] that of eight-and-
twenty sail, which this pirate had, had taken six-and-twenty of
them from him, so that he had with much ado escaped with those
only two remaining, wherein the most part of his men were hurt,
for which cause he was constrained to stay there seven days to have
them cured.   Now the present necessity enforcing us to take some
course, whatsoever it were, we were glad to agree for to serve under
him until such time as we might meet with some good opportunity
to get unto Malaca.   Those twenty days ended, wherein yet there
was no manner of reconciliation between us, but still continuing
in discord we embarked ourselves with this pirate, namely three
in the junk where he himself was, and five in the other, whereof
he had made a nephew of his captain.

Having left this island with an intent to sail unto a port called
Lailoo,[3] some seven leagues from Chincheo, we continued our
voyage with a good wind all along the coast of Lamau for the space
of nine days until that one morning when we were near to the river
of salt, which is about five leagues from Chabaquee, it was our ill
fortune to be assailed by a pirate, who with seven great junks fell
to fighting with us from six in the morning till ten of the clock
before noon, in which conflict we were so entertained with shot,
and pots full of artificial fire, that at last there were three sail
burnt, to wit, two of the pirate's and one of ours, which was the
junk wherein the five Portugals were, whom we could by no means
succour, for that then most of our men were hurt.   But at length
towards night, being well refreshed by the afternoon's gale, it
pleased our Lord that we escaped out of this pirate's hands.   In
this ill equipage wherein we were we continued our course for
three days together, at the end whereof we were environed by so
great and impetuous a tempest that the same night in which it

[1] Macau lies on a tongue of land and is gradually having its harbour more and
more silted up.   It is very possible that in Mendes Pinto's time it was a real
island; one still refers to Macau Island.   It was first occupied by the Portuguese
in 1586.
[2] Chao-chow.
[3] This seems to me to mean Swatow.

seized us we lost the coast, and because the violence of the storm would never suffer us after to recover it again we were forced to make with full sail towards the islands of the Lequios,[1] where the pirate, with whom we went, was well known, both to the king and those of the country; with this resolution we set ourselves to sail through the archipelago of these islands, where notwithstanding we could not make land, as well for that we wanted a pilot to steer the vessel, ours being slain in the last fight, as also because the wind and tide was against us.

Amidst so many crosses we beat up and down with labour enough from one rhumb to another for three-and-twenty days together, at the end whereof it pleased God that we discovered land, whereunto approaching to see if we could descry any appearance of a port or good anchorage, we perceived on the south coast near to the horizon of the sea a great fire, which persuaded us that there we might peradventure find some borough, where we might furnish ourselves with fresh water, whereof we had very great need. So we went and rode just before the island in seventy fathom, and presently we beheld two *almadias* [2] come towards us from the land with six men in them, who being come close to the side of our junk, and having complimented with us according to their manner, demanded of us from whence we came; whereunto having answered that we came from China with merchandise, intending to trade in this place if we might be suffered, one of the six replied that the *nautaquim*, lord of that island, called Tanixumaa,[3] would very willingly permit it upon payment of such customs as are usual in Japan, 'which is,' continued he, 'this great country that you see here before you.' At these news, and many other things which they told us, we were exceeding glad, so that after they had showed us the port, we weighed anchor, and went and put ourselves under the lee shore of a creek, which was on the south side, and where stood a great town named Miay-gimaa, from whence there came instantly aboard of us divers *paraoos* with refreshments, which we bought.

We had not been two hours in this creek of Miay-gimaa, whenas the *nautaquim*, prince of this island of Tanixumaa,[4] came directly to our junk, attended by divers gentlemen and merchants, who had brought with them many chests full of silver ingots, therewith to barter for our commodities; so after ordinary compliments passed on either side, and that we had given our word for his easiest coming aboard of us, he no sooner perceived us three Portugals, but he demanded what people we were, saying, that by our beards and faces we could not be Chinese. Hereunto the pirate answered that we were of a country called Malaca, whither many years

[1] Luchu Islands.   [2] See note, page 12.
[3] Tanegashima, a long, low, and cultivated island.   [4] The *daimio's* son-in-law.

before we were come from another land named Portugal, which
was at the further end of the world.[1]   At these words the *nautaquim* remained much amazed, and turning himself to his followers,
'Let me not live,' said he unto them, 'if these men here be not
the Chenchicogims, of whom it is written in our books that flying
on the top of the waters they shall from thence subdue the inhabitants of the earth, where God hath created the riches of the
world, wherefore it will be a good fortune for us if they come into
our country as good friends.'   Thereupon having called a woman
of Lequia, whom he had brought to serve as an interpreter between
him and the Chinese captain of the junk: 'Ask the *necoda*,' said
he unto her, 'where he met with these men, and upon what occasion
he hath brought them hither with him unto our country of Japan.'
The captain thereunto replied that we were honest men and merchants, and that having found us at Lampacau, where we had been
cast away, he had out of charity taken us in, as he used to do unto
all such as he met withal in the like case, to the end that God might
out of His gracious goodness be thereby moved to deliver him from
the danger of such violent tempests as commonly they that sail on
the sea are subject to perish in.

This saying of the pirate seemed so reasonable to the *nautaquim*,
that he presently came aboard of us, and because those of his train
were very many, he commanded that none but such as he named
should enter in.   After he had seen all the commodities in the junk
he sat him down in a chair upon the deck, and began to question
us about certain things which he desired to know, to the which we
answered him in such sort as we thought would be most agreeable
to his humour, so that he seemed to be exceedingly satisfied
therewith.   In this manner he entertained us a good while together,
making it apparent by his demands that he was a man very curious,
and much inclined to hear of novelties and rare things.   That
done, he took his leave of us and the *necoda*, little regarding the
rest, saying: 'Come and see me at my house to-morrow, and for a
present bring me an ample relation of the strange things of that
great world through which you have travelled, as also of the countries that you have seen, and withal remember to tell me how they
are called, for I swear unto you that I would far more willingly
buy this commodity than any that you can sell me.'

This said, he returned to land, and the next morning as soon as
it was day he sent us to our junk a great *paraoo*, full of divers sorts
of refreshments, as raisins, pears, melons, and other kinds of fruits
of that country.   In exchange of this present the *necoda* returned
him by the same messenger divers rich pieces of stuff, together with
certain knacks and rarities of China, and withal sent him word,

---

[1] They had told their nationality in this manner to the pirate, not being certain
how he would react to it.

that as soon as his junk should be at anchor and out of danger of the weather, he would come and wait on him ashore, and bring him some patterns of the commodities which we had to sell; as indeed the next morning he went on land, and carried us three along with him, as also some ten or eleven of the chiefest of the Chinese of his company, to the end that at this first sight he might settle a good opinion of himself in this people for the better satisfaction of that vanity whereunto they are naturally inclined; we went then to the *nautaquim's* house, where we were very well entertained, and the *necoda*, having given him a rich present, showed him the patterns of all the commodities he had, wherewith he rested so contented, that he sent presently for the principal merchants of the place, with whom the *necoda* having agreed upon a price for his commodities, it was resolved that the next day they should be transported from the junk unto a certain house, which was appointed for the *necoda* and his people to remain in till such time as he should set sail for China.

After all this was concluded the *nautaquim* fell again to questioning of us about many several matters, whereunto we rendered him such answers as might rather fit his humour than agree with the truth indeed, which yet we did not observe but in some certain demands that he made us, where we thought it necessary to make use of certain particulars altogether feigned by us, that so we might not derogate from the great opinion he had conceived of our country.[1] The first thing he propounded was, how he had learned from the Chinese and Lequios that Portugal was far richer, and of a larger extent, than the whole empire of China, which we confirmed unto him. The second, how he had likewise been assured, that our king had upon the sea conquered the greatest part of the world, which also we averred to be so; the third, that our king was so rich in gold and silver, as it was held for most certain that he had above two thousand houses full of it even to the very tops; but thereunto we answered that we could not truly say the number of the houses because the kingdom of Portugal was so spacious, so abounding with treasure, and so populous, as it was impossible to specify the same. So after the *nautaquim* had entertained us above two hours with this and the like discourse, he turned him to those of his train and said: 'Assuredly not one of those kings, which at this present we know to be on the earth, is to be esteemed happy, if he be not the vassal of so great a monarch as the emperor of this people here.'[2] Whereupon having dismissed the *necoda* and his company, he entreated us to pass that night on shore with him, for to satisfy the extreme desire that he had to be informed from us of many things

[1] Portuguese imperial expansion in the east depended very largely on Asiatics having a greatly exaggerated idea of the size and power of Portugal.
[2] Vassaldom is here viewed as a protection against less powerful aggressors.

of the world, whereunto he was exceedingly carried by his own
inclination; withal he told us that the next day he would assign us
a lodging next to his own palace, which was in the most commodious place of the town, and for that instant he sent us to lie
at a very rich merchant's house, who entertained us very bountifully
that night.

*Chapter XLIV.   The great honour which the nautaquim, lord of the
    isle, did to one of us for having seen him shoot with a harquebus,
    and his sending me to the king of Bungo; and that which passed
    till my arrival at his court*

THE next day the Chinese *necoda* disembarked all his commodities,
as the *nautaquim* had enjoined him, and put them into sure rooms
which were given him for that purpose, and in three days he sold
them all, as well for that he had not many, as because his good
fortune was such that the country was at that time utterly un-
furnished thereof, by which means this pirate profited so much,
that by this sale he wholly recovered himself of the loss of the
six-and-twenty sail which the Chinese pirate had taken from him;
for they gave him any price he demanded, so that he confessed unto
us that of the value of some five-and-twenty hundred taels which
he might have in goods, he made above thirty thousand.

Now as for us three Portugals, having nothing to sell, we
employed our time either in fishing, hunting, or seeing the temples
of these gentiles, which were very sumptuous and rich, whereunto
the bonzes who are their priests received us very courteously,
for indeed, it is the custom of those of Japan to be exceeding kind
and courteous.   Thus we having little to do, one of us, called
Diogo Zeimoto, went many times a-shooting for his pleasure in
a harquebus that he had, wherein he was very expert, so that going
one day by chance to a certain marsh, where there was great store
of fowl, he killed at that time about six-and-twenty wild ducks.
In the meantime these people beholding this manner of shooting,
which they had never seen before, were much amazed at it, insomuch that it came to the notice of the *nautaquim*, who was at that
instant riding of horses, and not knowing what to think of this
novelty, sent presently for Zeimoto, just as he was shooting in the
marsh, but when he saw him come with his harquebus on his
shoulder and two Chinese with him carrying the fowl, he was so
mightily taken with the matter as he could not sufficiently admire
it; for whereas they had never seen any gun before in that country,
they could not comprehend what it might be, so that for want of

understanding the secret of the powder, they all concluded that of necessity it must be some sorcery; thereupon Zeimoto seeing them so astonished, and the *nautaquim* so contented, made three shoots before them, whereof the effect was such that he killed one kite and two turtle-doves; in a word then, and not to lose time by endearing the matter with much speech, I will say no more, but that the *nautaquim* caused Zeimoto to get up on the horse's crupper behind him and so accompanied with a great crowd of people, and four ushers, who with battoons headed with iron went before him crying all along the streets: 'Know all men that the *nautaquim*, prince of this island of Tanixumaa, and lord of our heads, enjoins and expressly commands, that all persons whatsoever, which inhabit the land that lies between the two seas, do honour this *chenchicogim*, of the further end of the world, for even at this present and for hereafter he makes him his kinsman, in such manner as the *facharons* are, who sit next his person; and whosoever shall not do so willingly, he shall be sure to lose his head.' Whereunto all the people answered with a great noise: 'We will do so for ever.'

In this pomp Zeimoto being come to the palace gate, the *nautaquim* alighted from his horse, and taking him by the hand, whilst we two followed on foot a pretty way after, he led him into his court, where he made him sit with him at his own table, and to honour him the more, he would needs have him lodge there that night, showing many other favours to him afterwards, and to us also for his sake. Now Zeimoto conceiving that he could not better acknowledge the honour which the *nautaquim* did him, than by giving him his harquebus, which he thought would be a most acceptable present unto him on a day when he came home from shooting, he tendered it unto him with a number of pigeons and turtle-doves, which he received very kindly, as a thing of great value, assuring him that he esteemed of it more than of all the treasures of China, and giving him withal in recompense thereof a thousand taels in silver, he desired him to teach him how to make the powder, saying that without that the harquebus would be of no use to him, as being but a piece of unprofitable iron, which Zeimoto promised him to do, and accordingly performed the same.

Now the *nautaquim* taking pleasure in nothing so much as shooting in this harquebus, and his subjects perceiving that they could not content him better in anything than in this wherewith he was so much delighted, they took a pattern of the said harquebus to make others by it, and the effect thereof was such, that before our departure (which was five months and a half after) there was six hundred of them made in the country; nay, I will say more, that afterwards, namely the last time that the viceroy[1] Dom Afonso de Noronha sent me thither with a present to the king of Bungo,[2]

---

[1] That is, viceroy of India.   [2] The island of Kiushiu.

which happened in the year 1556, those of Japan affirmed, that in
the city of Fucheo,[1] being the chief of that kingdom, there were
alone thirty thousand; whereat finding myself to be much amazed,
for that it seemed impossible unto me that this invention should
multiply in such sort, certain merchants of good credit assured me,
that in the whole island of Japan there were above three hundred
thousand harquebuses, and that they alone had transported of
them in the way of trade to the country of the Lequios, at six several
times, to the number of five-and-twenty hundred; so that by
the means of that one, which Zeimoto presented to the *nautaquim*
in acknowledgment of the honour and good offices that he had done
him, as I have declared before, the country was filled with such
abundance of them, as at this day there is not so small a hamlet
but hath a hundred at the least; for as for cities and great towns,
they have them by thousands, whereby one may perceive what the
inclination of this people is, and how much they are naturally
addicted to the wars, wherein they take more delight than any other
nation that we know.[2]

We had been now three-and-twenty days in the island of Tanixumaa, where very contentedly we passed away the time, either in
fishing, fowling, or hunting, whereunto these people of Japan
are much addicted, whenas a vessel belonging to the king of
Bungo arrived in that port, in the which were divers men of
quality, and certain merchants, who as soon as they were landed
went to wait upon the *nautaquim* with their presents, according to
the usual custom of the country. Amongst them there was an
ancient man, very well attended, and unto whom the rest carried
much respect, that falling on his knees before the *nautaquim*
presented him with a letter and a rich cutlass [3] garnished with
gold, together with a box full of ventiloes, which the *nautaquim*
received with a great deal of ceremony. Then having spent some
time with him in asking of certain questions, he read the letter to
himself, and thereupon having remained a pretty while as it were
in suspense, and dismissed the bearer thereof from his presence,
with an express charge unto those about him to see him honourably
entertained, he called us unto him, and commanded the truchman [4]
that was thereby to use these words unto us: 'My good friends,
I entreat you that you will hear this letter read, which is sent me

[1] Fukuoka.
[2] Apart from the justness of this observation, it is interesting to note that
the Portuguese had visited Japan at a time of civil strife connected with the
Tokugawa regime.
[3] Most of the Japanese arts and crafts were borrowed from China. The
manufacture of ornamental swords was one of the most original crafts of that
military people.
[4] Hitherto Mendes Pinto had been among people who spoke or understood
Chinese, or dialects of it. An interpreter was again necessary now.

from my lord and uncle, and then I will let you know what I desire
of you'; so giving it to a treasurer of his, he commanded him to
read it, which instantly he did, and these were the contents of it:

'Thou right eye of my face, Hyascarangoxo, *nautaquim* of
Tanixuma, I, Oregemdoo, who am your father in the true love of
my bowels, as he from whom you have taken the name and being
of your person, king of Bungo and Facataa, lord of the great house
of Fiancima, Tosa, and Badou, chief sovereign of the petty kings
of the islands of Goto and Xamanaxeque,[1] I give you to understand, my son, by the words of my mouth, which are spoken of
your person, that some days since certain men coming from your
country have assured me that you have in your town three *chenchicogims* of the other end of the world, men that accommodate themselves very well with those of Japan, are clothed in silk, and usually
wear swords by their sides, not like merchants that use traffic,
but in the quality of persons that make profession of honour, and
which by that only means pretend to render their names im-
mortal;[2] moreover, I have heard for a truth, that these same men
have entertained you at large with all matters of the whole uni-
verse, and have affirmed unto you on their faith that there is
another world greater than ours inhabited with black and tawny
people,[3] of whom they have told you things most incredible to our
judgment, for which cause I infinitely desire you, as if you were
my son, that by Fingeandono, whom I have dispatched from hence
to visit my daughter, you will send me one of those three strangers,
which I am told you have in your house; the rather for that you
know my long indisposition, accompanied with so much pain and
grief, hath great need of some diversion. Now if it should happen
that they would not be willing thereunto, you may then assure them,
as well on your own faith as on mine, that I will not fail to return
them back in all safety; whereupon, like a good son that desires to
please his father, so order the matter that I may rejoice myself in
the sight of them, and so have my desire accomplished. What I
have further to say unto you, my ambassador Fingeandono shall
acquaint you with, by whom I pray you liberally impart to me the
good news of your person, and that of my daughter, seeing she is
as you know the apple of my right eye, whereof the sight is all the
joy of my face. From the house of Fucheo, the seventh *mamoque*
of the moon.'

After that the *nautaquim* had heard this letter read, 'The king
of Bungo,' said he unto us, 'is my lord and my uncle, the brother
of my mother, and above all he is my good father, for I call him by

[1] Perhaps Fukaye.
[2] Another example of the Japanese military spirit.
[3] Africa. Whether the Portuguese spoke of Africa as part of their empire
or not, we are not told, but they probably considered it as such at this time.

that name, because he is so to my wife, which is the reason that
he loves me no less than his own children, wherefore I count
myself exceedingly bound unto him, and do so much desire to
please him, that I could now find in my heart to give the best part
of my estate for to be transformed into one of you, as well for to
go unto him as to give him the content of seeing you, which out of
the knowledge I have of his disposition, I am assured he will value
more than all the treasures of China.   Now having thus acquainted
you with his desire, I earnestly entreat you to render yourselves
conformable thereunto, and that one of you two will take the pains
to go to Bungo, there to see that king whom I hold for my father
and my lord, for as for this other to whom I have given the name
and being of a kinsman, I am not willing to part with him till he
hath taught me to shoot as well as himself.'   Hereupon Cristóvão
Borralho and I, greatly satisfied with the *nautaquim's* courtesy,
answered him, that we kissed His Highness's hands for the exceeding honour he did us in vouchsafing to make use of us, and
seeing it was his pleasure so to do, that he should for that effect
make choice of which of us two he thought best, and he should not
fail to be suddenly ready for the voyage.   At these words, standing
a while in musing to himself, he looked on me, and said: 'I am resolved to send him there, because he seems not so solemn, but is of
a more lively humour, wherewith those of Japan are infinitely
delighted, and may thereby cheer up the sick man, whereas the
too serious gravity of this other,' said he, turning him to Borralho,
'though very commendable for more important matters, would
serve but to entertain [1] his melancholy instead of diverting it.'

Thereupon falling into merry discourse and jesting with those
about him, whereunto the people of Japan are much inclined,
Fingeandono arrived, unto whom he presented me, with a special
and particular recommendation touching the assurance of my
person, wherewith I was not only well satisfied, but had my mind
also cleared from certain doubts, which out of the little knowledge
I had of these people's humours, had formerly troubled me.   This
done, the *nautaquim* commanded two hundred taels to be given me
for the expense of my voyage, whereupon Fingeandono and I
embarked ourselves in a vessel with oars, called a *funce*, and in one
night having traversed all this island of Tanixumaa, the next
morning we cast anchor in a haven named Hiamangoo, from whence
we went to a good town called Quanquixumaa,[2] and so continuing
our course afore the wind, with a very fair gale, we arrived the day
ensuing at a very sweet place, named Tanora,[3] whence the morrow
after we went to Minato,[4] and so forward to a fortress of the king
of Bungo's called Osquy,[5] where Fingeandono stayed some time,

[1] Maintain.   [2] Kagoshima.   The ship evidently had business there.
[3] Toizaki.   [4] Miyazaki.   [5] Oita.

by reason that the captain of the place (who was his brother-in-law) found himself much indisposed in his health. There we left the vessel in which we came, and so went by land directly to the city, where being arrived about noon, Fingeandono, because it was not a time fit to wait upon the king, went to his own house.

After dinner having rested a little, and shifted himself into a better habit, he mounted on horseback, and with certain of his friends rode to the court, carrying me along with him, where the king was no sooner advertised of his coming, but he sent a son of his about nine or ten years of age to receive him, who, accompanied with a number of noblemen, richly apparelled, and his ushers with their maces going before him, took Fingeandono by the hand, and beholding him with a smiling countenance, 'May thy entrance,' said he unto him, 'into this house of the king my lord bring thee as much content and honour as thy children deserve, and are worthy, being thine, to sit at table with me in the solemn feasts.'

At these words Fingeandono prostrating himself on the ground, 'My Lord,' answered he, 'I most humbly beseech them that are in heaven above, which have taught thee to be so courteous and so good,[1] either to answer for me, or to give me a tongue so voluble, as may express my thankfulness in terms agreeable to thy ears for the great honour thou art pleased to do me at this present, for in doing otherwise I should offend no less than those ungrateful wretches which inhabit the lowest pit of the profound and obscure house of smoke.'

This said, he offered to kiss the cutlass which the young prince wore by his side, which he would by no means permit, but taking him by the hand, he led him to the king his father, unto whom, lying sick in his bed, he delivered a letter from the *nautaquim*, which after he had read, he commanded him to call me in from the next room where I stayed attending, which instantly he did, and presented me to the king, who entertaining me very graciously, 'Thy arrival,' said he unto me, 'in this my country is no less pleasing to me than the rain which falls from heaven is profitable to our fields that are sowed with rice.'

Finding myself somewhat perplexed with the novelty of these terms and this manner of salutation, I made him no answer for the instant, which made the king say to the lords that were about him: 'I imagine that this stranger is daunted with seeing so much company here, for that peradventure he hath not been accustomed unto it, wherefore I hold it fit to remit him unto some other time, whenas he may be better acquainted, and not be so abashed at the sight of people.'

Upon this speech of the king's I answered by my truchman, that whereas His Highness had said that I was daunted, I confessed

[1] His ancestors.

that it was true, not in regard of so many folks as were about me, because I had seen far many more, but that my amazement proceeded from the consideration that I was now before the feet of so great a king, which was sufficient to make me mute a hundred thousand years, if I could live so long; I added further, that those which were present there seemed to me but men, as I myself was, but as for His Highness, that God had given such great advantages above all, as it was His pleasure that he should be lord, and that others whould be mere servants, yea, and that I myself was but a silly ant in comparison of his greatness, so that His Majesty[1] could not see me in regard of my smallness, nor I in respect thereof be able to answer unto his demands.

All the assistants made such account of this mad[2] answer of mine, as clapping their hands by way of astonishment, they said unto the king: 'Mark, I beseech Your Highness, how he speaks to purpose; verily, it seems that this man is not a merchant, which meddles with base things as buying and selling, but rather a bonze, that offers sacrifices for the people, or if not so, surely he is some great captain that hath a long time scoured the seas.[3] 'Truly,' said the king, 'I am of the same opinion, now that I see him so resolute; but let every man be silent, because I purpose that none shall speak to him but myself alone, for I assure you that I take so much delight in hearing him talk, that at this instant I feel no pain.'[4]   At those words the queen and her daughters, which were set by him, were not a little glad, and falling on their knees, with their hands lifted up to heaven, they thanked God for this His great goodness unto him.

Chapter XLV.   The great mishap that befell the king of Bungo's son, with the extreme danger that I was in for the same; and what followed thereupon

A LITTLE after the king caused me to approach unto his bed, where he lay sick of the gout: when I was near him, 'I prithee,' said he unto me, 'be not unwilling to stay here by me, for it does me much good to look on thee and talk with thee; thou shalt also oblige me to let me know, whether in thy country, which is at the further end

[1] He was the *daimio* of Kjushiu, not the mikado.   Mendes Pinto, however, knew enough about life in the Far East to attribute a species of divinity to him.

[2] Cogan here has chosen an inappropriate adjective.   His answer was 'rough and gross,' rather than 'mad,' or so it seemed to him; the Japanese, however, found it a very fitting speech.

[3] Priests and warriors were the only two classes of society worthy of honour.

[4] Cogan omits the words 'so that that it may be that a while from now I shall eat somewhat.'

of the world, thou hast not learned any remedy for this disease wherewith I am tormented, or for the lack of appetite which hath continued with me now almost these two months without eating anything to speak of.'[1] Hereunto I answered that I made no profession of physic, for that I had never learned that art, but that in the junk, wherein I came from China, there was a certain wood, which infused in water healed far greater sicknesses than that whereof he complained, and that if he took of it, it would assuredly help him. To hear of this he was very glad, insomuch that transported with an extreme desire to be healed, he sent away for it in all haste to Tanixumaa, where the junk lay, and having used of it thirty days together, he perfectly recovered of this disease, which had held him so for two years together, as he was not able to stir from one place to another.

Now during the time that I remained with much content in this city of Fucheo, being some twenty days, I wanted not occasions to entertain myself withal; for sometimes I was employed in answering the questions, which the king, queen, princes, and lords asked of me, wherein I easily satisfied them, for that the matters they demanded of me were of very little consequence. Otherwhiles, I bestowed myself in beholding their solemnities, the temples where they offered up their prayers, their warlike exercises, their naval fleets, as also their fishing and hunting, wherein they greatly delight, especially in the high flying of falcons and vultures. Oftentimes I passed away the time with my harquebus in killing of turtles and quails, whereof there is great abundance in the country. In the mean season this new manner of shooting seemed no less marvellous and strange to the inhabitants of this land than to them of Tanixumaa, so that beholding a thing which they had never seen before, they made more reckoning of it than I am able to express, which was the cause that the king's second son, named Arichandono, of the age of sixteen or seventeen years, and whom the king wonderfully loved, entreated me one day to teach him to shoot, but I put him off by saying that there needed a far longer time for it than he imagined, wherewith not well pleased, he complained to his father of me, who to content the prince desired me to give him a couple of charges for the satisfying of his mind; whereunto I answered, that I would give him as many as his Highness would be pleased to command me. Now because he was that day to dine with his father, the matter was referred to the afternoon, howbeit then too there was nothing done, for that he waited on his mother to a village adjoining, whither they came from all parts on pilgrimage by reason of a certain feast, which was celebrated there for the health of the king.

[1] For other examples of the belief in the foreign healer, see Chapter XXVI, page 98, and the Shipwreck of the *São João*, page 259.

The next day this young prince came with only two young gentlemen waiting on him to my lodging, where finding me asleep on a mat, and my harquebus hanging on a hook by, he would not wake me till he had shot off a couple of charges, intending, as he told me afterwards himself, that these two shots should not be comprised in them I had promised him.   Having then commanded one of the young gentlemen that attended him to go softly and kindle the match, he took down the harquebus from the place where it hung, and going to charge it, as he had seen me do, not knowing how much powder he should put in, he charged the piece almost two spans deep, then putting in the bullet, he set himself with it to shoot at an orange-tree that was not far off, but fire being given, it was his ill hap that the harquebus brake into three pieces, and gave him two hurts, by one of the which his right-hand thumb was in a manner lost,[1] instantly whereupon the prince fell down as one dead, which the two gentlemen perceiving, they ran away towards the court, crying along in the streets that the stranger's harquebus had killed the prince.   At these sad news the people flocked in all haste with weapons and great cries to the house where I was. Now God knows whether I was not a little amazed when coming to awake I saw this tumult, as also the young prince lying along upon the floor by me weltering in his own blood without stirring either hand or foot.   All that I could do then was to embrace him in my arms, so beside myself as I knew not where I was.

In the meantime, behold the king comes in a chair carried upon four men's shoulders, and so sad and pale as he seemed more dead than alive; after him followed the queen on foot leaning upon two ladies, with her two daughters, and a many of women all weeping. As soon as they were entered into the chamber, and beheld the young prince extended on the ground, as if he had been dead, embraced in my arms, and both of us wallowing in blood, they all concluded that I had killed him, so that two of the company, drawing out their scimitars, would have slain me; which the king perceiving, 'Stay, stay,' cried he, 'let us know first how the matter goes, for I fear it comes further off, and that this fellow here hath been corrupted by some of those traitors' kindred, whom I caused to be last executed.'   Thereupon commanding the two young gentlemen to be called which had accompanied the prince, his son, thither, he questioned them very exactly.   Their answer was, that my harquebus with the enchantments in it had killed him.   This deposition served but to incense the assistants the more, who in a rage addressing themselves to the king, 'What need, sir, have you to hear more?' cried they; 'here is but too much, let him be put to a cruel death.'   Therewith they sent in all haste for the *jurubaca*, who was my interpreter to them; now for that upon the arrival of

[1] This is not well translated, as will later be seen.

this disaster he was out of extreme fear fled away, they brought him straitly bound to the king, but before they fell to examining of him, they mightily threatened him, in case he did not confess the truth; whereunto he answered trembling, and with tears in his eyes, that he would reveal all that he knew.

In the meantime being on my knees, with my hands bound, a bonze, that was president of their justice, having his arms bared up to his shoulders, and a poniard in his hand dipped in the blood of the young prince, said thus unto me: 'I conjure thee, thou son of some devil, and culpable of the same crime for which they are damned that inhabit in the house of smoke,[1] where they lie buried in the obscure and deep pit of the centre of the earth, that thou confess unto me with a voice so loud, that every one may hear thee, for what cause thou hast with these sorceries and enchantments killed this young innocent, whom we hold for the hairs and principal ornament of our heads.' To this demand I knew not what to answer upon the sudden, for that I was so far beside myself as, if one had taken away my life, I believe I should not have felt it; which the president perceiving, and beholding me with a terrible countenance, 'Seest thou not,' continued he, 'that if thou doest not answer to the questions I ask thee, that thou mayst hold thyself for condemned to a death of blood, of fire, of water, and of the blasts of the wind; for thou shall be dismembered into the air, like the feathers of dead fowl, which the wind carries from one place to another, separated from the body with which they were joined whilst they lived.' This said, he gave me a great kick with his foot for to rouse up my spirits, and cried out again: 'Speak, confess who they are that have corrupted thee? What sum of money have they given thee? How are they called? and where are they at this present?'

At these words being somewhat come again to myself, I answered him, that God knew my innocence, and that I took Him for witness thereof. But he, not contented with what he had done, began to menace me more than before, and set before my eyes an infinite of torments and terrible things; wherein a long time being spent, it pleased God at length that the young prince came to himself, who no sooner saw the king his father, as also his mother and sisters dissolved into tears, but that he desired them not to weep, and that if he chanced to die, they would attribute his death to none but himself, who was the only cause thereof, conjuring them moreover by the blood, wherein they beheld him weltering, to cause me to be unbound without all delay, if they desired not to make him die anew: the king, much amazed with this language, commanded the manacles to be taken off which they had put upon me; whereupon came in four bonzes to apply remedies unto him,

[1]Treason. Notice that Dante also puts traitors in the lowest part of hell.

but when they saw in what manner he was wounded, and that this thumb hung in a sort but by the skin, they were so troubled at it, as they knew not what to do; which the poor prince observing, 'Away, away,' said he, 'send hence these devils, and let others come that have more heart to judge of [1] my hurt, since it hath pleased God to send it me.' [2]

Therewith the four bonzes were sent away, and other four came in their stead, who likewise wanted the courage to dress him, which the king perceiving was so much troubled as he knew not what to do; howbeit, he resolved at length to be advised therein by them that were about him, who counselled him to send for a bonze called Teixeandono, a man of great reputation amongst them, and that lived then at the city of Facataa,[3] some seventy leagues from that place; but the wounded prince, not able to brook these delays,[4] 'I know not,' answered he, 'what you mean by this counsel which you give my father, seeing me in the deplorable estate wherein I am, for whereas I ought to have been dressed already, you would have me stay for an old rotten man, who cannot be here until one hath made a journey of a hundred and forty leagues both in going and coming, so that it must be a month at least before he can arrive; wherefore speak no more of it, but if you desire to do me a pleasure, free this stranger a little from the fear you have put him in, and clear the room of all this throng; he that you believe hath hurt me will help me as he may, for I had rather die under the hands of this poor wretch, that hath wept so much for me, than be touched by the bonze of Facataa, who at the age he is of, of ninety and two years, can see no further than his nose.'

Chapter XLVI. My curing the young prince of Bungo; with my return to Tanixumaa and embarking there for Liampoo

THE king of Bungo, being extremely grieved to see the disaster of his son, turned himself to me, and beholding me with a very gentle countenance, 'Stranger,' said he unto me, 'try, I pray thee, if thou canst assist my son in this peril of his life, for I swear unto thee if thou canst do it, I will make no less esteem of thee than of him himself, and will give thee whatsoever thou wilt demand of me.' Hereunto I answered the king that I desired His Majesty to

[1] This should be: 'do not exclaim continually about.'
[2] The nobility were guided rather by the somewhat stoical philosophy of Confucius, than by the religious beliefs connected with Buddhism or Shinto.
[3] Perhaps Osaka, near the capital of the emperor in Kioto.
[4] Though he still needed an interpreter, Mendes Pinto had been living among the Japanese long enough to follow the gist of what the prince was saying.

command all those people away, because the coil that they kept confounded me, and that then I would see whether his hurts were dangerous, for if I found that I was able to cure them, I would do it most willingly.   Presently the king willed every one to be gone, whereupon approaching unto the prince, I perceived that he had but two hurts—one on the top of his forehead, which was no great matter, and the other on his right-hand thumb, that was almost cut off.   So that Our Lord inspiring me, as it were, with new courage, I besought the king not to be grieved, for I hoped in less than a month to render him his son perfectly recovered.

Having comforted him in this manner, I began to prepare myself for the dressing of the prince, but in the meantime the king was very much reprehended by the bonzes, who told him that his son would assuredly die that night, and therefore it was better for him to put me to death presently, than to suffer me to kill the prince outright, adding further, that if it should happen to prove so, as it was very likely, [1] it would not only be a great scandal unto him, but also much alienate his people's affections from him.   To these speeches of the bonzes the king replied that he thought they had reason for that they said, and therefore he desired them to let him know how he should govern himself in this extremity.   'You must,' said they, 'stay the coming of the bonze Teixeandono, and never think of any other course, for we assure you in regard he is the holiest man living he will no sooner lay his hand on him but he will heal him straight, as he hath healed many others in our sight.'

As the king was even resolved to follow the cursed counsel of these servants of the devil, the prince complained that his wounds pained him in such sort as he was not able to endure it, and therefore prayed that any handsome [2] remedy might be instantly applied to them, whereupon the king, much distracted between the opinion of the bonzes and the danger that his son was in of his life, together with the extreme pain that he suffered, desired those about him to advise him what he should resolve on, in that exigent; not one of them but was of the mind, that it was far more expedient to have the prince dressed out of hand, than to stay the time which the bonzes spake of.

This counsel being approved of the king, he came again to me, and making very much of me, he promised me mighty matters if I could recover his son; I answered him with tears in my eyes, that by the help of God I would do it, and that he himself should be witness of my care therein.   So recommending myself to God, and taking a good heart unto me, for I saw there was no other way to save my life but that, I prepared all things necessary to perform the cure.   Now because the hurt of the right-hand thumb was most dangerous, I began with that, and gave it seven stitches,

---
[1] The original says 'clear that it would.'   [2] Handy, available.

whereas peradventure if a surgeon had dressed him, he would have given it fewer; as for that of the forehead, I gave it but five,[1] in regard it was much slighter than the other; that done, I applied to them tow wet in the whites of eggs, and so bound them up very close, as I had seen others done in the Indias. Five days after I cut the stitches, and continued dressing him as before, until that at the end of twenty days it pleased God he was thoroughly cured, without any other inconvenience remaining to him than a little weakness in his thumb. For this cause after that time the king and all his lords did me much honour; the queen also, and the princesses her daughters, presented me with a great many suits of silks, and the chiefest of the court with scimitars and ventiloes,[2] besides all which the king gave me six hundred taels, so that after this sort I received in recompense of this my cure above fifteen hundred ducats, that I carried with me from this place.

After things were past in this manner, being advertised by letters from my two companions at Tanixumaa, that the Chinese pirate, with whom we came thither, was preparing for his return to China, I besought the king of Bungo to give me leave to go back, which he readily granted me, and with much acknowledgment of the curing of his son he willed a *funce* to be made ready for me, furnished with all things necessary, wherein commanded a man of quality, that was attended by twenty of the king's servants, with whom I departed one Saturday morning from the city of Fucheo, and the Friday following about sunset I arrived at Tanixumaa, where I found my two comrades, who received me with much joy. Here we continued fifteen days longer, till such time as the junk was quite ready, and then we set sail for Liampoo,[3] which is a seaport of the kingdom of China, whereof I have spoken at large heretofore, and where at that time the Portugals traded. Having continued our voyage with a prosperous wind, it pleased God that we arrived safe at our desired port, where it is not be believed how much we were welcome by the inhabitants of the place.

[1] Cogan has 'four.'
[2] Cogan has 'other things,' instead of 'ventiloes.'
[3] This was, it will be remembered, Ning-Po.

V—THE TRAGIC HISTORY OF THE SEA
1552 AND 1585
(Translated by Charles David Ley)

Bibliographical

Navegação e lastimoso sucesso da perdiçam de Manoel de Sousa de Sepulveda. Lisbon. 1594.

Relação do naufragio da Nao San-Tiago, e Itinerario da gente, que nella se salvou. Lisbon. 1601.

História trágico-maritima em que se escrevem cronológicamente os naufrágios que tiverão as naos de Portugal, depois que se poz exercício á navegação da India. Lisbon. 1735.

THE TRAGIC HISTORY OF THE SEA

Account of the very notorious loss of the great galleon, the 'São João.' In which are told the great hardships and misadventures of the captain

MANOEL DE SOUSA SEPÚLVEDA

and the pitiful end to which he himself, his wife and children, and all the rest of his people came in the land of Natal, where they were cast on 24th June 1552.

Another shall come after, of good *fame*,
A *Knight*, a *Lover*, and a *lib'ral Hand*;
And with him bring a fair and gentle *dame*,
Knit *his* by LOVE, and HYMEN'S sacred Band.
In an ill hour, and to your loss and shame,
Ye come within the *Purlews* of *my* land;
    Which (kindly cruel) from the *sea* shall free you,
    Drowned in a *sea* of miseries to see you.

Sterv'd shall they see to death their *Children* deare;
Begot, and *rear'd*, in so great *love*. The black
Rude CAFRES (out of *Avarice*) shall teare
The *Cloathes* from the *Angellick Lady's* back.
Her dainty limbs of *Alabaster* cleare
To *Heate*, to *Cold*, to *Storm*, to *Eyes'* worse *Rack*
Shall be laid *naked*; after she hath trod
    (Long time) with her soft Feet the burning Clod.

Besides all this, *Their Eyes* (whose happier lot
Will be to scape from so much miserie)
This *Yoake* of LOVERS, out into the hot
And unrelenting *Thickets* turn'd shall see.
Ev'n *there* (when *Teares* they shall have squeez'd and got
From *Rocks* and *Desarts*, where no waters be)
    Embracing (*kind*) their *Souls* they shall exhale
    Out of the faire, but miserable Iayle.

Camões, *Os Lusíadas*, Canto V,
stanzas 46–8. Translated by
Richard Fanshawe (1665).

PROLOGUE

The manner of this shipwreck here related is such as to make
men greatly fear divine retribution, be good Christians, and bear
the fear of God before their eyes, not breaking His commandments.
For Manoel de Sousa was a noble and worthy gentleman, who, in
his time, had spent more than fifty thousand crusadoes in India on
giving food to many people, and on the good works he did to many
men; and yet, at the last, he came to end his life, as did his wife
and children, in great poverty and misfortune, amongst the Kaffirs,
without the wherewithal to eat, drink, and clothe himself. He
had, indeed, so many hardships to go through before his death
that they seem unbelievable to those who did not partake them.
But amongst these latter there was a certain Álvaro Fernandes,
boatswain's mate to the galleon, whom I met by chance here in
Mozambique in the year 1554, and who told me the whole story in
great detail.

Their story, then, may serve as a warning to all men. Therefore,
I have written down the hardships and death of this gentleman and
all his company, so that all those who travel by sea may continually
implore God's protection and Our Lady's intercession.—Amen.

*The shipwreck of the great galleon, the ' São João,' in the land of Natal
in the year* 1552

Manoel de Sousa (may God have mercy on his soul!) started from
Cochin [1] in this galleon on the third of February in the year fifty-
two on this ill-fated voyage. He sailed so late because he had been
to fetch cargo from Quilon. [2] Finding that there was a scarcity of
pepper he had laden about four thousand five hundred pounds [3]
there and then went on to Cochin to finish lading the amount of
seven thousand five hundred pounds in all. This he did with
great difficulty because of the war which was being waged in
Malabar. [4] Thus he departed homewards with this cargo, though
he could have taken twelve thousand pounds. But because the
ship carried only a small amount of pepper, that did not mean to
say that she was not very greatly burdened with other merchandise,

[1] Now in the province of Madras, on the north of Travancore, south-west
India, in fact.
[2] Some seventy miles to the south along the coast.
[3] Presumably pounds. The measure is not given in the original.
[4] The region of which the Portuguese centre at Calicut was the capital. The
new viceroy, Noronha, was a severe ruler and caused many abortive revolts
among the Asiatics under his control.

and that they would not have, for this reason, to take every care, seeing that overburdened ships are running a great risk.

On 13th April, Manoel de Sousa came in sight of the coast of the Cape[1] at thirty-two degrees.[2] They came so near in because it was so long since they had left India, and they were such a long time on their way to the Cape because of the worn-out sails they were using, which was one of the reasons, the principal one, in fact, of their being wrecked. Actually the pilot André Vaz had bent his course for the land round Cape Agulhas, but the captain, Manoel de Sousa, had asked him to keep nearer in to the land; so the pilot had done so, in order to fulfil the captain's wishes. And thus they came in sight of the land of Natal, and, with a light wind behind them, ran along the coast, constantly using the plumb-line and sounding depths until they came in sight of Cape Agulhas. The winds were so variable that, if one day they blew east, the next day they blew west. As late in the season as 11th May, while they were still north-east of the Cape of Good Hope, and at twenty-five miles from the coast, they were assailed by a wind coming from the west-north-west which was accompanied by frequent flashes of lightning. Near night-time the captain called the master and the pilot and asked them what was to be done in such weather, seeing that the wind was blowing against the prow. Both replied that the best plan was to make for land.

The reasons they gave for making for land were that the ship was very big and very long, that it was very greatly burdened with boxes and other goods, that they no longer had any other sails than those on the yards after the other equipment of sails had been carried away by a storm they had met with on the Line, and that their present ones were so torn that they were not to be trusted. For, if they stayed where they were, and if the weather then grew worse and they had to make for land, the wind might carry off the sails they had, and this would greatly endanger both their voyage and their safety, seeing that they had no others in the ship. Even those they were using were in such a way that it took as much time to mend them as it did to sail with them; the time they had spent lowering and patching up the sails had been one of the causes why they had not doubled the Cape[3] by now. Therefore their best plan was to make for land with the two foremast sails half furled, because if they used the head-sail only it was so old that the wind would quite certainly tear it off the yard, because of the great weight of the ship, whereas the two together would relieve each other. But while they were thus approaching the shore at some hundred and thirty leagues from the Cape, the wind veered so violently

[1] The shores of South Africa.
[2] Off the northern part of the coast of Natal.
[3] Of Good Hope.

to the north-north-east that it made them run to the south-south-west again.   Besides, the waves which bore down from the west and those which mounted up in the east so swamped the galleon that each time she rocked it seemed she was going to the bottom. They ran on like this for three days; at the end of them, the wind began to calm down a little, but the sea was still so rough and tossed the ship about so much that she lost three of the pintles from the helm; and it is the helm which determines whether a ship be lost or saved.   But nobody knew of this except the ship's carpenter, who had been to examine the helm and found those parts missing. He had gone to the master, one Cristóvão Fernandes da Cunha, the 'Pigmy,' and told it to him secretly.   He, being a good officer and a good man, had replied that such a thing ought not to be told either to the captain or to any other person, lest it should cause fear and panic on board.   And the carpenter had followed his advice.

Whilst they were in these difficulties, the wind came up again, (from the east-south-east, in a violent storm.   Then it seemed to them that it was God's will to make an end of the ship; as, later, it was.   So they made for land once again, using the same sail, but the helm made the ship heel, she could not be steered by it, she started to run alee.   The strong wind tore the mainsail off the main-yard.   When they saw that they had lost their sail and that they had no other to take its place, they all ran to take in the fore-sail, for they preferred to risk the waves striking the ship athwart to being left without any sails.   They had not quite finished lowering the foresail when the sea struck the ship athwart.   At the same time three such huge waves broke over her that the lurches she gave burst the rigging and the mast beams on the larboard side, so that only the three foremost ones were left.

As their rigging was broken and as they had no shrouds on the mast on that side, they fetched some rope to make some backstays with.   But, as they were at this work, the sea became so swollen that they decided their efforts were useless and that they would be better advised to cut down the mast, seeing how rough the sea was. The violence of the wind and sea would not let them make any reparations and not a man of them could keep his footing.

They had their axes in their hands and were beginning to fell the mainmast, when it broke away above the rings of the fiddle-blocks, as if they had felled it with one stroke, and the wind threw it into the sea to starboard, as if it were something very light, together with the top and the shrouds.   Then they cut the rigging and the shrouds on the other side and they all fell into the sea. Being now without their mast or their yards, they made a small mast out of the stump which was left them of the old one by nailing a piece of a spar to it and woolding this as best they might; to the spar they fastened a yard for the studding-sail.   They made a yard for a mainsail out of another spar, and began to furnish this main-yard with some pieces of old sails.   They also did as much for the foremast.   But all this was so patched up and weak that a very slight wind would have been enough to carry it all away.

When everything was ready, they hoisted the sails, the wind being south-south-west.   As the helm already had its three principal pieces missing, the ship could not be steered except with great difficulty, and they were already using the sheets instead of a helm.   And, as they went along thus, the wind grew stronger, and the ship ran to the leeward, and the wind drove them without their being able to control the ship with the helm or the sheets.   This time also the wind bore away the mainsail and its studding-sail.   When they saw they had lost their sails again, they had recourse to their fore-sail, but then the waves caught the ship athwart and she began to lurch.   The helm was rotten, and a wave which hit at it that moment broke it in the centre and bore half of it away; all the pintles were jammed into the gudgeons.   So we see that great care should be taken with the helms and sails of ships because of the many great trials which are to be met with when sailing along this route.

He who knows the sea well, or indeed any one who considers the matter fully, will understand the state of mind of Manoel de Sousa and his wife, and of the others, when they realized they were near the Cape of Good Hope in a ship without a helm, with no mast nor sails, and with nothing to make new ones of.   By now the ship lurched so much and took in so much water that they thought their best safeguard against going straight to the bottom would be to cut down the foremost mast which was splitting their ship open. They were just going to cut it when it was struck by a great wave which broke it at the mast-partner chocks and flung it into the sea for them without their having any further trouble than to cut its shrouds loose.   But in its fall the mast gave the bowsprit a heavy blow which knocked it off its block and threw practically all of it inside the ship.   Despite all, this was fortunate, for it left them with one mast.   Everything foretold greater hardships; for their sins, nothing availed them.   They had not seen land since they left the Cape,[1] but they must have been about fifteen to twenty leagues from it.

The ship began to be borne in the direction of the land, now that it was without masts, helm, or sails.   Manoel de Sousa and his officers were in a hopeless plight, but they determined to make a helm as best they could and to fit together some sort of makeshift sails out of some cloth they had with them as merchandise, so as to be able to reach Mozambique.   They at once set earnestly to work dividing the men, some to work on the helm, other to construct

---

[1] In this case Cape Agulhas is meant.

some kind of mast, and others to make some sort of sails; which all took ten days. They made the helm, but, when they began to fit it in they found it was too narrow and too short and, in fact, useless. Nevertheless, they hoisted what sails they had, in a last attempt to save themselves, and put in the helm, but it failed completely to steer the ship because it was not the same size as the other one the sea had washed away. Now, however, they came in sight of land. This was on 8th June. They prayed God to save them, being, as they were, so near the coast, with sea and wind bearing them landwards. For, indeed, there was no hope for them if they did not bring the ship ashore; otherwise, she would certainly sink to the bottom. She was all split open, and it was only by the miraculous help of God that she still kept afloat.

Thus Manoel de Sousa was very near land, though helpless. So he asked the opinion of his officers. They all said that the best manner of saving their lives from death at sea was to wait until they reached ten fathoms, and, when they sounded that depth, drop anchor, and launch the long-boat for them to disembark. They launched a small boat then and there with some men in it to examine the beach and find out which would be their best place to land in. They agreed that, after all had disembarked and come ashore in the long-boat or the smaller boat, such stores and arms as could be fetched should be; but to save any of the other goods would give rise to even greater risks, as the Kaffirs would steal them from them. In accordance with their plan, they went on approaching the coast amidst the noise of wind and sea, lengthening the ropes on one side and shortening them on the other; the helm would not steer the ship, and there were fifteen spans of water below decks. Near land they dropped the line, but still found the depth very great, so they let the ship run on. After a long time the smaller boat returned to the ship with the news that there was a beach near by where they could disembark if they could reach it, but that all the rest of the coast was jutting rocks and vast cliffs where they could not possibly be saved.

Indeed, it is very terrible for a man to think of! They were going to come aground in the country of the Kaffirs in the belief that they were safer there on land, dangerous as it was. So that we can see what hardships were in store for Manoel de Sousa, and his wife and children. Now that they had this information from the small boat they strove to go in a direction in which they might slowly approach the beach, till they reached the place they had been told of, where they found they were in seven fathoms, and cast anchor. Then they resolutely fitted instruments together for launching the lifeboat.

The first thing they did in the long-boat was to take another anchor and to cast it out onto the land. The wind was calmer now and the galleon was three bow-shots from the shore. Manoel de Sousa could see his galleon would go to the bottom, and that there was no help for it. So he called the master and pilot and told them that the first thing they were to do was to put him ashore with his wife and children, and twenty men to guard them; then they must go and fetch the arms, provisions, and powder out of the ship, and also some cambric cloth, in case there should be some means of purchasing provisions on land. Their aim would have to be to make themselves a rough fortification with barrels in that place, and to make a rough caravel [1] out of the wood of the ship, by which they could send word to Sofala.[2] But, as it was already written on high that this captain, his wife, his children, and all his company should meet their end, no plan could be thought of to which fortune would not be opposed. They had this idea of fortifying themselves there, but the wind came up again with great violence and the sea became so swollen that it drove the galleon in towards the shore, thus preventing them from doing anything of what they had intended. At this time, Manoel de Sousa, his wife and children, and about twenty men were on land, and all the rest were in the galleon. It is unnecessary to tell of the dangers the captain, his wife, and these thirty people went through in order to disembark. But since I must tell the truth of this sad story, I am bound to tell that the third time the small boat went to land it was lost, and some men were drowned, one of whom was the son of Bento Rodrigues. Until that time the long-boat had not been to land. They had not dared to send it with the sea so rough; the smaller boat had escaped those first two times on account of its lightness.

The master and pilot, and the other people in the ship, saw that the galleon was moving towards its land anchor, and understood that their sea-anchor had been broken by the drift underneath two days before. It was when the third day dawned that they realized that the galleon was only fastened by the land-anchor and that the wind was coming up. When the ship actually touched the bottom the pilot said to the others: 'My brothers, he who wishes to embark with me in the long-boat may do so, before the ship splits open and goes down.' Then he embarked and had the master put on board also, for the master was an old man and his courage had failed him because of his age. Though with great difficulty because of the great strength of the wind, about forty people embarked in the aforesaid long-boat. The sea was breaking so violently against the shore that it dashed the

[1] The light Portuguese caravels are the kind of craft most associated with the Portuguese Age of Discovery.
[2] Now in Portuguese East Africa. Captured by the Portuguese from the Arabs at the beginning of the century. One of their most important ports at that time.

long-boat in pieces against the beach.   But Our Lord was not willing
for anyone from this boat-load to die, which was a miracle because
the sea overturned them before they came to land.

The captain, who had disembarked the day before, went along
the beach cheering the men.   When he could, he took them by the
hand and led them to the fire he had made, because the cold was
very great.[1]   Nearly five hundred people were left in the ship,
namely, two hundred Portuguese and the rest, slaves.   Amongst
those left behind were Duarte Fernandes, the galleon's boatswain,[2]
and the guardian.   As the ship was by now constantly striking
against the ground, it seemed prudent to them to ease the anchor
by hand and allow the ship to run straight in to land.   They did
not want to cut it, lest the ebb should draw them out into the deep
water again.   After the ship went aground she soon broke apart,
one half being from the mast forwards, and the other from the mast
to the stern.   In about an hour those two pieces had become four,
the holes in the ship were broken wide open, and the goods and
boxes came floating to the surface.   The people in the ship made
for land on top of the boxes and wood.   More than forty Portuguese
and seventy slaves flung themselves into the sea and were drowned.
The rest were borne to land on the waves, or, in some cases, under
them, as it pleased Our Lord.   Many were wounded by the nails
and the wood.   Four hours later, the galleon was all broken up,
and not even a piece as long as two feet was to be found, though
the sea threw it all on shore in that great storm.

They say the goods in the galleon, both those belonging to the
king and those of private persons, were worth a thousand pieces of
gold.   For since India was discovered till then no ship had left
it so richly freighted.   But, as the ship had been broken into so
many fragments, Manoel de Sousa could not make the craft
he wished, for no long-boat was left nor anything out of which
he could have constructed a caravel.   So that he had to make
a different plan.

The captain now saw, as did all his company, that there was no
possibility of embarking.   So that, in consultation with his officers
and the gentlemen of the party, who were Pantaleão de Sá, Tristão
de Sousa, Amador de Sousa, and Diogo Mendes Dourado of
Setúbal, he decided to stay some days on that beach they had
reached from the galleon, until those who were sick had recovered,
seeing that they had water there.   Thus they made their defences
out of some chests and barrels, and stayed there twelve days.   All
that time no negroes came from the land to speak to them, though

[1] This shows that it must have been night-time, since it would not have been
cold during the day.   See the story of the *Santiago*, page 281.
[2] This is the 'boatswain's mate' referred to in the Prologue.   His full name
was Alvaro Duarte Fernandes.

during the first three days nine Kaffirs had appeared on a hill,
and stayed there for two hours, but without speaking to us, and
they had gone away again as if amazed.   Two days later it seemed
best to send a man with one of the galleon's Kaffirs [1] to see if they
could find some negroes to come and parley with them about selling
them provisions.   But their two messengers went around for two
days without finding a living soul, only some deserted straw huts,
by which they understood that the negroes had fled in fear.   Also,
they found arrows [2] sticking into some of the houses, which, it
is said, is the Kaffirs' sign of war.   Then they returned to the
encampment.

Three days afterwards, while they were still in the place to which
they had escaped from the galleon, seven or eight Kaffirs leading
a cow [3] appeared on a hill.   The Christians made them signs to
come down, and the captain went to speak to them.   When the
negroes were fairly cornered they made signs that they wanted
iron.   Then the captain sent for half a dozen nails and showed them
to them, and they were very pleased to see these, and came nearer
our men and began to bargain for the price of the cow.   Everything had been settled when five Kaffirs appeared on another hill
and began to call out to them in their language not to give the cow
in exchange for nails.   Immediately the Kaffirs went away, taking
the cow with them and not saying a word.   And the captain was
unwilling to take the cow away from them, though he was in great
need of it for his wife and children.

Thus he waited awhile, carefully on the watch.   He got up three
or four times every night to inspect the watches, which was a great
hardship for him.   In short, they all waited twelve days, until the
health of the party was recovered.   At the end of this time, he saw
they were ready to move on.   Then he called a council to decide
what they should do.   And, before they discussed the matter,
he spoke to them as follows:

'Gentlemen and friends, you can clearly see the state we are
reduced to for our sins.   I truly believe that my own alone would
have been enough for us to have been submitted to these great
privations you see we are undergoing.   But Our Lord is pitiful,
and He was so merciful to us that He willed that we should not
sink to the bottom in that ship, despite the great quantity of water
which we had below decks.   His will be done, for it is His object
to lead us to a Christian country, and may their souls be saved who
end their lives in the trials of our quest.   These days we have spent
here were necessary, as you see, gentlemen, for our sick to recover

---

[1] These would have been members of some Bantu tribe.
[2] These may have been of wood or of iron.   The negroes knew the use of
iron from its introduction to farthest Africa through ancient Egypt.
[3] Also introduced through ancient Egypt and Ethiopia.

their health. But now, God be praised, they are ready to move.
Therefore I have called you together here so that we may decide
what path we are to take to safety; since our determination to build
some craft or other has been frustrated, seeing we were not able to
save anything at all from the ship for that end. As, then, gentlemen and brothers, your lives are at stake as well as mine, it would not
be right to do or decide anything without asking the advice of all.
I ask one favour of you, not to abandon me or leave me if I cannot
travel as fast as the fastest of you because of my wife and children.
And may God in His mercy help us all.'

After he had spoken in this manner and they had disputed the
path they ought to take, they decided there was nothing else for it
but to make their way as best they could along those beaches in the
direction of the river Lourenço Marques had discovered,[1] and all
promised never to leave him. They put their plan into practice
straight away. It must have been a hundred and eighty leagues
to that river by the coast, but they travelled more than three
hundred, because of the many circuits they made in their attempts
to cross the rivers [2] and marshes they found in their way and in
afterwards, returning to the sea. It took them in all five months
and a half.

They began to move off from the beach (which was at thirty-one
degrees) [3] where they had been wrecked, on 7th June '53. In
the vanguard went André Vaz and his company carrying a banner
with a crucifix. Then came Manoel de Sousa with his wife and
children, and eighty Portuguese, and slaves; Dona Leonor, the
captain's wife, was carried by slaves, in a litter. Immediately
behind them followed the master of the galleon with the seamen
and the female slaves. Pantaleão de Sá came in the rearguard
with the rest of the Portuguese and of the slaves, about two
hundred people. Altogether they were about five hundred people,
a hundred and eighty of whom were Portuguese. They proceeded
like this for a month, enduring great hardships and great hunger
and thirst. All this time they ate nothing but the rice which had
been rescued from the galleon and some jungle fruits, for they
found no other food in the country, nor any one to sell it to them.
So that they went through privations which can neither be believed
nor written.

In all that month they must have gone a hundred leagues. Yet,
because of the huge circuits they made to cross the rivers, they
cannot have travelled even thirty leagues along the coast. By now
they had lost ten or twelve people. One of Manoel de Sousa's

---

[1] The Maputa, some fifty miles from the town in Portuguese East Africa
which now bears his name. Or, perhaps, the Limpopo. See note on page 252.
[2] The Tugela, the Umvolosi, and other lesser rivers.
[3] Somewhat to the south of where Durban now stands.

children, a bastard son of ten or twelve years of age who was very weak with hunger, had been left behind, he and a slave who was carrying him on his back.   When Manoel de Sousa asked for him and they told him he was about half a league behind, he nearly went out of his mind; for he had imagined the child had lagged behind in the rearguard with his uncle, Pantaleão de Sá (as he had done on other occasions), and, as a result, he had lost him.   He at once promised five hundred crusadoes to any two men who would go back and look for him.   But nobody would accept, it being nearly nightfall, and because of the lions and tigers,[1] who, had they seen any man out behind the others, would have eaten him straight away.   The captain was obliged not to leave the path he was following, and had to leave his son in that manner, though it was like leaving the light of his eyes to him.   Whence it may be seen how many hardships this gentleman had to undergo before his own death.   António de Sampaio, nephew of the late Governor of India Lopo Vaz de Sampaio, and five or six other Portuguese and some slaves were also lost, purely through hunger and the trials of the journey.

By now they had had a few skirmishes, but the Kaffirs had always been put to flight.   Diogo Mendes Dourado had been killed in an encounter in which he had fought bravely to the death, like a gallant knight.   What with their wakefulness and hunger and weariness their trials were so great that they were weaker every day. Every day one or two people dropped behind along those beaches or in that jungle, unable to go on; and these were immediately eaten by the tigers, or by the serpents, of which there were a great many in that land.   And certainly to see those men left behind every day in those deserts was a cause of great sorrow and misery to all. For he who was to be left behind would tell the others he had been journeying with, parents, brothers, maybe, or friends, to go on their way and to pray to the Lord God for him.   It was pitiful to them to see their relation or their friend left behind, and to be unable to do anything for him, and to know that in a very short time he would be eaten by savage beasts.   And, if this is painful to hear, how much more painful must it have been to those who saw it and lived through it.

Thus they went on their way in the greatest distress.   Sometimes they had to go inland into the wilds to look for food, or to cross rivers, then return to the sea coast where they had to climb up very high mountains or down very dangerous ones.   And, as if these hardships were not enough, the Kaffirs added others.   In this way they journeyed for about two months and a half, and they were so hungry and so thirsty that on most of those days very strange

---

[1] For 'tigers,' we ought to read 'leopards.'

things happened, some of the most noteworthy of which I shall recount.

It often happened that these people sold each other a pint pitcher of water for ten crusadoes; and for a cauldron which held two gallons they asked a hundred crusadoes. As this sometimes gave rise to disorders the captain took to sending for a cauldron of it, since the company had no larger vessels, and paying a hundred crusadoes to the man who went to fetch it. The captain then portioned it out with his own hand, and what he took for his wife and children cost him eight and ten crusadoes the pint. Later he portioned out the next one in the same way, so that they were never in difficulties for it, because after the money which had been made out of that water one day, there was always somebody to fetch it the next day, to take that risk for self-interest. Besides which they suffered great hunger and would pay dearly for any fish that was found on the beach or for any animal from the hills.

Thus they went along by daily stages, short or long according to the nature of the country they had to go through, but always under-going the trials I have spoken of. They must have been travelling for three months since they had first decided to set out for that river discovered by Lourenço Marques, which provides the ships' watering-place of Boa Paz. For many days they had only had the fruits they found by chance to sustain them, and toasted bones. Often snake-skins were sold in the encampment for fifteen crusadoes. Even when they were dry, they threw them into water and then ate them as they were.

When they went along the beaches they lived on shell-fish or fish thrown up by the sea. In the end they came across a Kaffir, an old man, who was a chief of two villages. He seemed to them a man of merit, and so he was, as can be seen by the welcome he gave them. He told them not to go on any further, but stay with him, and he would supply them as best he could. And, indeed, if supplies were lacking in that country, it was not because the land would not yield them, but because the Kaffirs only sow very little, and eat nothing but the wild cattle they kill.

So it was that this Kaffir king greatly importuned Manoel de Sousa and his people to remain with him. He told them he was at war with another king whose lands they would have to pass through, and that he wanted their help. If they went on ahead they were certain to be robbed by that king, who was more powerful than he was. In fact, he made every effort to prevent their going on further, both because of the advantage and support he hoped for from them, and because of the experience he had already had of the Portuguese through Lourenço Marques and António Caldeira's having been there. These two latter had named him Garcia de Sá, as he was old, and very like the man, and, also, good (for it cannot be doubted that there are good and bad in all nations). It was because he was so that he welcomed and honoured the Portuguese, and made every effort he could to prevent their going on any further, telling them that they would be robbed by the king he was at war with. They delayed there six days, considering the matter. But it seems that it was determined that Manoel de Sousa and the greater part of his company should meet with their end on this journey, and they would not follow the advice of this kinglet when he warned them.

When the king saw that the captain was determined to go on, he asked him for some men of his company to help him, before they departed, against a king in the country behind them. Manoel de Sousa and the other Portuguese were of the opinion that they could not do otherwise than as he asked, both because of his good deeds and the welcome they had received from him, and also so as not to give offence to him, since they were in his power and that of his people. For these reasons the captain asked his brother-in-law, Pantaleão de Sá, to go with twenty Portuguese to help their friend, the king. Pantaleão de Sá, with these twenty men and with five hundred Kaffirs and their captains, went back six leagues across the country they had come through, and fought the rebellious Kaffir and took all his cattle, which are their spoils of war, and brought it back to the encampment where Manoel de Sousa and the king were. This took them five or six days.

Thus Pantaleão de Sá and his men came back from the war they had gone to for the kinglet's sake, and rested after their labours. The captain again asked his officers' opinion about their departure. Their opinion was of little value, seeing that they decided to go on until they discovered Lourenço Marques's river and did not realize that they were already on its banks. The river flows into Boa Paz, and it has three arms which all lead into the same estuary, and they were on the banks of the first. Yet, though they saw a red mark, which was a sign that the Portuguese had already been there, their evil destiny blinded them and they only wished to go onwards. Now they had to cross the river and could not do it except in canoes,[1] because it was broad. There were seven or eight canoes fastened by chains in the river, which the captain wished to try and lay hands on and use for crossing the river; for the king, who greatly wanted to keep them with him and tried by every means to prevent their crossing, was not willing to give them the boats. For this reason the captain sent some men to see if they could lay hands on the canoes. Two came back and said it was a difficult matter. The others lagged behind purposely, loosened one of the canoes, embarked in it, and went away down the river, leaving their captain behind. He then realized it was

---

[1] *Almadias.* See page 12.

impossible to cross the river except with the king's consent. So he begged the king to let him be taken across to the other side in the canoes and said he would pay the people well who took him. Besides, Manoel de Sousa gave the king some of his arms, so that he should let them go and order them to be taken across the river.

On that, the king went with him in person. As the Portuguese feared some act of treachery on crossing the river, the captain, Manoel de Sousa, asked the king and his men to return home and to allow him and his people to cross the river freely, only accompanied by the negroes in the canoes. The negro kinglet had no ill intentions, rather did he wish to help them as far as it lay in his power; it was easy to persuade him to return to his place. He went away at once and let them cross freely. Then Manoel de Sousa ordered thirty men to cross to the other bank in the canoes with three muskets. Immediately the thirty men had reached the other bank, the captain went over with his wife and children and all the others after him. No one was robbed on that occasion, and they at once grouped themselves for proceeding on their way.

They had been travelling towards the second river for five days, and they must have gone thirty leagues, when they reached the middle river.[1] There they found negroes who directed them to the sea, it being then sunset. From the banks of the river they saw two large canoes. They made their camp there on a stretch of sand where they slept that night. This river was brackish, and there was no fresh water around there, only further back. They felt such thirst in the camp that they were in great straits that night. Manoel de Sousa wished to send for some water, but nobody was willing to go for it for less than a hundred crusadoes the cauldronful. For all that, he sent them, and they made two hundred out of it each day. Had he not consented, he would have been hard put to it.

They had to suffer all this thirst, even though they had so little to eat, as I said before. It was the Lord's will that water should be all the provisions they had. Whilst they were still at that encampment, on the next day near nightfall, some negroes arrived in three canoes. These told them, through one of the negresses in the encampment, who was beginning to understand a little, that a ship with men in her like them had been there but had now gone. Then Manoel de Sousa had them asked if they would take them across to the other side. The negroes replied that it was already night (Kaffirs will do nothing at night-time), but that they would take them across next day if they were paid for it. As soon as it was dawn, the negroes came in four canoes. For the price of a few nails, they began to take the people across. First

---

[1] The Komati. The author seems to have supposed that the Maputi and Komati were part of some huge delta of the Limpopo.

the captain had some men taken across to guard their passage. Next, he himself embarked in a canoe, with his wife and children, so as to wait for the rest of his company on the other side. With him went three other canoes loaded with people.

It is also said that he was not in his right mind by then because of frequent lack of sleep and the great anxieties of the journey, which always weighed heavier on him than on all the others. Being in that state and fearing the negroes would play him false, he seized his sword, pulled it out, saying: 'Dogs, where are you taking me to?'

When the negroes saw the naked sword they leapt into the sea and left him there in danger of being drowned. On which his wife and others who were with him begged him not to hurt the negroes, for if he did they would all be lost. And truly, any one who had known Manoel de Sousa and his urbanity and kindliness would certainly have said he was not altogether in his right mind had he seen the cultivated and courteous captain behaving thus. From that time on he was never able to command his people as well as he had been able to before. When they reached the other shore, he complained greatly of his head and they bound cloths round it. Finally, the whole company was assembled together again.

They were ready to move on again, but they saw a band of Kaffirs coming. On which they prepared to fight if necessary, thinking the negroes had come to rob them. The band drew near; they began to parley, and the Kaffirs asked our people who they were and what they wanted. Our people replied that they were Christians and that they had been wrecked, and they asked them to guide them to a broad river [1] which lay on ahead. Moreover, if the Kaffirs had provisions, let them bring them and they should be paid for them. The negroes replied, through a negress who came from Sofala, that if they required supplies they should come with them to a place where their king was, and that he would give them a good welcome.

At this time there must still have been some hundred and twenty in the company. Dona Leonor now went on foot as well, and, though she was a delicate young noblewoman she walked along those rough difficult pathways like any strong countryman. Indeed, she very often comforted the women who were with her, and helped to carry her children. (This was after there were no slaves to carry her litter.) It would really seem that the Lord in His mercy came to her aid. If not, how could a weak woman, unaccustomed to hardships, make her way along such rough pathways, suffering such hunger and thirst? For they had by now walked over three hundred leagues, because of their long detours.

Let us return to our story. On hearing the king was near by,

[1] The Limpopo.

the captain and his company let the Kaffirs guide them, and went
with them very quietly to the place the negroes had told them of,
though God knows what hunger and thirst they endured.   It was
a league's journey to the place where the king was.   When they
arrived, the Kaffir sent word to them not to enter the place (they
are very secretive about these things) but to go towards some trees
they had shown to them, where he would send them something to
eat.   Manoel de Sousa did as he was asked, feeling that he was in
a country not his own, and because he did not know so much about
the Kaffirs as we do now, after his wreck and that of the *São
Bento* [1]; for a hundred men with muskets could cross the whole
Kaffir country—they are more afraid of these than of the devil
himself.

Whilst they were reposing in the shade of the trees in this way,
the negroes began to bring them some food to buy with nails.
They stayed there five days.   They thought they would be able
to remain there until a ship came from India; that was what the
negroes said, too.   Manoel de Sousa asked the Kaffir king for a
house to shelter him and his wife and children.   The Kaffir replied
that he would give him one, but that his people could not all
stay there with him since they could not be fed, owing to the lack
of sufficient provisions in that country.   Let him stay there with
his wife and children and some other people of his choosing, and
the rest could be divided up amongst different places.   He would
order them to be given food and houses until a ship came.

We can see that the king had evil intentions in all this by what
he did afterwards; which adds proof to the opinion that the
Kaffirs fear muskets.   For, though the Portuguese had only five
muskets in all, and were a hundred and twenty in number and
practically dead with hunger, the Kaffir did not dare to fight them,
but separated them from one another by sending them to different
places, so that he might rob them.   And they, not realizing how
much better it would have been not to be separated, gave themselves up to fate and did what the king who meant to destroy them
wished, though they had not taken the advice of the kinglet who
told them the truth and had been as good to them as he could.
By which men may see that they should not think they can ever
decide or direct what they do; rather must they put everything into
the hands of the Lord God.

So the Kaffir king came to an agreement with Manoel de Sousa
that the Portuguese should be portioned out amongst several
villages or other places, so that they could be fed.   He told him

[1] The *São Bento* was also wrecked in Natal shortly afterwards.   The shipwrecked party wandered over the same country, and had even more harassing, if
less fatal, experiences.   Its fate is the second narrative of the *História tràgico-
marítima*: that of the *São João* provides the first.

he had captains of his own there who would take charge of the
people, that is to say that each would be responsible for feeding
those who were entrusted to him! this, however, was impossible
if he did not order the Portuguese to leave their weapons behind,
because the Kaffirs were afraid of these when they saw them.
He would have the muskets put into a certain house and give them
back to them when the Portuguese ship came.

Because Manoel de Sousa was by now very ill and not in his
perfect mind, he did not reply as he would have done had he had
his wits about him.   His answer was that he would consult with
his people.   But, because the hour had come in which he was to
be robbed, he spoke to them and told them that he was not going
to go any further; some help would come, either in the form of a
ship, or by some other means the Lord might ordain.   The river
they were on [1] was the one discovered by Lourenço Marques,
as his pilot, André Vaz, said.   Any who wanted to go on might
do so if they thought fit.   He could not, out of love to his wife
and children, for his wife was very much weakened by these great
hardships and neither could go any further nor had slaves to carry
her.   Therefore his decision was that if God wished to make an
end of him and his family His will should be done.   But he asked
those who went on to bring or send word if they came across any
Portuguese shipping.   Let those who wished to remain with him
remain; whatever was in store for him would be in store for them.
Moreover, it was necessary to give up their arms so that the negroes
could trust them and not think they were thieves who came to rob;
this they must do to relieve the great hunger with which they had
been afflicted for so long.   Which shows that Manoel de Sousa
who suggested this and those who consented to it were not altogether responsible for their actions, for, had they considered,
they would have understood that the negroes had never molested
them as long as they had firearms.   Then the captain ordered the
arms to be given up, though his hopes of being saved, after God,
lay in them.   This was done against the wishes of some of them
and completely against those of Dona Leonor.   For nobody
protested except her, though it was of little avail to her.   She said:
'You are giving up the arms.   Now I know that I am lost, and all
these people.'   The negroes took the arms and carried them off
to the Kaffir king's house.

The Kaffirs' treachery had been planned beforehand and, as soon
as they saw that the Portuguese had no weapons, they began to
separate them and rob them and take them through the jungle in
the groups they had been sorted into.   When they reached the
appointed places they stripped them, and left them with nothing on

[1] The Komati.   They were, in fact, slightly to the north-east of the present
town of Lourenço Marques.

them and drove them out, beating them severely. Manoel de
Sousa did not go in any of these groups. He, and his wife and
children, the pilot André Vaz, and about twenty other people,
stayed with the king because they had a great quantity of jewels
and precious stones and coins. It is said that what that company
brought all that way with it was worth more than a hundred thousand crusadoes. As soon as Manoel de Sousa and his wife and those
twenty other people had been separated from the rest they were
immediately robbed of all they had brought with them, though the
king did not strip them. He told him that he might go away at
once in search of his company, for he did not wish to do him any
more harm, nor hurt his person or that of his wife. When this
happened to Manoel de Sousa he must have seen very clearly
what a great mistake he had made in giving up the arms. But he
had to do what they told him, for it was not in his power to do
otherwise.

The other members of the company, ninety in all, including
Pantaleão de Sá and three other gentlemen, though they had all
been separated from each other and robbed and stripped by the
Kaffirs to whom they had been apportioned by the king, managed
to come together again, little by little, because they were not far
from each other. So they started out again together, beaten,
despondent, without arms, clothes, or money to buy food with,
and without their captain.

They now no longer looked like men; they had no one to lead
them, and, in their disorder, they travelled quite out of the right
path. No council was held any more, nor was there any one
capable of calling one together. Some went through the jungle;
others went over the mountains; they spread hither and thither
and at last each of them only cared for finding some way of preserving his life, either amongst the Kaffirs or amongst the Moors.
But, as they were now completely lost, I shall speak of them no
more, but return to Manoel de Sousa, and his unfortunate wife,
and his children.

When Manoel de Sousa found he had been robbed and then
sent away by the king to look for his company, and that he had no
money, arms, or people that could have wielded them, he felt
the wrong which had been done him deeply; and that despite the
fact that his head had been disordered for some days. But if he
did so, can we imagine what a most delicate woman would feel
brought face to face with such trials and such need, above all, when
she saw her husband in that state, unable either to command any
more or to take thought for his children. But she, being a woman
of intelligence, took the advice of the men she still had with her,
and they began to go through the jungle with no help and stay
but God. At this time, André Vaz the pilot was still in her com-

pany, and the boatswain,[1] who never left her, and one or two
Portuguese women, and some female slaves.   Whilst they went
along they decided it would be best to follow the track of the
ninety despoiled men who were two days' journey on ahead.   By
now Dona Leonor was very weak, sad, and disconsolate, because
she saw how ill her husband was, and because she found the
others were so far off that she thought it impossible ever to join
them.   To think of it is a thing to break one's heart.   As they
went along thus the Kaffirs again came upon the captain, his wife,
and the few people who were in their company and stripped them
there without leaving anything on them.   When they were both left
like that, with two very young children with them, they com-
mended themselves finally to the Lord.[2]

Here they say that Dona Leonor would not let herself be stripped,
but defended herself with buffets and blows, for she was of a nature
to prefer being killed by the Kaffirs to being left naked before all
the people.   There is no doubt, even, but that her life would have
been over if Manoel de Sousa had not begged her to let herself
be stripped, reminding her that all were born naked, and, as it was
God's will, she should not now refuse to be so, too.   One of their
great trials was seeing those two little children of theirs there
crying and asking for food whilst they, the parents, were unable to
help them.   When Dona Leonor was left without clothes, she flung
herself on the ground immediately and covered herself completely
with her hair, which was very long.   She made a hole in the sand
in which she buried herself up to the waist and never arose from it
again.   Manoel de Sousa then turned to an old nurse of hers who
had been left with a torn shawl and asked her for it to cover Dona
Leonor with, and she gave it to him.   For all that, Dona Leonor
never again consented to arise from the spot on which she had
flung herself down when she had been left naked.

Truly I do not know who could consider this without great pity
and sadness.   Here was a most noble woman, the daughter and the
wife of very honourable gentlemen, most cruelly and ignominiously
used!   When the men who were still in their company saw Manoel
de Sousa and his wife naked they moved away a little, being ashamed
to see their captain and Dona Leonor so.   Then she said to André
Vaz the pilot: ' You see the state we are in and that we cannot go on
any further and that we must end our lives here, for our sins.   Go
on your way, save yourselves, and commend us to God.   If you
reach India or Portugal at some future time, tell them how you left
Manoel de Sousa and myself and our children.'   They, seeing it
was not in their power to alleviate their captain's exhaustion, nor

---

[1] Álvaro Duarte Fernandes.   See pages 240 and 246.
[2] Literally, 'They gave thanks to God.'   God must be thanked both for
fortune and misfortune.

the poverty and misery of his wife and children, went off through
the jungle to save their lives as best they might.

After André Vaz had left Manoel de Sousa and his wife, Duarte
Fernandes the boatswain of the galleon stayed with them, as did
some female slaves; three of these were afterwards saved and went
to Goa where they told how they had seen Dona Leonor die.
Though Manoel de Sousa was not in his right mind he did not
forget the great need of eating his wife and children were in. He
was limping from a wound the Kaffirs had given him in his leg,
but, nevertheless, he went out wounded as he was into the jungle
to find fruit for them to eat. On his return he found Dona Leonor
very weak with hunger and weeping, for, after the Kaffirs had
stripped her, she had never arisen from that place, nor ceased
weeping. And he found one of the children dead, and buried
him in the sand with his own hands. The next day, Manoel de
Sousa again went out into the jungle to look for fruit, and, when he
returned, Dona Leonor had died, and the other child, and the five
slaves were weeping over her with violent cries.

They say that when he found her dead he did nothing but make
the slaves retire and sit down near her with his head in his hands
for the space of half an hour, without weeping or saying anything.
His eyes were fixed on her, and he paid little heed to the child.
When that space of time was over, he arose and began to dig a
hole in the sand with the help of the slaves. Still not speaking a
word, he buried her and his son with her. When this was ended, he
again took the same path which he had taken when he had gone to
look for the fruits, saying nothing to the slaves. He went into the
jungle and they never saw him again. It would seem beyond doubt
that, as he wandered through the jungle, he must have been eaten by
the lions and tigers. So husband and wife ended their lives, after
six months' journey with great trials through the lands of the Kaffirs.

Those who escaped of all this company, both of those who had
remained with Manoel de Sousa when he was robbed and of the
ninety who had gone on ahead, must have been some eight Portuguese, fourteen men slaves, and three of the women slaves who
were with Dona Leonor when she died. Amongst the eight
Portuguese were Pantaleão de Sá, Tristão de Sousa, the pilot
André Vaz, Baltazar de Sequeira, Manoel de Castro, and Álvaro
Fernandes. As they wandered over the countryside without hopes
of ever reaching a Christian land, a ship came into that river in
which a relation of Diogo de Mesquita's was going to trade in
ivory. Hearing the news that there were Portuguese lost in that
land he sent for them and ransomed them in exchange for beads.
Each person cost twoscore beads, which are the things the negroes
value most. And if Manoel de Sousa had been alive at that time
he would have been ransomed also. But it seems it was for the

good of his soul otherwise, since such was the Lord's will. Those who were saved reached Mozambique [1] on 25th May 1553.

Pantaleão de Sá wandered for a long time through the lands of the Kaffirs. He reached the palace [2] almost exhausted by hunger, nakedness, and the trials of so long a journey. When he reached the door of the palace he begged the people of the palace to obtain some relief from the king for him. They refused to ask him, but excused themselves on account of the great illness the king had long been suffering. The illustrious Portuguese asked them what illness that was, and they replied, a sore on his leg which was so beyond treatment and so festered that they expected his death at any time. He listened attentively and asked them to let the king know of his coming, for he said he was a doctor and that he could perhaps restore him to health. [3] They were very glad to hear it and went in at once to tell the news to the king. The king instantly asked them to bring Pantaleão de Sá in. He, when he saw the wound, said to the king: 'Take good heart. You will easily recover your health.' He went out and began to think over the task he had undertaken. He could not even escape from that situation alive, for he knew of no sort of treatment to apply to the king, seeing that he had learned rather to take lives than to cure complaints and save people. Thinking thus, despairing of life, and preferring to die once than many times, he pissed on the ground, thus making a little mud, and went in to put it on the almost incurable sore. That day went by; on the following the illustrious Sá expected to receive his own death sentence and saw no hope of life either for himself or for the king. But the courtiers came out with a huge commotion, wishing to carry him around on their shoulders. He asked them the cause of their unexpected gaiety, and they replied that all the suppuration of the sore had disappeared because of the medicament which had been put on it, and that only the flesh now showed, in a good, healthy state. The supposed doctor went in, and, when he saw that it was as they had related, he ordered the treatment to be continued. In this manner the king recovered his perfect health in a few days' time. In view of this, besides other honours, they placed Pantaleão de Sá on an altar, and the king, worshipping him like a divinity, asked him to stay in his palace; and he offered him the half of his kingdom, and, if not that, he would do whatever he wished. Pantaleão de Sá refused his offer, and told him he had to return to his own people. The king ordered a great quantity of gold and precious stones to be brought, with which he plentifully rewarded him, and ordered his men to accompany him to Mozambique.

[1] This town had become a Portuguese possession early in the century.
[2] One is led to the conclusion that this was a Moorish, not a Kaffir palace.
[3] See notes on pages 98 and 231.

Account of the wreck of the 'Santiago' in the year 1585, and the journeyings of those who were saved from it. Written by Manoel Godinho Cardoso.

On Wednesday, 1st April, 1585, the *Santiago* left Lisbon with other ships bound for India. The admiral was Fernão de Mendonça, the pilot Gaspar Gonçalves, and the master Manoel Gonçalves. She set sail between eight and nine o'clock, but later cast anchor opposite Santa Catarina de Ribamar, where they stayed for that day, there not being enough wind. On the Thursday the ships moved off towed by galleys. But, as the wind was too rough, they anchored again. The flagship and the *Santo Alberto* were now at the end of the bar, and the others at the tower of São Gião. On the Friday, the two foremost ships crossed the bar with their topsails furled and waited for the companions they had left behind. But the latter lacked the wind that had impelled the former, and were unable to cross that day. So the two ships went on their way and they never saw the others again.

From that Friday until the Monday in Holy Week they were sometimes becalmed and sometimes rolling from one side to the other. The wind often changed, and on the Tuesday they entered what is called the Valley of Mares, and began to feel the fury of the sea there. The calm ended in a long relentless storm. They were nearly lost, because the wind began to blow up from all quarters, and the seas were so swollen that, though the *Santo Alberto* was sailing within hail of the flagship, they could at times not see her for the great mountains of water that rose between the two ships; or again, they saw her lifted so high on those waves that the flagship seemed swallowed in those gulfs.

The storm lasted all that day and was so violent that many wished themselves back in Lisbon. And some, even of the boldest, thought that they should seek harbour at Bayona,[1] owing to the great risk they were undergoing in such turbulent waters. Indeed in whatever direction the prow turned it was always struck by the waves. But what made them most afraid was seeing the foremast of the *Santo Alberto* break. This ship thereupon made for Lisbon and indeed the officers in the flagship feared lest the same disaster should happen to them. But Our Lord willed the winds to die down, by virtue of the Agnus Dei and the relics they had dipped into [2] the sea.

On the Thursday morning they sighted two sails, a large one and a small one. Thinking they were French they got ready to fight them, though they had not come prepared for that sort of thing. Besides most of them having been seasick, the decks were

---

[1] A little harbour in Galicia.

[2] It may be they threw them into the sea. See note 2 on page 265.

obstructed with barrels and cases (as they always are at the beginning of a voyage), and the muskets were rusty with the rain, and everything was in such disorder that, courageous as our soldiers are, if the enemy had managed to board them, they would have been in great straits.   But Our Lord was merciful; because at dinner-time they learned that one of them was a ship from India. They approached her and she proved to be a caravel from Sezimbra going to the Canary Islands.   They heard that the other was an English ship which had followed behind her like a shadow, and had not departed a stone's throw from her until the previous day. Since this news put them at ease they fell again into the seasickness fear had taken from them, and this was a great hindrance to performing the holy offices on those days as the priests wished. All the same, they celebrated tenebrae under the quarter-deck, where the altar was.

On the Thursday morning there was Mass, and in the afternoon the washing of the feet with a sermon by Father Pedro Martins, of the Company of Jesus, and, at night, a procession with a sermon on the Passion by Father João Gonçalves.   On the Friday morning, the ceremony of the adoration of the cross was celebrated, but the sea was so rough and the ship heaved so much that, instead of the deacon and sub-deacon, two men stood at the altar holding up the priest who was performing the ceremony lest he should fall.

On the Saturday, that is, twelve days after they had embarked, Our Lord was pleased to send them a good, steady wind.   So that they escaped from the hazards of this first trial.   And this added in no small manner to the joy and solemnity with which they celebrated Our Lord's Resurrection.   On Easter morning they made a procession round the deck and fired several pieces of artillery.   Then there was Sung Mass.   Though it was celebrated without the Holy Sacrament,[1] the congregation heard it devoutly, for the storm was now over and it was as if they had, with Christ, returned to life from the death they had all seen before their eyes.

Friar Thomas Pinto, of the Order of Preachers, who was to be an inquisitor in India, and his companion, Friar Adrião de S. Jerónimo, were travelling in this ship; besides Father Pedro Martins, Father Pedro Álvares, Father João Gonçalves, Father Sapata, Brother Manoel Ferreira, and Brother Manoel Dias, all of the Company of Jesus.   Father Pedro Martins arranged with them all that, as there were so many clerics on board, there should be Mass every Sunday and Saint's Day.   And from then onwards so it was, and Mass was also said for Our Lady every Saturday, besides on many other days because of the great zeal there was for her.   And it was also celebrated so continuously on Fridays that sailors who had made that voyage for fifteen or twenty years

[1] This was then a rule for Masses at sea.

said that in no ship had there ever been so many and such solemn
divine services as in that one.

When some Saint was to be honoured they chose a master of the
ceremonies to organize the festival.   Each of these masters coveted
being considered the best organizer.   Sometimes there was choral
music with organ and harp for evensong and Mass, and several
displays of tapestried leather which was going to be sold in India.
Orders were also given for somebody to be elected every week as a
warden for the poor when they were taken ill.   The first week the
captain took this work on himself.   And he and the two after
him performed the work with such care that all after them could
not but be charitable and liberal.   So it seemed better to have one
special warden for the whole voyage.   So that Father Sapata was
made prefect of the sick with the task of finding everything necessary for them by means of charity.   Because, though the captain
wished to provide for the sick at his own cost and told the priest
not to ask any one else for anything, many worthy men who were
in the ship begged that the poor should be cared for by the charity
of all, since they too wanted to contribute their part.   And so
it was done in common.

Now, gambling cannot be totally banished from ships however
much preaching there may be.   Father Sapata, not wishing the
players to have to pay for those games in Purgatory, went around
the ship from table to table, telling them to play a portion of their
money for the sick in restitution for certain excesses there were in
their play.   Every one accepted this because he spoke with courtesy
and authority.   The very first round they played they put aside a
portion for the sick.   By the time he went away there were so many
large portions collected that, besides the sick, he was able to help
many poor soldiers and buy them clothes for the common stock.
So I think that, after God's will, this was the principal cause of
there being very few ill people on this voyage, till they were wrecked.
And only one man died and he was not one of the poor the priest
was caring for.   Because, in general, those who die in these ships
are poor devils who come on board dead with hunger and naked to
sun, wind, and stars.

The principal needs of every one were thus provided for.   Father
Pedro Álvares took charge of religious instruction, and on Easter
Sunday Father Pero Martins had wanted to begin the series of
sermons.   But on the Saturday he was taken ill with a burning
ague of a rather serious nature.   However, God was pleased to
remove their anxieties because, after being bled three times, the
fever left him in a week.

They continued on their voyage with a good wind and reached
the coast of Guinea.   The calms in that region are well known
to sailors who go to India.   They began at three degrees to the

north of the equator and continued to three or four to the south
of it.   This took them seventeen days.   They crossed the line
on 27th May, in such disagreeable, burning heat that the heat of
the Alentejo [1] is like the cold of Norway in comparison with it,
During this calm they had a great fright.   They sighted a sail.
They thought she must have come from India, for it seemed to
them that a French ship would not have come so far south.   They
sent seven or eight men in the skiff.   But she did not want to be
known and shot at them with a cannon to make them turn back.
And indeed she very nearly sent them to the bottom.

Having passed the line, three or four degrees to the south of it,
some winds blew up which the sailors call 'general' because when
ships go to India they generally come across them there.   And
sometimes they are so contrary that they drive the ships towards
the Brazilian coast, and they are in great danger of being lost on
the many shoals there are in those parts, called the Abrolhos.
But God delivered them from that danger and they sailed between
the islands of Martim Vaz.[2]   And that is the best course, since it is
far away from the Brazilian Abrolhos.

They saw these islands on the eve of St. Anthony.   There was
as much joy in the ship as if they had seen the bar at Goa.[3]   There
was even somebody who asked if those islands had roots to them
to the bottom of the sea, or if they floated like buoys.   This pleasure,
like all others in the world, ended in sadness, when the winds that
had propelled them through the islands dropped.   The wind had
blown for four days, but from then onwards the breeze was against
the prow, which then heaved up and down, or there was so little
that it seemed as if Our Lord was holding the ship back, unable to
decide to bear her on to the disastrous shipwreck which was
waiting for her.

From the islands of Martim Vaz onwards they began to find
forecasts of an ill-fated journey, for there they came across a fish
and nobody knew what fish it was.   It was like a not very big
whale, sombre-looking and evil-countenanced, and it frightened
away all the other fish that came with the ship.   And it never left
them until the night they were wrecked.   Even on the evening
before the wreck, some of the men saw it in front of the ship throwing up great spurts of water, as if it was pleased, or maybe as if it
was warning them of what was going to happen.

But, despite all these becalmings and forebodings, what never
calmed down were the acts of devotion and divine services; or

[1] The great plains of Portugal.
[2] The Martim Vaz rocks lie at some distance to the east of the Brazilian island
of Trinidad, about 10 degrees from the mainland.   This passage in Godinho
inclines one to think that Cabral's discovery of Brazil may have really been an
accident and not intentional as many have thought.
[3] The principal city in Portuguese India.

rather, they increased.   Thus they celebrated the Saints' Days that
come at that time of the year, such as St. Anthony, St. John the
Baptist, St. Peter and St. Paul, and some others, with the greatest
solemnity possible at sea.   To speak of one of them in particular,
I shall describe that of Corpus Christi in detail.   Some days before
the festival, four masters of the ceremonies were chosen for the
task of furnishing as well as they could the necessary things for
the procession.   On the Wednesday evening they made a sort of
chapel with the tapestried leather beyond the quarter-deck, where
they raised an altar with a silken cloth of various colours and two or
three pictures which had not been brought out before because they
belonged to private persons who were very piously taking them from
Portugal to India.   They set up a big Agnus Dei flanked on either
side with many little golden angels with painted candles in their
hands, not to speak of the waxen ones which were burning in silver
candlesticks on the altar.   When the time came they sang evensong
to the organ, and during the Magnificat a priest went up, preceded
by lighted torches, to cense the altar, for which purpose a censer
had been made of a little brazier of glazed earthenware with some
pieces of wire as chains.

On Thursday, when Mass was over, they had a procession.
Though they lacked the principal element of solemnities and devo-
tions, the Blessed Sacrament, they tried as far as possible to collect
together everything else that is used on that particular morning
in this kingdom.   They constructed a cross, with its silken covering; this was carried at the head of the procession by a youth dressed
in a surplice.   Behind the cross came the rejoicings and dances
which the officers of the ship performed in honour of the Blessed
Sacrament.   At the tail of the procession went the clerics with the
singers and then the priest who had said Mass under a pallium
made specially for that day, with the Agnus Dei in his hands,
accompanied by two children dressed as angels with lanterns in
their hands.   They proceeded with many candles and torches
to the other altar carefully arranged in the prow, where the priest
halted and put down the Agnus Dei, and the dancers recited their
lines.

They also acted the temptations of Christ in the wilderness, the
first at the beginning of the procession, the second in the forecastle,
when they arrived there, and the third near the quarter-deck,
just before retiring.   At the end of everything they cast the devil
down into a fire, as if he was being sent to hell after Christ's victory.
Moreover, so that this procession should not lack its proper accom-
paniments, they fought with a wooden bull; [1] this helped not a little

[1] The kind that bull-fighters still use for training and practice.   It is wheeled
towards the fighter, who must avoid it and go through all the various passes
with it.

ι drawing the common sailors and riff-raff to the yards of the
ιteen sail, thus leaving the deck free for the procession to proceed
ι better order.

So they celebrated the day of Corpus Christi with these rejoicings
nd solemnities, and with a great devoutness, which they all felt,
ι the midst of the waves of the sea (a dwelling suited only to fish),
nd showed their great desire to honour the Sacrament and their
ιigh dedication to divine worship.   And indeed it inspired greater
ιevoutness to see a procession like this, with all its poverty and
ιts earthenware censer, than to see the solemn ones in this kingdom
ωith all their ornaments of silver and brocade.   The clerics of the
Company also celebrated their festival on this day.   For a fort-
night they had recommended confession in their sermons and in
their private conversations.   Nearly all followed their advice,
and most confessed themselves completely, for their whole lives.
It seems they already foresaw the need they would be in, in two
months' time, of having confessed themselves fully.

But to return to the voyage.   With the lulls and the little wind,
as I say, they reached the Cape of Good Hope on 12th July.   They
hoped that by the 14th, which was St. Bonaventure's day, that
the boatswain would have good luck in rounding [1] the Cape.   But the
little wind they had died down, and they spent ten or fifteen days
there without being able to make the sixty leagues that were needed
to pass it.   Here the boatswain and some of the sailors who had
gone in the same ship the year before told how they had dipped
Father Pedro da Silva of the Company of Jesus into the sea in
those parts. [2]

Having rounded the Cape, they reached the coast of Natal.   I
think it must have been given that name because he who escapes
from the great storms which arise beyond the promontory may,
with reason, be said to have been reborn.   Such was certainly their
experience, for in the two or three days they had spent rounding
the Cape they had met with such a wind that it had borne down all
the sails except the studding-sail, which they had bound tight
round the forecastle, and the officers said that they had made
fifty leagues a day.   But immediately afterwards the lulls came on
as before, which put them in danger of having to take the outer
course.   As he wanted to run between the island of S. Lourenço [3]
and the mainland, the captain ordered the food and water in the

[1] There is a play upon words here: 'Bonaventura' is the name of the Saint,
and they hope that on that day they will have 'boa viagem,' a good journey.
[2] It is generally supposed that they threw him in, because of the superstition
that it is unlucky to have a priest on board; or he may have died during the
voyage.   I, however, hold that they dipped him into the sea to appease the
waters, as they had dipped the relics, and as they were to dip another man later
(after our extract ends).
[3] Madagascar.

ship to be examined to see if they could last out to Cochin, if the
inner route to Goa could not be taken.   They seemed sufficient,
so he consulted with the officers and the most experienced of the
men and also called the inquisitor and Father Pedro Martins.
They agreed as follows: If the little west wind that was then
blowing died down and if the north wind came on before they
reached a reef called the Jew's Shoal, because the ship of a converted Hebrew discovered it (they called her the Jewish ship, after
her owner), which shoal is at twenty-two degrees, they would
take the outer course, for it was getting late in the year and, if they
took the inner course, they would risk having to winter in Mozambique.   To seal this agreement they drew up a document which
every one signed except Father Pedro Martins, who refused to
vote because he said that he could not give his opinion on the matter,
not having any previous knowledge of either of the routes.

In this connection, something must be related which, whether it
was a prophecy or a great and hidden judgment of God's—as it
afterwards seemed—I know not.   Generally, in the journey they
call the outer course,[1] there are many cases of illness, swelling of the
feet and the gums,[2] and so many deaths that the men who have
made the journey say that more than a hundred people die every
year they undertake it, not to speak of the hunger and thirst which
those on board who are poor suffer.   Some persons on the ship
who were carrying merchandise for sale feared that, as it was
already late in the year, if they took the inner course they would
have to winter in Mozambique.   Therefore they talked urging
the advantages of taking the outer course, and put the gains that
would accrue to them from going to India that year before the lives
and health of many who were poor would lose on the voyage.

So the discussion ended in a decision that they should take the
outer course, provided the wind continued scarce until they had
passed the reef.   But Father Pedro Álvares often said that he was
very much afraid that God would carry them to Mozambique
and oblige them to winter there, so that the poor would live and
the rich lose more than they had hoped to win by deaths among
the poor; thus those would be punished who wished to take the
outer course because they accounted the small profits they might
draw from this above the great harm it would do to the lives and
health of the poor.   And, in the end, they did winter in Mozambique, and, after not wishing to lose a little of the much they had,
they lost all, and even had to spend the beginning of the winter in
the land of the Kaffirs, naked, bare-footed, half dead with hunger,
longing to go and satisfy its qualms in Mozambique.

The date on which this discussion took place must have been
about the 4th to the 6th August.   Since they had received so many

[1] West of Madagascar.   [2] Scurvy.

special mercies from God by the intercession of the Blessed Virgin throughout the course of the voyage, they felt very confident that, on the day on which she had been taken to Heaven, enough wind would come for them to go on their way; so, on the day of the Assumption,[1] Father Pedro Martins took out an image of St. Luke, which they put on the altar during the Mass and Father João Gonçalves's sermon. For the evening litany the priest ordered the image to be put on the altar again and that nine of the youngest children in the ship should be collected and stand there with lighted candles every day that octave whilst the litany was being sung, to the end that by these means, people should be aroused to ask and hope with greater confidence for the arrival of favourable weather for continuing their journey by the intercession of the Virgin. These efforts were not fruitless, since, on the second day after the Assumption of the Virgin, a strong wind blew up behind them. They were all pleased at this and began to speak of still being able to put in at Mozambique to provision themselves with victuals and water.

On 18th August, as also on the day before, they had seen some albatrosses, which birds always keep close to land so as to make their nests there.[2]   The pilot calculated that they were near the Jew's Shoal.   On the 19th, he took the position of the sun and found that they were at twenty-two degrees and a third, and should be about seven or eight leagues from the shoal to the north-east, in which direction they were sailing.   At this point, the ship's officers greatly disagree in their account of the plan they followed. They all tell different stories and every one tries to clear himself of the blame of the wreck and shift it on to the others.   For my part I do not know what happened at their discussion and, even if I did know, I should be loath to write anything condemning any one on so serious a head.   I truly believe that, in these affairs, we have greater reason to fear the hidden judgments of God and praise the secret plan by which His divine providence permits all these things than to blame the improvidence of men.   So let me leave aside the opinions which every one says he expressed, and the foresight he displayed, and tell of the disastrous wreck just as it happened.

Everybody was very happy on the afternoon of that day, for all believed they had passed the shoal.   And, at the appointed time, all who were not on watch went to their berths overjoyed to think of the fine weather which, the sailors said, they would have till they reached Goa.   But, when all were in the depths of their first sleep and the sails were all swollen with the swiftest and most

---

[1] 15th August.
[2] This is not the case.   Especially in the region of the Cape of Good Hope, these birds are to be seen a long way from land.

K 986

favourable wind they had had for the whole journey, by God's
equable and hidden judgment, for our sins, the ship ran clean onto
the shoal.   Because God had blinded the eyes of the sailors who
watched from the bowsprit and the soldiers who watched from the
yard, so that they did not see the foam breaking on the shoal, and
He had stopped their ears so that they should not hear the roaring
of the waves in the silence of the night, breaking on the rocks so
furiously that they could be heard for two leagues around.

When the ship struck it gave three most frightful knocks, and
the bottom of the ship was immediately cast up above the water
because of the great roughness of those submerged rocks, and soon
the waves cast it firmly onto the shoal.   The upper part of the
ship was also cast up onto the reef.   Two of the decks were
broken to splinters by it, and two others were cast up onto the
rocks together with all their sails because of the strength of the
wind.   All judged it a miracle that two decks of a sailing ship
without a hold should ride where no one would ever have suspected
even a small ship could pass.   The mast broke at its base under the
deck round the partner because of the impetus with which the
ship had been travelling.   They cut its shrouds and it snapped
again and fell completely away.   But one thing is certain, if the
wind had been a whit less strong everybody in the ship would have
gone to the bottom in a trice.   As I said before, a whale had
followed the ship from the islands of Martim Vaz to the shoal
where she struck, and, on the day the ship was wrecked he had gone
before her, as if guiding her to some disaster.

What made this wreck all the more horrible was that it took place
at night, in such darkness that they could hardly see one another.
The screams and confusion amongst the people there were terrific,
coming as they did from men who found themselves without any
hope of aid in the midst of the roaring seas, with death before their
eyes in a more tragic and horrible form than was ever imagined in
past shipwrecks.   The breaking up of the ship, the cracking of the
wood which was all being ground to nothing, the falling of masts
and spars, made so terrible a noise and clatter that to those who
write of it afterwards it seems impossible to recall.[1]   All the
people there now cared for nothing but the salvation of their
souls, for their bodies seemed totally lost, and they begged for
confession from the clerics who were in the ship, with many
tears and groans, but so little restraint or order that they all wished
to confess at the same time and so loudly that they could all hear
each other, except in the case of some noblemen and gentlemen
who confessed themselves in secret.   There was such a haste
for confession that one man, who could not wait, began by saying
to one of the clerics that he should hear his confession and, without

[1] The author had been present.

further delay, told his sins out aloud, sins which were so grave and so great that the priest had to put his hand in front of his mouth, shouting to him to be silent and he would hear his confession immediately. And when the man had been confessed, he called out to the priest from a distance, asking him to absolve him, so distracted was he at the coming of death.

The priests in the ship turned this affliction to great profit by the examples of patience they gave to all. Friar Thomas Pinto, who had retired to the highest part of the ship, was wounded on the head by an iron instrument which fell on him. He attended to the office of confession in great pain, holding his hand on the wound. Before dawn, the confession of everybody in the ship had been heard, which was more than four hundred and fifty souls. After the confession the clerics made many addresses encouraging all to resign themselves to Our Lord's will. Litanies were said and a general confession of faith and everything else necessary for the salving of consciences. So things continued until the moon came out, very fine and resplendent, about two hours before morning. Till then people had been in such darkness that they could hardly see one another close at hand, but when they saw the clarity and the splendour of the moon it made such an impression on them that they began to raise their voices and call on Our Lady, saying that they saw her in the moon.

Day began to break and many now said that they saw land, and some affirmed it was the mainland. But when it was quite light they saw that they were altogether mistaken, since what had seemed land and trees were the lids of the ship's hatchways all broken up, and barrels and boxes which had been carried away and had struck at that point because it was shallower. They saw the shoal, which was formed as follows:

This shoal is round, but with a tendency to run from north-west to south-west, which gives it an ovoid shape. The sea broke over it to the north-east but all the rest was sheltered. In the centre of this reef there is a basin or lake which is about two leagues across. In some parts it must be three or four fathoms deep, and, in other parts, two or less. The reef must be a league long from where it begins to where it runs into the lake. And the whole shoal must be four leagues across and twelve round, more or less. At high tide there are two or three spans of water above the rocks; at low tide there was no footing, generally speaking, till two leagues and a half, or barely three, away from the ship. From east to north run many rocks all in a row, three of the highest of which stand off to the north-east and, when seen from a distance, seem to be islands. The whole reef and lagoon are full of a quantity of white, red, and green coral. It shades off from white into brown, from brown to pink, and afterwards to red. None is perfect. The

red is so soft that if you put your hand on it it crumbles at once
and what is left looks like congealed blood.   Every one was cut by
the coral because walking on it is like walking on thin glass.   The
wounds were poisoned and took the colour of the coral, and it seems
that even the water in which the coral is formed is poisonous.

[*There follows a long discussion whether this reef was really the
Jew's Shoal or not.*]

Returning to the unhappy story of the wreck, the two decks
which were caught on the rocks were immediately broken up, so
that the poop, prow, and side now formed a triangle.   It was not a
complete triangle because there was a small opening on the northern
side from which some rafts afterwards made away. A great pool was
formed in the midst of these three parts of the ship, which at high
tide was deeper than the very tallest man's height.   At low tide
it was up to the knee.   The skiff put off to sea at once with the
admiral, Manoel Gonçalves the boatswain, the passengers Manoel
Rodrigues and Vicente Jorge, Diniz Ramos the ship's barber, and
the foremen of the caulkers with some sailors, nineteen in all,
and amongst them a child of nine, Vicente Jorge's son, whom his
father had hidden there by stealth.   They said they were going to
inspect the shoal and see if they could sight land and that they
would come back very soon.   Friar Thomas Pinto also entered
the skiff, with a ship's compass in his hand, but the admiral begged
him to leave it, swearing to him with many solemn oaths that he
would come back for him and that he was only going to sound the
shoal and see if they could sight land.   Friar Thomas Pinto left
the boat, because he trusted the admiral's oaths, and because he
wished to pacify the disorder and unrest which might have arisen.
Many noblemen and gentlemen who were preparing to enter the
skiff did not attempt to do so when they saw Friar Thomas Pinto
leave it.
    However, the skiff went, and those who remained found them-
selves all unprotected amongst huge waves roaring on all sides,
seeing nothing except the sky and the sea and the scattered remains
of the beautiful structure which their ship had been.   Then they
understood what a great mistake it had been to let the skiff go without giving any more thought to the matter.   Because, if they had
had it, with it and the boat that they built afterwards, the men
would have taken more heart and made more, better, and more
perfect rafts, and more people would have been saved.   The skiff
did not come back, though it is known that the admiral very
insistently asked the boatswain and his other companions to return.   But they would not and the admiral was much grieved, but
indeed, he had to obey in the distress he was in.

About this time they calculated who was missing and found that ten or twelve had been killed who had been in the cabins or under the decks, or had been broken by the iron-work which had fallen on them. As many more died that morning, because they covetously left the ships in search of goods which they saw high and dry, or of exposed parts of the ship from which they could make rafts. But the pull out to sea was so strong that it carried them out and drowned them.   The waves broke very fiercely over the reef and washed off immediately with great violence to the north-east, in which direction the sea seemed to be running.

That morning there were many tears and many signs of contrition and repentance for sins.   Litanies were said.   All asked for God's mercy.   Many gave themselves great blows with many signs of feeling and sorrow.   Others brought pictures of Our Lady and placed them as high up as they could where all could see them, and all fell on their knees and with great and ceaseless cries and sobs and tears asked Our Lady to help them in their so horrible afflictions.   And indeed they no longer asked for anything but help for their souls, because they had given up all hope of saving their bodies.

When he saw these misfortunes, a lad, captive [1] of a passenger, Manoel Rodrigues, began to make great rejoicings, laughing and eating sweetmeats of which there were a great quantity in the ship, and jumping very happily into the pool in the middle of the ship. He swam and dived there, as sure of himself and as fearless as if he were swimming in the river in Lisbon, and he jested at the others saying that he was free now and owed nobody anything.   Whence we see that brutishness sometimes produces the same effects in barbarians as learning and philosophy in the civilized, because not to show sadness and desperation at that state of things a man must have been either a pilot [2] or a beast.

As everybody had said, this was the richest and best-furnished ship which had left the country for many years.   The top deck was strewn with great quantities of pieces of eight, not counting many sacks of them which they had thrown into the sea.   They trod money under their feet without attaching any value to it, though, indeed, covetousness was so strong in one or two of the common people that they filled their sacks with the gold coins, which they meant to take away and save on the rafts they made.

On the first and second days after the wreck they did not set any store by the long-boat, though many tried to repair it, for they most of them thought that if there was any hope of being saved it would be by the rafts they were piecing together.   At this time everybody was going about bound with two or three ropes to

[1] An Asiatic or an African.
[2] This refers to the proverbial calm of ships' pilots in danger.

be tied on to the rafts, and, after winding the ropes many times
round their waists they wound them as many times again round
their necks, in order to be able to move more freely. It was
such a sad sight that they seemed thus all condemned to death
with halters round their necks.   On this same day one of the ship's
sides broke open and, as if it was giving birth, threw out the boat
with a third part missing.   The waters threw it on to the shallowest
part of the reef and it came aground three gunshots from the ship.
The first to venture out to it was a Genoese nobleman called
Scipio Grimaldi.   Some of the sailors went to see it and said that
there was no means of repairing it.   But others decided to stay in
it, and made a signal with a little flag to those in the ship telling
them to come to them, because the boat was still serviceable.
And many did so, including Duarte de Melo, a gentleman from
Bassein, and Diogo Rodrigues Caldeira.   The pilot and others
elected Duarte de Melo captain, by general consent, and that
gentleman was certainly worthy of that and greater honours.

Having made this choice they turned their minds very seriously,
as indeed the moment demanded, to the reparations to the boat.
They mended the poop with planks of boxes caulked with shirts
and Flemish cheese soaked in pitch, using the end of a knife.
Indeed they caulked most of it with the same cloth and cheese,
for it was in a bad state and let in the water from nearly all sides.
They also used five or six wooldings from the mast, but, even so,
that was not enough to keep out the water, and they had to keep
two buckets constantly going to bail it out, which gave a great
amount of work.   That was while the boat was still on the shoal,
just to keep it upright.   Afterwards, when it sailed, there were
always four pails going.   And all those who could took their turn
at them.

Those who were in the boat whilst it was being repaired suffered
greatly from hunger and thirst, because they did not drink more
than twice a day, each having his own turn of unwatered wine with a
slice of cheese or quince jelly.[1]   They slept the first night with water
up to their waists.   The second they were very crowded in the boat
because there were many of them, though there was less water,
and some were outside the boat leaning against it with water up to
their chests.   They were engaged in this work from the Tuesday
afternoon to the Thursday.   Friar Thomas Pinto took with him
Jerónimo da Silva, the boatswain's mate on the ship, to see the boat
and judge whether he ought to trust himself to it or to the rafts, some
of which were very well made.   It seemed to both of them that
the boat was safer.   So Jerónimo da Silva immediately gave orders
to bring victuals, water, wine, biscuits, cheese, quince jelly,

---

[1] A favourite 'sweet' in Portugal and Spain, taken with a knife and fork at
the end of meals.

and some other jams from the ship.   The spritsail was patched up from a sheet and another piece of linen.   The mast was made of a handspike, the yard of two stays, the spritsail mast of three stays, the yard of two.   Later they mended the yard of the main-mast with another bar, and made the yard-arms of two stay-heads. The shrouds were made of fishing-tackle and wires, and the cable of twelve sailor's bowlines and a linen cord thirty-eight poles in length twisted like a rope, the grapnel of six brass chocks together with a sack of three hundred crusadoes.   Two paddles served as a rudder and gave great trouble in handling.

They waited for the tide.   But many people from the ship, when they saw Friar Thomas Pinto and the boatswain's mate leave her, went to where the boat was.   As there were many of them, those in the boat feared they might have great difficulty in putting out to sea, as often happens on these occasions.   To avoid this, Captain Duarte de Melo had the lucky inspiration of asking Friar Thomas Pinto to take their weapons from those people by some peaceful means and tell them to give them up to him out of their great respect for him, and thus they might avoid those misfortunes which are common in shipwrecks.   Friar Thomas Pinto asked them very gently for their weapons, and many gave them up to him, though there were some who did not wish to do so.   But Friar Thomas Pinto had so much authority over the seamen that when he placed his hand gently on some of those who refused they gave them up.   This permitted those in the boat to embark more peacefully and safely, for there was no doubt that people who found themselves helpless and left to drown in the middle of the sea in the next half-hour or less would have stuck at nothing if they had had weapons in their hands.

By this time the tide had risen greatly and five rafts which had been made came up to the side of the boat, in which those hoping to be saved in it embarked with great difficulty because, at the sword's point, the crew refused entry to those who came to ask for it, since there was no help for it.   Some women who had been in the ship clung to the boat, but were wounded by those in it, just as the men who tried to force an entry were.   The spectacle on that day was the saddest and most pitiful that could be seen. The reef was covered with people whom neither those in the boat nor those on the rafts would admit.   The tide was rising, and they could no longer stand, so that those who could not swim very soon began to drown.   And those who could swim were drowned even if they kept off death a little while.   A very large number of men were swimming, some to the rafts, others to the boat. And thus all were drowned, including two women who were going out to the rafts on which many others were.   A boy of fifteen swam nearly half a league, and reached the boat, which had now moved

far out from where the others were swimming.   They put a sword
out to stop him, but he had no fear of it in that extremity and, in
fact, gripped it as if it was a cable.   And he did not let go till they
took him in, though he paid for it with a deep wound in his hand.
Those who were travelling in the boat looked back at the ruins of
the ship and its broken hatches and saw that there were still
many people on them, all with red bonnets on their heads and
red surtouts like reapers' jackets made of scarlet cloth and some
coloured silk there were in the ship, which would have been a
beautiful sight to see at some happier time.   The rafts were also
very plainly visible and looked like pinnaces with sails of green,
crimson, and other coloured damask.

The boat continued on its journey and arrived at night near the
rocks which have been already mentioned, two leagues and a half
from where it had begun its journey.   As they were sailing by them
the people in the boat still thought for a long time they were islands
until they saw them from very near at hand and realized they were
rocks.   They were covered with people who had gone from the ship
to seek refuge on them, choosing rather to end their days there than
in the water.   When the boat had reached this point night had come
on.   It was so cold that the very temperature would have been
enough to kill them all, and that night was followed by other
extraordinarily cold ones.   At this point the most horrible sight
of the whole shipwreck was seen, for both those on the rafts and
those on the rocks, hoping to find refuge in the boat, left them and
came naked, up to their chests in water, crying out all night because
of the coldness of the water and their unbearable agonies.   Nothing
could be heard except sighs, groans, and pitiful supplications.   They
shrieked to those in the boat to help them, calling on many by
their names and telling them the terrible state they were in.   One
of those who called out most was Dom Duarte de Meneses, cousin
by marriage of the captain, Fernão de Mendonça.   But his petitions
were not heard, nor those of Rui Mendes de Carvalho, a man of
noble birth.   On the other hand, they took in the master-gunner
of the ship at the very first word he said.

The next morning was Friday, the 23rd of the month.   When
the people in the boat were about to start, the pilot was strongly of
opinion, and so were the boatswain's mate and some of the sailors
(and the first spoke to the captain, Duarte de Melo, on the matter)
that the boat could not sail with so many people, and he, the pilot,
said it could not sail with so many people and that he did not
dare put out to sea with more than forty-six or forty-seven people
on board.   And it seemed to some, who had taken command of the
boat, that the boatswain's mate had not kept a proper reckoning
of those in it, since the boat was much weighed down.   So they
agreed amongst themselves to throw some people into the sea.

and that only they should consider and decide who were to be condemned.   Those of this party told Duarte de Melo what the pilot had said and the reckoning the boatswain's mate had ordered to be made.   The captain, Duarte de Melo, showed true Christian feeling and did not know how the execution of such a cruel plan could be avoided.   However, he sent four or five men to count the people that were in the boat.   They had naked swords in their hands so as the more easily to enforce the sentence and wretched fates of those condemned.

They flung seventeen people out of the boat.   Amongst them was Jorge Figueira, a man noble both in reputation and in rank, who had worked on the repairing of the boat like a ship's hand from the very first day they had thought of using it till the time it sailed.   When was it decided that anyone should be thrown into the sea, the executioners flung him in immediately, though Duarte de Melo gave him leave to speak if he wished to, and thus showed some humanity towards him and mitigated the severity of the sentence.   Eleven people had already been flung into the sea, when someone in the boat, whose name shall be omitted to avoid scandal, said that it was not just that, when so many people were being thrown into the sea, two brothers, honourable men from Lisbon, Gaspar Ximenes and Fernão Ximenes, should be spared. What that person said created great surprise, for Gaspar Ximenes and Fernão Ximenes being very honourable men, and having behaved themselves well, had many friends in the boat.   Though there were some that approved of what that person said.   Those who had given the sentence consulted together and decided that one of them should be thrown into the sea.   And the executioner seized Gaspar Ximenes who, though he was the elder, was smaller and thinner than his brother.   Whilst these diligent servants were carrying him along, his brother, Fernão Ximenes, moved by brotherly love, rushed up to him, seized him by the jacket, and snatched him away from them all.   He told them to let him speak to Duarte de Melo, and clinging tightly to his brother with both hands, turned to Duarte de Melo and said to him: 'Ah, Senhor Duarte de Melo, is there no help for it but that one of us should be cast into the sea?' Duarte de Melo's only reply was to weep and shrug his shoulders, to show him that it could not be otherwise.   Fernão Ximenes replied with great spirit—which God gave him, because what he did was more His work than the work of man.   He asked that, if it could not be otherwise, his brother might be saved, as being the elder and like a father to his sisters, and that he, Fernão Ximenes, might be thrown into the sea.   When he said this they threw him in.   And he was as brave as if he had been thrown out near a shore full of friendly people, whereas it was really a hostile sea more than a hundred and twenty leagues from the nearest land.   For this high-minded youth

* K 986

remembered rather the obedience he owed to his elder brother who had been a father to him, and the care and well-being of his mother and sisters and their needs, than how he could save his own life. And he trusted in God's loving-kindness to have mercy on his soul.

This gallant action was indeed worthy of being eternally recorded in the memories of men, since the spirit of love was more exalted here than in the loving contest of Pylades and Orestes. And very seldom can a brother have given his life for another as bravely as this one did. But, being so notable and charitable a deed, the Lord God did not long leave it unpaid. Indeed, He repaid him that same day. All those who had been thrown out of the boat had gone to some high rocks, and they called out to Fernão Ximenes asking him if he wished to come there. But he replied that he would await his fate where he was. So he mounted a little rock, where the water was up to his neck and underneath it was very precipitous. He saw the ship begin to weigh anchor and sail away. As, like nearly everybody, he had put on two shirts, he tried to pull them off so as to make ready to swim. As he tugged them over his head a great wave coming up beneath him made him lose his footing on the rock. Thus he was in the deep sea with his head caught up in the shirts. And, as he afterwards recounted, when he found himself in that state, at grips and face to face with death, he tugged so furiously and forcibly that, being young and strong, he split the shirts completely open in front. In this way his head was free, though he still wore the shirts on his arms. He swam back to the rock, where he took them off altogether, and then struck out in pursuit of the boat. He continued swimming for more than three hours, forcing his way through very strong currents and calling loudly and lamentingly on Our Lord Jesus Christ, and on the Most Blessed Virgin, His Mother, beseeching them to aid him in that awful struggle. His brother, Gaspar Ximenes, was in the boat, lamenting continuously because of the pitiful pass his brother had come to, from whom so shortly before he had received such a proof of love. And now he could only repay it with tears and groans. In consequence, a friend of his came up and told him gently that he must be silent, because every one in the boat was so irritated with hearing him that they said they would fling him into the sea too, so as to hear him no more. Thus Gaspar Ximenes felt obliged to keep silence, only he wept in his heart and asked for God's mercy, and prayed with great devotion for the intercession of Our Lady of the Pleasures of the parish of St. Christopher in Lisbon, where both of them had been brought up.[1]

[1] Now the part of Lisbon, to the west, where lies the largest cemetery, the Cemetery of the Pleasures (*Prazeres*).

Our Lord permitted the hour to come in which He would pay the young man for the so charitable deed he had done. When he could hardly keep afloat for the effort of swimming, the same men that had condemned him to be flung out of the boat demanded that he should be taken in, in God's name, though, if it was necessary to the sailing of the boat to fling him out again, they would do so. They called out that he could come on board, but they had to hold out a stay for him to cling to, which he did. So they pulled him into the boat. He was all swollen with water. They turned him head downwards and he disgorged a great quantity of it. Seeing himself free from death, he gave great thanks to God and Our Lady of the Pleasures, of whom he was a great votary. Afterwards, he began to bail out with a bucket, with others who were doing the same, and continued to do this work until the day on which they went ashore. Besides Fernão Ximenes two others were taken in again who had been thrown out of the boat. None of the clerics in the boat interfered in these executions, hearing the commands of the captain and those of his party, though they were very sorry about it, and because it was very foreign to their profession. The leaders must have understood this, because, on all accounts, they avoided speaking to the clerics on this subject. Therefore the latter found it best to keep silent.

Still sailing along by the shoal where the ship had been wrecked, they saw under water a most beautiful field of coral, most of it green, with some red intermixed; for the water was so clear here that they could see the very smallest stones at the bottom of the sea. They also saw some diminutive hills of two or three spans in circumference, with some leaves of coral as long as a man's finger, and three times as broad, of an extraordinarily fine green, but this gave them very little joy in the midst of all their horrible misfortunes. Here they wished to fling into the sea the under-cooper, who had worked very hard on the repairs to the boat. When the poor man saw there was no help for it, he asked them to give him a slice of quince jelly. They gave it to him, and after that he drank a gulp of wine and let himself be thrown into the sea. He went straight to the bottom and was never seen again.

Amongst those thrown into the sea was one lad who followed swimming for a long way in the wake of the boat and begged again and again to be taken in and refused to go away, saying that Our Lady had appeared to him and told him that the boat would be saved. Therefore he asked them to take him in for giving them such good news. He insisted for so long and said so much that those who were in command of everything were moved to pity and took him and another sailor in.

[*There follows a list of the fifty-seven people in the boat.*]

It seemed a miracle that fifty-seven people could reach land in two-thirds of a boat, bound with ropes, and letting in so much water on all sides that four pails, working day and night, could not empty it out; but even so, it succeeded in crossing a hundred leagues or more of open sea. But if the boat's reaching land is to be deemed a miracle (as indeed it was), by God's mercy it could also miraculously have carried those who had been thrown from it into the sea. But let us leave this subject and resume the thread of our story. Two days after their departure they pieced together two small sails of green and crimson velvet which were very necessary to the sailing of the boat. The victuals they had were delivered over to Friar Thomas Pinto to portion out among all the different people every day, and he had a sailor who was a very worthy man to assist him in this very important task. The rule was that everybody should be given daily as much biscuit as he could hold in his hands, a slice of quince jelly, and a glass of well-watered wine. As there was very little water, it was only given to invalids. In this way, they made shift, though their thirst was very great, because the wine did not quench the thirst of those who were not accustomed to it, and some said that it even increased it. They were so crowded in the boat that they could not even move, lying, as they did, one on top of the other. The cold at night was unbearable, and by day they were all parched with the tropical heat. The sailors who were looking after the sheets of the spritsail were so overcome with sleep that there was no means of making them keep awake at night, so that the boat frequently caught the wind athwart. Friar Thomas Pinto always kept a sharp eye on the sailors and on those who were working the buckets, because the safety of the boat seemed to depend on those two groups of people, after God. Every day they said a litany, and all recommended themselves continually to God's keeping, for only in Him was there any hope of safety. Despite these agonizing straits, in the midst of such evident danger, there was no lack of scandalous incidents among the people in the boat, though they were in the condition which has been described, with only God's mercy able to help them and with death before their eyes every moment. There were great and extraordinary oaths, quarrels and words of hate, and threats for when they got to land, though it was so far off and so ill deserved after all these disorders.

In this way they travelled a week, always going towards the north-north-west. On Wednesday, 28th August, the sea had churned-up sand in it, which made it look as though it was not very far to the bottom. So they dropped the line and found a depth of fifteen fathoms, then twelve, eight, six. They sounded six fathoms without yet seeing land. On the next morning, Thursday the 29th, they could see land clearly and the boat touched the bottom three hours after midday. However, they could not reach the land without danger, because, as the land there is lower than the water, they did not see that the sea was rolling until they were right in the roll of it. The waves were very big and came from a distance, roaring and breaking very far from the shore. And the boat was as we have already described it. With all these perils it seemed as if there was nothing for it but to fold their arms and give themselves up completely to death. They thought they were in a worse situation than any before. The pilot and boatswain gave up all hope, and called on Our Lady, not without tears. The waves all struck the poop of the boat, and if they had struck it sideways there would have been no chance of being saved. Then two men, who felt confidence in themselves because they could swim, jumped out of the boat. The water came up to their waists, and they were carried in towards the land by the strong roll of the sea, but they reached it without danger. The boat moved in further until it grounded altogether, and then those in it left it without danger.

Having left these trials by sea, they began to experience those which were waiting for them on the land. For, on the same day as they disembarked, some Kaffirs fell on them and stripped them all, and gave two assagai-thrusts to Friar Thomas Pinto and wounded a sailor in the eye. Now that they were free from the dangers of the sea, this was the hospitable treatment they found on the land they had all been longing for so much. The Kaffirs, after making this assault, took away Jorge Soeiro and Fernão Rodrigues Caldeira by force. The rest that remained went along the beach to the east, without knowing where they were or where they were going to. They afterwards learned that the boat had grounded between Luranga and Quizungo. It was now nearly night, the cold was very great, and they were all naked and had no shelter of any sort. It was a pitiful sight to see people in such a state, including grave and learned prelates, many gentlemen and noblemen, and others, so unprotected, on a savage shore, with the sea on the one hand whose furious waves still terrified them, and, on the other, a land of such cruel enemies as these Kaffirs are.

In this way they walked on for three hours of the night, but the unbearable cold, and so many days' hunger and thirst, and their weariness had so weakened them that they could not go another step. Thus they took shelter by a sand-hill on the beach where they spent the greater part of the night, covered up with sand, in holes they had made for themselves. When the morning of Friday, the 30th, broke, they continued to walk along the beach, feeling great hunger and thirst. But they could not find any water, nor anything to eat except some wild beans which grew right out of the sand. But some would not eat these, because they thought

they were poisonous.   However, many did so, being greatly pressed
by hunger, but they paid for it soon with painful vomits and other
discomforts which followed.   As the sun had come up they hoped
to find some warmth after the cold, but it was like leaving snow for
fire, because the sun was so hot in a few hours that it roasted them.
And it peeled the skin from all their arms and shoulders to such an
extent that they could not even bear to touch them with their own
hands.

They went on walking in this way until ten o'clock, when some
Kaffirs came to meet them, led by a negress who smiled constantly
and signed to them in a friendly manner to follow her.   They
gave the negroes some caps they were still wearing, but the nature
of those savages is such that they were not content with what
they were given, but even robbed them of some pieces of cloth
they had been able to save the day before.   They followed the
Kaffirs inland and, at a short distance, came to a marshy pool of
very impure water, but they could not resist entering it.   They
were all so tortured by thirst that, though they drank more earth
than water, it seemed to them that they were drinking cool water
from the river Douro or the Minho.   The negroes cried out and
made signs to them not to drink, giving them to understand that the
water was poisonous, but nobody stopped drinking for that reason.
Their thirst was such that even blows could not drive them away.

They went on, and reached some villages they call Patay, in the
district of the Quizungo River, which is so well known to our
countrymen.   Less than a league from this river, they came to a
village, into which the Kaffirs led them.   In it there was a very
old negro, who was its chief and the husband of the negress who
had come up to them.   This negro received them well, and, after
they had sat down, he ordered a bough of green Indian figs to be
set before them, which they ate stewed.   After the figs came some
maize flour which tasted very good to them then.   Meanwhile
more maize was being cooked and in great quantities.   Some
thought that this would be the Kaffirs' dinner, but these last
gave it to everybody.   Thus they were hospitably served, and
indeed this food seemed a banquet to them.   But from then on
the Kaffirs began to cut down their rations, so that in a very few
days they reached the extreme limits of hunger.   And there were
many days on which each of them did not eat more than a small
green fig, or, more properly speaking, a thoroughly unripe one.   At
this period, they ate pumpkin rinds and maize flour of which they
sometimes made cakes.   But as they were sticky, yet difficult to
keep together, they had to be wrapped in fig-leaves, like curd
cheese at home.   Then they roasted them on the embers, and ate
them when they were still only half roasted, so great were their
pangs of hunger.   And when there was enough of this flour for

everybody to make himself even a small cake, they thought they were lucky in their dinner.

They suffered great hunger here. The negroes only gave them two spoonfuls of cooked maize all day, and would not allow them to go to the woods to fetch fruit or herbs, because they kept them in a small circle amongst some fig-trees, like prisoners. And if one of them moved a stone's throw from the others, they forced him to go straight back to his prison, sometimes with blows. The shelter at night was insufficient. These negroes had some huts, raised on stakes of an ell in height, which they used as granaries. Everybody from the boat had to take refuge under two of these at night, and, though there were always some left outside, they were so cramped that many could not sleep all night. The bed was of grasses which were so rough that they left their impress all over their bodies. They had to suffer all this in a state of nakedness, and, as it was still winter in those parts, the cold was very great. They were fortunate in having a fire all night, because there is plenty of wood in that country, and it is so good that when it is green it burns better than even dry wood in Portugal. But, since the cold penetrated to the very marrow of their bones, if one part of them was warmed, the other felt frozen. Whence they learned how mistaken are those who say: 'It is never cold in the torrid zone,' which, it seems, can only be applied to those who actually live on the equator. And, in those lands, the cold did not last longer than an hour after the sun rose, and all the rest of the day till sunset was unbearably hot. They twice tried to escape, but the negroes made them turn back, meeting them on the way, armed with assagais and bows, and shouting. And then they stripped them of any remnant of a shirt or doublet that our men had hidden from their former robbings.

One day, whilst they were in this miserable state, a negro arrived with a hat of black taffeta on his head. This caused them all as great a pleasure as if they had seen a Portuguese. They all went out to receive him. The negro took off his hat and, with a sad look on his face, like one who was sorry to see them in that miserable state, he spoke to them in Portuguese. He told them not to be overcome, because it was all God's will, though it pained him to see them in so wretched a condition. He was called a *bano*; he was a nephew of the *bano* or sheik of Luranga, and he brought them letters from Fernão Rodrigues Caldeira and another Portuguese and orders to take them away from there. Then he gave them the letters. One was for Diogo Rodrigues Caldeira, brother of Fernão Rodrigues, and the other for them all. They recounted how the negroes had taken them off by force when their boat grounded. The very next day they had been brought to Luranga, which was near by. They had been well treated by the sheik there, and they

had persuaded him to send this nephew of his to look for them
with a sufficient ransom to be able to bring them back with him.

This negro at once began to negotiate all their ransoms, but
could not come to any understanding with the Kaffirs in whose
power they were. The negro went away without speaking to them
again. As they afterwards learned, he did this because he did not
want to hear the complainings of those unhappy people, and he
was determined to come back better provided. They were all
much disheartened at the negro's departure, not knowing whether
he would come back or not. But Friar Thomas Pinto encouraged
them all to expect the negro's return, for he had a high opinion of
him and defended it. However, they all thought it would be useful,
now they knew in which direction Luranga was, and that the distance was short, to send a couple of their companions there to
explore the territory and negotiate their ransom with the *bano*. For
this purpose they chose Afonso Gomes, who had been destined to
be captain-general of the Melinde [1] coastal region, and a sailor called
Gonçalo Francisco. And because they delayed a long time sending word of what had happened—for it had been generally understood that one of them should come back with news of what luck
they had had—they sent two more, Friar Adrião de São Jerónimo,
of the Order of Preachers, companion of Friar Thomas Pinto; and
Manoel Ferreira, a brother of the Company of Jesus, and Manoel
de Basto, ship's notary, also went with them. They had to go
by stealth, because the Kaffirs would not have given leave. And,
even before they had set out, another two had gone in the same
manner, Dom João de Meneses, son of Dom Francisco de Meneses,
and Manoel da Silva, a sailor.

After Friar Adrião left, nine or ten went away on the same night.
But they did an ill service to those who remained, because the
negroes, realizing what had happened, came up shouting and very
angry on the day after they had left. And they put all the rest
into a little enclosed hut, like cattle, where they had not even
room to sit down and were forced to remain standing though dropping with weariness. As to those who were leaning against the
wall, the sharp-edged stones cut into their naked flesh very severely.
This was one of the greatest trials they underwent in all their
misfortunes, because there were some very intelligent men amongst
them who were convinced the Kaffirs had put them there in order
to set fire to the house and burn them all. This impression was
increased when they heard a sailor who had been left outside calling
out very pitifully that they were strangling him. What had
happened was that two Kaffir lads had tied a rope round the poor
man's neck and were dragging him along by it, meaning rather to
frighten him than to kill him. But, as the sailor had his hands

[1] Malindi.

free, he loosened the noose, and thus protected himself from them. As the intention of the Kaffirs was to torment him, the game ended by their jerking at his neck a number of times.

Whilst they were in this condition, they gave up most of their time to prayer and spiritual addresses. They made all those promises and vows people do make in these mortal straits, they asked each other pardon and those who hated each other or had quarrelled became friends. Even in those unhappy days there had been relations broken between some of them, for human weakness is such that, though within sight of death, it will not retreat an inch in matters of honour.

Friar Thomas Pinto persuaded them all, in an address he made them, of the reasons for their all being resigned to that state God had been pleased to bring them to. He showed them how the soul benefited by this disposition. He told them they had never had more occasion for confidence, and for hoping their lives would be saved, as they all so greatly wished, than at present. Because, since all sources from which help could come were cut off, that was the surest sign and argument that Our Lord would succour them by His mercy. It was in such times that His mercy was most fully manifested, for His greater glory. And so it was, for, when they had given up all hope of help, a negro from Luranga arrived that afternoon with a letter from Friar Adrião and Brother Manoel Ferreira, in which they said they had reached Luranga, and that the bearer was carrying the young *bano* on his shoulders with enough ransom to rescue them all and take them with him.

The joy such good news caused them all after they had been face to face with death, is indescribable. The *bano* came with three negroes to arrange the ransom of every one for thirty garments. So they left Quizungo at midnight on Wednesday, the 12th September. They travelled the rest of the night, and at noon on the next day, the 13th, arrived at Luranga, at a distance of eight leagues from where they had started from. In Luranga, they were well received by the *bano*.[1] This negro must have been about eighty years old, and was large of limb and of a fine appearance. All that land is subject to him and his brothers and nephews. They are a truly noble family. They are the best-natured and most gentlemanly negroes in all this land. They are much feared by their neighbours, who can take no liberties with them. They are content with what they have, and so they live in great peace and quiet.

Their chief business and commerce with the Portuguese is in ivory and the fruits of the earth, which are plentiful and excellent there. The Portuguese bring them cloths which they wear, tin, and beads. The land is so rich and fertile that anything would

[1] The old *bano*.

grow there if it was planted. The plantations are big and the women cultivate them, though with more care than the men do in our country. The women clear away the brushwood, dig, sow, and gather the crops; [1] the men eat, walk about, and talk. For this reason the women in that country are more or less avaricious, and the men generous. The land gives much rice, finer maize than in Portugal, millet, beans, sesame, and yams. They have palm-trees and many coco-nuts, but they only know how to use these by drinking their milk, eating their pulp, and making curries of their juice. They do little breeding, either of hens or of horned cattle, though the land makes very good pasture. But, as the people there do not care to work, they prefer to take their ease at dances and festivals rather than mind their farms, and they are content with such common food as rice, maize, and vegetables. They also eat mice and snakes, which they consider very good and laugh at us for not eating them. Sometimes they hunt, and catch buffaloes, stags, and gazelles. And if they can trap apes and tigers, they eat them also. Some of the Portuguese tried tiger's flesh and said it had not a bad taste. There are many tigers, ounces,[2] lions, ele-phants, and so many civet cats that the woods often stink of them, though they contain many fine-scented flowers like musk, honey-suckle, and other sweet-smelling plants which adorn them.

The Luranga River is admirable. It has an excellent mouth and bar. It must contain fish, but the negroes do not fish, or when they do, it is only for little fish in the pools near the bank. And in some creeks made by the river the negroes fish with cloths they put into the water and catch little fishes, which they put in the curries they eat with maize and rice. In religion, these people worship one God alone, believe in the immortality of the soul, and do not deny God's providence. They believe there are devils. They are very blasphemous, because, if their harvests are not successful or anything distasteful to them occurs, they speak ill of God and say He has done what He ought not to, and other such things. A nephew of Friar Thomas Pinto died in this country. Some of the chief negroes, wishing to console him, told him that God had treated him very badly and that he ought not to trust Him, because He was wicked. Friar Thomas Pinto, though much overcome, spoke out in God's honour, and told them what it was needful they should know of the matter, and convinced them easily, because they are not men given to many answers and replies.

Their ceremonies are for the dead at their burials. When any of these negroes dies, the first thing they do is this: One of the nearest relations comes out of the dead man's house and begins

---

[1] The plough was unknown there at that time.
[2] Misnamed, like the 'tigers.' The ounce inhabits mountainous districts and is unknown in South Africa.

to weep for him in a loud voice. And the whole village, men and women, run up shrieking when they hear his cries, and begin a very sad lamentation in sing-song voices, which made the Portuguese very sorry for them, so that they too wept. One of the chief among them intones the lamentation and the others respond. And the way they respond is something like the end of a line of poetry. This lamentation lasts about an hour. Meanwhile the corpse is shrouded, almost as among us, in a blue cloth, and bound round on all sides with strips of the same cloth. They bury all his weapons with him, bows, arrows, assagais. Those who accompany him also carry their weapons. They throw maize, rice, beans, and other vegetables into his grave; on top of the grave they put the bed he used to sleep in and the three-legged stool he used to sit on.

They then burn the house of the dead man and also all the furniture it had, because not only may they not keep anything he had, they may not even touch it. And, if they do touch it by any chance, they may not go into their own houses without first having gone to wash themselves in the sea or in the river. Everything they touch before washing can no longer be used and must of necessity be burned. They carry the ashes of the house which has been burned on some half-burned sticks and place them on the tomb of the dead man. They mount a stick on it with a white flag which remains for some days.

They weep for the dead man every day for a week. They begin at midnight. One always commences by wailing the lamentation, and the other voices gradually join in. Thus they proceed in the way which has already been described. If there is a very close relation of the dead man in any village near by, he goes out alone at night for that week and makes the lamentation alone, as Father Thomas Pinto and Duarte de Melo observed when they were the guests of one of the *bano's* sons, on the other side of the river. Whilst they were sleeping in his house one night, he got up and made such a pitiful lamentation that it broke their hearts to hear him. At dawn, they go to the tomb of the dead man, and scatter maize, beans, and flour round him, uttering some special words, and they put some of the flour over one of his eyes so that it hides part of his cheek. They asked these heathens [1] what they prayed or said when they performed this ceremony. They replied that they placed their lands and other possessions under the protection of their dead, who, they believe, can help them in those matters.

Such are the ceremonies they perform for the dead. As for weddings, they usually have two wives, and some, if they are noblemen, have concubines. A virgin who is going to be married, when

[1] Literally 'some Moors,' but we must remember that Portuguese writers use the term 'Moor' pretty generally for all heathens.

her marriage has been agreed upon, leaves the village, as if sent into exile, and remains a whole month away from it, sorrowing for her honour, which she must lose; though she may go home to sleep at night, and can be visited by everybody at dawn.   When the month is over, two or three negresses begin dancing early in the morning, and others come and join in, so that by noon they have made a great circle of dancers.   Meanwhile they play many *atabales*, and everything which is to be given to the bride is first hung round the necks of the drummers.   Every one present gives her rice, maize, beans, millet, figs, and a quantity of flour, each competing to go up to her first.   They put flour on her face so that the greater part of it is covered up, including the left eye.[1]   The festival ends in the evening with the bridegroom taking the bride home, and she is considered his lawful wife.

The negresses have a pleasing appearance, though the fact that they have their cheeks and lower lips pierced spoils them considerably.   The rich women put round pieces of lead the size of a halfpenny in them, and the poor ones, instead of lead, put wooden pegs, like the stoppers of wine-skins, which make them very ugly indeed.

They have many feast-days.   They have superstitions about them, too, because they observe the ceremony of not eating anything on them; but they drink all through the day and night, though the chief part of the festival is at night.   So from the time the festival begins to when it ends they are always drunk. They dance, play instruments, and fight together; they make many gestures and grimaces, and they are covered with branches like satyrs, so that they look like the soldiers of Bacchus when he conquered India.   Their wine is of two kinds.   The commonest is of maize, with other ingredients.   But they have a better one made of a fruit they call a *pudoh*, which has a sour but very pleasant flavour, unfermented, and is sweet and tasty fermented.   There were Portuguese who tried both, and said they had not a bad taste.   These people put a deal of faith in their enchantments and casting of lots, which, it seems, they get from the Moors,[2] who are great sorcerers; these lots are known to consist in some kind of geomancy.[3]   To discover thefts they usually arrange a dance of many negresses together, who sing certain words.   They dance so much that they seem mad or possessed by demons in the diabolical fury of their dance.   At the end of this they say the devil enters into one of them and reveals who did the theft.

Government among these negroes is a very mild affair.   Each

---

[1] It is not quite clear from the Portuguese whether it is the bride's face or those of the guests which are so covered.
[2] Here the term is used more appropriately for Mohammedans.
[3] A complicated use of lines and circles.

village has a head they call *fumoh*.   He settles differences verbally, and there are generally very few of them; but if the *fumohs* are in doubt about anything, the *bano* decides the case in consultation with the other *fumohs*, who meet in a small square in front of the *bano's* house.   They were given to making great salutations.   They have to make so many when they pay a visit, that a good space of time is spent in compliments to each other before they speak of the business they have come about.   They have a good, very gentle disposition and showed great compassion for the misfortunes of the Portuguese.

This was what they learned of the religion and customs of those negroes.   Whilst the Portuguese were with them they gave what they could—though it was in greater quantities the first days— so that those fifty-seven persons could not have received such loving and charitable hospitality even in Portugal.   In the end, as there were so many Portuguese, they could not provide them with everything necessary, but still they gave what they had. They portioned out the Portuguese amongst themselves.   Some chanced to have rich hosts, others had not such good fortune.

[*The narrative now becomes more confused.   Most of the Portuguese in this party reached their own land, finally, and others who had been left at the shoal also managed to escape on rafts.*]

VI—THE JESUITS IN ABYSSINIA, 1625–34

(Translated, with Preface, by Samuel Johnson)

Bibliographical

TRANSLATIONS: *A Short Relation of the River Nilo.* (No translator's name.) 1673.

In *Relation historique de l'Abissinie.* . . . By Joachim Le Grand. Paris. 1728.

A Voyage to Abyssinia. (Translated by Samuel Johnson, but anonymously.) London (really, Birmingham). 1735.

THE JESUITS IN ABYSSINIA

Preface to the Translation of Father Lobo's Voyage to Abyssinia
(By Samuel Johnson)

The following relation is so curious and entertaining, and the dissertations that accompany it so judicious and instructive, that the translator is confident his attempt stands in need of no apology, whatever censures may fall on the performance.

The Portuguese traveller, contrary to the general vein of his countrymen, has amused the reader with no romantic absurdities or incredible fictions: whatever he relates, whether true or not, is at least probable; and he who tells nothing exceeding the bounds of probability, has a right to demand that they should believe him who cannot contradict him.

He appears by his modest and unaffecting narration to have described things as he saw them, to have copied nature from the life, and to have consulted his senses, not his imagination. He meets with no basilisks that destroy with their eyes; his crocodiles devour their prey without tears; and his cataracts fall from the rock without deafening the neighbouring inhabitants.

The reader will here find no region cursed with irremediable barrenness, or blest with spontaneous fecundity; no perpetual gloom or unceasing sunshine; nor are the nations here described either devoid of all sense of humanity, or consummate in all private and social virtues; here are no Hottentots without religion, polity, or articulate language; no Chinese perfectly polite, and completely skilled in all sciences: [1] he will discover what will always be discovered by a diligent and impartial inquirer, that wherever human nature is to be found there is a mixture of vice and virtue, a contest of passion and reason; and that the Creator doth not appear partial in his distributions, but has balanced in most countries their particular inconveniences by particular favours.

In his account of the mission, where his veracity is most to be suspected, he neither exaggerates overmuch the merits of the Jesuits, if we consider the partial regard paid by the Portuguese to their countrymen, by the Jesuits to their society, and by the papists to their Church, nor aggravates the vices of the Abyssinians; but if the reader will not be satisfied with a popish account of a popish mission, he may have recourse to the *History of the Church of Abyssinia*, written by Dr. Geddes, in which he will find the actions and sufferings of the missionaries placed in a different light, though the same in which Mr. Le Grand,[2] with all his zeal for the Roman Church, appears to have seen them.[3]

[1] A reference to Mendes Pinto, presumably.
[2] J. le Grand or Legrand, historian (1653–1733).
[3] Johnson goes on to discuss Le Grand's *Dissertations on Abyssinia*, published in the same volume.

Chapter IV. An account of the religion of the Abyssins [1]

YET though there is a great difference between our manners, customs, civil government, and those of the Abyssins, there is yet a much greater in points of faith; for so many errors have been introduced, and engrafted into their religion, by their ignorance, their separation from the Catholic Church, and their intercourse with Jews, Pagans, and Mahometans, that their present religion is nothing but a kind of confused miscellany of Jewish and Mahometan superstitions, with which they have corrupted those remnants of Christianity which they still retain.

They have, however, preserved the belief of our principal mysteries: they celebrate with a great deal of piety the passion of Our Lord, they reverence the Cross, they pay a great devotion to the Blessed Virgin, the Angels, and the Saints; they observe the festivals, and pay a strict regard to the Sunday. Every month they commemorate the Assumption of the Virgin Mary, and are of opinion that no Christians beside themselves have a true sense of the greatness of the Mother of God, or pay her the honours that are due to her. There are some tribes amongst them (for they are distinguished like the Jews by their tribes), among whom the crime of swearing by the name of the Virgin is punished with forfeiture of goods, and even with loss of life; they are equally scrupulous of swearing by St. George. Every week they keep a feast to the honour of the Apostles and Angels; they come to Mass with great devotion, and love to hear the Word of God.[2] They receive the Sacrament often, but do not always prepare themselves by confession.[3] Their charity to the poor may be said to exceed the proper bounds that prudence ought to set to it, for it contributes to encourage great numbers of beggars, which are a great annoyance to the whole kingdom, and as I have often said, afford more exercise to a Christian's patience than his charity: for their insolence is such, that they will refuse what is offered them, if it be not so much as they think proper to ask.

Though the Abyssins have not many images they have great numbers of pictures, and perhaps pay them somewhat too high a degree of worship.[4] The severity of their fasts is equal to that of the primitive Church. In Lent they never eat till after sunset. Their

[1] The Abyssinian Church was originally part of the Jewish Church. King Soloman and the Queen of Sheba were traditionally the ancestors of the emperors. Queen Candace's eunuch, baptized by St. Philip, first brought news of Christianity to the country.

[2] The services were conducted in old Abyssinian, a language which had fallen into disuse in everyday life.

[3] They were, at any rate, always supposed to confess before receiving the Sacrament, which they took in both kinds.

[4] In this they resembled the Orthodox Church.

fasts are the more severe, because milk and butter are forbidden them, and no reason or necessity whatsoever can procure them a permission to eat meat, and, their country affording no fish, they only live on roots and pulse.   On fast-days they never drink but at their meat, and the priests never communicate till evening, for fear of profaning them.   They don't think themselves obliged to fast till they have children either married or fit to be married, which yet doth not secure them very long from these mortifications, because their youths marry at the age of ten years, and their girls younger.

There is no nation where excommunication carries greater terrors than among the Abyssins, which puts it in the power of the priests to abuse this religious temper of the people, as well as the authority they receive from it, by excommunicating them, as they often do for the least trifle in which their interest is concerned.

No country in the world is so full of churches, monasteries, and ecclesiastics [1] as Abyssinia; it is not possible to sing in one church or monastery without being heard by another, and perhaps by several.   They sing the psalms of David, of which, as well as the other parts of the holy scriptures, they have a very exact translation in their own language, in which, though accounted canonical, the books of the Maccabees are omitted.   The instruments of music made use of in their rites of worship are little drums, which they hang about their necks, and beat with both their hands; these are carried even by their chief men, and by the gravest of their ecclesiastics.   They have sticks likewise with which they strike the ground, accompanying the blow with a motion of their whole bodies.   They begin their concert by stamping their feet on the ground and playing gently on their instruments, but when they have heated themselves by degrees, they leave off drumming and fall to leaping, dancing, and clapping their hands, at the same time straining their voices to their utmost pitch, till at length they have no regard either to the tune or the pauses, and seem rather a riotous than a religious assembly.[2]   For this manner of worship they cite the psalm of David, 'O clap your hands all ye nations.'[3] Thus they misapply the sacred writings, to defend practices yet more corrupt than those I have been speaking of.

They are possessed with a strange notion that they are the only true Christians in the world; as for us, they shunned us as heretics, and were under the greatest surprise at hearing us mention the Virgin Mary with the respect which is due to her, and told us that we could not be entirely barbarians, since we were acquainted with

---

[1] There were a very large number of monks and nuns.
[2] This induced fervour was probably of Jewish origin.   Similar fervour shown by Saul and by David will be remembered in the book of Samuel.
[3] Psalm xlvii.

the Mother of God. It plainly appears that prepossessions so
strong, which receive more strength from the ignorance of the
people, have very little tendency to dispose them to a reunion [1]
with the Catholic Church.

They have some opinions peculiar to themselves about Purgatory,
the creation of souls, and some of our mysteries. They repeat
baptism every year, they retain the practice of circumcision, they
observe the sabbath, they abstain from all those sorts of flesh
which are forbidden by the Law. Brothers espouse the wives of
their brothers, and, to conclude, they observe a great number of
Jewish ceremonies. [2]

Though they know the words which Jesus Christ appointed to be
used in the administration of baptism, they have without scruple
substituted others in their place, [3] which makes the validity of their
baptism and the reality of their Christianity very doubtful. They
have a few names of Saints the same with those in the Roman
martyrology, but they often insert others, as *Zama la Cota*, the
Life of Truth, *Ongulari*, the Evangelist, *Asca Georgi*, the Mouth of
St. George.

To bring back this people into the enclosure of the Catholic
Church, from which they had been separated so many ages, was
the sole view and intention with which we undertook so long and
toilsome a journey, crossed so many seas, and passed so many
deserts, with the utmost hazard of our lives. I am certain that we
travelled more than seven thousand leagues before we arrived at our
residence at Maigoga.

We came to this place, anciently called Fremona, [4] on 21st June, [5]
as I have said before, and were obliged to continue there till
November, because the winter begins here in May, and its greatest
rigour is from the middle of June to the middle of September.
The rains that are almost continually falling in this season make it
impossible to go far from home, for the rivers overflow their banks,
and therefore in a place like this, where there are neither bridges
nor boats, are, if they are not fordable, utterly impassable. Some
indeed have crossed them by means of a cord fastened on both
sides of the water, others tie two beams together, and placing themselves upon them, guide them as well as they can, but this experi-

---

[1] The first dissension had been over the Council of Chalcedon, in which matter,
as in all religious questions, they had been governed by Alexandria.

[2] These had remained over from the days of Abyssinian Judaism.

[3] Other accounts do not bear this out. The Jesuits claimed that the
Abyssinians baptized not in the name of the Trinity, but 'in the waters of
Jordan.'

[4] There seems to be some mistake here. The 'ancient' name—the Abyssinian one—was Maigoga. It was the Jesuits who renamed it after Frumentius,
the first missionary to Abyssinia. It was their headquarters.

[5] 1625.

ment is so dangeous that it hath cost many of these bold adventurers
their lives.   This is not all the danger, for there is yet more to be
apprehended from the unwholesomeness of the air, and the vapours
which arise from the scorched earth at the fall of the first showers,
than from the torrents and rivers.   Even they who shelter themselves in houses find great difficulty to avoid the diseases that proceed from the noxious qualities of these vapours.   From the
beginning of June to that of September, it rains more or less every
day.   The morning is generally fair and bright, but about two hours
after noon the sky is clouded, and immediately succeeds a violent
storm, with thunder and lightning flashing in the most dreadful
manner.   While this lasts, which is commonly three or four hours,
none go out of doors.   The ploughman upon the first appearance
of it unyokes his oxen, and betakes himself with them into covert.
Travellers provide for their security in the neighbouring villages,
or set up their tents; everybody flies to some shelter, as well to
avoid the unwholesomeness as the violence of the rain.   The
thunder is astonishing and the lightning often destroys great
numbers, a thing I can speak of from my own experience, for it
once flashed so near me that I felt an uneasiness on that side for
a long time after; at the same time it killed three young children,
and having run round my room went out, and killed a man and
woman three hundred paces off.   When the storm is over the
sun shines out as before, and one would not imagine it had rained
but that the ground appears deluged.   Thus passes the Abyssinian
winter, a dreadful season, in which the whole kingdom languishes
with numberless diseases, an affliction which, however grievous,
is yet equalled by the clouds of grasshoppers, which fly in such
numbers from the desert, that the sun is hid and the sky darkened;
whenever this plague appears, nothing is seen through the whole
region but the most ghastly consternation, or heard but the most
piercing lamentations, for wherever they fall, that unhappy place
is laid waste and ruined, they leave not one blade of grass, nor any
hopes of a harvest.

God, who often makes calamities subservient to His will, permitted this very affliction to be the cause of the conversion of
many of the natives, who might have otherwise died in their
errors; for part of the country being ruined by the grasshoppers
that year in which we arrived at Abyssinia, many, who were forced
to leave their habitations and seek the necessaries of life in other
places, came to that part of the land where some of our missionaries were preaching, and laid hold on that mercy which God
seemed to have appointed for others.

As we could not go to court before November, we resolved that
we might not be idle, to preach and instruct the people in the
country; in pursuance of this resolution I was sent to a mountain,

two days' journey distant from Maigoga. The lord or governor of the place was a Catholic, and had desired missionaries, but his wife had conceived an implacable aversion both from us and the Roman Church, and almost all the inhabitants of that mountain were infected with the same prejudices as she. They had been persuaded that the Hosts which we consecrated and gave to the communicants were mixed with juices strained from the flesh of a camel, a dog, a hare, and a swine, all creatures which the Abyssins look upon with abhorrence, believing them unclean, and forbidden to them as they were to the Jews. We had no way of undeceiving them, and they fled from us whenever we approached. We carried with us our tent, our chalices and ornaments, and all that was necessary for saying Mass. The lord of the village, who, like other persons of quality throughout Ethiopia, lived on the top of a mountain, received us with very great civility. All that depended upon him had built their huts round about him, so that this place compared with the other towns of Abyssinia seems considerable. As soon as we arrived he sent us his compliments, with a present of a cow, which among them is a token of high respect. We had no way of returning this favour but by killing the cow, and sending a quarter smoking, with the gall, which amongst them is esteemed the most delicate part. I imagined for some time that the gall of animals was less bitter in this country than elsewhere, but upon tasting it, I found it more; and yet have frequently seen our servants drink large glasses of it with the same pleasure that we drink the most delicious wines.

We chose to begin our mission with the lady of the village, and hoped that her prejudice and obstinacy, however great, would in time yield to the advice and example of her husband, and that her conversion would have a great influence on the whole village, but having lost several days without being able to prevail upon her to hear us on any one point, we left the place, and went to another mountain, higher and better peopled. When we came to the village on the top of it where the lord lived, we were surprised with the cries and lamentations of men that seemed to suffer or apprehend some dreadful calamity; and were told, upon inquiring the cause, that the inhabitants had been persuaded that we were the devil's missionaries, who came to seduce them from the true religion, that foreseeing some of their neighbours would be ruined by the temptation, they were lamenting the misfortune which was coming upon them. When we began to apply ourselves to the work of the mission, we could not by any means persuade any but the lord and the priest to receive us into their houses; the rest were rough and untractable to that degree that, after having converted six, we despaired of making any farther progress, and thought it best to remove to other towns where we might be better received.

We found, however, a more unpleasing treatment at the next place, and had certainly ended our lives there, had we not been protected by the governor and the priest, who, though not reconciled to the Roman Church, yet showed us the utmost civility; the governor informed us of a design against our lives, and advised us not to go out after sunset, and gave us guards to protect us from the insults of the populace.

We made no long stay in a place where they stopped their ears against the voice of God, but returned to the foot of that mountain which we had left some days before; we were surrounded, as soon as we began to preach, with a multitude of auditors, who came either in expectation of being instructed, or from a desire of gratifying their curiosity, and God bestowed such a blessing upon our apostolical labours, that the whole village was converted in a short time. We then removed to another at the middle of the mountain, situated in a kind of natural parterre or garden. The soil was fruitful, and the trees that shaded it from the scorching heat of the sun gave it an agreeable and refreshing coolness. We had here the convenience of improving the ardour and piety of our new converts, and at the same time of leading more into the way of the true religion. And indeed our success exceeded the utmost of our hopes; we had in a short time great numbers whom we thought capable of being admitted to the sacraments of baptism and the Mass.

We erected our tent and placed our altar under some great trees, for the benefit of the shade; and every day before sunrising my companion and I began to catechize and instruct these new Catholics, and used our utmost endeavours to make them abjure their errors. When we were weary with speaking, we placed in ranks those who were sufficiently instructed, and passing through them with great vessels of water, baptized them according to the form prescribed by the Church. As their number was very great, we cried aloud: 'Those of this rank are named Peter, those of that rank Anthony,' and did the same amongst the women, whom we separated from the men. We then confessed them, and admitted them to the Communion. After Mass we applied ourselves again to catechize, to instruct, and receive the renunciation of their errors, scarce allowing ourselves time to make a scanty meal, which we never did more than once a day.

After some time had been spent here, we removed to another town not far distant, and continued the same practice. Here I was accosted one day by an inhabitant of that place where we had found the people so prejudiced against us, who desired to be admitted to confession. I could not forbear asking him some questions about those lamentations which we heard upon our entering into that place. He confessed with the utmost frankness

and ingenuity that the priests and religious had given dreadful
accounts both of us and of the religion we preached, that the unhappy people was taught by them that the curse of God attended
us wheresoever we went, that we were always followed by the
grasshoppers, that pest of Abyssinia, which carried famine and
destruction over all the country: that he, seeing no grasshoppers
following us when we passed by their village, began to doubt of
the reality of what the priests had so confidently asserted, and was
now convinced that the representation they made of us was calumny
and imposture.   This discourse gave us double pleasure, both as
it proved that God had confuted the accusations of our enemies
and defended us against their malice without any efforts of our own,
and that the people who had shunned us with the strongest detesta-
tion were yet lovers of truth and came to us on their own accord.

Nothing could be more grossly absurd than the reproaches which
the Abyssinian ecclesiastics aspersed us and our religion with.
They had taken advantage of the calamity that happened the year
of our arrival; and the Abyssins, with all their wit, did not consider that they had often been distressed by the grasshoppers
before there came any Jesuits into the country; and indeed before
there were any in the world.

Whilst I was in these mountains I went on Sundays and Saints'
Days sometimes to one church and sometimes to another; one day
I went out with a resolution not to go to a certain church where I
imagined there was no occasion for me, but before I had gone far,
I found myself pressed by a secret impulse to return back to that
same church.   I obeyed the influence, and discovered it to proceed from the mercy of God to three young children who were
destitute of all succour, and at the point of death.   I found two
very quickly in this miserable state; the mother had retired to
some distance that she might not see them die, and when she saw
me stop, came and told me that they had been obliged by want to
leave the town they lived in, and were at length reduced to this
dismal condition, that she had been baptized, but that the children
had not.   After I had baptized and relieved them, I continued
my walk, reflecting with wonder on the mercy of God, and about
evening discovered another infant, whose mother, evidently a
Catholic, cried out to me to save her child, or at least, that if I
could not preserve this uncertain and perishable life, I should give
it another certain and permanent.   I sent my servant to fetch
water with the utmost expedition, for there was none near, and
happily baptized the child before it expired.

Soon after this, I returned to Fremona, and had great hopes of
accompanying the patriarch [1] to the court; but, when we were

_____

[1] That is, the Portuguese patriarch sent by Rome to replace the Alexandrian
patriarch.   His name was Afonso Mendes.

almost setting out, received the command of the superior of the mission to stay at Fremona, with a charge of the house there, and of all the Catholics that were dispersed over the kingdom of Tigre, an employment very ill proportioned to my abilities.   The house of Fremona has always been much regarded, even by those emperors who persecuted us; Sultan Segued [1] annexed nine large manors to it for ever, which did not make us much more wealthy, because of the expensive hospitality which the great conflux of strangers obliged us to.   The lands in Abyssinia yield but small revenues, unless the owners themselves set the value upon them, which we could not do.

The manner of letting farms in Abyssinia differs much from that of other countries.   The farmer, when the harvest is almost ripe, invites the *chumo* or steward, who is appointed to make an estimate of the value of each year's product, to his house, entertains him in the most agreeable manner he can, makes him a present, and then takes him to see his corn.   If the *chumo* is pleased with the treat and present, he will give him a declaration or writing to witness that his ground, which afforded five or six sacks of corn, did not yield so many bushels, and even of this it is the custom to abate something; so that our revenue did not increase in proportion to our lands, and we found ourselves often obliged to buy corn, which indeed is not dear, for in fruitful years forty or fifty measures weighing each about twenty-two pounds may be purchased for a crown.

Besides the particular charge I had of the house of Fremona, I was appointed the patriarch's grand vicar, through the whole kingdom of Tigre.   I thought that to discharge this office as I ought, it was incumbent on me to provide necessaries as well for the bodies as the souls of the converted Catholics.   This labour was much increased by the famine which the grasshoppers had brought that year upon the country.   Our house was perpetually surrounded by some of those unhappy people, whom want had compelled to abandon their habitations, and whose pale cheeks and meagre bodies were undeniable proofs of their misery and distress.   All the relief I could possibly afford them could not prevent the death of such numbers, that their bodies filled the highways; and to increase our affliction, the wolves, having devoured the carcasses and finding no other food, fell upon the living; their natural fierceness being so increased by hunger, that they dragged the children out of the very houses.   I saw myself a troop of wolves tear a child of six years old in pieces before I or any one else could come to its assistance.

While I was entirely taken up with the duties of my ministry,

[1] Selten Sagad, the then emperor of Abyssinia.   He tried to introduce Roman Catholicism into the country, but it proved too unpopular.

the viceroy of Tigre received the commands of the emperor, to search for the bones of Don Christopher de Gama.[1] On this occasion it may not be thought impertinent to give some account of the life and death of this brave and holy Portuguese, who, after having been successful in many battles, fell at last into the hands of the Moors, and completed that illustrious life by a glorious martyrdom.[2]

Chapter VII. They discover the relics.   Their apprehension of the Galles.[3]   The author converts a criminal and procures his pardon

WE took with us an old Moor, so enfeebled with age that they were forced to carry him (he had seen, as I have said, the sufferings and death of Don Christopher de Gama), and a Christian who had often heard all those passages related to his father, and knew the place where the uncle and nephew of Mahomet [4] were buried, and where they interred one quarter of the Portuguese martyr. We often examined these two men and always apart; they agreed in every circumstance of their relations, and confirmed us in our belief of them by leading us to the place, where we took up the uncle and nephew of Mahomet as they had described.   With no small labour we removed the heap of stones which the Moors, according to their custom, had thrown upon the body, and discovered the treasure we came in search of.   Not many paces off was the fountain where they had thrown his head with a dead dog, to raise a greater aversion in the Moors.   I gathered the teeth and the lower jaw.   No words can express the ecstasies I was transported with, at seeing the relics of so great a man, and reflecting that it had pleased God to make me the instrument of their preservation, so that one day, if our holy Father the Pope shall be so pleased,[5] they may receive the veneration of the faithful. All burst into tears at the sight: we indulged a melancholy pleasure in reflecting what that great man had achieved for the deliverance of Abyssinia from the yoke and tyranny of the Moors; the voyages he had undertaken, the battles he had fought, the victories he had won, and the cruel and tragical death he had suffered.   Our first

---

[1] The son of Vasco da Gama, who had come to assist the Abyssinians against the Moors.
[2] An account of his death and of the Moorish wars follows.
[3] The Mohammedan tribe which harried the Abyssinians much as the Philistines in biblical times did the Jews.
[4] The Moorish chieftain against whom Gama had fought.
[5] If Gama is sainted.   It is, however, strange that the neck and jaw were here as the head had been carried to Zebid by the Mohammedans.

moments were so entirely taken up with these reflections, that we were incapable of considering the danger we were in of being immediately surrounded by the Galles. But as soon as we awaked to that thought, we contrived to retreat as fast as we could; our expedition, however, was not so great but we saw them on the top of a mountain ready to pour down upon us. The viceroy attended us closely with his little army, but had been probably not much more secure than we, his force consisting only of foot, and the Galles entirely of horse, a service at which they are very expert. Our apprehensions at last proved to be needless, for the troops we saw were of a nation at that time in alliance with the Abyssins.

Not caring, after this alarm, to stay longer here, we set out on our march back, and in our return passed through a village where two men who had murdered a domestic of the viceroy lay under an arrest; as they had been taken in the fact, the law of the country allowed that they might have been executed the same hour, but the viceroy, having ordered that their death should be deferred till his return, delivered them to the relations of the dead, to be disposed of as they should think proper. They made great rejoicings all the night, on account of having it in their power to revenge their relation, and the unhappy criminals had the mortification of standing by to behold this jollity and the preparations made for their execution.

The Abyssins have three different ways of putting a criminal to death; one way is to bury him to the neck, to lay a heap of brambles upon his head, and to cover the whole with a great stone. Another is to beat him to death with cudgels. A third, and the most usual, is to stab him with their lances. The nearest relation gives the first thrust, and is followed by all the rest according to their degrees of kindred, and they to whom it does not happen to strike while the offender is alive dip the points of their lances in his blood, to show that they partake in the revenge. It frequently happens that the relations of the criminal are for taking the like vengeance for his death, and sometimes pursue this resolution so far that all those who had any share in the prosecution lose their lives.

I, being informed that these two men were to die, wrote to the viceroy for his permission to exhort them, before they entered into eternity, to unite themselves to the Church. My request being granted, I applied myself to the men, and found one of them so obstinate that he would not even afford me an hearing, and died in his error. The other I found more flexible, and wrought upon him so far that he came to my tent to be instructed. After my care of his eternal welfare had met with such success, I could not forbear attempting something for his temporal, and by my endeavours matters were so accommodated that the relations were willing to grant his life on condition he paid a certain number of cows, or the value. Their first demand was of a thousand, he offered them five, they at last were satisfied with twelve, provided they were paid upon the spot. The Abyssins are extremely charitable, and the women on such occasions will give even their necklaces and pendants, so that, with what I gave myself, I collected in the camp enough to pay the fine, and all parties were content.

Chapter VIII. The viceroy is offended by his wife. He complains to the emperor but without redress. He meditates a revolt, raises an army, and makes an attempt to seize upon the author

WE continued our march, and the viceroy, having been advertised that some troops had appeared in a hostile manner on the frontiers, went against them; I parted from him and arrived at Fremona, where the Portuguese expected me with great impatience. I reposited the bones of Don Christopher de Gama in a decent place, and sent them the May following to the viceroy of the Indies, together with his arms which had been presented me by a gentleman of Abyssinia, and a picture of the Virgin Mary, which that gallant Portuguese always carried about him.

The viceroy, during all the time he was engaged in this expedition, heard very provoking accounts of the bad conduct of his wife, and complained of it to the emperor, entreating him either to punish his daughter himself, or to permit him to deliver her over to justice, that, if she was falsely accused, she might have an opportunity of putting her own honour and her husband's out of dispute. The emperor took little notice of his son-in-law's remonstrances, and the truth is the viceroy was somewhat more nice in that matter than the people of rank in this country generally are. There are laws, 'tis true, against adultery, but they seem to have been made only for the meaner people, and the women of quality, especially the *ouzoros* or ladies of the blood-royal, are so much above them, that their husbands have not even the liberty of complaining; and certainly to support injuries of this kind without complaining requires a degree of patience which few men can boast of. The viceroy's virtue was not proof against this temptation; he fell into a deep melancholy, and resolved to be revenged on his father-in-law. He knew the present temper of the people, that those of the greatest interest and power were by no means pleased with the changes of religion and only waited for a fair opportunity to revolt; and that these discontents were everywhere heightened by the monks and clergy. Encouraged by these reflections he was always talking of the just reasons he had to complain of the emperor, and gave them sufficient room to understand that if they would appear in his party he would declare himself for the ancient religion and put himself at the head of those who should take arms in the defence of it.   The chief and almost the only thing that hindered him from raising a formidable rebellion was the mutual distrust they entertained of one another, each fearing that as soon as the emperor should publish an act of grace or general amnesty, the greatest part would lay down their arms and embrace it; and this suspicion was imagined more reasonable of the viceroy than of any other.   Notwithstanding this difficulty, the priests, who interested themselves much in this revolt, ran with the utmost earnestness from church to church levelling their sermons against the emperor and the Catholic religion: and that they might have the better success in putting a stop to all ecclesiastical innovations, they came to a resolution of putting all the missionaries to the sword; and that the viceroy might have no room to hope for a pardon, they obliged him to give the first wound to him that should fall into his hands.

As I was the nearest, and by consequence the most exposed, an order was immediately issued out for apprehending me, it being thought a good expedient to seize me and force me to build a citadel, into which they might retreat if they should happen to meet with a defeat.   The viceroy wrote to me, to desire that I would come to him, he having, as he said, an affair of the highest importance to communicate.

The frequent assemblies which the viceroy held had already been much talked of; and I had received advice that he was ready for a revolt, and that my death was to be the first signal of an open war.   Knowing that the viceroy had made many complaints of the treatment he received from his father-in-law, I made no doubt that he had some ill design in hand; and yet could scarce persuade myself that after all the tokens of friendship I had received from him, he would enter into any measures for destroying me.   While I was yet in suspense, I dispatched a faithful servant to the viceroy with my excuse for disobeying him; and gave the messenger strict orders to observe all that passed and bring me an exact account.

This affair was of too great moment not to engage my utmost endeavours to arrive at the most certain knowledge of it, and to advertise the court of the danger.   I wrote, therefore, to one of our fathers who was then near the emperor, the best intelligence I could obtain of all that had passed, of the reports that were spread through all this part of the empire, and of the disposition which I discovered in the people to a general defection; telling him, however, that I could not yet believe that the viceroy, who had honoured me with his friendship, and of whom I never had any thought but how to oblige him, could now have so far changed his sentiments as to take away my life.

The letters which I received by my servant and the assurances he gave me that I need fear nothing, for that I was never mentioned by the viceroy without great marks of esteem, so far confirmed me in my error that I went from Fremona with a resolution to see him. I did not reflect that a man who could fail in his duty to his king, his father-in-law, and his benefactor, might without scruple do the same to a stranger, though distinguished as his friend; and thus sanguine and unsuspecting continued my journey, still receiving intimation from all parts to take care of myself. At length when I was within a few days' journeys of the viceroy, I received a billet in more plain and express terms than anything I had been told yet, charging me with extreme imprudence in putting myself into the hands of those men who had undoubtedly sworn to cut me off.

I began upon this to distrust the sincerity of the viceroy's professions, and resolved, upon the receipt of another letter from the viceroy, to return directly. In this letter, having excused himself for not waiting for my arrival, he desired me in terms very strong and pressing to come forward and stay for him at his own house, assuring me that he had given such orders for my entertainment as should prevent my being tired with living there. I imagined at first that he had left some servants to provide for my reception, but being advertised at the same time that there was no longer any doubt of the certainty of his revolt, that the Galles were engaged to come to his assistance, and that he was gone to sign a treaty with them, I was no longer in suspense what measures to take, but returned to Fremona.

Here I found a letter from the emperor, which prohibited me to go out, and the orders which he had sent through all these parts directing them to arrest me wherever I was found, and to hinder me from proceeding on my journey. These orders came too late to contribute to my preservation, and this prince's goodness had been in vain, if God, whose protection I have often had experience of in my travels, had not been my conductor in this emergency.

The viceroy, hearing that I was returned to my residence, did not discover any concern or chagrin as at a disappointment, for such was his privacy and dissimulation that the most penetrating could never form any conjecture that could be depended on about his designs, till everything was ready for the execution of them. My servant, a man of wit, was surprised as well as everybody else, and I can ascribe to nothing but a miracle my escape from so many snares as he laid to entrap me.

There happened during this perplexity of my affairs an accident of small consequence in itself, which yet I think deserves to be mentioned, as it shows the credulity and ignorance of the Abyssins. I received a visit from a religious, who passed, though he was blind, for the most learned person in all that country; he had the whole scriptures in his memory, but seemed to have been at more pains to retain than understand them; as he talked much, he often took occasion to quote them, and did it almost always improperly. Having invited him to sup and pass the night with me, I set before him some excellent mead, which he liked so well as to drink somewhat beyond the bounds of exact temperance. Next day, to make some return for this entertainment, he took upon him to divert me with some of those stories which the monks amuse simple people with, and told me of a devil that haunted a fountain, and used to make it his employment to plague the monks that came thither to fetch water, and continued his malice, till he was converted by the founder of their order, who found him no very stubborn proselyte till they came to the point of circumcision; the devil was unhappily prepossessed with a strong aversion from being circumcised, which, however, by much persuasion he at last agreed to, and afterwards taking a religious habit, died ten years after with great signs of sanctity. He added another history of a famous Abyssinian monk, who killed a devil two hundred feet high and only four feet thick, that ravaged all the country; the peasants had a great desire to throw the dead carcass from the top of a rock, but could not with all their force remove it from the place, but the monk drew it after him with all imaginable ease, and pushed it down. This story was followed by another of a young devil that became a religious of the famous monastery of Aba-Gatima. The good father would have favoured me with more relations of the same kind, if I had been in the humour to have heard them, but, interrupting him, I told him that all these relations confirmed, what we had found by experience, that the monks of Abyssinia were no improper company for the devil.

Chapter IX. The viceroy is defeated and hanged. The author narrowly escapes being poisoned

I DID not stay long at Fremona, but left that town and the province of Tigre, and soon found that I was very happy in that resolution, for scarce had I left the place, before the viceroy came in person to put me to death, who, not finding me as he expected, resolved to turn all his vengeance against the father Gaspard [1] Pais, a venerable man, who was grown grey in the missions of Ethiopia, and five other missionaries, newly arrived from the Indies. His design

_____
[1] Gaspar.

was to kill them all at one time without suffering any to escape; he therefore sent for them all, but one happily being sick, another stayed to attend him; to this they owed their lives, for the viceroy, finding but four of them, sent them back, telling them he would see them all together. The fathers, having been already told of his revolt, and of the pretences he made use of to give it credit, made no question of his intent to massacre them, and contrived their escape so that they got safely out of his power.

The viceroy, disappointed in this scheme, vented all his rage upon Father James, whom the patriarch had given him as his confessor; the good man was carried, bound hand and foot, into the middle of the camp: the viceroy gave the first stab in the throat, and all the rest struck him with their lances, and dipped their weapons in his blood, promising each other that they would never accept of any act of oblivion, or terms of peace, by which the Catholic religion was not abolished throughout the empire, and all those who professed it either banished or put to death. They then ordered all the beads, images, crosses, and relics which the Catholics made use of to be thrown into the fire.

The anger of God was now ready to fall upon his head for these daring and complicated crimes; the emperor had already confiscated all his goods and given the government of the kingdom of Tigre to Keba Christos, a good Catholic, who was sent with a numerous army to take possession of it. As both armies were in search of each other, it was not long before they came to a battle. The revolted viceroy Tecla Georgis placed all his confidence in the Galles his auxiliaries. Keba Christos, who had marched with incredible expedition to hinder the enemy from making any entrenchments, would willingly have refreshed his men a few days before the battle, but finding the foe vigilant, thought it not proper to stay till he was attacked, and therefore resolved to make the first onset; then presenting himself before his army without arms and with his head uncovered, assured them that such was his confidence in God's protection of those that engaged in so just a cause, that though he were in that condition and alone, he would attack his enemies.

The battle began immediately, and of all the troops of Tecla Georgis only the Galles made any resistance, the rest abandoned him without striking a blow. The unhappy commander, seeing all his squadrons broken and three hundred of the Galles with twelve ecclesiastics killed on the spot, hid himself in a cave, where he was found three days afterwards with his favourite and a monk. When they took him they cut off the heads of his two companions in the field, and carried him to the emperor; the procedure against him was not long, and he was condemned to be burnt alive. Then imagining that, if he embraced the Catholic faith, the intercession of the missionaries with the entreaties of his wife and children might procure him a pardon, he desired a Jesuit to hear his confession, and abjured his errors.   The emperor was inflexible both to the entreaties of his daughter and the tears of his grandchildren, and all that could be obtained of him was that the sentence should be mollified, and changed into a condemnation to be hanged. Tecla Georgis renounced his abjuration, and at his death persisted in his errors.   Adero, his sister, who had borne the greatest share in his revolt, was hanged on the same tree fifteen days after.

I arrived not long after at the emperor's court and had the honour of kissing his hands, but stayed not long in a place where no missionary ought to linger, unless obliged by the most pressing necessity; but being ordered by my superiors into the kingdom of Damote, I set out on my journey, and on the road was in great danger of losing my life by my curiosity of tasting a herb which I found near a brook, and which, though I had often heard of it, I did not know.   It bears a great resemblance to our radishes: the leaf and colour were beautiful and the taste not unpleasant; it came into my mind when I began to chew it, that perhaps it might be that venomous herb against which no antidote hath yet been found, but persuading myself afterwards that my fears were merely chimerical, I continued to chew it, till a man accidentally meeting me and seeing me with a handful of it, cried out to me that I was poisoned; I had happily not swallowed any of it, and throwing out what I had in my mouth, I returned God thanks for this instance of His protection.

I crossed the Nile the first time in my journey to the kingdom of Damote.   My passage brought into my mind all that I had read either in ancient or modern writers of this celebrated river; I recollected the great expenses at which some emperors had endeavoured to gratify their curiosity of knowing the sources of this mighty stream, which nothing but their little acquaintance with the Abyssins made so difficult to be found.   I passed the river within two days' journey of its head, near a wide plain which is entirely laid under water when it begins to overflow the banks.   Its channel is even here so wide that a ball shot from a musket can scarce reach the farther bank.   Here is neither boat nor bridge, and the river is so full of hippopotames or river-horses, and crocodiles, that it is impossible to swim over without danger of being devoured.   The only way of passing it is upon floats which they guide as well as they can with long poles.   Nor is even this way without danger, for these destructive animals overturn the floats, and tear the passengers in pieces.   The river-horse, which lives only on grass and branches of trees, is satisfied with killing the men, but the crocodile, being more voracious, feeds upon the carcasses.

* L 986

But since I am arrived at the banks of this renowned river, which I have passed and repassed so many times, and since all that I have read of the nature of its waters and the causes of its overflowing is full of fables, the reader may not be displeased to find here an account of what I saw myself or was told by the inhabitants.

Chapter X. A description of the Nile [1]

THE Nile, which the natives call Abavi, that is, the Father of Waters, rises first in Sacala, a province of the kingdom of Goiama, which is one of the most fruitful and agreeable of all the Abyssinian dominions. This province is inhabited by a nation of the Agaus, which but only call themselves Christians, for by daily intermarriages they have allied themselves to the Pagan Agaus, and adopted all their customs and ceremonies. These two nations are very numerous, fierce, and unconquerable, inhabiting a country full of mountains, which are covered with woods and hollowed by nature into vast caverns, many of which are capable of containing several numerous families and hundreds of cows; to these recesses the Agaus betake themselves when they are driven out of the plain, where it is almost impossible to find them and certain ruin to pursue them. This people increases extremely, every man being allowed so many wives as he hath hundreds of cows, and it is seldom that the hundreds are required to be complete.

In the eastern part of this kingdom on the declivity of a mountain, whose descent is so easy that it seems a beautiful plain, is that source of the Nile, which has been sought after at so much expense of labour, and about which such variety of conjectures hath been formed without success. This spring, or rather these two springs, are two holes each about two feet diameter, a stone's cast distant from each other; the one is but about five feet and an half in depth (at least we could not get our plummet farther, perhaps because it was stopped by roots, for the whole place is full of trees); of the other, which is somewhat less, with a line of ten feet we could find no bottom, and were assured by the inhabitants that none ever had been found. 'Tis believed here that these springs are the vents of a great subterraneous lake, and they have this circumstance to favour their opinion, that the ground is always moist, and so soft that the water boils up underfoot as one walks

---

[1] Lobo may well have been the second European to visit this source. The first was Father Pais some years previously. This was the Blue Nile, still called the Abai by the Abyssinians. The Nile proper rises in the Victoria Nyanza.

upon it; this is more visible after rains, for then the ground yields and sinks so much, that I believe it is chiefly supported by the roots of trees that are interwoven one with another: such is the ground round about these fountains. At a little distance to the south, is a village named Guix, through which the way lies to the top of the mountain, from whence the traveller discovers a vast extent of land, which appears like a deep valley, though the mountain rises so imperceptibly that those who go up or down it are scarce sensible of any declivity.

On the top of this mountain is a little hill which the idolatrous Agaus have in great veneration. Their priest calls them together at this place once a year, and having sacrificed a cow, throws the head into one of the springs of the Nile; after which ceremony, every one sacrifices a cow or more, according to their different degrees of wealth or devotion. The bones of these cows have already formed two mountains of considerable height, which afford a sufficient proof that these nations have always paid their adorations to this famous river. They eat these sacrifices with great devotion, as flesh consecrated to their deity. Then the priest anoints himself with the grease and tallow of the cows, and sits down on a heap of straw, on the top and in the middle of a pile which is prepared; they set fire to it, and the whole heap is consumed without any injury to the priest, who, while the fire continues, harangues the standers-by, and confirms them in their present ignorance and superstition. When the pile is burnt, and the discourse at an end, every one makes a large present to the priest, which is the grand design of this religious mockery.

To return to the course of the Nile, its waters, after the first rise, run to the eastward for about a musket-shot, then turning to the north, continue hidden in the grass and weeds for about a quarter of a league, and discover themselves for the first time among some rocks, a sight not to be enjoyed without some pleasure by those who have read the fabulous accounts of this stream delivered by the ancients, and the vain conjectures and reasonings which have been formed upon its original, the nature of its water, its cataracts, and its inundations, all which we are now entirely acquainted with and eye-witnesses of.

Many interpreters of the Holy Scriptures pretend that Gihon, mentioned in Genesis,[1] is no other than the Nile, which encompasseth all Ethiopia; but as the Gihon had its source from the terrestrial paradise, and we know that the Nile rises in the country of the Agaus, it will be found I believe no small difficulty to conceive how the same river could arise from two sources so distant from each other, or how a river from so low a source should spring

[1] 'And the name of the second river [out of Eden] is Gihon: the same is it that compasseth the whole land of Ethiopia.'—Gen. ii. 13.

up and appear in a place perhaps the highest in the world; [1] for if we consider that Arabia and Palestine are in their situation almost level with Egypt, that Egypt is as low if compared with the kingdom of Dambia as the deepest valley in regard of the highest mountain, that the province of Sacala is yet more elevated than Dambia, that the waters of the Nile must either pass under the Red Sea or take a great compass about, we shall find it hard to conceive such an attractive power in the earth as may be able to make the waters rise through the obstruction of so much sand, from places so low, to the most lofty region of Ethiopia.

But leaving these difficulties, let us go on to describe the course of the Nile. It rolls away from its source with so inconsiderable a current, that it appears unlikely to escape being dried up by the hot season, but soon receiving an increase from the Gemma, the Keltu, the Bransu, and other less rivers, it is of such a breadth in the plain of Boad, which is not above three days' journeys from its source, that a ball shot from a musket will scarce fly from one bank to the other. Here it begins to run northwards, deflecting, however, a little towards the east for the space of nine or ten leagues, and then enters the so much talked of lake of Dambia, called by the natives Barhar Sena, the Resemblance of the Sea, or Bahar Dambia, the Sea of Dambia. It crosses this lake only at one end, with so violent a rapidity, that the waters of the Nile may be distinguished through all the passage, which is six leagues. Here begins the greatness of the Nile. Fifteen miles farther, in the land of Alata, it rushes precipitately from the top of a high rock, and forms one of the most beautiful waterfalls in the world. I passed under it without being wet, and resting myself there for the sake of the coolness, was charmed with a thousand delightful rainbows which the sunbeams painted on the water in all their shining and lively colours. The fall of this mighty stream from so great a height makes a noise that may be heard to a considerable distance; but I could not observe that the neighbouring inhabitants were at all deaf; I conversed with several, and was as easily heard by them as I heard them. The mist that rises from this fall of water may be seen much farther than the noise can be heard. After this cataract, the Nile again collects its scattered stream among the rocks, which seem to be disjoined in this place only to afford it a passage. They are so near each other that in my time a bridge of beams, on which the whole imperial army passed, was laid over them. Sultan Segued hath since built here a bridge of one arch in the same place, for which purpose he procured masons from India. This bridge, which is the first the Abyssins have seen on the Nile, very much facilitates a communication between the

[1] It was at one time believed that the terrestrial paradise was in Ethiopia.
[2] Lake Tsana.

provinces and encourages commerce among the inhabitants of his empire.

Here the river alters its course, and passes through many various kingdoms; on the east it leaves Begmeder, or the Land of Sheep, so called from great numbers that are bred there (*beg* in that language signifying sheep, and *meder* a country). It then waters the kingdoms of Amhara, Olaca, Choaa, and Damote, which lie on the left side, and the kingdom of Goiama which it bounds on the right, forming by its windings a kind of peninsula. Then entering Bezamo, a province of the kingdom of Damote, and Gamarcausa, part of Goiama, it returns within a short day's journey of its spring, though to pursue it through all its mazes and accompany it round the kingdom of Goiama is a journey of twenty-nine days. So far, and a few days' journeys farther, this river confines itself to Abyssinia, and then passes into the bordering countries of Fazulo and Ombarca.

These vast regions we have little knowledge of: they are inhabited by nations entirely different from the Abyssins; their hair is like that of the other blacks, short and curled. In the year 1615, Rassela[1] Christos, lieutenant-general to Sultan Segued, entered those kingdoms with his army in a hostile manner, but being able to get no intelligence of the condition of the people, and astonished at their unbounded extent, he returned without daring to attempt anything.

As the empire of the Abyssins terminates at these deserts, and as I have followed the course of the Nile no farther, I here leave it to range over barbarous kingdoms, and convey wealth and plenty into Egypt, which owes to the annual inundations of this river its envied fertility. I know not anything of the rest of its passage, but that it receives great increases from many other rivers, that it has several cataracts like the first already described, and that few fish are to be found in it, which scarcity doubtless is to be attributed to the river-horses and crocodiles, which destroy the weaker inhabitants of these waters, and something may be allowed to the cataracts, it being difficult for fish to fall so far without being killed.

Although some who have travelled in Asia and Africa have given the world their descriptions of crocodiles and hippopotamus or river-horse; yet as the Nile has at least as great numbers of each as any river in the world, I cannot but think my account of it would be imperfect without some particular mention of these animals.

The crocodile is very ugly, having no proportion between his length and thickness; he hath short feet, a wide mouth, with two rows of sharp teeth, standing wide from each other, a brown skin so fortified with scales even to his nose that a musket-ball cannot

[1] This suggested the name 'Rasselas' to Johnson. He was the emperor's brother and an ardent Roman Catholic, which later earned him banishment.

penetrate it.   His sight is extremely quick and at a great distance.
In the water he is daring and fierce, and will seize on any that
are so unfortunate as to be found by him bathing; who if they
escape with life, are almost sure to leave some limb in his mouth.
Neither I, nor any with whom I have conversed about the crocodile, have ever seen him weep, and therefore I take the liberty of
ranking all that hath been told us of his tears amongst the fables
which are only proper to amuse children.

The hippopotamus or river-horse grazes upon the land and
browses on the shrubs, yet is no less dangerous than the crocodile.
He is the size of an ox, of a brown colour without any hair; his tail
is short, his neck long, and his head of an enormous bigness; his
eyes are small, his mouth wide, with teeth half a foot long; he
hath two tusks like those of a wild boar, but larger; his legs are
short, and his feet part into four toes.   It is easy to observe from
this description that he hath no resemblance of a horse, and indeed
nothing could give occasion to the name, but some likeness in his
ears, and his neighing and snorting like a horse when he is provoked
or raises his head out of water.   His hide is so hard that a musket
fired close to him can only make a slight impression, and the best-
tempered lances pushed forcibly against him are either blunted
or shivered, unless the assailant has the skill to make his thrust
at certain parts which are more tender.   There is great danger in
meeting him, and the best way is, upon such an accident, to step
aside and let him pass by.   The flesh of this animal doth not
differ from that of a cow, except that it is blacker and harder
to digest.

The ignorance which we have hitherto been in of the original
of the Nile hath given many authors an opportunity of presenting
us very gravely with their various systems and conjectures about
the nature of its waters and the reason of its overflows.

It is easy to observe how many empty hypotheses and idle
reasonings the phenomenons of this river have put mankind to the
expense of.   Yet there are people so bigoted to antiquity, as not
to pay any regard to the relation of travellers who have been upon
the spot, and by the evidence of their eyes can confute all that the
ancients have written.   It was difficult, it was even impossible
to arrive at the source of the Nile by tracing its channel from the
mouth; and all who ever attempted it, having been stopped by the
cataracts,[1] and imagining none that followed them could pass
farther, have taken the liberty of entertaining us with their own
fictions.

It is to be remembered likewise, that neither the Greeks nor

---

[1] This was the case with Herodotus, who reached the first cataract.   He says
that he went as far up as Elephantine (the modern Aswan or Assuan), where the
first cataract is situated; 'beyond that obtaining information by hearsay' (ii. 29).

Romans, from whom we have received all our information, ever carried their arms into this part of the world, or ever heard of multitudes of nations that dwell upon the banks of this vast river; that the countries where the Nile rises, and those through which it runs, have no inhabitants but what are savage and uncivilized; that before they could arrive at its head, they must surmount the insuperable obstacles of impassable forests, inaccessible cliffs, and deserts crowded with beasts of prey, fierce by nature, and raging for want of sustenance. Yet if they who endeavoured with so much ardour to discover the spring of this river had landed at Mazna [1] on the coast of the Red Sea, and marched a little more to the south than the south-west, they might perhaps have gratified their curiosity at less expense, and in about twenty days might have enjoyed the desired sight of the source of the Nile.

But this discovery was reserved for the invincible bravery of our noble countrymen, who, not discouraged by the dangers of a navigation in seas never explored before, have subdued kingdoms and empires where the Greek and Roman greatness, where the names of Caesar and Alexander were never heard of; who first steered a European ship into the Red Sea through the Gulf of Arabia and the Indian Ocean, who have demolished the airy fabrics of renowned hypotheses, and detected those fables which the ancients rather chose to invent of the sources of the Nile than to confess their ignorance. I cannot help suspending my narration to reflect a little on the ridiculous speculations of those swelling philosophers, whose arrogance would prescribe laws to nature, and subject those astonishing effects which we behold daily to their idle reasonings and chimerical rules. Presumptuous imagination! that has given being to such numbers of books, and patrons to so many various opinions, about the overflows of the Nile. Some of these theorists have been pleased to declare it as their favourite notion, that this inundation is caused by high winds which stop the current, and so force the water to rise above its banks and spread over all Egypt. Others pretend a subterraneous communication between the ocean and the Nile, and that the sea being violently agitated swells the river. Many have imagined themselves blessed with the discovery when they have told us that this mighty flood proceeds from the melting of snow on the mountains of Ethiopia, without reflecting that this opinion is contrary to the received notion of all the ancients, who believed that the heat was so excessive between the tropics that no inhabitant could live there. So much snow and so great heat are never met with in the same region. And, indeed, I never saw snow in Abyssinia, except on Mount Semen in the kingdom of Tigre, very remote from the Nile, and on Namera, which is indeed not far distant, but where there never

---

[1] On modern maps the place is called Massawa or Massaua.

falls snow sufficient to wet the foot of the mountain when it is
melted.

To the immense labours and fatigues of the Portuguese mankind is indebted for the knowledge of the real cause of these inundations so great and so regular.   Their observations inform us
that Abyssinia, where the Nile rises and waters vast tracts of land,
is full of mountains, and in its natural situation much higher than
Egypt; that all the winter, from June to September, no day is
without rain; that the Nile receives in its course all the rivers,
brooks, and torrents which fall from those mountains; these necessarily swell it above the banks, and fill the plains of Egypt with
the inundation.   This comes regularly about the month of July,
or three weeks after the beginning of a rainy season in Ethiopia.
The different degrees of this flood are such certain indications of
the fruitfulness or sterility of the ensuing year, that it is publicly
proclaimed in Cairo, how much the water hath gained each night.
This is all I have to inform the reader of concerning the Nile,
which the Egyptians adored as the deity in whose choice it was to
bless them with abundance, or deprive them of the necessaries
of life.

*Chapter XI.   The author discovers a passage over the Nile.   Is sent
into the province of Ligonous, which he gives a description of.
His success in his mission.   The stratagem of the monks to encourage the soldiers.   The author narrowly escapes being burned*

WHEN I was to cross this river at Boad, I durst not venture myself
on the floats I have already spoken of, but went up higher in
hopes of finding a more commodious passage.   I had with me
three or four men that were reduced to the same difficulty with
myself.   In one part, seeing people on the other side, and remark-
ing that the water was shallow, and that the rocks and trees which
grew very thick there contributed to facilitate the attempt, I leaped
from one rock to another till I reached the opposite bank, to the
great amazement of the natives themselves, who never had tried
that way; my four companions followed me with the same success,
and it hath been called since the Passage of Father Jerome.

That province of the kingdom of Damote, which I was assigned
to by my superior, is called Ligonous, and is perhaps one of the
most beautiful and agreeable places in the world; the air is healthful
and temperate, and all the mountains, which are not very high,
shaded with cedars.   They sow and reap here in every season, the

ground is always producing, and the fruits ripen throughout the year: so great, so charming is the variety, that the whole region seems a garden, laid out and cultivated only to please. I doubt whether even the imagination of a painter has yet conceived a landscape as beautiful as I have seen. The forests have nothing uncouth or savage, and seem only planned for shade and coolness. Among a prodigious number of trees which fill them, there is one kind which I have seen in no other place, and to which we have none that bears any resemblance. This tree, which the natives call *ensetè*, is wonderfully useful; its leaves, which are so large as to cover a man, make hangings for rooms and serve the inhabitants instead of linen for their tables and carpets. They grind the branches and the thick parts of the leaves, and when they are mingled with milk find them a delicious food; the trunk and the roots are even more nourishing than the leaves or branches, and the meaner people, when they go a journey, make no provision of any other victuals. The word *ensetè* signifies the tree against hunger, or the poor's tree, though the most wealthy often eat of it. If it be cut down within half a foot of the ground, and several incisions made in the stump, each will put out a new sprout, which, if transplanted, will take root and grow to a tree. The Abyssins report that this tree, when it is cut down, groans like a man, and on this account call cutting down an *ensetè* killing it. On the top grows a bunch of five or six figs, of a taste not very agreeable, which they set in the ground to produce more trees.

I stayed two months in the province of Lingonous, and during that time procured a church to be built of hewn stone, roofed and wainscoted with cedar, which is the most considerable in the whole country. My continual employment was the duties of the mission, which I was always practising in some part of the province, not indeed with any extraordinary success at first, for I found the people inflexibly obstinate in their opinions, even to so great a degree, that when I first published the emperor's edict requiring all his subjects to renounce their errors and unite themselves to the Roman Church, there were some monks who, to the number of sixty, chose rather to die by throwing themselves headlong from a precipice than obey their sovereign's commands: and in a battle fought between these people that adhered to the religion of their ancestors, and the troops of Sultan Segued, six hundred religious, placing themselves in the head of their men, marched towards the Catholic army with the stones of the altars upon their heads, assuring their credulous followers, that the emperor's troops would immediately at the sight of those stones fall into disorder and turn their backs. But as they were some of the first that fell, their death had a great influence upon the people, to undeceive them and make them return to the truth. Many were converted after the battle,

and when they had embraced the Catholic faith, adhered to that
with the same constancy and firmness with which they had before
persisted in their errors.

The emperor had sent a viceroy into this province whose firm
attachment to the Roman Church, as well as great abilities in
military affairs, made him a person very capable of executing the
orders of the emperor, and of suppressing any insurrection that
might be raised to prevent those alterations in religion which they
were designed to promote. A farther view in the choice of so
warlike a deputy was, that a stop might be put to the inroads of
the Galles, who had killed one viceroy, and in a little time after
killed this.

It was our custom to meet together every year about Christmas,
not only that we might comfort and entertain each other, but
likewise that we might relate the progress and success of our
missions, and concert all measures that might farther the conversion of the inhabitants. This year our place of meeting was the
emperor's camp, where the patriarch and superior of the missions
were. I left the place of my abode, and took in my way four
fathers, that resided at the distance of two days' journeys, so that
the company, without reckoning our attendants, was five. There
happened nothing remarkable to us till the last night of our journey,
when taking up our lodging at a place belonging to the empress,
a declared enemy to all Catholics, and in particular to the missionaries, we met with a kind reception in appearance, and were lodged
in a large stone house covered with wood and straw, which had
stood uninhabited so long that great numbers of red ants had taken
possession of it; these, as soon as we were laid down, attacked us
on all sides, and tormented us so incessantly, that we were obliged
to call up our domestics. Having burnt a prodigious number of
these troublesome animals, we tried to compose ourselves again,
but had scarce closed our eyes before we were awaked by the fire
that had seized our lodging. Our servants, who were, fortunately,
not all gone to bed, perceived the fire as soon as it began, and
informed me who lay nearest the door. I immediately alarmed
all the rest, and nothing was thought of but how to save ourselves
and the little goods we had, when, to our great astonishment, we
found one of the doors barricaded in such a manner that we could
not open it; nothing now could have prevented our perishing in
the flames, had not those who kindled them omitted to fasten that
door near which I was lodged. We were no longer in doubt that
the inhabitants of the town had laid a train and set fire to a neighbouring house, in order to consume us; their measures were so well
laid that the house was in ashes in an instant, and three of our
beds were burnt which the violence of the flame would not allow
us to carry away. We spent the rest of the night in the most dismal

apprehensions, and found next morning that we had justly charged the inhabitants with the design of destroying us, for the place was entirely abandoned, and those that were conscious of the crime had fled from the punishment. We continued our journey, and came to Gorgora,[1] where we found the fathers met, and the emperor with them.

Chapter XII. The author is sent into Tigre; is in danger of being poisoned by the breath of a serpent; is stung by a serpent; is almost killed by eating anchoy. The people conspire against the missionaries, and distress them

MY superiors intended to send me into the farthest parts of the empire, but the emperor overruled that design and remanded me to Tigre where I had resided before; I passed in my journey by Ganete Ilhos, a palace newly built and made agreeable by beautiful gardens, and had the honour of paying my respects to the emperor who had retired thither, and receiving from him a large present for the finishing of a hospital which had been begun in the kingdom of Tigre. After having returned him thanks I continued my way, and in crossing a desert two days' journeys over, was in great danger of my life, for, as I lay on the ground, I perceived myself seized with a pain which forced me to rise, and saw about four yards from me one of those serpents that dart their poison at a distance.[2] Although I rose before he came very near me, I yet felt the effects of his poisonous breath, and, if I had lain a little longer, had certainly died; I had recourse to bezoar, a sovereign remedy against these poisons which I always carried about me. These serpents are not long, but have a body short and thick, and their bellies speckled with brown, black, and yellow; they have a wide mouth, with which they draw in a great quantity of air and, having retained it some time, eject it with such force, that they kill at four yards' distance; I only escaped by being somewhat farther from him. This danger, however, was not much to be regarded in comparison of another which my negligence brought me into. As I was picking up a skin that lay upon the ground, I was stung by a serpent, that left his sting in my finger; I at least picked an extraneous substance about the bigness of a hair out of the wound which I imagined was the sting. This slight wound I took little notice of, till my arm grew inflamed all over; in a short time the poison infected my blood, and I felt the most terrible convulsions,

[1] Another Jesuit centre, where Father Pais had built two churches.
[2] A snake of this species was brought to the zoological gardens in London in 1927.

which were interpreted as certain signs that my death was near and inevitable. I received now no benefit from bezoar, the horn of the unicorn, or any of the usual antidotes, but found myself obliged to make use of an extraordinary remedy which I submitted to with extreme reluctance; this submission and obedience brought the blessing of heaven upon me. Nevertheless, I continued indisposed a long time, and had many symptoms which made me fear that all the danger was not yet over: I then took cloves of garlic, though with a great aversion both from the taste and smell; I was in this condition a whole month, always in pain, and taking medicines the most nauseous in the world, at length youth [1] and a happy constitution surmounted the malignity, and I recovered my former health.

I continued two years at my residence in Tigre, entirely taken up with the duties of the mission, preaching, confessing, baptizing, and enjoyed a longer quiet and repose than I had ever done since I left Portugal. During this time one of our fathers, being always sick, and of a constitution which the air of Abyssinia was very hurtful to, obtained a permission from our superiors to return to the Indies; I was willing to accompany him through part of his way, and went with him over a desert at no great distance from my residence, where I found many trees loaded with a kind of fruit called by the natives *anchoy*, about the bigness of an apricot, and very yellow, which is much eaten without any ill effect. I therefore made no scruple of gathering and eating it, without knowing that the inhabitants always peeled it, the rind being a violent purgative; so that eating the fruit and skin together I fell into such a disorder as almost brought me to my end. The ordinary dose is six of these rinds, and I had devoured twenty.

I removed from thence to Debaroa, fifty-four miles nearer the sea, and crossed in my way the desert of the province of Saraoe: the country is fruitful, pleasant, and populous; there are greater numbers of Moors in these parts than in any other province of Abyssinia, and the Abyssins of this country are not much better than the Moors.

I was at Debaroa when the prosecution was first set on foot against the Catholics. Sultan Segued, who had been so great a favourer of us, was grown old, and his spirit and authority decreased with his strength. His son, who was arrived at manhood, being weary of waiting so long for the crown he was to inherit, took occasion to blame his father's conduct, and found some reason for censuring all his actions; he even proceeded so far as to give orders sometimes contrary to the emperor's. He had embraced the Catholic religion, rather through complaisance than conviction or inclination; and many of the Abyssins who had done the

[1] He was twenty-nine.

same waited only for an opportunity of making public profession of the ancient erroneous opinions, and of reuniting themselves to the Church of Alexandria.   So artfully can this people dissemble their sentiments, that we had not been able hitherto to distinguish our real from our pretended favourers, but as soon as this prince began to give evident tokens of his hatred, even in the lifetime of the emperor, we saw all the courtiers and governors who had treated us with such a show of friendship declare against us and persecute us as disturbers of the public tranquillity, who had come into Ethiopia with no other intention than to abolish the ancient laws and customs of the country, to sow divisions between father and son, and preach up a revolution.

After having borne all sorts of affronts and ill-treatments we retired to our house at Fremona, in the midst of our countrymen, who had been settling round about us a long time; imagining we should be more secure there, and that at least during the life of the emperor, they would not come to extremities or proceed to open force.   I laid some stress upon the kindness which the viceroy of Tigre had shown to us, and in particular to me; but was soon convinced that those hopes had no real foundation, for he was one of the most violent of our persecutors.   He seized upon all our lands, and advancing with his troops to Fremona, blocked up the town. The army had not been stationed there long before they committed all sorts of disorders, so that one day a Portuguese, provoked beyond his temper at the insolence of some of them, went out with his four sons, and wounding several of them forced the rest back to their camp.

We thought we had good reason to apprehend an attack: their troops were increasing, our town was surrounded, and on the point of being forced; our Portuguese therefore thought that without staying till the last extremities, they might lawfully repel one violence by another, and sallying out to the number of fifty, wounded about threescore of the Abyssins, and had put them to the sword, but that they feared it might bring too great an odium upon our cause.   The Portuguese were some of them wounded, but, happily, none died on either side.

Though the times were by no means favourable to us, every one blamed the conduct of the viceroy, and those who did not commend our action made the necessity we were reduced to of self-defence an excuse for it.   The viceroy's principal design was to get my person into his possession, imagining that if I was once in his power, all the Portuguese would pay him a blind obedience. Having been unsuccessful in his attempt by open force, he made use of the arts of negotiation, but with an event not more to his satisfaction.   This viceroy being recalled, a son-in-law of the emperor's succeeded, who treated us even worse than his predecessor had done.

When he entered upon his command, he loaded us with kindnesses, giving us so many assurances of his protection, that while
the emperor lived we thought him one of our friends; but no sooner
was our protector dead, than this man pulled off his mask, and
quitting all shame, let us see that neither the fear of God nor any
other consideration was capable of restraining him when we were
to be distressed.   The persecution then becoming general, there
was no longer any place of security for us in Abyssinia; where we
were looked upon by all as the authors of all the civil commotions,
and many councils were held to determine in what manner they
should dispose of us.   Several were of opinion that the best way
would be to kill us all at once, and affirmed that no other means
were left of re-establishing order and tranquillity in the kingdom.

Others more prudent were not for putting us to death with so
little consideration, but advised that we should be banished to one
of the isles of the lake of Dambia, an affliction more severe than
death itself.   These alleged in vindication of their opinions that
it was reasonable to expect, if they put us to death, that the viceroy
of the Indies would come with fire and sword to demand satisfaction.   This argument made so great an impression upon some of
them, that they thought no better measures could be taken than
to send us back again to the Indies.   This proposal, however, was
not without its difficulties, for they suspected that when we should
arrive at the Portuguese territories, we would levy an army, return
back to Abyssinia, and under pretence of establishing the Catholic
religion, revenge all the injuries we had suffered.

While they were thus deliberating upon our fate, we were
imploring the succour of the Almighty with fervent and humble
supplications, entreating Him in the midst of our sighs and tears
that He would not suffer His own cause to miscarry, and that
however it might please Him to dispose of our lives, which, we
prayed, He would assist us to lay down with patience and resigna-
tion worthy of the faith for which we were persecuted, He would
not permit our enemies to triumph over the truth.

Thus we passed our days and nights in prayers, in affliction, and
tears, continually crowded with widows and orphans, that sub-
sisted upon our charity, and came to us for bread when we had not
any for ourselves.

While we were in this distress we received an account that the
viceroy of the Indies had fitted out a powerful fleet against the
king of Mombasa, who having thrown off the authority of the
Portuguese, had killed the governor of the fortress, and had since
committed many acts of cruelty.   The same fleet, as we were informed, after the king of Mombasa was reduced, was to burn and
ruin Zeila, in revenge of the death of two Portuguese Jesuits, who
were killed by the king in the year 1604.   As Zeila was not far

from the frontiers of Abyssinia, they imagined that they already saw the Portuguese invading their country.

The viceroy of Tigre had inquired of me a few days before how many men one India ship carried, and being told that the complement of some was a thousand men, he compared that answer with the report then spread over all the country, that there were eighteen Portuguese vessels on the coast of Adel, and concluded that they were manned by an army of eighteen thousand men; then considering what had been achieved by four hundred, under the command of Don Christopher de Gama, he thought Abyssinia already ravaged or subjected to the king of Portugal. Many declared themselves of his opinion, and the court took its measures with respect to us from these uncertain and ungrounded rumours. Some were so infatuated with their apprehensions that they undertook to describe the camp of the Portuguese, and affirmed that they had heard the report of their cannons.

All this contributed to exasperate the inhabitants, and reduced us often to the point of being massacred. At length they came to a resolution of giving us up to the Turks, assuring them that we were masters of a vast treasure, in hope that after they had inflicted all kinds of tortures on us, to make us confess where we had hid our gold or what we had done with it, they would at length kill us in rage for the disappointment. Nor was this their only view, for they believed that the Turks would by killing us kindle such an irreconcilable hatred between themselves and our nation, as would make it necessary for them to keep us out of the Red Sea, of which they are entirely masters: so that their determination was as politic as cruel. Some pretend that the Turks were engaged to put us to death as soon as we were in their power.

Chapter XIII. The author relieves the patriarch and missionaries, and supports them. He escapes several snares laid for him by the viceroy of Tigre. They put themselves under the protection of the prince of Bar

HAVING concluded this negotiation they drove us out of our houses and robbed us of everything that was worth carrying away, and not content with that, informed some banditti that were then in those parts of the road we were to travel through, so that the patriarch and some missionaries were attacked in a desert by these rovers with their captain at their head, who pillaged his library, his ornaments, and what little baggage the missionaries had left, and might have gone away without resistance or interruption, had they satisfied themselves with only robbing, but when they began to fall upon the missionaries and their companions, our countrymen, finding that their lives could only be preserved by their courage, charged their enemies with such vigour, that they killed their chief and forced the rest to a precipitate flight. But these rovers, being acquainted with the country, harassed the little caravan till it was past the borders.

Our fathers then imagined they had nothing more to fear, but too soon were convinced of their error, for they found the whole country turned against them, and met everywhere new enemies to contend with and new dangers to surmount. Being not far distant from Fremona where I resided, they sent to me for succour; I was better informed of the distress they were in than themselves, having been told that a numerous body of Abyssins had posted themselves in a narrow pass, with an intent to surround and destroy them. Therefore, without long deliberation, I assembled my friends, both Portuguese and Abyssins, to the number of fourscore, and went to their rescue, carrying with me provisions and refreshments, of which I knew they were in great need. These glorious confessors I met as they were just entering the pass designed for the place of their destruction, and doubly preserved them from famine and the sword. A grateful sense of their deliverance made them receive me as a guardian angel. We went together to Fremona, and being in all a patriarch, a bishop, eighteen Jesuits, and four hundred Portuguese, whom I supplied with necessaries, though the revenues of our house were lost, and though the country was disaffected to us, in the worst season of the year. We were obliged for the relief of the poor, and our own subsistence, to sell our ornaments and chalices, which we first broke in pieces, that the people might not have the pleasure of ridiculing our mysteries by profaning the vessels made use of in the celebration of them; for they now would gladly treat with the highest indignities what they had a year before looked upon with veneration.

Amidst all these perplexities, the viceroy did not fail to visit us and make us great offers of service in expectation of a large present. We were in a situation in which it was very difficult to act properly; we knew too well the ill intentions of the viceroy, but durst not complain, or give him any reason to imagine that we knew them. We longed to retreat out of his power, or at least to send one of our company to the Indies, with an account of the persecution we suffered, and could without his leave neither do one nor the other.

When it was determined that one should be sent to the Indies, I was at first singled out for the journey, and it was intended that I should represent at Goa, at Rome, and at Madrid the distresses and necessities of the mission of Ethiopia. But the fathers, reflecting afterwards that I best understood the Abyssinian language and was most acquainted with the customs of the country, altered their opinions, and continuing me in Ethiopia either to perish with them or preserve them, deputed four other Jesuits, who in a short time set out on their way to the Indies.

About this time I was sent for to the viceroy's camp, to confess a criminal, who, though falsely, was believed a Catholic, to whom after a proper exhortation I was going to pronounce the form of absolution, when those that waited to execute him told him aloud that if he expected to save his life by professing himself a Catholic, he would find himself deceived, and that he had nothing to do but prepare himself for death. The unhappy criminal had no sooner heard this, than rising up he declared his resolution to die in the religion of his country, and being delivered up to his prosecutors, was immediately dispatched with their lances.

The chief reason of calling me was not that I might hear this confession; the viceroy had another design of seizing my person, expecting that either the Jesuits or Portuguese would buy my liberty with a large ransom, or that he might exchange me for his father, who was kept prisoner by a revolted prince. That prince would have been no loser by the exchange, for so much was I hated by the Abyssinian monks, that they would have thought no expense too great to have gotten me into their hands, that they might have glutted their revenge by putting me to the most painful death they could have invented. Happily, I found means to retire out of this dangerous place, and was followed by the viceroy almost to Fremona, who being disappointed, desired me either to visit him at his camp, or appoint a place where we might confer. I made many excuses, but at length agreed to meet him at a place near Fremona, bringing each of us only three companions. I did not doubt but he would bring more, and so he did, but found that I was upon my guard, and that my company increased in proportion to his. My friends were resolute Portuguese, who were determined to give him no quarter if he made any attempt upon my liberty: finding himself once more countermined he returned ashamed to his camp, where a month after, being accused of a confederacy in the revolt of that prince who kept his father prisoner, he was arrested and carried in chains to the emperor.

The time now approaching in which we were to be delivered to the Turks, we had none but God to apply to for relief; all the measures we could think of were equally dangerous; resolving nevertheless to seek some retreat where we might hide ourselves either altogether or separately, we determined at last to put ourselves under the protection of the prince John Akay, who had defended himself a long time in the province of Bar against the power of Abyssinia.[1]

[1] He had indeed never made a formal submission to the emperor.

After I had concluded a treaty with this prince, the patriarch and all the fathers put themselves into his hands, and being received with all imaginable kindness and civility, were conducted with a guard to Adicota, a rock excessively steep, about nine miles from his place of residence. The event was not agreeable to the happy beginning of our negotiation; for we soon began to find that our habitation was not likely to be very pleasant. We were surrounded with Mahometans, or Christians who were inveterate enemies to the Catholic faith, and were obliged to act with the utmost caution. Notwithstanding these inconveniences, we were pleased with the present tranquillity we enjoyed and lived contentedly on lentils and a little corn that we had, and I, after we had sold all our goods, resolved to turn physician, and was soon able to support myself by my practice.

I was once consulted by a man troubled with an asthma, who presented me with two *alquieres*, that is, about twenty-eight pound weight of corn, and a sheep; the advice I gave him, after having turned over my books, was to drink goat's urine every morning. I know not whether he found any benefit by following my prescription, for I never saw him after.

Being under a necessity of obeying our *acoba* or protector, we changed our place of abode as often as he desired it, though not without great inconveniences, from the excessive heat of the weather, and the faintness which our strict observation of the fasts and austerities of Lent as it is kept in this country [1] had brought upon us. At length wearied with removing so often, and finding that the last place assigned for our abode was always the worst, we agreed that I should go to our sovereign and complain.

I found him entirely taken up with the imagination of a prodigious treasure affirmed by the monks to be hidden under a mountain. He was told that his predecessors had been hindered from discovering it by the demon that guarded it, but that the demon was now at a great distance from his charge, and was grown blind and lame; that having lost his son, and being without any children, except a daughter that was ugly and unhealthy, he was under great affliction, and entirely neglected the care of his treasure; that if he should come, they could call one of their ancient brothers to their assistance, who being a man of a most holy life would be able to prevent his making any resistance. To all these stories the prince listened with unthinking credulity. The monks, encouraged by this, fell to the business, and brought a man above a hundred years old, whom, because he could not support himself on horseback, they had tied on the beast and covered him with black wool.

[1] It is interesting to see that, despite many points of disagreement, the Jesuits still conformed to certain of Abyssinia's religious customs, when working there.

He was followed by a black cow designed for a sacrifice to the demon of the place, and by some monks that carried mead, beer, and parched corn to complete the offering.

No sooner were they arrived at the foot of the mountain, than every one began to work; bags were brought from all parts to convey away the millions which each imagined would be his share.   The *xumo* who superintended the work would not allow any to come near the labourers, but stood by, attended by the old monk, who almost sung himself to death.   At length, having removed a vast quantity of earth and stones, they discovered some holes made by rats or moles; at sight of which a shout of joy ran through the whole troop: the cow was brought and sacrificed immediately, and some pieces of flesh were thrown into these holes.   Animated now with assurance of success, they lose no time, every one redoubles his endeavours, and the heat, though intolerable, was less powerful than the hopes they had conceived.   At length, some not so patient as the rest were weary and desisted.   The work now grew more difficult, they found nothing but rock, yet continued to toil on, till the prince, having lost all temper, began to inquire with some passion when he should have a sight of this treasure, and after having been sometime amused with many promises by the monks, was told that he had not faith enough to be favoured with the discovery.

All this I saw myself, and could not forbear endeavouring to convince our protector how much he was imposed upon; he was not long before he was satisfied that he had been too credulous, for all those that had so industriously searched after this imaginary wealth within five hours left the work in despair, and I continued almost alone with the prince.

Imagining no time more proper to make the proposal I was sent with, than while his passion was still hot against the monks, I presented him with two ounces of gold and two plates of silver, with some other things of small value, and was so successful that he gratified me in all my requests, and gave us leave to return to Adicora, where we were so fortunate to find our huts yet uninjured and entire.

About this time the fathers who had stayed behind at Fremona arrived with the new viceroy, and an officer, fierce in the defence of his own religion, who had particular orders to deliver all the Jesuits up to the Turks, except me, whom the emperor was resolved to have in his own hands alive or dead.   We had received some notice of this resolution from our friends at court, and were like-wise informed that the emperor their master had been persuaded that my design was to procure assistance from the Indies, and that I should certainly return at the head of an army.   The patriarch's advice upon this emergency was that I should retire into the woods, and by some other road join the nine [1] Jesuits who were gone towards Mazna; I could think of no better expedient, and therefore went away in the night between the 23rd and 24th April with my comrade, an old man very infirm and very timorous. We crossed woods never crossed, I believe, by any before; the darkness of the night and the thickness of the shade spread a kind of horror round us; our gloomy journey was still more incommoded by the brambles and thorns which tore our hands; amidst all these difficulties I applied myself to the Almighty, praying Him to preserve us from those dangers which we endeavoured to avoid, and to deliver us from those to which our flight exposed us. Thus we travelled all night till eight next morning without taking either rest or food; then imagining ourselves secure, we made us some cakes of barley meal and water, which we thought a feast.

We had a dispute with our guides, who they thought [2] had bargained to conduct us for an ounce of gold, yet when they saw us so entangled in the intricacies of the wood that we could not possibly get out without their direction, demanded seven ounces of gold, a mule, and a little tent which we had; after a long dispute we were forced to come to their terms. We continued to travel all night and to hide ourselves in the woods all day; and here it was that we met the three hundred elephants I spoke of before. [3] We made long marches, travelling without any halt, from four in the afternoon to eight in the morning.

Arriving at a valley where travellers seldom escape being plundered, we were obliged to double our pace, and were so happy as to pass it without meeting with any misfortune, except that we heard a bird sing on our left hand—a certain presage among these people of some great calamity at hand. As there is no reasoning them out of superstition, I knew no way of encouraging them to go forward but what I had already made use of on the same occasion, assuring them that I heard one at the same time on the right. They were, happily, so credulous as to take my word, and we went on till we came to a well, where we stayed awhile to refresh ourselves. Setting out again in the evening, we passed so near a village where these robbers had retreated, that the dogs barked after us. Next morning we joined the fathers who waited for us. After we had rested ourselves some time in that mountain, we resolved to separate and go two and two, to see for a more convenient

---

[1] When they were last mentioned, on p. 323, they were four.
[2] Presumably a printer's error for 'though they.'
[3] A reference to the opening sentence of Chapter II: 'There are so great numbers of elephants in Abyssinia, that in one evening we met three hundred of them in three troops; as they filled up the whole way, we were in great perplexity a long time what measures to take; at length, having implored the protection of that Providence that superintends the whole creation, we went forwards through the midst of them, without any injury.'

place where we might hide ourselves. We had not gone far before we were surrounded by a troop of robbers, with whom, by the interest of some of the natives who had joined themselves to our caravan, we came to a composition, giving them part of our goods to permit us to carry away the rest, and after this troublesome adventure arrived at a place something more commodious than that which we had quitted, where we met with bread, but of so pernicious a quality, that after having ate it we were intoxicated to so great a degree, that one of my friends, seeing me so disordered, congratulated my good fortune of having met with such good wine, and was surprised when I gave him an account of the whole affair. He then offered me some curdled milk very sour, with barley-meal, which we boiled and thought it the best entertainment we had met with a long time.

Chapter XIV. They are betrayed into the hands of the Turks; are detained awhile at Mazna; are threatened by the bassa of Suaquem. They agree for their ransom and are part of them dismissed

SOME time after we received news that we should prepare ourselves to serve the Turks, a message which filled us with surprise, it having never been known that one of these lords had ever abandoned any whom he had taken under his protection; and it is on the contrary one of the highest points of honour amongst them, to risk their fortunes and their lives in the defence of their dependants who have implored their protection. But neither law nor justice were of any advantage to us, and the customs of the country were doomed to be broken when they would have contributed to our security.

We were obliged to march in the extremity of the hot season, and had certainly perished by the fatigue, had we not entered the woods which shaded us from the scorching sun. The day before our arrival at the place where we were to be delivered to the Turks, we met with five elephants that pursued us, and if they could have come to us, would have prevented the miseries we afterwards endured, but God had decreed otherwise.

On the morrow we came to the banks of a river, where we found fourscore Turks that waited for us armed with muskets. They let us rest awhile, and then put us into the hands of our new masters, who, setting us upon camels, conducted us to Mazna; their commander, seeming to be touched with our misfortunes, treated us with much gentleness and humanity; he offered us coffee, which we drank, but with little relish. We came next day to Mazna in so wretched a condition, that we were not surprised at being hooted by the boys, but thought ourselves well used that they threw no stones at us.

As soon as we were brought hither, all we had was taken from us, and we were carried to the governor, who is placed there by the bassa of Suaquem. Having been told by the Abyssins that we had carried all the gold out of Ethiopia, they searched us with great exactness, but found nothing except two chalices, and some relics of so little value that we redeemed them for six sequins. As I had given them my chalice upon their first demand, they did not search me, but gave us to understand that they expected to find something of greater value which either we must have hidden, or the Abyssins must have imposed on them. They left us the rest of the day at a gentleman's house who was our friend, from whence the next day they fetched us to transport us to the island,[1] where they put us into a kind of prison, with a view of terrifying us into a confession of the place where we had hid our gold, in which, however, they found themselves deceived.

But I had here another affair upon my hands which was near costing me dear. My servant had been taken from me and left at Mazna to be sold to the Arabs; being advertised by him of the danger he was in, I laid claim to him, without knowing the difficulties which this way of proceeding would bring upon me. The governor sent me word that my servant should be restored me upon the payment of sixty piastres, and being answered by me that I had not a penny for myself, and therefore could not pay sixty piastres to redeem my servant, he informed me by a renegade Jew, who negotiated the whole affair, that either I must produce the money or receive a hundred blows of the batoon.[2] Knowing that those orders are without appeal, and always punctually executed, I prepared myself to receive the correction I was threatened with, but, unexpectedly, found the people so charitable as to lend me the money. By several other threats of the same kind they drew from us about six hundred crowns.

On 24th June we embarked in two galleys for Suaquem, where the bassa resided; his brother, who was his deputy at Mazna, made us promise before we went that we would not mention the money he had squeezed from us. The season was not very proper for sailing, and our provisions were but short. In a little time we began to feel the want of better stores, and thought ourselves happy in meeting with a *gelve*, which, though small, was a much

[1] It is on this island that the modern town of Massawa is situated. It is joined to the mainland by a causeway.
[2] Bastinado. The favourite form of punishment amongst the Islamites.

better sailer than our vessel in which I was sent to Suaquem to procure camels and provisions.[1]   I was not much at my ease, alone among six Mahometans, and could not help apprehending that some zealous pilgrim of Mecca might lay hold on this opportunity in the heat of his devotion, of sacrificing me to his prophet.

These apprehensions were without ground.   I contracted an acquaintance which was soon improved into a friendship with these people; they offered me part of their provisions, and I gave them some of mine.   As we were in a place abounding with oysters, some of which were large and good to eat, others more smooth and shining in which pearls are found, they gave me some of those they gathered.   But whether it happened by trifling our time away in oyster catching, or whether the wind was not favourable, we came to Suaquem later than the vessel I had left, in which were seven of my companions.

As they had first landed they had suffered the first transports of the bassa's passion, who was a violent tyrannical man, and would have killed his own brother for the least advantage, a temper which made him fly into the utmost rage at seeing us poor, tattered, and almost naked; he treated us with the most opprobrious language, and threatened to cut off our heads.   We comforted ourselves in this condition, hoping that all our sufferings would end in shedding our blood for the name of Jesus Christ.   We knew that the bassa had often made a public declaration before our arrival, that he should die contented if he could have the pleasure of killing us all with his own hand; this violent resolution was not lasting, his zeal gave way to his avarice, and he could not think of losing so large a sum as he knew he might expect for our ransom; he therefore sent us word that it was in our choice either to die or to pay him thirty thousand crowns, and demanded to know our determination.

We knew that his ardent thirst of our blood was now cold, that time and calm reflection and the advice of his friends had all conspired to bring him to a milder temper, and therefore willingly began to treat with him; I told the messenger, being deputed by the rest to manage the affair, that he could not but observe the wretched condition we were in, that we had neither money nor revenues, that what little we had was already taken from us; and that therefore all we could promise, was to set a collection on foot, not much doubting but that our brethren would afford us such assistance as might enable us to make him a handsome present according to custom.

This answer was not at all agreeable to the bassa, who returned an answer that he would be satisfied with twenty thousand crowns, provided we paid them on the spot, or gave him good securities for the payment.   To this we could only repeat what we had said

[1] This was before he visited Abyssinia.

before. He then proposed to abate five thousand of his last demand, assuring us that unless we came to some agreement, there was no torment so cruel but we should suffer it, and talked of nothing but impaling and flaying us alive; the terror of these threatenings was much increased by his domestics, who told us of many of his cruelties. This is certain, that some time before, he had used some poor pagan merchants in that manner, and had caused the executioner to begin to flay them, when some Brahmin, touched with compassion, generously contributed the sum demanded for their ransom. We had no reason to hope for so much kindness, and having nothing of our own, could promise no certain sum.

At length, some of his favourites whom he most confided in, knowing his cruelty and our inability to pay what he demanded, and apprehending that if he should put us to the death he threatened, they should soon see the fleets of Portugal in the Red Sea, laying their towns in ashes to revenge it, endeavoured to soften his passion and preserve our lives, offering to advance the sum we should agree for, without any other security than our words; by this assistance, after many interviews with the bassa's agents, we agreed to pay four thousand three hundred crowns, which were accepted on condition that they should be paid down, and we should go on board within two hours. But changing his resolution on a sudden, he sent us word by his treasurer that two of the most considerable among us should stay behind for security, while the rest went to procure the money they had promised. They kept the patriarch, and two more fathers, one of which was above fourscore years old, in whose place I chose to remain prisoner, and represented to the bassa that being worn out with age, he perhaps might die in his hands, which would lose the part of the ransom which was due on his account, that therefore it would be better to choose a younger in his place, offering to stay myself with him, that the good old man might be set at liberty.

The bassa agreed to another Jesuit, and it pleased Heaven[1] that the lot fell upon Father Francis Marques. I imagined that I might with the same ease get the patriarch out of his hand, but no sooner had I begun to speak, but the anger flashed in his eyes, and his look was sufficient to make me stop and despair of success. We parted immediately, leaving the patriarch and two fathers in prison, whom we embraced with tears, and went to take up our lodging on board the vessel.[2]

[1] Lobo is not expressing thankfulness. He means, 'Heaven willed.'
[2] The patriarch and his companions suffered further hardships, but were finally ransomed.

VII. OVERLAND RETURN FROM INDIA, 1663

(Translated by Charles David Ley)

Bibliographical

Relação do novo caminho que fez por terra e mar o Padre Manoel Godinho, vindo da India para Portugal. Lisbon. 1665.

OVERLAND RETURN FROM INDIA

Chapter XIX. How I left Basra with three companions. Three Arabs who were going to Samawah¹ join us. I relate my journey day by day

I HAD bought the horses we needed for myself, for the Portuguese I had engaged there, and for the interpreter (since the guide, or *shauter* as he is called in the Arabian tongue, rode on a Persian mare he had). The packs had been filled with biscuits which were so badly cooked that they tasted of dough, a piece of cheese, and some onions—that was all that could be taken and all there would be for the five days during which we did not reckon on reaching a village. The *chikels* were prepared, too: these are water-skins which hang from the pommel of the saddle. We took corn on the horses' croups for them to eat over the same number of days. We now only lacked the *shauter*, Agi Deb, to mount and go on our way. But he was not long in coming, for, at five in the morning of the appointed day, 9th April 1663, he rode in through the gates with a lance in his right hand. He was dressed as a beggar, for he did not wish to risk wearing better clothes, and he told us to go. Then I went to the church to take my leave of its patron saint, the Virgin Mother, and afterwards of Friar Brás de Santa Barbara, to whom I was under a great obligation for his religious and honourable treatment during the days in which I was lodged at his house. He accompanied me to the gates of the city to the west, and there we gave each other our farewell embraces. We four, two dressed in the Turkish and two in the Arab fashion, mounted our horses, and made our way through the gates of the city. We were all armed with weapons, and with patience to bear the inclemencies of the sun, and of the desert sands which begin immediately outside the gates to the west of Basra. The *shauter* had his lance; the *truchman* (as they call the interpreter in Turkish and Arabic) had two pistols and a carbine; the Portuguese, pistols and muskets; I, pistols and a carbine. This was not counting the scimitars we all hung from a part of the saddle under our legs, and an iron mace tied on the other side as well. They had by now learned in the city that there were people who were going to adventure into the desert (until then we had kept them from knowing it, to avoid the Alarves being advised of it by their spies), and that those adventurers were Franks (as they call the Christians, and Christendom they call Frankland) and well armed. So three Arabs from the desert

¹ A town on the Euphrates, then a village.

333

country near the Euphrates came up behind us mounted on their mares. When they came up to us they told us that they would accompany us as far as Samawah, which was six days' journey from there. Each of them had a lance in his hand, as is their custom. At the beginning I was nervous about their company, for I feared they would play us false when we least expected it. But the *shauter* assured me that they were peaceable people; they dared not go alone to their native place, nor had they been able to find a ship bound for there, so that they had sought out our company. This reassured me somewhat and I offered to take them with me to wherever they wished. Thus we see how dangerous this route is, if three Arabs who are natives of the desert do not dare to take it unaccompanied.

All that day we went on without resting. The sun was excessively hot and there was no wind. My lack of practice in riding and the fierceness of the horses themselves, which there was no holding in, caused me great pain. And all this was only the first taste of the desert. In the afternoon we made our way down to our right, where the Euphrates lay and a village near it called Der. We came in sight of this place, and our Arab companions made straight towards it. My *shauter* followed and I shuddered, for I had been told in Basra to buy corn for five days because it would take us as long as that to get to the first village, and now I saw we were bound for this one which was full of very expert robbers who, if they do not rob you when you go in, lie in wait for you when you come out. I did not neglect informing my *shauter* of my fears, but he calmed and encouraged me by saying that our Arab companions had friends in the village and that its governor was a great friend of his. Besides, above all, he must accompany them because they had asked him to do so. These arguments did not satisfy me, but I had to agree with the *shauter*, and so I let myself go on between fear and hope. We entered the village, which was of low, single-storeyed, brown houses of baked earth, inhabited by Arabs still under the dominion of the pasha of Basra. There we sought out the governor's house and courtyard, which are opposite the gates and enclosed by mud walls. We dismounted and fastened our horses to some stakes which were planted in the ground in the courtyard for that purpose. Afterwards we found a corner where we could sit on our packs and weapons, all our capital, in fact; this was what the *shauter* advised us to do first of all. Soon the governor came out and asked us who we were and where we were going to. We replied that we were Franks from India, and that we had been sent for by the *topegi baxi* of Damascus to serve the Grand Signior [1] as bombardiers. *Topegi* is the same as generalissimo, and the *topegi* of Damascus is a Greek Christian.

_____
[1] The sultan of Turkey was the overlord of all this region.

We answered the governor's questions and he sent for bitter curds, dates, and cakes, saying that these would serve as refreshment till supper time.   On this, a renegade Kaffir from Mozambique, who had been a captive of the Portuguese in Muscat [1] for many years, came up to me and asked me on the governor's behalf what I should like to have for supper, since he wished to make me welcome to the best of his ability.   I thanked him for his kindness and politeness and excused myself from choosing the meal by saying that I found all Arab dishes exceedingly tasty.

About the hour of angelus eighteen Turkish horsemen entered the same courtyard, well armed, having muskets with their matches lit in their right hands, and scimitars and pistols in their belts. They had iron maces on the sides of their saddles, and they all had their fuses ready.   In the middle of this troop came the ensign with a small though broad flag on a lacquered staff; the colour of the flag was green and red.   On one side it had the new moon with some stars embroidered in its hollow; in the upper corner near the staff it had a man's open hand.   On the other side, there was a sword with a cross-shaped hilt from which issued two blades with very sharp points at a distance from each other.   The governor received them with the same refreshments as we had had.   Supper followed for all, and consisted of four dishes stewed in their manner. Hunger made this manner of theirs appear better than ours.   As a savoury we had fresh grasshoppers [2] fried in butter, which is a very good thing for dessert.   When we had finished, the governor ordered his servants to give rice to all the horses, ours and the Turks'.   The latter, however, did not wish to accept this and were very angry that he did not give them corn.   Nor was their testiness confined to refusing the rice, but they insolently burst out into many insults against the governor's servants.   They even affronted him himself, as if he lawfully owed them his good treatment of them and corn for their horses.   The governor took offence, for he was an old Arab whose long beard deserved respect; so he called to his men, who swarmed in, with toasted sticks,[3] like mosquitoes. The Turks saw that things were taking a bad turn and they saddled their horses quickly; the hooves of these stood them in good stead in their flight towards Basra where they were going to enlist under the pasha, who was alarmed about the war in Germany,[4] for which people were now being collected in Babylon and Diarbekr [5] or Mesopotamia.

We rested a little, but when the moon appeared we took our way

[1] A coastal town in south-eastern Arabia, which had been an important Portuguese naval base till it was taken by the Persians in 1648.
[3] Or locusts.
[2] Staves pointed and hardened by fire.
[4] The Austrian struggle against Turkey.
[5] In Kurdistan.

out into the wilds where nothing was to be seen but loose sand and
desert country.   When 10th April dawned the sun came out hotter
than it had ever been before over those sands.   We at once began
to feel the heat, and no less than that, a killing thirst.   The *chikels*
of water we had brought were used up; none of the company had a
drop left.   The worst of all was that there was no hope of coming
across any more until well into the night, and the time was now
midday.   I put bullets into my mouth to moisten my tongue.
The expedient was useless because the very lead seemed to have
lost its moistness.   My Portuguese cleared his throat and spat,
and brought out blood, his thirst was so great.   It was now that
repentance came for having chosen such a route; now that regret
came for not having gone along by the river, whose waters I figured
to myself to be the best in the world.   Oh, how many fountains
came into my thoughts!   How many pools and springs came up
before my imagination!   My memory was charged with the fountains of Bangani, of Murmugan, and the Pillar Well in Goa; the
reservoir of Bassaim, that of Corlem in Salsette; the pool of
Siracer in Tanna, the water of the Mangate in Cochin, and of
Manapar in the Pearl Fisheries,[1] and others that I had seen and
drunk from.   My eyes roamed forward to see if they could catch
a glimpse of some water.   At every step it seemed to me that I saw
a river ahead; this is an illusion all this desert gives to the eyes,
for though it is all plains stretching out of sight, distinguished from
one another only by a few hills of shifting sand, the traveller figures
to himself that the plain which he sees far off is a lake or a running
river.   Even when I had been once deceived, that did not prevent
me from being deceived on other occasions, and I was very angry
when my companions undeceived me by saying that what had
appeared was not a river but a likeness of one.

I went along, or rather, I let my horse carry me on, groaning
and sighing for some hours, being nearer the after-life than the
water I longed for.   At three o'clock in the afternoon we found a
lake near a mosque.   The horses first had scent before we had
sight of the water.   When they smelt it, they broke into a gallop,
and nobody could hold them back, for the thirst worked its effects
on them also.   On getting into the water my horse dropped down.
I could no longer bear the thirst, flies, and heat, so I pulled myself
off the horse; I floundered in the mud and came out of it all wet.
We wished to quench our thirst, but the water was not fresh but
brackish, and so much so that they say that when Friar Cipriano,
a Franciscan, drank of it, he burst at once.   We saw his half-buried
bones there.   I felt some freshness inside with the water which
entered the pores of my body.   But when my thirst redoubled

[1] Places in Portuguese India the author remembers.   Some of them had
already passed out of Portuguese hands.

afterwards, I suffered the very pains of death. None of my companions spoke a word, for they were each intent on finding some way of alleviating the thirst they were suffering. One Arab hung his tongue out like a dog for the wind to freshen it, but, as there was not a breath of wind, he became much sadder than before. Another lifted his *chikel* many times to his mouth, as if the smell of water was enough to quench thirst. At last, more dead than alive, we caught sight of an Arab herdsman who was pasturing some goats in that desert. We made straight towards him at full speed, persuaded that he would have water either where he was or near him. We found him at a reedy pond, but this was of such a nature as I had never seen water of before; it was as warm as a hot spring, and it did not quench the thirst. However, we drank of it and rested a little; we washed our faces and gave our horses a drink. At sunset we reached some Arab tents where they gave us fresh milk and cold water. I should have liked to stay that night with them, but we had to go on our way again, because my companions feared those very charitable Arabs. By nine at night we finally came to Dacrirey, a fortress in those parts which belongs to the pasha of Basra and which is capable of standing a siege. The walls are high, though they are of baked earth, and there is a good garrison. It is situated on the Euphrates in the place where it winds about like a snake. We did not wish to enter the fortress, both so as not to pay the customary sum and because it was already night. But we stayed at the house of a farmer who gave us everything he had in the house for supper. Besides supper, he ordered carpets to be laid down for us to use as beds. When this had been done he warned us to be on our guard at night against the tigers, who were so persistent and so bloodthirsty that they took the cattle and beasts of burden from inside the house. As we were sleeping outside the house we had to keep an even more careful guard. We tied up the horses at our feet, and we took turns as sentinels through the four watches of the night.

At about dawn the farmer got up to prepare a breakfast of chicken for us. After we had breakfasted, we went on our way, not through the wilds again, but along by the Euphrates. For we thought that it was better to run the risk of being robbed than that of dying of thirst and heat. So we went along in sight of the water which had been lacking to us the day before. It is thus that need and abundance change about. On this day at ten o'clock we had sight of a village, but the *shauter* did not want us to enter it, so that we should not be known, he entered it alone, to buy some eggs. At about four in the afternoon I was in signal danger of my life as I crossed a stream which flows out of the Euphrates. I wished to be the first to ride through this ford, and I was borne down by the current to beyond the pass. I reached the other bank on horseback, for the horse swam well.   But when I wished to land the bank was so steep that the horse could find no place for his feet and beat his chest against the slope.   He was thrown back by his own strength, and fell, and I fell off the saddle and, to help me the more, my mantle caught my feet.   God was willing for the horse to make straight for one of the banks, where he clung to the land and they were able to guide him along by the reins to where the ground was lower.   I had breasted my way through the current as best I could and swam across to the other side.   On this occasion the water soaked all the papers I had on me, except the most important letters which kept dry because they were sealed up.   As night came up over us, we entered a place called Chalouchie and sought lodging in the governor's courtyard.   He made us welcome with that liberality in which these Arabs exceed any other nation.   For supper he gave us freshly cooked fish with raisins, some herbs which spiced it, bread, sour milk, dates, and cheese.   He ordered corn to be put down for the horses.   And for all this he only asked me for some charges of gunpowder.

Here I do not want to omit telling what happened to me with some Turks I found there who had come from Babylon.   They came up to me as soon as I had dismounted and asked leave to see the fire-arms I had placed in a corner.   The governor gave me a glance to tell me not to let them touch them.   But I let some of them do so.   They did not tire of seeing them nor of praising the Franks for their cultivation and ingenuity.   What surprised them most was to see that each of my arms was charged with two or more bullets, because they do not fire more than one from theirs.   After the arms, they came to look at my breviary, for I had begun to pray.   The first to ask me what book it was was the governor.   I replied it was the Mossafo of Isai.   ('Mossafo' is the same as sacred book in Arabic, and 'Isai' is Christ.)   They at once all took it and kissed it, and lifted it up to their eyes many times, and praised the beauty of the binding and the perfection of our printing presses, of which they have none.   Later they ran through it, leaf by leaf, looking for sacred pictures and designs.[1]   They asked me the names and mysteries of the figures they saw.   I explained these to them; though a Turk who was present and who must once have been a Christian explained them better in their language.   They were all very glad to see the birth of Christ, the adoration of the Magi, the Ascension, and other sacred mysteries depicted.   But they were scandalized to see a design of the most blessed Trinity, and a picture of the death and passion of Christ, because they do not believe in the threefold nature of God, nor that Christ died; they say that God saved Him from the hands of the Jews and bore Him off

---

[1] The 'sacred pictures' were intended for devotion; the 'designs' for contemplation.

body and soul to heaven, deceiving the Jews with a phantasmal body which He left them in place of Christ's. Arguing from these tales the Turks threw it in my face that the Mussulmans paid greater honour to Isai than the Nazarenes did. For these last insulted His memory by proclaiming that He died on a cross, while the first had a care of His credit and defended the opinion that He rose to heaven alive. Here I took the opportunity of showing how full of lies their Mossafo was, since it taught that Christ had not died, when there was nobody else in the world, except the Mussulmans, who could believe such a tale. They began to feel injured, and I, so as not to be injured, left off talking and retired to the place where I was to spend the night.

In the early morning of the following day we left this place with two more Turks in our company. On this day's journey we met more than fifty Turks on horseback and very well armed. They were travelling in formation, with broad banners. When they caught sight of us and we of them we made towards each other, not in a straight line, but as if circling round. At last, when they came up near us they greeted us with their 'Salam alecon,' and we replied with the customary 'Alecon salama.' They then asked who the white people were, which when they knew, they galloped along in a line a couple of times as a sign of courtesy, and went away. At night we went to sleep in a village named Elarga. When it was time for it, supper came, sent by the governor of the place. He also sent to say that there were many robbers there, so that we ought to keep a guard over our goods and horses. He was not content with warning us, but also sent three of his porters to sleep near our horses. It was not necessary to take turns to watch that night, for we were all wakeful and no one slept a single hour because of the fleas. There were as many of them in the house as in the street, and in the street as in the house.

On the fifth day of our journey we reached a large and well populated place called Ennegeb. But we refrained from entering it, not wishing to lose time, or to pay a certain sum of *patacas* [1] which is there exacted from travellers. At night we went to a village which is called Samawah and was the village of the three Arabs who were our companions. An Arabian widow whom my *shauter* knew received us and exceeded Sareptana [2] in her hospitality. Our very fathers and mothers would not have done the kindnesses to us she did for the day and a half we stayed on in her house, both to rest ourselves, and because the *shauter* wished to change his mare. He needed a fresher one of better mettle, for the one he had was very tired. I needed a day of rest more than any of them, because a crop of boils which had shot up

[1] Pieces of eight, dollars.
[2] Probably the Samaritan woman.

on the third day of the journey tormented me so that to mount
my horse was a torture.

On the 15th April we had breakfast and were provided with
victuals for ourselves and corn, for the three days we should spend
in the desert before we entered any village. So we left this
Samawah and made off into the wilds. That day we came to two
hills in the midst of great plains, and on one of them we found half
a fresh fish, which must have been left there by one of those great
birds of the size of large sheep which there are in this desert.
We were going down the first hill when suddenly we spied four
men on horseback and one on foot. I at once went forward to
gain knowledge of them in the way I have already said is customary
among the Arabs. But they did not make the signal of friendship;
on the contrary, they came towards us at full speed, without slacken-
ing their pace. Seeing this, I turned to my companions and we
backed our horses flank to flank like a cross, put in powder, and
cocked our pistols and carbines. The Arab horsemen, who were
well armed after their own style, skirted by us without taking their
eyes off us. Then they drew up their mares and called to the
shauter. I was not willing to let him go alone. So we all made
towards them and started to parley. They first asked who we
were. When they knew this, they asked also how we had dared
to take that route, being so few in number and foreigners. I told
our people to reply that as we had no goods we were not afraid of
robbers, nor of being killed either; for we had many good offensive
and defensive weapons with us; and, besides, there could not be
any men barbarous enough to wish to lose their own lives merely
in order to take ours. Having heard this reply, they asked for
tobacco and went away.

We can only have gone a short way after leaving the Arabs when
the shauter's mare fell down suddenly as if dead. He made haste
at once to cut its nostrils and cut something like an acorn out of
the tear-ducts of its eyes. He then threw ground salt into its eyes
and nostrils. After this it recovered again and could go on its
way. On that day I saw the wind blow the sands into the air, making them look like the smoke from a furnace. But we speeded
our horses and avoided the danger. About five in the afternoon, we came across a fresh lake, which was the home of many
large birds. I wanted to take a shot at them, but, in order not to
be heard by the Arabs, who frequent these places where there is
water, I forbore to do so. We left the lake and went to sleep in a
bare little range of hills, if indeed it can be said that we slept and
not rather that we stayed awake all night guarding our horses against
the tigers who passed by us in bands to go and drink at the lake.

On the following day, we found water in a number of holes. By
ten o'clock at night we caught sight of a high tower built on a piece

of rising ground as a beacon to those who travel over this desert.   It can be seen for many leagues and it deceives the eyes of those who see it from far away in a remarkable manner; for it seems at first to be very close; then you are convinced that it is retreating from you.   After we had covered the distance, we came in sight of Ba Ali.   It is a fine city surrounded by walls of baked earth on a wide plain in the midst of that desert.   Its many towers and soaring pyramids, which are higher than the walls, seem marvellous to travellers.   This city is well provided with provisions, fruits, and delicacies in great plenty.   The ground there does not give them of itself, for it will not yield them, but people come from every other place to sell them there.   It would lack water if money and inventiveness had not brought this from the Euphrates by underground pipes which run for three leagues in length.   It is visited by all kinds of Mahometans, because of the body of Ali, Mahomet's son-in-law, which is buried in it and not in Mexeta as Tenreiro and Friar Gaspar de São Bernardino write.   Considering they say that Mexeta is in Mesopotamia, I do not know how they did not remark that Ali was buried in a city in Arabia, where he was killed by the orders of Mauhia.[1]   João de Barros writes more correctly that the city in which Ali was interred was first called Cufa,[2] and that the Moors later changed its name to Mazad Ali, that is to say, the house of Ali.[3]   The Arabs call it Ba Ali, which has the same meaning.

This Ali was the second caliph by Mahound's nomination;[4] but, as I have told before, he was not allowed to take possession. He is one of the four interpreters of the Koran, who were Abubekr, Omar, Othman, and Ali.   The sect called Melchia is founded on the interpretation of Abubekr, and this the Moors revere; the sect called Hanefia is founded on Omar's interpretation, and the Turks observe it; the Arabs follow Othman's, which is called Buanesia; Ali's is called Immemia; it is the one which differs most from the others, and the Persians have embraced it.   Together with Ali, some of his grandsons, the sons of Hosain, are buried in the principal mosque of this city.   A saddled and bridled horse is to be seen in the public square at all times.   The Persians say that it is waiting for Mahomet Mahadim, Ali's grandson, the one who, in their opinion, has not yet died but will come on horseback to settle all the differences there are about their law between Arabs, Persians, and Turks, and to convert the whole world to their sect. When they wish to light the candles in the principal mosque,

[1] Muawiyah.
[2] Kufa or Cufa, about twenty-five miles south of the ruins of Babylon; founded by the caliph Omar.   From it the Arabic characters designated Cufic are named.
[3] Ali was murdered in 660 by three conspirators, of whom one called Abdurrahman aimed the death-blow.   Ali was then caliph.
[4] The other three 'interpreters' were all caliphs before Ali.

the horse is brought there and they offer it to Ali, begging him to
send his grandson with dispatch.   The Persians do not hold this
city in less reverence than Medina where the body of their false
prophet lies.   They are continually coming from Persia on pilgrimage to this holy sepulchre of his.   In the days when the Persian
was lord of Babylon, he was also lord of Ba Ali.   But now it is the
Turk's, who keeps a garrison there and officials empowered to
mulct every one who goes on that pilgrimage so many *patacas*.
They do not let any one enter the city, so the *shauter* told me.

For this reason, and also because it seemed nonsense to me to
give Turks *patacas* in order to see the sepulchre of Ali, I followed
the *shauter's* advice, he being of the opinion that we might sleep
within sight of the city.   All that night we saw lamps in the towers
of their mosques, because it was the season of Ramadan,[1] which is
the Moors' Lent, during which they fast all the day, spending the
greater part of it at home.   As soon as the stars come out they
begin to eat and continue till dawn, spending the night in banquets,
comedies, and jollity; for the solemn prohibition of Turks from
going out into the streets at night is withdrawn, and therefore,
at this season, they do not shut the gates of each street.   I shall
relate what else there is to tell of this Ramadan or Lent of theirs
when I reach Aleppo, where I was on the day of their Easter,
which they call Bairam.[2]   At this point I will observe that one
could go from this city to Ana without passing through Babylon, in which manner the way would be greatly shortened; but
there would be the disadvantage of having of necessity to go
through the places which are most dangerous for their robbers;
at the same time, there would be a great lack of water until such
time as one reached the Euphrates.   I wanted to take this route,
but the *shauter* did not dare, and gave as his reason that it could
only be attempted on dromedaries or camels, for they can bear
thirst better than horses; also, we should be certain to come across
Arabs.

So we resolved on travelling to Babylon and crossing over on to
the other bank of the Euphrates.   Before dawn we mounted and
took the road which goes from Ba Ali to Belile.   We met many
people going to visit this last holy city of theirs.   Two leagues
distant from it, we saw a sumptuous mosque with high, proud
towers adorned in a thousand marvellous ways, but it was in a
solitary and unpopulated spot.   It had many doors and great walls.
Inside, it was dark and divided into many rooms.   Ali was in this
mosque praying when they killed him, according to what João de

---

[1] A yearly fast, called the 'Blessed Month.'   The fast is a hard one, as
no food or drink of any sort may be taken during daylight, and even saliva
may not be swallowed designedly.
[2] The first or greater Bairam, called 'the Festival and the Sacrifices.'

Barros writes. A little further on from this mosque two Arabs met us. They revealed at once by their foolish questions that they were the spies for others who lay in ambush. However, when they were aware of the weapons we had, they did not dare to molest us. Towards evening, we reached Belile, a big and populous city, placed both on the far and near sides of the Euphrates, which cuts it in two and waters its broad corn-fields. This city has a pleasing approach from this side, from Arabia, enriched with pyramids and high towers. I did not see any orchards, but I saw some fields of fresh vegetables, and some date-palms. We went to sleep in a beautiful caravanserai on the other side of the river, which we crossed by a bridge of boats.

On 18th April we took our way along the highway from Belile to Babylon. At night we halted at a caravanserai (it is like a large cloister of a monastery, with a number of cells on top of it to house the travellers and a number of stables below for the camels and horses). This one was near a small village where only poor people lived. It is a magnificent and very costly piece of work; it can lodge two thousand horses. As there is no water in this village, the caravanserai has a watering-room with twelve thick brass pipes which can be turned on and off like bathroom gutters, and which give men, cattle, and beasts of burden all the water they may require. The name of the caravanserai is Birnous. There are many servants in it for the travellers. I found there many pilgrims or rather fakirs from India, Turkey, and Persia who were going to Babylon to visit the sepulchres of their saints.

It was the 19th April at the time of noon when we came in sight of that famous city, which now preserves only the name of Babylon—even this it has lost with its greatness, for the Turks, Persians and Arabs call it Baghdad instead of Babylon.[1] At two o'clock in the afternoon we entered Rachish, a village on the banks of the Tigris, opposite Babylon just as Cacilhas is opposite Lisbon, though not so far away from it, for the river Tigris does not flow so wide there as the Tagus does here. It had, on a rough calculation, six hundred inhabitants. The pasha Azen Vazir ennobled it with an ample inn, and with a square and a mosque of the finest marbles brought from Mosul, which was the Nineveh of old times. We did not make a stay in this village but at once crossed over to the other bank by a bridge of thirty-seven boats, which was fastened on both sides by thick iron chains to strong and firm stone pedestals. After we had passed over the bridge, the janizaries [2] who take the toll for crossing came out to meet us and asked us who we were. The *shauter* replied that we were Franks who had been called upon

[1] Godinho was not, of course, in Babylon but in Baghdad.
[2] A Turkish order of infantry formed in 1326, and abolished in 1820.

by the *topegi baxi* of Damascus to serve as bombardiers to the grand signior. They believed this and let us enter without paying anything. I went to be the guest of the Reverend Father, Friar Jean Baptiste, a bearded Capuchin from France who acts as superior to some monks of his order there and does God great service, if not by converting Turks, at any rate by keeping some oriental Christians in the Roman faith and by reclaiming others who are schismatical.

Chapter XXII. The stay I made in Babylon; leaving it, I continue my journey to Ana in great danger

I ONLY rested a day and a half in Babylon, if indeed it can be said I rested and did not rather toil to obtain the many things necessary for my journey, which would now be much more trouble-some than it had been up to then, both because we should have to undergo a greater lack of water and because we were bound to meet the Alarves. As nobody takes the land route from Basra to Babylon, the pirates do not weary themselves very greatly watching the desert there; but from Babylon to Aleppo there are Turkish *kafilas* or caravans and travellers they wait for, and sometimes they even take the money going to Constantinople, however large a convoy it has with it. The first thing I decided on was to redeem two hundred *patacas* for which I had a letter from Basra to a banian[1] called Mangi, who does traffic in Babylon, and is in con-tact with the banians of India. I went to ask him for them. He, because there were Turks and Arabians present, said that he could not give them to me. But he brought them to my house after-wards and said that he had not given them to me in his because if those Arabs had known I had money they would have either given word to the robbers or acted on their own account. With this money I bought a horse for my interpreter, whose own had been tired out by the time we had reached there; also three skin bottles for carrying water, which we hung under the horses' bellies; thirty fathoms of cord to draw water out of very deep wells; some few pounds of *caoe*,[2] a ground and toasted seed the Mahometans

---

[1] Hindoo trader.
[2] A form of cocoa, a drink not introduced into Europe till the eighteenth century. The seed was known in England in 1708; the beverage in 1788 or earlier.

drink in hot water; and some tobacco leaves and other things of that nature to give to the Alarves if I could, by any chance, bring them to any agreement with me. Having bought these things, I bargained again with my *shauter* for him to guide me to Aleppo and he agreed to do so, as he had already had proof of my strength and that I could bear the hardships. Though, indeed, he advised me to go in a caravan which was leaving there two days later for Aleppo and made its daily halts at Nineveh, Nisibi, Cochassar, and Orfa, which is a safer route than the one through Ana, despite its detours. I did not take his advice. I paid him what I owed him for having guided me to Babylon, and left the thirty *patacas* we had just bargained for for the journey to Aleppo, in the care of the banian Mangi. I took my leave of the Capuchin fathers, got on my horse, and ordered my companions to mount; these were, as I have already said, the *shauter*, the interpreter, and the Portuguese.

On the 25st April we left Babylon by the same bridge of boats which I wrote of when I described how I arrived there. I told every one we were going to Damascus to seek out the *topegi*. We had already left Rachish behind us when a janizary came running after us with a round staff in his hand, yelling out to us to stop. I did not wish to obey him, for I feared that he would want us to say farewell in *patacas*, but the *shauter* expected to be passing that way on other occasions and feared to offend the janizary, so he waited for him, and we with him. He came up and asked us for two *patacas* per head, though his only claim to them was the staff he had. We brought the price on our own heads down as far as possible, and, at the end of all our calculations and arguments he came to accept fifteen *shaes* (coins of that country) which made five *patacas*, and so he went away. This country of the Turks is such that there is nobody to appeal to about an injustice of this kind without risking the loss of one's money, and incurring a fine into the bargain, though indeed I believe that our country is like theirs in this respect. We had gone two leagues when we saw the outline of a man on a hillock not far from our path. As we approached we recognized it to be an Arab. When he realized that he might be distinguished he went down the hillock and crept along close to the ground. As we came alongside the hillock, we saw that there were some people lying on its flanks on the other side. This was their look-out from which they watched to see if the caravan or any people had come out from Babylon for them to assault. So we fired off two carbines, in order that they should know that we had seen them, and pressed on all together. Near there we came across a stream from which the horses drank and from which we filled our *chikels* and skins. Then, without more delay, as the place was dangerous, we again got on horseback and went on our way. We slept that night

in the middle of a plain, in great fear of the lions and tigers, who
are bloodthirsty in those parts. The horses slept near us as
usual, tethered at our feet. At about eleven at night, the interpreter, who was taking the first watch, awoke us saying: 'Tiger!
Tiger!' By that time the horses had huddled together firing
their hoof-artillery against the tiger, who was preparing for
his leap. We seized our scimitars and the *shauter* his lance. We
did not seize our fire-arms, because we were as afraid of being
heard by the Alarves if we fired and they should happen to be
near us, as we were of being set upon by the tigers. We went
towards the only one we saw and went between it and the
horses, rather seeking to defend ourselves than to attack it.
God was willing for it to be awed by us and it went away.
We were left in fear that it would come back in company.
But either it found no companions, or it found a better
prey.

On the second day of the journey, the 22nd April, we found water
in a little slough which was the home of strangely large birds of the
shape of ducks, but with backs of a burnt ochre colour, a red
breast, black wings, a white neck, and a steel-coloured beak. We
caught one of these large birds by hand, for it could not get
onto its feet to fly. Many corpses of these great ducks lay by the
side of this slough, some of them recently dead, others dead a long
time ago. My curiosity made me measure one of their spines, and
I calculated it was nine spans in length. The tigers kill these birds,
and keep them there as in a larder for their incidental needs. We
waded into the mud to take in some water; because the slough was
drying up and leaving a miry patch at the sides. The *shauter* was
filling a skin, either with water or mud, I do not know which,
when there we saw a huge tiger coming straight towards him; we
quickly took hold of the horses, and the *shauter* of his lance. The
tiger was parched with thirst, took no notice of our hubbub, went
down to drink, and, after quenching his thirst, lay quietly in the
water with his eyes fixed on us. We cried to him to go away, but
he took no notice of that. We aimed our carbines at him, but to
no purpose. At last he wearied of looking at us and infuriating
us, turned his back on us, and went a musket-shot away. Some
did not fail to wish to shoot at him. However, we were not certain
that what he might do would be not to die at once, but to let us
know how savage a wounded tiger can be, so we desisted. When
the tiger had moved off, we took in water. We left the pathless-
ness of that desert and came onto a road which goes to Ana. We
came onto it by night, and spent the rest of the night in the
hollow of a hillock where we made a fire which we struck from
the flint of a pistol to roast a hare the *shauter* had woken with the
point of his lance. It had been sleeping near a bush, and one could

truly say of this hare what Virgil sings of his Orontes, that he met his death in a sleep.[1]

At dawn on 23rd April we found the fresh track of a *kafila* or caravan. We went on following this caravan until we came up to it, and it consisted of camels, and a few other beasts of burden. It had only corn that it was taking from Babylon to Ana, where there is none. Not many men went with it, both because it was small and because the journey was short and they were taking a great risk. As soon as they caught sight of us they thought they were lost, judging that we were Alarve robbers. They threw their packs on the ground, to make a parapet of them, and stood waiting for us with bows and arrows in their hands. Since we perceived their fear, we began to wheel about, from which they understood we came in peace. Their foreman left his train or *kafila* and came to us on an ass which bore him as swiftly as if it had been a horse. He greeted us and offered us corn for our horses, asking us to accompany him to Ana, where he would pay us for this favour which he hoped we would grant him. I ordered the blind man's answer to be given to him—we would see. On this day, and the day before, we found some strips of thin white marble in the desert which stretch for many leagues. They are not deep, but rise out of the surface of the ground, and are of the thickness of a brick.

We had only been travelling in company a little way when we espied an Arab on horseback to the left, coming along driving two oxen before him. We made straight towards him and asked him for the news about that desert. He answered that formerly a hundred and twenty mounted Alarves had coursed along that road every day, but that he did not know where they were now. For his part, he was repairing to his hut with this spoil which some pillaging he and others had done had yielded him. His pack was examined and he had four roasted cakes in it, which are a great luxury in that desert. The Arab went off without them, bewailing his existence because his hut was still a long way off, ten leagues' journey; but, as he travelled lighter, he could arrive sooner. A bit further on after this meeting, we found many horsemen's tracks all over the roadway, and there was no sign of the horses being shod, which showed that these were hostile people. We at once consulted as to what it would be most fitting to do to avoid a meeting. I requested the *shauter* to leave the caravan and travel at full speed away from the road where the greatest danger was. This request of mine had very forcible arguments in its favour.

---

[1] Godinho appears to be confusing the drowning of Orontes in the first book of the *Aeneid* with that of Aeneas's pilot Palinurus, who falls asleep at the helm and tumbles overboard at the end of the fifth book.

The first was that the robbers in that desert do not usually follow the tracks of horses, because they consider they will not be able to catch up with them; but they do follow those of caravans, since they know very well that they travel slowly. My second argument was that those Alarve robbers infested the road and would come on us sooner or later; this would not happen if we made off towards Ana across the desert. The *shauter* did not fail to agree with me. But interest and expediency prevailed with him and he replied that it did not fit his reputation to leave the caravan in its danger, and fail to do what its foreman, who was a friend of his, asked us. He said we should be safer if we went with it; as if it had been one of the large Babylonian ones. And now, that it may be seen what contrary means God often takes to achieve His ends, and how human reason should be guided by divine providence, I shall relate what happened on the second day.

I was displeased with the *shauter* for not having done what I wanted in the matter of leaving the road and the caravan, and we all went along together travelling slowly down a slope which led to the river Euphrates. We had hardly descended this slope when we noticed, far off in the midst of a spacious plain, a great dust thrown up by a body of horsemen; but we did not know if it was coming towards or going away from us, as we saw it at a great distance. We dismounted in all haste, and with no less haste the people of the caravan unloaded their camels and asses. We climbed a bank and waited for the enemy behind a barrier of our beasts and baggage. The enemy would of necessity have to go through a narrow pass between a hill and the river which I always recall whenever I reach Barrocas da Rainha on my way from Santarém to Golegã.[1] By now the enemy had made back to the hiding-places it had near there, without noticing us. Thus we were relieved from this danger (into which we should inevitably have fallen if the *shauter* had been persuaded by my arguments and left the *kafila* to travel more quickly, for those robbers had only a very short while ago gone by the same point where we were waiting for them now); and we sat on the bank of the river Euphrates in the shade of some willows there were there, whilst the foreman of the caravan roasted on some burning coals a cake he had made of flour with his own rough hands.

We had not managed to have an hour's rest in the shade before the camel-drivers called out: 'Arabi dus, Arabi dus,' which means 'Arab robbers, Arab robbers.' I and the others seized our arms. We cocked our pistols and carbines and climbed to take up our position in the narrow pass I have already spoken of between a hill and the river. On this occasion the Portuguese was so overcome by dismay that he went to hide among the thickest willows.

[1] A spot on the Tagus, some miles inland from Lisbon.

He gave up everything for lost and his only idea was to take his horse with him, as if his life was not more effectively lodged in his weapons and in courage than in flight. The Arabs who were coming were only four in number, and one of them was the sheik or head of the troops we had seen in the distance. My interpreter desired them to draw up. But they took little notice of his request and continued to come on, until two bullets whistling past their ears made them draw rein and frightened them. They cried out that they were friends and made the signal of peace, circling round with their horses. We then received them in friendship, offering them some of the cake we had with us for dinner, dates, and onions from our pack. They ate of all these things with a good will, and they also accepted a little tobacco I gave them with the same. At the end of the meal I asked them where they came from. They replied that they came from the country round Hella, an ancient city now half in ruins, and that they were taking back a large capture they had made from a very rich Turk who had been going to Babylon to take up the office of cadi and who had had with him six camels loaded with Indian garments, and plenty of opium, lacquer, and copper. All this they had taken from him, and he had been left dead with two slaves of his because they had offered resistance and killed one of their Arabs first. When they had given this account of themselves they rose and went to take a look at the baggage of our little caravan, and they took whatever pleased them from it without its owner saying a word. They also saw my fire-arms, which I held in my hands while I showed them. They wanted my water-skin because it made the water good. But I answered them that that was just the reason I wanted it. They were much surprised that I put so many bullets into a single carbine; and they asked me why there were so many of them. When they heard that it was so as to kill ten Arabs at a shot they turned away their faces and said: 'Allah starfalah, God forfend.' After having taken a look at what there was in the caravan, the Arabs wanted to go away to their robbers' dens which were near there, behind a hillock. But I would not let them go without some security that their people would not attack us before we reached the city of Ana. They asked for twenty *patacas* for the security. They were given fifteen, some of them false, some of them good, along with other things. The sheik gave me his little crook, saying: 'You can travel in safety. If the horsemen of another sheik come out on you, tell them that you met me and show them this little crook of mine, which they will respect. My name is Sheik Burisha.' When he had said this they disappeared in no time at all, leaving the road and making for a sandy waste in which there was neither path nor track. We travelled with all speed the rest of the day. Our fear that they would catch up with us when they discovered how they had been deceived about the *patacas* was greater than our trust in their little crook. However, since they handle very little money they know very little about it. At nightfall we retired from the road, bore to our right, and went to hide or rest between two hills.

About midnight the moon came out, and we came out with it from our hiding-place. We urged on our camels as fast as possible for fear of those devilish Arabs. At dawn we found we had one companion too many amongst us and he was an Arab, evil-featured, ragged, and bare. It seemed to me that he was a spy, and it seemed to every one that it would be a good thing to treat him as such. But the foreman, who knew for his sins how revengeful the Arabs were, came to the help of this one and saved him from a good beating. When he was asked who he was, he replied he was a merchant who had come from Babylon and been robbed the day before with many others of his company who were still prisoners in the tents of the robbers; he had escaped that night, because his master had not bound him securely. It is true, anyhow, that he fled from us also on the following night. That day we ate sumptuously, for we hunted a gazelle, and a tiger shared a wild boar with us; which he had killed within view of us, and not without its costing him some blood, for it was a hard fight and the wild boar knew very well how to defend itself. The thing happened in this way. We arrived at the Euphrates at about eleven o'clock in the morning, as the river had twisted away from the road the day before. Here we found a large tiger before us with his tail raised on high, his mouth open, all afire, and jumping from time to time on a piece of mud (for so the wild boar he was fighting with seemed to us at first sight, because it was very well armed with layers of mud, one over the other). The camels stopped; we who were on horseback went forward in order to see the fight closer at hand. The pig had its back against a willow, its tusks well sharpened, and three fingers deep of dry mud all over its body. The maddened tiger struggled to draw it away from its position. But when the tiger saw his efforts were useless he jumped on to its back with one bound and used his claws, thinking he would come away with the hide and the hair, but he found that he had only taken off mud and hair. He repeated the bound again and again until he had completely torn that muddy mail off the boar's back, though with little damage to anything beside. As soon as the wild boar found it was disarmed, it ran to the river to cover itself with mud again. But the tiger came on to its back again and tore it in two with his claws. After killing it, he lay down beside it licking a wound, the only one that he had received in that battle. When he thought it was time, he ate what he could and left a part for us, which was enough for the only ones of us who could eat that meat, which is forbidden by the law of Mahound; though the *shauter* could not restrain himself.

At about four in the afternoon, we reached a place where we found recent signs of many horses having been stationed a short while before. We counted these by the stakes they had been tethered to; which were still in the ground. Thus I thanked God for having delivered me from such evident danger through the delay accompanying the *kafila* had caused us. For the rest of the day and part of the night we travelled by the river, which is broad and deep there. The multitude of wild boar we saw that day was unbelievable, as also the multitude of wild asses which came to drink in the Euphrates. We slept near it for the part of the night when we were not travelling. As day dawned on 25th April, we continued on our way, which led us straight into Ana by eight in the morning.

Chapter XXIII. The famous city of Ana is described and another journal of my travels is given, up to the time when I reached Aleppo

THE city of Ana, in former days capital and head of the whole desert, but which is now more desert than town, is situated on the two banks of the river Euphrates, which passes through the middle of it near two rocks which protect its flanks on both sides and do not let it extend. This is the reason why that city has so few roads, but those it has are so long that it takes an hour to go along one road on horseback. The town is not walled, nor could it be, because its streets run into the rock at one end and its houses jut into the river on the other. The buildings are all formed like high castles, with battlements round their terraces; most of them are of earth, though there are quarries there. As their escutcheon over the doors they have a Chinese or Persian plate inset into the wall. The best thing in Ana is its orchards and gardens, which are supplied with water from the Euphrates, and which abound in European fruits and flowers. In this city I saw some olive-trees as fine as ours, and they use their oil for lamps. They have not much cultivated land, though they have a fair number of wheat fields. Corn for the horses comes to them from Babylon. In the middle of the city, between the two sides of the city, there is an island of the size of the castle in Lisbon;[1] it is walled all round with earthen or baked adobe walls which are half ruined, as are also the buildings which are inside the walls. This city belonged first to the Arabs, then the Turks took it. This is the reason why its inhabitants are especially harassed by the Arabs, as being usurpers of what was

[1] The Castelo de São Jorge, which is on a prominent position on a hill. Though it has no moat, it is about the usual size of a medieval moated castle.

once theirs.   The river is not crossed by a stone bridge, nor by a
bridge of boats as in Babylon, but by a large, well ballasted boat,
of size enough to hold fifteen loaded camels.   As there is only one
ferry-boat, the caravan from Babylon uses it for a week or more
when it passes that way.   When the people of the place pass from
one bank to the other, they do not always go in the boat; sometimes
they go on inflated skins which they paddle with their hands,
though certainly the current carries them a long way down.   The
Euphrates is three hundred and twenty paces wide here.   The
inhabitants are chiefly Arabs, tame Arabs as we might say, Turks,
and Jews who they say stayed there after their transmigration
from Babylon.   All these people live by spinning cloth of camel's
hair.   There used to be very rich merchants in this city, but they
have all moved to Damascus and Aleppo because of the late wars
between the Turks and the Persians.   Here I saw water-wheels
moved by the current of the river, which raised up the water to
a height of sixty spans.

Now, as we arrived at the first road on the far side of Ana,
many women and children came out to meet us to ask for news
of those coming in the caravan, because they had had very bad news
the day before.   When we told them they had just come in safely,
they ran out onto the highway with great rejoicings to meet their
men.   We at once crossed the river and went to lodge at the house
of a weaver who was a friend of the *shauter's*, and who also behaved
towards us honourably as a friend on that one day, 25th April,
which we spent in Ana in order to give our horses a little pasturage.
We ordered biscuits to be made for the packs, kneaded with butter
to make them softer. This biscuit cost me very dear, for it caused me
great vexation and in addition I was obliged to give the *shauter* two
gold pieces.   It happened like this: I told my three companions
each to put as much biscuit as they could carry into their packs.
None of them wanted to load their horses, and the *shauter* wished
least of all to load his mare; so they left me to carry what they
were going to eat.   I was angry, and the *shauter* was angry
with me, though he had no reason to be so, and I could not
quiet him until I had put two gold pieces into his hand, as if I had
done him an injury.   However, I saw very clearly that it was not
his good graces I was buying with them, but my life, which depended on his faithfulness.   It is what he who hopes for good
fortune on these roads must do.   Those who are mean either arrive
here robbed or remain there dead.

In that place I was caused even greater vexation by the news of
the thefts and hostile acts the Arabs committed daily; no one
escaped being robbed and killed whether they went by land or by
the river.   I spoke to a Turk there who had come down the river
from Pir in a boat loaded with goods which they had taken from him;

and they had kept him captive until he had procured a ransom of
two thousand *patacas*; two days before he had been freed from their
power.   He and the others in that town affirmed as a certain and
well-known fact that the large caravan from Babylon which had
left it three months before was detained and surrounded by them,
though they had already been given sixteen thousand *patacas*;
but they had asked for the same again.   Nobody now went out
beyond the city gates, for they were terrified at such determined
enemies.   The news cut me to the heart, but, for all that, I did not
show this to those who gave it me; I told them that I was not afraid
of the Arabs, and that, if any of them wanted to go along with me,
I would go surety for them with my life.   To avoid giving information to the spies the robbers have in that city, as in the others,
I gave out that I should not leave there without having given a
week's pasturage to the horses.

When we knew what was happening in the desert, the four of us
took counsel.   Opinions were given that we should return to
Babylon or stay on in Ana, because all else was evidently to risk
our lives.   These opinions had against them that the return to
Babylon was also risky and that a delay in Ana would last a year,
until another large caravan came from Babylon.   When all this
had been considered, a decision was taken to continue our journey
early in the morning of the following day so that there would not be
time for the Arabs to have notice of our going.   If we could we
would join the caravan which was being held up at about a day and
a half's journey from there.   After we had taken this decision,
my *shauter* turned to me and said: 'Now you will see how well
I know these deserts.   I shall so guide you that neither will the
Alarves see us nor we see them.   All the same, have your arms all
ready, because it may be we shall have need of them.'

In the early morning of the following day, 25th April, we took
the high road out of Ana, with our packs and skins full, and our
arms slung round us.   A Turk sallied forth to meet us, and asked
us for two *patacas* each.   I gave them because it was customary
to do so, but only after lamenting my poverty.   For in these lands,
just as travellers must know how to spend, so they must also know
how to conceal their possessions and never let it be understood
that they have money or that they part with it easily.   I always
kept money shared out among my companions, so that, when
anybody had to be paid, I asked them to lend me some.   After
the Turk had gone, a servant or guard of the governor's came
running along behind us calling out for the *shauter*.   This last
went to him and left us waiting.   As we knew later, all this was to
ask if we were people who had anything worth taking.   The
shauter answered that we were poor Franks who had made our way
to Babylon by asking charity; we had bought the horses we went on

with the alms given by some Christians there; and that he was guiding us for God's sake. God was pleased for the governor to believe the *shauter* and let us go on. The dwellers in the road we were going along, both men and women, came to the doors and windows of their houses and said: 'Where are you going, fellows? Do you want to be killed or robbed by thieves? Do you not know what is happening? They are just beyond the city gates there. You are going to have a fine journey of it, and you will say so too afterwards. These Franks are obstinate fellows!' Once we got outside the city, we climbed a hill behind it from which we had a view of a very broad plain stretching out of sight, and we were relieved, for we could see nothing of any Alarves. However, so as to be safer, we struck off to the left of the direct route, leaving it on our right. Then we journeyed across melancholy stretches of loose sand until we finally came to a hole or lair which seemed to have been a lion's den. We kindled a fire and boiled a great number of *grandulins'* or *cattas'* eggs and truffles we had found in the desert that day. At night seven tigers visited us in a band and, if they had not been heard a long way off by the horses, we should have suffered a misfortune. They found us ready at the door of the lair, with our horses gathered in, and this made them abandon their evil intentions.

On the following day at daybreak, after travelling some leagues we came across a little well of water, left there from the winter, with some banks around it. The horses drank, and we filled our skins. When we had finished watering, the *shauter* told us that on that day's journey we should have to go through the most dangerous part of the desert, because our way would be between the dwelling-place of the prince of the Arabs and the spot where the caravan was held up. We ought to give the horses the reins and gallop all day. It was necessary to do this to escape from the very evident peril we should be in in either of two cases: first, if the mounted scouts who were encircling the caravan caught sight of us; secondly, if we came across any Arabs going from the caravan to their dwelling-place. He also recommended us always to travel in pairs, in the Arab fashion, and not one behind another, so that if they saw us in the distance, they would think we were their people. We did this, and the horses on that occasion proved that they were Arab horses, for, despite being worn out with so long a journey, almost dead with thirst and hunger, and loaded with corn, packs, arms, water-skins, and our persons, they did not halt in their career from the morning until two o'clock in the afternoon. During that time we travelled over the eight most dangerous leagues of country. Though it is certainly true that the horse of the Portuguese, because it was old and ate sparingly, was so exhausted by this course that we had to abandon it two days later.

Towards evening we reached a hill which looked out over an extensive plain in which the *shauter* said he had found two very deep wells when he had passed by that way before. But these would certainly be Alarve outposts since they went there to give drink to their horses. So we dismounted and went singly, so as not to be seen, to explore the country. We distinguished seven horses in the very place where the *shauter* had announced the wells to be. We consulted on what we ought to do in our position, whether we ought to flee before they saw us or go out to meet them. No one thought flight safe, since, as it would have to be back to where we had been in such peril, it would be like escaping from one danger into an even greater one. Making towards these seven was not difficult; but we were intimidated by our anxiety lest when close at hand the seven should prove to be twenty. The policy of enforced valour at length prevailed; so we charged our fire-arms, cocked the triggers of the pistols in our belts, and made towards them. As soon as they saw us making straight towards them, the nine, as they turned out to be, mounted and came for us like lightning without either their or our making signs of peace. When they came within hailing distance we asked them who they were and bade them stay where they were. They did not reply, but skirted by us, noticed our arms, and stopped at once. We rode up to the wells, which we found dry and choked, so we continued on our way without further delay. Before we had covered much ground, the Alarves, who had consulted together, rushed on us at the gallop with their lances levelled against us. The four of us made a cross-formation, with our horses backed flank to flank, so as to protect ourselves from all four quarters. But, before they came within a lance's length, we fired seven bullets from a musket and two carbines amongst them, to which God gave such expedition that they made them stop quickly. They at once turned their backs on us and made off, not nine now but seven, leaving us very much afraid that they had gone away to look for others. This fear made us gallop as far in the afternoon as we had in the morning until we reached a mount of sand the top of which had formerly been used by the Alarves as a tethering-ground for cattle. Since it had been all manured by the animals, we found plenty of fresh grass on it, which was a miracle in that desert. It was a splendid place in which to give pasturage to the horses, who by now had no more corn. But our fear of being overtaken by those enemies made more impression on us than the comforts the spot offered. We mowed some of that grass with knives. Each put his truss on his horse's croup, and we made on till we came to a shelter where we halted about nine at night, without having rested either an hour or a jot that day.

On that same day of 27th April, at about four o'clock in the afternoon, we saw the sun suddenly become as white as snow; it

was rayless and lustreless, and did not hurt our eyes at all when
we looked at it.   It was as though that shining planet had felt a
sudden faintness.   For a long time I did not take my eyes off it
as I travelled, but its brightness did not hurt them now.   One
cannot look at the very moon so freely as one could then at the sun.
So if the sun had had the least blemish, it could have then been
made out.   It was not even so high above the earth as on other days
at the same time.   After it had continued so for half an hour, a thick
cloud took it as it were in its arms, and withdrew it from our sight,
leaving us amazed at this strange happening.

We spent the whole night on the watch, and, when the dawn of
28th April came, we resumed our route and passed across in
sight of Rahab before it was day.   Rahab is a city and fortress
set on a high place in the midst of a broad countryside, at two
leagues' distance from the Euphrates.   This last in the beginning
passed near its walls and enriched it with its water and the commerce there was on the river.   But later it took another course
and withdrew to the distance I have said.   Now it is a poor city,
inhabited by Arabs subject to the Turk who live by their beasts
and their husbandry.   David refers to this city in the eighty-seventh
psalm, when he says that Babylon and Rahab knew God: 'Memor
ero Rahab, et Babylonis scientium me.' [1]   At a cannon-shot from
this Rahab there is a lake of not very good water and it is the water
the city drinks.   The Arabs and Turks recount of it that it communicates underground with the well called Zamzan [2] which is
worshipped in Mecca and enclosed inside a very great temple.
They boast of this that it comes from the fountain which sprung
up under the feet of Ishmael when he was perishing of thirst in the
desert.[3]   Many religious persons continually draw water from this
well to give to the pilgrims for them to wash their bodies with,
for these people hold that this water washes and cleanses the
soul from all sins.   The proof these barbarians bring forward to
make one believe that their lake communicates with the well is
founded on a certain story about a hadji or pilgrim to Mecca whose
bowl had fallen in the well of Zamzan and he a long time later
came across it in the lake of Rahab.   We did not drink the waters
of this lake because we were afraid of being seen from the city
and obliged to pay many *patacas*, as the custom is when foreigners

---

[1] The Authorized Version translates: 'I will make mention of Rahab and
Babylon to them that know me ' (v. 4).
[2] The well Zem or Zemzem in the House of Allah, the great shrine at Mecca.
The water is counted miraculous and is only used for drinking and religious
ablution.
[3] A reference to the wanderings of Hagar with her young son in the wilderness of Beer-sheba.   'And God opened her eyes, and she saw a well of water;
and she went, and filled the bottle with water, and gave the lad drink'
(Gen. xxi. 19).

pass in caravans.   Feeling dead with our two days' thirst, we slept the night in the country.

On 29th April the rain fell on us for several hours.   The wind was so strong, too, that it drove us out of our course as if we had been small sailing-ships in a storm.   It was not even possible for us to travel for a great part of the day, so we spent that time in a stretch of bare country on our horses until the storm was over.   By nine at night we reached a deep well from which we drew water in all haste, for we found signs around it of people having been there.   We then went on for about three leagues, when we dismounted between two hillocks.   I do not say we slept, because the ground was flowing with the water of the rain I have spoken of and our clothes were fountains it flowed from, too.   This discomfort and our fear served as supper and sleep for us.   May God give nights like that to the enemies of His religion.   It must have been at the hour of midnight when we heard some figures, who were passing by, speaking Arabic.   The night was dark and dreadful, we were unmounted, our horses were worn out, the magazines of our fire-arms were damp, and nearly all the powder had been wetted.   All these things together prompted us merely to try not to be heard.   And it was God's pleasure that the figures should go on their way without seeing us.   We learned in Thaibe on the following day that they were sixty Alarves on thirty dromedaries who had ravaged that country and the country round Rahab with the robberies they had committed of beasts and from the people crossing from one city to the other.   Then we understood the mercy that God had shown us in sending the rain of the day before.   Though it had been a trouble to us, it had also been our safeguard against those robbers, for they had left the well and the road in order to take shelter from it.   It is, however, quite true that, if it had not been for the rain, we should have had a resource against them; for the superiority of our weapons would have prevailed against the swiftness of their dromedaries.

On the next day, 30th April, at nine o'clock in the morning, we sighted a very magnificent square building, many parts of which were in ruins, all of very fine marble, with columns, water-conduits, fortifications, and halls.   The porticos were of Corinthian design, and indeed the whole building seemed the very temple of Solomon. The natives say that when the French crossed over to the conquest of the Holy Land, they destroyed those lands so completely that they did not leave even the memory of what they were before. On the highest tower of this building I saw many eagles and other birds of a remarkable size.   Half a league from here stands the town of Thaibe on a steep hill; it is surrounded by plastered walls; over the principal gate it has a small bronze cannon, but there is no other ordnance in all the town fortifications, since they have

only the Alarves to fear. The inhabitants are Arabs, as is the
governor himself, and they live on their agriculture and their
camel-breeding. They have no arable lands, farms, or orchards
there, not even trees, though the stream which runs near the walls
would be able to give water for them; but the ground is very
unfertile. St. Epiphanius writes that Elijah was born there, basing
this on the saying of Jehu in the fourth book of Kings, chapter
nine: 'Sermo Domini est, quem locutus est per servum suum
Heliam Thesbiten.' [1] It is quite true that both Holy Scripture
and St. Epiphanius call it Tishbish and not Thaibe. But this
variation must be a corruption of language and not a difference of
place. Because if Elijah, as St. Epiphanius writes, was born in the
Arab country, there is no place in the whole of Arabia with a name
more like Tishbish than this place called Thaibe.

Its inhabitants were very much amazed at our telling them that
we had not fought with the Arabs on the dromedaries, against whom
they had sent to beg cavalry from the pasha of Aleppo. These
Tishbites were living in such fear of them that they had not even
put the camels out to graze for several days. We were housed at
an acquaintance of the *shauter's*. We had hardly dismounted
when the governor of the place came in at the doot. He was a
stout-built man, with a long beard, and uncovered breasts as
big as a woman's, bare-footed and bare-legged, and well known to
some of the Europeans who had passed by there, not for his virtues,
but as the cruellest robber in all Arabia. I, too, knew him by
reputation. So, as soon as they told me who he was, I pretended
to be moneyless and ill used. I received him with as much
courtesy and kindness as if there had been a great friendship
between us. I gave him *caoe*, tobacco, and an embroidered
handkerchief. He drank the *caoe* and smoked a little without
speaking; and, at such a time as he wished to go home, he called
the *shauter* aside and asked him what people we were, where we
came from, where we were going to, and what capital we had. The
shauter told him the truth about everything. Then he went off
to supper, pledging himself to come back, though we neither
asked that of him nor wished it. He returned shortly afterwards with several of his people, who fell upon the *caoe*, it being
something they seldom had. So I pulled all there still was of it
out of the pack and divided it amongst them, pleading my poverty
as an excuse for the smallness of the present. At this the governor
smiled and said to me: 'We know very well that you are rich.
If you were not you could hardly make this journey with all its
expenses. The poor, or those who have little, come along with the
caravans begging for alms, or only paying for their own expenses.

[1] 'This is the word of the Lord, which he spake by his servant Elijah the
Tishbite' (2 Kings, ix. 36).

You have brought these companions with you from Basra at your own expense, and yet you want to put it into our heads that you are poor? But let us have a look at your purse.' Saying this, he commanded his men to bring up our packs, which were both baskets and bags to us. I pretended this did not trouble me, and ordered the interpreter to show him everything we brought in the packs. Then I turned to the governor and ran my hands down his beard (which is amongst them a sign of goodwill and a witness to the humbleness of one who begs) and I implored him not to be so stern to a man who had betaken himself to this town of his trusting in his nobleness and gentility when he could have stayed outside it. As to the customary rights, I would pay them. Besides this, he might expect a great token of gratitude from me on my return journey from Aleppo.[1] It was this hope which persuaded the devilish governor, however much he pretended his change was due to my civil behaviour, and he ordered his men to stop their inspection of my packs. For the time being I contented him with ten *patacas* and one of my horses' saddles which he coveted because of its unusual workmanship. Thus I was at liberty to continue my way next day.

We left Thaibe on 1st May. Three of us were on horseback and my Portuguese was on a donkey because his horse had been tired out. On that day's journey we entered the land of Syria and, for that reason, we found water in various places. We passed the night in the open. On the second day's travelling, we saw an immense number of storks and gazelles;[2] these last covered the earth as the first did the sky. Thirteen Turks were out on horseback hunting the gazelles; each of them had his falcon. The hunter flies this from his wrist and it goes to perch on the head of the gazelle which it flusters with its wings and picks at her eyes in such a way that the poor thing is stupefied and takes more account of the beak which is tormenting her than of the lance which threatens her life. So she lies down and thus affords place and time to the hunter to come up to her and kill her. On the night of this day we slept in Miloua, a town inhabited by Turks and a few Arabs. We stayed with these last, and they housed us more charitably than safely; for all night we watched our horses against the Turks, who in that place rob travellers, for all the world like wild Arabs. On the morning of 3rd May we went along by the side of a very big lake of fresh water, from which salt is taken to the great surprise of every one. But it is not less surprising that the dew from heaven, when it falls on the leaves of certain trees which are sometimes found near the Euphrates, changes to as acrid a salt

---

[1] There was not going to be any return journey, naturally. But the governor does not seem to have realized that Godinho was a European going to Europe.
[2] He was in the part of the world where gazelles are commonest.

as that of Setúbal or Alcácer. By three o'clock in the afternoon, we reached the farms round Aleppo, soon after which we came to the city. It was twenty-five days since we had left Basra and we had rested one in Samawah, a day and a half in Babylon, nearly a day in Thaibe, and another in Ana. But before we repair to Aleppo, I shall write a chapter or relation of the several ways which can be taken by land from India to Europe, with all the warnings and precautions necessary.